CONTENTS

ABBREVIATIONS

AIL	Anti-Internment League
ASU	Active Service Unit
BSP	British Socialist Party
CIA	Central Intelligence Agency
CPGB	Communist Party of Great Britain
DUP	Democratic Unionist Party
EPA	Emergency Powers Act
FRFI	*Fight Racism! Fight Imperialism!*
GAA	Gaelic Athletic Association
ICJP	Irish Commission for Justice and Peace
ICTU	Irish Congress of Trade Unions
ILP	Independent Labour Party
IMG	International Marxist Group
INLA	Irish National Liberation Army
IRA	Irish Republican Army
IRSP	Irish Republican Socialist Party
ISM	Irish Solidarity Movement
ITGWU	Irish Transport and General Workers Union
ITUC	Irish Trade Union Congress
LAW	Loyalist Association of Workers
LCAI	Labour Committee Against Internment
LCI	Labour Committee on Ireland
MRF	Military Reconnaissance Force
MUFTI	Minimum Use of Force Tactical Intervention
NCCL	National Council for Civil Liberties
NIC/ICTU	Northern Ireland Committee – Irish Congress of Trade Unions
NICRA	Northern Ireland Civil Rights Association
NILP	Northern Ireland Labour Party
NUPE	National Union of Public Employees
NUR	National Union of Railwaymen
OUP	Official Unionist Party
PAC	Prisoners Aid Committee
PAF	Protestant Action Force
PTA	Prevention of Terrorism Act

RAC   Relatives Action Committee
RCG   Revolutionary Communist Group
RTE   Radio Telefis Eireann
RUC   Royal Ulster Constabulary
SAS   Special Air Services
SDF   Social Democratic Federation
SDLP   Social Democratic and Labour Party
SLP   Socialist Labour Party
SNHDC   Stoke Newington and Hackney Defence Campaign
SWP   Socialist Workers Party
TOM   Troops Out Movement
TUCAR   Trade Union Campaign Against Represson
UDA   Ulster Defence Association
UDR   Ulster Defence Regiment
UUAC   United Unionist Action Council
UUUC   United Ulster Unionist Council
UVF   Ulster Volunteer Force
UWC   Ulster Workers Council
WRP   Workers Revolutionary Party (Britain)

PREFACE

In November 1980 *Fight Racism! Fight Imperialism!* printed the first article of what was intended to be a series of three articles on the Irish question. The series, under the title 'The Communist Tradition on Ireland' was in fact to run to seventeen issues and was completed in November 1982. That series constitutes the bulk of this book. It has been edited and slightly reordered, small additions and corrections have been made and a postscript was added in November 1983. The political argument and material in the book has not been significantly changed from the articles.

The articles were written because of the urgent need to mobilise British people in support of the Irish prisoners' struggle for political status. The first article, 'Marx and Engels on Ireland', appeared very soon after the first hunger strike had begun. The introduction to that article made the political standpoint of the series very clear:

'Today with the hunger strike in the H-Blocks, the need to understand and act upon the revolutionary significance of the Irish war is more urgent than ever.

'The communist tradition on Ireland holds a wealth of theoretical, political and tactical lessons for us today. For communists the question of Irish self-determination stands at the heart of the British revolution. This is as true today as it was when Marx first stated it over a hundred years ago. Now as then, Irish liberation is the precondition for the British revolution. Communists, as these articles will show, have always stood for the fullest freedom for the Irish people and have waged a determined struggle against those opportunists in the working class movement who have repeatedly betrayed that struggle.'

The series of articles grew in length precisely because of the lessons the history of the Irish people's struggle for freedom contained and offered to those prepared to study it in any detail. Deeper study had, after all, forced Marx and Engels to reverse their earlier standpoint on the relation between the Irish and British revolution. And if, as Marx and Engels argued, the Irish revolution stands at the heart of the British revolution, then undoubtedly its history from their time until today would be full of vital lessons for any developing revolutionary movement in Britain.

As the history of each period was examined in turn, it established a number of important political conclusions. Firstly, that British imperialism cannot play a progressive role in Ireland. Secondly, that the failure of the British working class to make 'common cause' with the Irish people's struggle for freedom has undermined the struggle for socialism in both Britain and Ireland, and significantly strengthened reaction in Britain itself. Finally, that any developing revolutionary movement in Britain has a great deal of a theoretical, political and tactical character to learn from the Irish people's struggle for freedom.

Ireland: the key to the British revolution examines the history of the Irish people's struggle for freedom from the late 1840s to the present day. Basing itself on the theoretical and practical activity of Marx and Engels on the Irish question, it examines this history in the context of the struggle for socialism, and establishes that Ireland *is* the key to the British revolution. It shows how Lenin further developed the position laid down by Marx and Engels in the concrete context of imperialism as a world wide system. As a result of this understanding Lenin was one of the few socialists who grasped the revolutionary significance of the Easter Rising and Connolly's role in it.

The lessons drawn by Marx, Engels, Connolly, Lenin and the Communist International from the Fenian Movement, the Dublin lock out, the Easter Rising, the War of Independence, the Civil War and the partitioning of Ireland are used as the basis for a detailed analysis of the latest period of the Irish national revolution: 1969–1983. This forms the major part of the book and demonstrates that the Provisional Republican Movement continues the traditions of the Irish revolutionary national movement of the earlier period.

This book shows that at every crucial stage of the Irish struggle for self-determination the British working class movement has failed to make 'common cause' with the Irish people. It has proved incapable of decisively challenging its own reactionary pro-imperialist Labour and trade union leadership. As a consequence it has not only held back the

Irish national revolution but also has fatally undermined its own struggle for socialism in Britain.

Finally this book argues that new revolutionary forces have emerged in Britain which are capable of uniting with the Irish people and winning other sections of workers to an alliance with the Irish national liberation movement against British imperialism. It remains true today, as in Marx's day, that the emancipation of Ireland is the precondition for the British socialist revolution.

In a book written about the German revolutionary Eugene Leviné (1883–1919), Rosa Leviné-Meyer wrote, in a passage she attributed to Lenin:

'It is another of those misconceptions to believe that we can have an unbiased view in matters of class struggle. Our judgement is built from the start on the premise of the sanctified present social order; it has been instilled into us for generations. The so-called objectivity is therefore in the last analysis a stand against revolutionary changes – against the working class. To be really "objective" we must first decide on which side we stand: with the oppressed or with the tenacious champions of the privileged minority.'

Ireland: the key to the British revolution takes sides. In the struggle between the Irish people and British imperialism it stands fully behind the Irish people. It stands with the oppressed and against the 'tenacious champions of the privileged minority'.

This book could not have been written without the collective efforts of my comrades and friends in the Revolutionary Communist Group. It is the result of discussion, debate and the political activity of the RCG and its supporters on the Irish question. I have used material first published in *Revolutionary Communist, Hands Off Ireland!* and *Fight Racism! Fight Imperialism!* as the basis for many of the arguments in this book. Without the help, encouragement and strenuous practical efforts of many comrades – editing, typing, proofing etc – *Ireland: the key to the British revolution* could never have appeared.

Special thanks are due to Terry Marlowe. From the very first article to the edited version of the articles used in this book, all the major arguments have been discussed thoroughly with him. He has painstakingly gathered together source material from newspapers and magazines which has been used for writing a number of chapters. The postscript is based on a speech given by me to the Irish Solidarity Movement Conference of November 1983 – it was jointly written with Terry Marlowe. Without doubt this book could never have been completed without his very significant contribution.

Finally, my thanks to my comrades and friends at Red Lion Setters who spared no efforts in giving me help and encouragement to publish both the original articles in *Fight Racism! Fight Imperialism!* and this book.

DAVID REED
February 1984

PART ONE

THE COMMUNIST TRADITION

KARL MARX

CHAPTER ONE

MARX AND ENGELS ON IRELAND

'The policy of Marx and Engels on the Irish question serves as a splendid example of the attitude the proletariat of the oppressor nation should adopt towards national movements, an example which has lost none of its immense practical *importance . . . '*

VI Lenin[1]

Over 100 years ago Marx and Engels laid the foundation for a consistent communist standpoint on Ireland. Through their work on Ireland in the First International they were able to develop a proletarian policy towards national liberation movements not only for the British working class but for the international working class movement as a whole. That policy has lost none of its *practical* importance for the struggle to build a communist movement today.

THE EARLY POSITION

Over a period of 20 years there was to be a fundamental shift in Marx and Engels' position on the national question. Their deep study of the relation between Britain and Ireland was decisive in the change of standpoint.

At first Marx and Engels thought that Ireland would be liberated not by the national movement of the oppressed nation but by the working class movement of the oppressor nation. While British democracy, Engels argued in 1848, would advance much more rapidly as its ranks were filled by 'two million brave and ardent Irish',[2] Irish liberation would come about as a result of the victory of the Chartist movement. The Chartists – the first broad mass revolutionary movement in England based on the working class – had called for the repeal of the Act of

Union of Britain and Ireland in their second Petition to Parliament in 1842 (signed by 3½ million people). And in numerous petitions they had protested against the draconian Irish Coercion Bill 1847 imposed by the English Parliament. In an address printed in the first issue of *The Northern Star* for 1848, Feargus O'Connor the Chartist leader called upon the Irish people to fight alongside the English working class and the Chartists to win the six points of The People's Charter. Engels' comments on this address and on the record of the Chartist movement express the earlier standpoint.

> 'There can be no doubt that henceforth the mass of the Irish people will unite ever more closely with the English Chartists and will act with them according to a common plan. As a result the victory of the English democrats, and hence the liberation of Ireland, will be hastened by many years ... '[3]

The early position of Marx and Engels not only applied to the actual conditions then existing between Britain and Ireland but also represented their general view of the development of capitalism and its worldwide expansion.

For Marx and Engels the modern working class, itself the product of capitalist development, was the really revolutionary class. It had no interests in the existing property relations – capitalism. The hostility between nations and the exploitation of some nations by others was also the product of the existing property relations. For this reason only the victory of the working class over the bourgeoisie could lead to the liberation of oppressed nations.

The greater the development of capitalism, the more heightened is the class struggle and therefore the political consciousness of the working class. The class struggle in England, the most developed capitalist country, was therefore the key to the liberation of oppressed peoples. This was given substance by the revolutionary character of the Chartist movement. Marx and Engels made these points clear in speeches in November 1847 on Poland.

> 'Of all countries, England is the one where the contradiction between the proletariat and the bourgeoisie is most highly developed. The victory of the English proletarians over the English bourgeoisie is, therefore, decisive for the victory of all the oppressed over their oppressors. Hence Poland must be liberated not in Poland but in England. So you Chartists must not simply express pious wishes for the liberation of nations. Defeat your own internal enemies and

you will then be able to pride yourselves on having defeated the entire old society.'[4]

Further, and following on from the point made so far, the worldwide expansion of British industrial capital was seen to play a progressive role in developing the productive forces in the oppressed nations. While attacking the barbaric methods of English colonial rule, Marx and Engels, nevertheless, saw in the destruction of obsolete non-capitalist societies and methods of production a progressive development. Marx expressed this view in 1853 in relation to India.

'England, it is true, in causing a social revolution in Hindostan, was actuated only by the vilest interests, and was stupid in her manner of enforcing them. But that is not the question. The question is, can mankind fulfil its destiny without a fundamental revolution in the social state of Asia? If not, whatever may have been the crimes of England she was the unconscious tool of history in bringing about that revolution.'[5]

This was essentially the early position. The emancipation of the oppressed peoples would be brought about through the victory of the working class in the oppressor nation. The role of the oppressed peoples themselves is seen as a secondary one.

The further development of capitalism and the working class movement in England forced on Marx and Engels a very significant change of view. And it was through an analysis of the relation between Britain and Ireland that Marx and Engels developed the new standpoint.

THE REVOLUTIONARY POSITION ON IRELAND

In December 1869 in a letter to Engels about how he would raise the Irish issue in the General Council of the First International, Marx wrote:

'The way I shall put forward the matter next Tuesday is this: that quite apart from all phrases about "international" and "humane" *justice for Ireland* – which are taken for granted in the *International Council* – it is in the direct and absolute interest of the English working class to get rid of their present connection with Ireland.... For a long time I believed that it would be possible to overthrow the Irish regime by English working-class ascendancy. I always expressed this point of view in the *New York Tribune*. Deeper study has now convinced me of the opposite. The English working class will *never accomplish anything* before it has got rid of Ireland. The lever must be applied in Ireland. That is why the Irish question is so important for the social movement in general.'[6]

Whereas two decades earlier the liberation of Ireland was to be achieved in the course of the victory of the English working class, now the relation was reversed. The liberation of Ireland was the precondition for the victory of the English working class. What brought about this remarkable shift of view?

The explanation lies in a number of important changes which took place over the period of 20 years from 1848. Essentially they are (1) the path of economic development of Ireland under English colonial rule and its effect on the national liberation movement in Ireland. (2) The class relationships in Britain following the defeat of the Chartist movement.

For reasons we shall outline below, it so happened that over the 20 year period the national liberation movement in Ireland assumed revolutionary forms, while the working class movement in Britain not only lost its revolutionary drive with the defeat of the Chartist movement but also fell under the influence of the liberal bourgeoisie for a long period of time.

ENGELS' TOUR OF IRELAND

In 1856 Engels went on a tour of Ireland. His experience of that tour undoubtedly started the process which eventually forced the change of view. In a letter to Marx he lays down the basis for the change of view. He points out first the systematic and all-pervading repression everywhere. 'I have never seen so many gendarmes in any country' with a 'constabulary, who are armed with carbines, bayonets and handcuffs.' Second he comments on the existence of a parasitical layer which mediates English colonial rule and lives off the crushing poverty of the peasantry.

'Gendarmes, priests, lawyers, bureaucrats, country squires in pleasing profusion and a total absence of any industry at all, so that it would be difficult to understand what all these parasitic growths live on if the distress of the peasants did not supply the other half of the picture.'[7]

Third, he points to the artificial character of the development of Ireland, which, geared to the interest of the English colonial power, actually creates poverty for the mass of the Irish people. 'How often

have the Irish started out to achieve something, and every time they
have been crushed, politically and industrially'. And finally he points
out that 'the so-called liberty of English citizens is based on the
oppression of the colonies'.[8]

THE LAND QUESTION AND THE FENIAN MOVEMENT

1846—49 saw the ravages of the famine in Ireland. The Irish 'famine'
strikingly demonstrated how the colonising power creates poverty in
the country it oppresses. The potato, which was the staple diet for the
Irish peasantry, was struck with blight. Ireland was short only of potatoes and otherwise full of food in the form of oats, wheat, butter, eggs
sheep and pigs, all of which continued to be exported to England on a
considerable scale. The people starved and died in their hundreds of
thousands. About a million people died from malnutrition and disease.
Another million were forced to emigrate. Large districts of Ireland
were depopulated and the abandoned land was turned into pasture by
the English and Irish landlords. As a direct result of the 'famine' the
population of Ireland was almost halved in 20 years, from over 8 million to less than 5 million. A popular saying of the time made the essential point 'God sent the blight, the English sent the famine'.

The repeal of the Corn Laws in 1846 led to a fall in the price of corn
—a major Irish crop—and this meant that many Irish peasants could
not pay their rent. They were evicted off the land—a process which
increased depopulation. Finally the passing of the Encumbered Estates
Act (1849) swept away debt-ridden estates which had to be sold off to
pay creditors. Land concentration and the replacing of tillage by pas-
turage were the dominant features of this period. And in the absence of
any compensating industrial development this meant that the Irish
peasant masses were faced with a life-and-death struggle to survive
having been robbed of their land. This was what Marx was referring to
in December 1867 when he said:

> 'what even those Englishmen who side with the Irish, who concede
> them the right to secession, do not see—is that the regime since 1846,
> though less barbarian in form, is in effect destructive, leaving no
> alternative but Ireland's voluntary emancipation by England or life-
> and-death struggle'.[9]

The Irish question, said Marx, is therefore not simply a nationality
question but a question of land and existence—a social question
as well. 'Ruin or revolution is the watchword'.

In Ireland the bourgeois Repeal Association led by Daniel O'Connell split when the revolutionary democratic leaders – John Mitchel, James Fintan Lalor and others – formed the Irish Confederation in January 1847. Mitchel, Lalor and their supporters supported armed struggle; the establishment of an independent Irish Republic; destruction of the landlord system and giving the land to the peasantry; and links with the Chartist movement. These leaders organised the 1848 rising which was crushed by the British colonial authorities. The survivors of the 1848 rising went on to form the Fenian movement on the same revolutionary democratic basis. The Fenian movement, founded in the USA in 1857 and soon to spread to Ireland, combined the armed struggle against colonial oppression with the struggle against the eviction of Irish tenants from the land. It was this that gave it its revolutionary character. The Fenians organised the 1867 rising.

Marx summed up his position in a letter to Engels on 30 November 1867:

'What the English do not yet know is that since 1846 the economic content and therefore also the political aim of English domination in Ireland have entered into an entirely new phase, and that, precisely because of this, Fenianism is characterised by a socialistic tendency (in a negative sense, directed against the appropriation of the soil) and by being a lower orders movement.'[10]

The national liberation movement in Ireland by the mid-1860s had assumed revolutionary forms. This however, only deals with the situation in Ireland. We now must turn to examine the effect of English colonial rule on the class struggle in England.

THE IRISH NATIONAL REVOLUTION AND THE ENGLISH WORKING CLASS

The English ruling class was divided into two main sections – the landed aristocracy and the bourgeoisie. The major political issues of the day involved conflicts between these two sections of the ruling class. The working class had in fact used these conflicts in order to forward its own interests, such as in the struggle for the 10 Hours Bill.

With this background in mind we can begin to see the significance of the other central points Marx and Engels made about English colonial rule in Ireland. First not only was Ireland a bastion of power for the English landed aristocracy but it was also a point of *unity* between both sections of the ruling class.

The exploitation of Ireland was 'one of the main sources of the English aristocracy's material welfare: it is its greatest moral strength'. And the domination of England over Ireland was 'the great means by which the English aristocracy maintains its *domination in England herself*'.[11]

The English bourgeoisie also benefited from English domination over Ireland. It had a common interest with the aristocracy in turning Ireland into mere pasture land which provided the English market with food and wool at the 'cheapest possible prices'.

But secondly it also had an even more important interest. The concentration of land and the eviction of the Irish peasantry off the land meant that Ireland steadily supplied England with its surplus population and 'this forces down wages and lowers the moral and material condition of the English working class'. Irish immigrants were forced to live in conditions of unimaginable degradation and squalor.

And most important of all! The forced emigration of impoverished Irishmen to England divided the proletariat into two hostile camps. In January 1870 Marx wrote:

'...in all *the big industrial centres in England* there is profound antagonism between the Irish proletariat and the English proletariat. The average English worker hates the Irish worker as a competitor who lowers wages and the *standard of life*. He feels national and religious antipathies for him. He regards him somewhat like the *poor whites* of the Southern States of North America regard their black slaves. This antagonism among the proletarians of England is artificially nourished and supported by the bourgeoisie, it knows that this scission is the true secret of maintaining its power.'[12]

The English worker sees himself as a member of the *ruling* nation in relation to the Irish. In doing so he turns himself 'into a tool of the aristocrats and capitalists of his country *against* Ireland, and thus strengthening their domination *over himself*'. The *antagonism* between the English and the Irish worker is 'the *secret of the impotence of the English working class*, despite its organisation'.[13] These words ring true today. The English working class by identifying with ruling class policy on Ireland strengthens the domination of the ruling class over itself.

The Irish peasant driven off the land formed an oppressed layer of the working class in England. They were looked down upon by sections of the English working class. The working class movement was therefore divided by national antagonism, while the ruling class were united around their common interests in the plunder of Ireland.

This led to Marx's third major point. A working class revolution in England required as a preliminary condition the overthrow of the English landed aristocracy. And that, said Marx, remained impossible because the aristocracy's position in England was invulnerable as long as 'it maintains its strongly entrenched outposts in Ireland'. However the landed aristocracy was most vulnerable in Ireland. The very process which had increased its wealth in Ireland has created a revolutionary opposition to its rule. The Irish peasantry was forced to fight for national independence in order to regain the source of its existence – the land. The Fenian movement was therefore a central threat to the landed aristocracy and hence to a section of the English ruling class. That is why Marx said 'the lever must be applied in Ireland'. Unless the working class in England supported the Fenian movement by calling for the separation of Britain from Ireland, the working class would 'never accomplish anything'. A conclusion that has lost none of its force today.

Marx made the further point that 'Landlordism in Ireland is maintained solely by the *English army*'. It alone prevents an agrarian revolution taking place. And that Ireland was the only pretext for the English government retaining a *big standing army* which, if need be, could be used against the English workers after having done its military training in Ireland.[14] Again a point worth noting for our understanding of the Irish question today.

Marx and Engels' support, through their work in the First International, for the Irish liberation movement was not only to oppose the brutality of English rule on the grounds of 'sympathy' or 'international justice'. As Marx wrote to Kugelmann on 29 November 1869:

> '...both my utterance on this Irish amnesty question and my further proposal to the General Council to discuss the attitude of the English working class to Ireland and to pass resolutions on it have of course other objects besides that of speaking out loudly and decidedly for the oppressed Irish against their oppressors.'[15]

Those 'other objects' were precisely to separate the policy of the working class with regard to Ireland most definitely from the policy of the ruling class. Only by making 'common cause with the Irish' and taking the initiative in dissolving the Act of Union could the working class lay down the basis for its own emancipation. This was inevitably to put Marx into conflict with those opportunist leaders of the English labour movement who wanted to follow Gladstone and the leaders of the liberal bourgeoisie. The Irish question then as today posed the very *practical* question of the struggle against opportunism in the labour movement. As Engels was to remark much later in 1888, on being asked about the attitude of the English workers to the Irish movement:

> 'The masses are *for* the Irish. The organisations and the labour aristocracy in general, follow Gladstone and the liberal bourgeois and do not go further than these.'[16]

Unless the working class were broken from their opportunist leaders who were hand in glove with the ruling class on Ireland, the English working class 'would never accomplish anything'.

THE FIRST INTERNATIONAL AND IRELAND

Marx and Engels not only regarded the Irish question as critical for the class struggle in England but also internationally. England, the dominant world power at that time, was the 'most important country for the workers' revolution' being the 'only country in which the material conditions for this revolution have developed up to a certain degree of maturity'. To hasten the social revolution in England said Marx, in a letter to Meyer and Vogt on 9 April 1870, 'is the most important object of the International'. The sole means of doing this is to make Ireland independent. Marx explained in a letter to the Lafargues on 5 March 1870:

> 'To accelerate the social development in Europe, you must push on the catastrophe of official England. To do so, you must attack her in Ireland. That's her weakest point. Ireland lost, the British "Empire" is gone, and the class war in England, till now somnolent and chronic will assume acute forms . . . '[17]

Therefore the task of the International was everywhere to put the 'conflict between England and Ireland in the foreground, and everywhere to side openly with the Irish'.[18]

The International took up the Irish question on many occasions. It played a leading role in defending the Irish liberation struggle and fighting for the rights of Fenian prisoners.

In 1865 the Fenians made plans for an armed uprising but due to the activities of informers this did not take place, and some of the leaders of the movement were arrested. The Fenian newspapers were suppressed and Habeas Corpus suspended. The General Council of the International supported a campaign started in England in defence of

Fenian prisoners. Then as now the British government treated the Irish political prisoners in the most barbaric fashion. Of note was the Pentonville separate system where the prisoners were kept in solitary confinement and not allowed any association. Any breach of discipline was met by flogging and a regime of bread and water in a dark cell for 28 days. Many prisoners were driven insane by this system. The H-Blocks, the control units, the beatings of Irish political prisoners in our day show how little has changed.

The General Council made sure that wide publicity was given in the press to the barbaric treatment of Irish prisoners, and it supported appeals to collect funds for families of Irish prisoners. Jenny Marx played a crucial role in exposing the treatment of the Fenian prisoners.[19]

In February–March 1867, the armed uprising, for which the Fenians had long prepared, suffered defeat. Many leaders were arrested and put on trial. On 18 September 1867, in Manchester, an armed attack on a police van was organised to release two Fenian leaders. Their escape was a success but during the clash a police officer was killed. Large numbers of Irishmen were soon arbitrarily rounded up. Five were put on trial for their lives accused of killing the policeman. In this patently rigged trial they were all found guilty and sentenced to death. A wave of protest in England and Ireland took place. Marx and his supporters won the International to a call for the commutation of the death sentence.

In the discussion which took place at that time in the General Council of the International, Dupont, a supporter of Marx defended the Fenian movement. He attacked those 'English would-be liberators' who argued that 'Fenianism is not altogether wrong' but asked why they did not employ 'the legal means of meetings and demonstrations by the aid of which we have gained our Reform Bill?' Dupont gave an answer that still serves for those English 'would-be liberators' of the Irish people today.

'What is the use of talking of legal means to a people reduced to the lowest state of misery from century to century by English oppression. . . Having destroyed all – life and liberty – be not surprised that nothing should be found but hatred to the oppressor. Is it well for the English to talk of legality and justice to those who on the slightest suspicion of Fenianism are arrested and incarcerated, and subjected to physical and mental tortures? . . . The English working men who blame the Fenians commit more than a fault, for the cause of both peoples is the same; they have the same enemy to defeat – the territorial aristocracy and the capitalists'.[20]

A bitter debate took place in the Reform League – a movement for Suffrage reform which had six members of the General Council on its standing committee – over a letter in which its President, Beales, while approving the objects of the Fenians had condemned their tactics. He was attacked on the Council of the League and most strongly by members who sat on the General Council of the International – Lucraft, Odger and Weston, the former being prominent British trade union leaders. The Irish they maintained had every right to use force since force was used to deny them their freedom.[21]

A widespread attack in the Press on the Reform League, and Lucraft and Odger in particular, for encouraging Fenian assassins followed. This pleased Marx greatly. As he wrote to Engels on 2 November 1867:

'You will have seen what a row "our people" kicked up in the Reform League. I have sought in every way to provoke this manifestation of the English workers in support of Fenianism.'[22]

After this the bourgeois radical leaders in the Reform League put pressure on Odger and Lucraft to withdraw their statement. At the next meeting of the League's Council Lucraft and Odger went back on their position saying that they had been misunderstood. This highlighted the problems which would later need to be confronted.

Nevertheless there was great support among the working class for the Fenians, which caused Engels to remark in a letter to Kugelmann on 8 November 1867:

'...the London proletarians declare every day more and more openly for the Fenians and, hence – an unheard-of and splendid thing here – for, first, a violent and, secondly, an anti-English movement.'[23]

In spite of the widespread campaign, three of the Fenian prisoners were brutally executed. Engels' comments on this also apply today:

'The Southerners (in the American Civil War) had at least the decency to treat Brown as a *rebel*, whereas here everything is being done to transform a political attempt into a common crime'.[24]

The next major campaign on the issue of Irish prisoners occurred towards the end of 1869. The International helped to organise a mass demonstration in London, estimated at nearly 100,000 people, in support of the demand for amnesty for Irish political prisoners. A discussion took place in the International in November 1869 in the period when Marx put forward the revolutionary position on Ireland.

At these sessions of the General Council Marx, in supporting the Irish struggle, drove a wedge beween the labour movement and Gladstone. In calling for an amnesty for Irish political prisoners, Marx attacked the hypocrisy of Gladstone who during the election had 'justified the Fenian insurrection and said that every other nation would have revolted under similar circumstances' and after being elected had done nothing. Further when faced with a popular amnesty movement and a petition of 200,000 signatures calling for an amnesty he again did nothing. He tried to excuse himself on the grounds that 'the prisoners have not abandoned their designs which were cut short by imprisonment'. Gladstone, Marx said, 'wants them to renounce their principles, to degrade them morally'.[25] Exactly what the British government is trying to do today.

Marx also told the General Council how Dr M'Donnell's letters objecting to the treatment of untried prisoners in Mountjoy led to his dismissal and the promotion of the official who had suppressed his letters. Little has changed when we remember the attempt of the British authorities to smear Robert Irwin, the police surgeon, because of his revelations about torture of Irish prisoners in the period leading to the Bennett Report (see chapter 12).

To Gladstone's argument that the 'Fenians were tried according to lawful custom and found guilty by a jury of their own countrymen' Marx replied:

'If a poacher is tried by a jury of country squires he is tried by his countrymen. It is notorious that the Irish juries are made up of purveyors to the castle whose bread depends upon their verdict. Oppression is always a lawful custom.'[26]

Judges in Ireland, he told the General Council, cannot be independent as their promotion depends on how they serve the government. Today the British have done away with even the pretence of justice. They leave the decision of guilt and sentencing to loyalist judges.

Marx ended his contribution by proposing a resolution which accused Gladstone of 'deliberately insulting the Irish nation', attacked the conduct of the government and supported the amnesty movement.

The discussion of Marx's contribution is important. The attack on Gladstone was clearly too much for some of the English members of the General Council. Odger objected to demands made on the government for the 'unconditional release' of the prisoners. While being himself, of course, for their release he argued 'it is impolitic to proceed in that way, it prejudices the case'. He then went on to defend Gladstone. Marx in answer to Odger reminded him that the resolution was one of support for the Irish and a review of the conduct of the government, and that 'it is more important to make a concession to the Irish people than to Gladstone'.[27]

Mottershead regretted that Englishmen applauded the statement of Marx. Ireland he said, could not be independent. It would undermine the security of Britain. 'If we relinquish our hold, it would only be asking the French to walk in'. He then went on to defend Gladstone. The issue of the security of Britain was to be critical to the Labour Party position in 1920–1 (see chapter 4).

Three English trade unions left the International because of its principled position on the Fenians. While this certainly shows the political bankruptcy of these unions, the debates also show the important effect which Marx's revolutionary stand in support of the Irish had in exposing the opportunist leaders of the British labour movement.

NATIONALISM AND INTERNATIONALISM

There is still one more important dispute which took place in the International on the Irish question. This time it was Engels who put forward the internationalist standpoint. At the Council Meeting of 14 May 1872, John Hales, an English trade unionist and secretary to the General Council, opposed the formation of *Irish* nationalist branches of the International in England. He argued that such branches went against the 'fundamental principle of the Association' which was 'to destroy all semblance of nationalist doctrine'. Further the formation of Irish branches in England 'could only keep alive that national antagonism which . . . existed between the people of the two countries'.[28]

Engels' reply to Hales is of great importance. His essential argument was that in the case of the Irish, true internationalism must necessarily be based upon a distinct national organisation which had as its first and most pressing duty the national independence of Ireland. He argued that it was an insult to Irish working men to ask them to submit to a British Federal Council.

'If members of a conquering nation called upon the nation they had conquered and continued to hold down to forget their specific nationality and position, to "sink national differences" and so forth, that was not Internationalism, it was nothing else but preaching to them submission to the yoke, and attempting to justify

and to perpetuate the dominion of the conqueror under the cloak of
Internationalism. It was sanctioning the belief, only too common
among the English working men, that they were superior beings
compared to the Irish . . .'[29]

He argued that if the motion were adopted 'after the dominion of the
English aristocracy over Ireland, after the dominion of the middle class
over Ireland, (the Irish) must now look forth to the advent of the
dominion of the English working class over Ireland'. Engels was fully
aware that the antagonism between the Irish and English working class
in England had been 'the most powerful means by which class rule was
upheld in England'. Now, he said, for the first time when there were
possibilities of English and Irish workers acting together in their joint
interests, the International was being asked to dictate to the Irish. They
were being told that they must not carry on the movement in their own
way but submit to be ruled by an English Council.

The Hales motion was put and lost with only one voting in favour.
Engels' intervention had prevented the International undermining its
own cause among Irish workers.

Engels' intervention was to be clearly vindicated in November 1872.
The Irish members of the International in London decided to organise
a massive demonstration in Hyde Park to demand a general amnesty
for Irish prisoners. They contacted all London's democratic organisations and set up a committee which included McDonnell (an Irishman),
Murray (an Englishman) and Lessner (a German) – all members of the
last General Council of the International. There was a new regulation
in force which gave the government the right to control public meetings
in London's parks. Two days written notice had to be given of such
meetings, indicating the names of the speakers. The Irish, said Engels
in his report of the event, 'who represent the most revolutionary element of the population' were not prepared to submit to this regulation
seeing it as an attack on one of the people's rights. The committee
unanimously agreed to this stand.

The massive demonstration took place as arranged, some 35,000
being there and hearing 'forceful' speeches demanding a general
amnesty and a repeal of the Coercion Laws. This was the first time an
Irish demonstration had been held in Hyde Park. It was also the first
time the English and Irish sections of the population had united in
friendship. As Engels said 'this gratifying fact is due principally to the
influence of the last General Council of the International, which has
always directed all its efforts to unite the workers of both peoples on a

basis of complete equality'. He ended his report of the demonstration by saying that the Irish through their energetic efforts had saved the right of the people of London to hold meetings in parks 'when and how they please'.[30]

NOTES

1   Lenin, *Collected Works (LCW)* Moscow 1964 Volume 20 p. 442.
2   Marx K and Engels F, *Ireland and the Irish Question (MEOI)* Moscow 1978 p. 57.
3   *MEOI* pp. 59–60.
4   Marx K and Engels F, *Collected Works (MECW)* London 1976 Volume 6 p. 389.
5   *MECW*, London 1979 Volume 12 p. 132.
6   *MEOI* pp. 397–8.
7   *ibid* p. 93.
8   *ibid* p. 94.
9   *ibid* p. 136.
10   *ibid* p. 157.
11   Marx to Meyer and Vogt 9 April 1870, *MEOI* pp. 406–9 for this and other quotes below.
12   *MEOI* p. 254.
13   *ibid* p. 408.
14   *ibid* p. 255.
15   *ibid* p. 394.
16   *ibid* p. 460.
17   *ibid* p. 404.
18   *ibid* p. 408.
19   *ibid* pp. 496–522.
20   *ibid* pp. 486–7.
21   See Collins H and Abramsky C, *Karl Marx and the British Labour Movement* London 1965 p. 132.
22   *MEOI* p. 153.
23   *ibid* p. 155.
24   *ibid* p. 155.
25   *ibid* pp. 162–3
26   *ibid* p. 165.
27   *ibid* p. 168.
28   *ibid* pp. 527–8.
29   *ibid* p. 419.
30   *ibid* pp. 423–5.

CHAPTER TWO

THE SOCIALIST REVOLUTION AND THE RIGHT OF NATIONS TO SELF-DETERMINATION

The period from the end of the First International to the founding Conference of the Third (Communist) International was a decisive one for the working class movement world-wide. In this period a fundamental change in the nature of the capitalist system took place. Capitalism entered its imperialist phase.

IMPERIALISM AND THE WORKING CLASS

What was true of the relationship of Britain and Ireland in the later part of the nineteenth century was mirrored all over the world with the development of imperialism as a world system. By the turn of the century capitalism, in its relentless drive for profits, had entered its imperialist phase – a world-wide system of colonial oppression and financial domination of the overwhelming majority of the world by a small number of imperialist countries. Imperialism divides the world into oppressed and oppressor nations. It also divides the working class. A handful of imperialist countries obtain high monopoly profits out of the brutal exploitation of oppressed peoples world-wide. Out of these 'super-profits' imperialism is able to create and sustain a small privileged and influential layer of the working class in the imperialist countries whose conditions of life isolate it from the suffering, poverty and temper of the mass of the working class. Such workers, a labour aristocracy, constitute the social base of opportunism in the working class movement. So critical was this development for the working class movement and so great the damage done to the interests of the working class as a result of the activities of these opportunist layers that Lenin, at the Second Congress of the Communist International (1920), said that:

'Opportunism is our principal enemy. Opportunism in the upper ranks of the working-class movement is not proletarian socialism but bourgeois socialism. Practice has shown that the active people in the working class movement who adhere to the opportunist trend are better defenders of the bourgeoisie than the bourgeoisie itself. Without their leadership of the workers, the bourgeoisie could not remain in power.'[1]

These developments in the working class movement occurred in the major imperialist countries at the turn of the century. However, in Britain they took place a lot earlier. In the nineteenth century the British bourgeoisie managed to split the British working class movement.

In the middle of the nineteenth century Britain already revealed at least two major distinguishing features of imperialism, vast colonies and monopoly profits. Because of its monopoly in the world market the profits of British capital were very high. These 'super-profits' allowed a relatively privileged standard of life for an aristocracy of labour – for a minority of skilled well-paid workers. These workers were organised in narrow, self-interested craft unions and they isolated themselves from the mass of the working class. They looked down on the unskilled worker. Politically this labour aristocracy supported the Liberals, who they looked to for the political and economic reforms thought necessary to guarantee their continued advancement and to secure their privileged existence. They were contemptuous of socialism, regarding it as 'utopian'. It is indicative of the political influence of this layer that Lenin could remark, with justification even in 1913, that 'nowhere in the world are there so many liberals among the advanced workers as in Britain'.[2]

In the last quarter of the nineteenth century things began to change. Britain's monopoly power was being challenged by American, German and French capitalism. The economic basis of the narrow petit bourgeois trade unionism and liberalism among the British workers was being undermined. The previously tolerable conditions of life gave way to extreme want as the cost of living rose and real wages fell. The class struggle intensified and this period saw the emergence and development of socialist organisations. The unskilled workers, encouraged and aided by the socialists, were organised in the wave of the New Unionism which swept Britain at the end of the nineteenth century. In 1889 the Gas Workers Union and the Dockers Union were founded under the leadership of Will Thorne, Tom Mann and Ben Tillett. The next 25 years saw the inevitable conflict between the mass of the

IKBR–C

working class and the Liberal-Labour leadership which dominated the political and trade-union organisations of the labour movement.

IMPERIALISM AND COLONIAL POLICY

As Britain's economic superiority was being challenged, the opportunism of the leaders of the British labour movement necessarily took on the form of national chauvinism – a defence of the 'nation'. To retain their privileged position they needed to maintain their alliance with the bourgeoisie. This opportunist leadership of the labour movement therefore supported, in one form or another, the colonial policy of their 'nation'. Lenin pointed out the importance of this development in 1907, in an article on the Congress of the Second International held at Stuttgart that year.

'The British bourgeoisie... derives more profit from the many millions of the population of India and other colonies than from the British workers. In certain countries this provides the material and economic basis for infecting the proletariat with colonial chauvinism. Of course, this may be only a temporary phenomenon, but the evil must nonetheless be clearly realised and its causes understood in order to be able to rally the proletariat of all countries for the struggle against such opportunism.'[3]

At Stuttgart a major difference emerged in the Second International on the question of colonial policy. While all parties to the dispute, *of course*, rejected the present methods of capitalist colonial policy, a resolution was placed before the Congress which departed significantly from previous positions. It stated in its opening paragraph that:

'The Congress notes that the benefits and necessity of the colonies are grossly exaggerated, especially for the working class. However, the Congress does not, in principle and for all times, reject all colonial policy, which, under a socialist regime, may have a civilising effect.'[4]

The dispute centred around this part of the resolution and the Congress almost split on the issue. 128 rejected this part of the resolution and with it the possibility of any so-called 'socialist' colonial policy. 107 voted for it and there were 10 abstentions. The English delegation split, 14 votes being given in favour of 'socialist' colonial policy including that of Ramsay MacDonald (Independent Labour Party), who spoke in favour, and 6 were against including the Social Democratic

Federation – an indication of the division in the British movement yet to come. All the Russian delegation voted against, a pointer to the revolutionary stand to be made by the Russian movement in the future.

At this Congress what was later to be called the Social-Democratic (evolutionary-socialist) trend in the international movement – a trend which encompassed the Fabians, the British Labour Party and most of the ILP – emerged as a significant force. Bernstein, a member of the German Social Democratic Party, expressed their opportunist stand with its clear racist overtones when he said:

'There can be no question of defending the capitalist colonial policy. All of us are its opponents, the question is merely how we give expression to this opposition . . .

'We must not assume a purely negative standpoint . . . on the question of colonial policy, but instead must pursue a positive socialist colonial policy. (Bravo!) We must get away from the utopian idea that aims at simply leaving the colonies. The final consequence of that view would be to return the United States to the Red Indians. (disturbance in meeting) The colonies are there. We must put up with this fact. A certain guardianship of cultured peoples over non-cultured peoples is a necessity, which should also be recognised by socialists . . .

' . . . A great part of our economic system is based on the exploitation of resources from the colonies which the natives would not know what to do with. For this reason, we must adopt the majority resolution (on socialist colonial policy).'[5]

While the Congress narrowly defeated Bernstein's position there was a fundamental split in the international movement. This split was finally consolidated when the main parties of the Second International supported the First Imperialist War. The revolutionary trend in the working class movement was to carry through its consistent opposition to all colonial policy and its support for the right of nations to self-determination, to an opposition to imperialist war. This trend eventually founded the Third (Communist) International in 1919.

Given this dispute and the later developments, we need to understand why the attitude of socialists to the national question is such a decisive factor in determining the outcome of the socialist revolution. And why the revolutionary struggle for socialism has to be linked up with a revolutionary programme on the national question.

SOCIALISTS AND THE RIGHT OF NATIONS TO SELF-DETERMINATION

Many socialists argue against all nationalism on the grounds that they are 'internationalists'. But this is to turn internationalism into a lifeless and reactionary abstraction. This avoids confronting the reality of imperialism: the fact that the world has been divided into oppressor and oppressed nations and that national oppression has been extended and intensified. It also ignores the split in the working class movement. One section, the labour aristocracy, has been corrupted by the 'crumbs that fall from the table' of the imperialist bourgeoisie, obtained from the super-exploitation and brutal oppression of the people from oppressed nations. The other, the mass of the working class, cannot liberate itself without uniting with the movement of oppressed peoples against imperialist domination. Only such an alliance will make it possible to wage a united fight against the imperialist powers, the imperialist bourgeoisie, and their bought-off agents in the working class movement. This means the working class fighting in alliance with national liberation movements to destroy imperialism *for the purpose of the socialist revolution*.

The unity of all forces against imperialism can only be achieved on the basis of *the* internationalist principle 'No nation can be free if it oppresses other nations'. This is expressed through the demand of the right of nations to self-determination. Far from being counterposed to the socialist revolution, it is precisely to promote it that communists are so insistent on this demand. This demand recognises that class solidarity of workers is strengthened by the substitution of voluntary ties between nations for compulsory, militaristic ones. The demand for complete equality between nations, by removing distrust between the workers of the oppressor and oppressed nations, lays the foundation for a united international struggle for the socialist revolution. That is, for the only regime under which complete national equality can be achieved.

> 'To insist upon, to advocate, and to recognise this *right* (of self-determination) is to insist on the equality of nations, to refuse to recognise *compulsory* ties, to oppose all state privileges for any nation whatsoever, and to cultivate a spirit of complete class solidarity in the workers of the different nations.'[6]

Our 'internationalists', when confronted with these arguments, are forced to adopt yet another line of approach. Of course, they say, we support the right of nations to self determination, but as 'socialists' we are opposed to bourgeois and/or petit bourgeois nationalism. Once again they avoid the reality of national oppression. They ignore the fact that, as Lenin pointed out, the *actual* conditions of the workers in the oppressed and in the oppressor nations are not the same from the standpoint of national oppression. The struggle of the working class against national oppression has a twofold character:

'(a) first, it is the "action" of the nationally oppressed proletariat and peasantry *jointly* with the nationally oppressed bourgeoisie *against* the oppressor nation; (b) second, it is the "action" of the proletariat, or of its class-conscious section, in the oppressor nation *against* the bourgeoisie of that nation and all the elements that follow it.'[7]

Let us examine these two points in turn.

In general, all national movements are an alliance of different class forces which unite together for the purpose of achieving national freedom. The bourgeoisie in the oppressed nation supports the struggle for national freedom only in so far as it promotes its own class interests. For this class, national freedom means the freedom to exploit its own working class, to accumulate wealth for itself, to establish itself as a national capitalist class. If, at any point, the struggle for national freedom threatens the conditions of capitalist exploitation itself, the bourgeoisie will abandon the national struggle for an alliance with imperialism.

The working class supports the struggle for national freedom as part of its struggle to abolish all privilege, all oppression and all exploitation – this being the precondition of its own emancipation. The working class policy in the national movement is to support the bourgeoisie only in a certain direction, but it never coincides with the bourgeoisie's policy. For this reason, the working class only gives the bourgeoisie *conditional* support. Insofar as the bourgeoisie of the oppressed nation fights the oppressor, the working class strongly supports its struggle. As Lenin so clearly argued in 1914:

'The bourgeois nationalism of *any* oppressed nation has a general democratic content that is directed *against* oppression, and it is this content that we *unconditionally* support.'[8]

Insofar as the bourgeoisie of the oppressed nation stands for its own bourgeois nationalism, for privileges for itself, the working class opposes it.

The important thing for the working class is to ensure the development of its class. The bourgeoisie is concerned to hamper this development by pushing forward its own class interests at the expense of the working class. The outcome of this clash of interests in the national struggle cannot be determined in advance. It depends on the concrete context in which the struggle for national freedom takes place.

The guiding light for the working-class movement is clear. The working class rejects all privileges for its 'own' national bourgeoisie, and its 'own' nation. It is opposed to compulsory ties between nations standing firmly for the equality of nations. In the oppressor nation, the working class can *only* express this position by insisting on the right of nations to self-determination. And it does this in the interest of international working class solidarity. A refusal to support the right of nations to self-determination must mean in practice support for the privileges of its own ruling class and its bought-off agents in the working class movement. Therefore, support for the right of nations to self-determination is the *only* basis for a united struggle against national oppression and imperialism, and for the socialist revolution. Whether the exercise of this right takes the form of complete separation or not hinges on the conduct of the working class and the socialist movement in the oppressor nation. The history of the Irish struggle for self-determination underlines this.

Marx and Engels had at first expected that the English working class, having overthrown capitalism in England, would then go on to free Ireland. After 1848, however, the English proletariat lost its revolutionary drive and fell under the influence of the Liberals while the national liberation movement in Ireland developed and assumed revolutionary forms. Marx and Engels, therefore, called upon the English working class 'to make common cause with the Irish' and support the dissolution of the forced Union of Ireland and England in the interest of their *own* emancipation. As Marx wrote in January 1870:

> 'The transformation of the present *forced Union* (that is to say, the slavery of Ireland) into an *equal and free Confederation*, if possible, or into complete Separation, if necessary, is a *preliminary condition* of the emancipation of the English working class.'[9]

Whether the dissolution of the *forced Union* would take the form of complete separation or a free federal relationship would depend on the manner in which it was carried out. A 'free confederation' was a possibility if the emancipation of Ireland was achieved in a revolutionary manner and was fully supported by the English working class. Such a solution to the historical problem of Ireland, as Lenin pointed out, would have been in the best interest of the working class and 'most conducive to rapid social progress'.[10] Such close links between the proletariat in Ireland and England would have played a decisive role in a united international struggle for the socialist revolution in Europe. However, this was not to be. The failure of the British working class movement to support the Dublin workers in 1913 made it clear that the interests of the Irish working class could only be advanced through Ireland's complete separation from Britain. The long held view of that great revolutionary socialist, James Connolly, was to be confirmed. As he argued in 1916 a few weeks before the Easter Rising:

' . . . is it not well and fitting that we of the working class should fight for the freedom of the nation from foreign rule, as the first requisite for the free development of the national powers needed for our class? It is so fitting.'[11]

Socialists in Britain would soon be put to the test. The right of the Irish people to self-determination could only mean for socialists *complete separation* and, as Lenin argued, socialists could not, without ceasing to be socialists, reject such a struggle in whatever form, right down to an uprising or war. The years to the partition of Ireland were to show how the working-class movement in Britain failed to support the national struggle in Ireland. Imperialism and war not only split the working-class movement but also divided the national movement in Ireland into a revolutionary and a reactionary wing. The British working class movement did not support the revolutionary wing of the national movement in Ireland and in failing to do so betrayed both its own interests and those of the Irish working class.

In the period from the defeat of the Fenian rising in 1867 to the partition of Ireland and the Irish civil war, Ireland again took on a decisive importance for the British working class. For the ability of the working class to break from its own opportunist leadership and so move in a revolutionary direction was to be measured by its support for the Irish revolution.

NOTES

1   Lenin, *On Britain* Moscow n.d. p. 523. See also *LCW* Volume 31 p.231. For the development of Lenin's position on imperialism, see 'Imperialism, the Highest Stage of Capitalism' *LCW* Volume 22 pp. 185–304 and 'Imperialism and the Split

in Socialism' *LCW* Volume 23 pp. 105–20 (both available as separate pamphlets).

2 Lenin, *LCW* Volume 19 p. 370. For the development of the labour aristocracy in Britain in this period see David Reed, 'Marx and Engels: The Labour Aristocracy, Opportunism and the British Labour Movement' *Fight Racism! Fight Imperialism!* No 27 March 1983.

3 Lenin, *LCW* Volume 13 p. 77.

4 International Socialist Congress, Proposals and Drafts of Resolutions 18–24 August 1907, published by the International Socialist Bureau. Our translation from the German. The quotes are taken from the Plenary Session and Commission on the Colonial Question.

5 *ibid*. See also Bernstein E, *Evolutionary Socialism* (1899) – English translation, New York 1961, for the full development of Bernstein's opportunist and racist standpoint.

6 Lenin, 'On the Question of National Policy' *LCW* Volume 20 p. 223.

7 Lenin, 'A Caricature of Marxism and Imperialist Economism' *LCW* Volume 23 p. 62.

8 Lenin, 'The Right of Nations to Self-determination' *LCW* Volume 20 p. 412. Most of the arguments in this section are taken from Lenin's writings on the national question. The most important articles are available in pamphlet form.

9 Marx K and Engels F, *Articles on Britain* Moscow 1975 pp. 356–7. See also *MEOI* p. 255.

10 Lenin, *LCW* Volume 20 p. 441.

11 Connolly J, 'The Irish Flag' in *Labour and Easter Week* Dublin 1966 p. 175. Also in James Connolly *Selected Writings* London 1973 p. 145.

PART TWO

THE FIGHT FOR AN
IRISH REPUBLIC

JAMES CONNOLLY

CHAPTER THREE

HOME RULE

HOME RULE AND THE LAND QUESTION

After the defeat of the Fenian uprising in 1867, the opposition to British rule in Ireland mainly came through the Land League and Parnell's leadership of the Irish (Home Rule) Party in the British House of Commons. The last years of the 1870s saw bad harvests in Ireland and famine soon threatened again. The peasantry organised in Michael Davitt's Land League resisted evictions and seized land from the landlords – the land war had begun. They were supported by the Irish Republican Brotherhood which had secretly reorganised in 1873. Parnell became President of the Land League, so reinforcing his parliamentary campaign and 'obstruction' tactics in the House of Commons with the implied threat of a resort to violence if efforts to obtain Home Rule should fail. The Irish Party also held the balance of power between the Liberal and Conservative Parties, so the Irish question could not be pushed aside.

Gladstone's response to this was typical of the British ruling class – coercion mixed with partial reform. Exactly the policy the British ruling class were to adopt in our own period in the early 1970s when faced with a resurgence of revolutionary nationalism in Ireland. It was designed to crush the revolutionary wing of the movement and bring closer to British policy the reformist wing.

In August 1881 a conciliatory Land Act was passed giving some fixity of tenure to the Irish peasantry and creating Land Courts for establishing fair rents but falling far short of the demands of the Land League. In October 1881 the Land League was proclaimed illegal, meetings were broken up by the police, *habeas corpus* was suspended and over 1,000 people were imprisoned including Davitt and Parnell.

In 1882 a deal was concluded between Gladstone and Parnell for a 'peaceful' settlement of the land question through improvements to the Act and a repeal of the Coercion Act then in force. The political prisoners were released. Soon after, the new Chief Secretary and the Under-Secretary for Ireland were assassinated in Phoenix Park, Dublin. The Crimes Act 1882 was passed which more or less introduced martial law again in Ireland – this was the fifty-seventh Special Act dealing with Irish resistance to British rule since the Act of Union in 1801. And so it went on.

In 1886 Gladstone's first Home Rule Bill, a concession forced out of the British government by the revolutionary land war, was introduced into parliament offering the Irish limited self-government. It was defeated by an alliance of Liberal Unionists and the Conservative Party, backed by the promised use of violent resistance to Home Rule by the Orange Lodges of Belfast. The latter were given great encouragement by none other than Lord Randolph Churchill of the Conservative Party. New elections saw the Conservative Party come to power.

The activities of the Land League continued and a perpetual Coercion Act – the Crimes Act 1887 – was introduced. Five thousand people were charged under the Act in 3 years. Parnell died in 1891. A new Home Rule Bill was introduced by Gladstone in 1893 but was defeated by the veto of the House of Lords. Gladstone retired in 1894 and the issue of Home Rule in the British Parliament retreated into the background.

The Land Act 1903 offered a Government loan to tenant-farmers to buy their land and to repay the government over a period of, in the main, less than 70 years. As Lenin pointed out, the Liberals' 'system of land-purchase at a "fair" price' means that the tenant-farmer will continue to pay for many years 'millions upon millions to the British landlords as a reward for their having robbed him for centuries and reduced him to a state of chronic starvation'.[1] As a result of the Land Acts the land question ceased to be the dominant issue. It became one component among others in the struggle which was to build up over the next 15 years – that of a fight for an Irish Republic. In this period a new force – the Irish working class – was to take up the struggle.

IRISH LABOUR CONFRONTS BRITISH IMPERIALISM

The debates in the First International had already shown that many of the leaders of the English trade-unions were not prepared to criticise Gladstone and the Liberals for their policy on Ireland. In the last quarter of the nineteenth century the trade-union and labour leaders drew even closer to the Liberals standing as Liberal candidates and supporting Liberal policy. Even in 1906, 25 out of 29 constituencies won by the newly formed Labour Party were won with the help of the Liberals.

The end of the nineteenth century saw the rise of the new Unions of unskilled workers. They had been founded and promoted by Socialists in conditions when faith in the capitalist system was being severely shaken. They began to challenge the domination over the labour movement of the Liberal-Labour leadership of the old aristocratic unions. The next 20 years would see this struggle take place. *The Irish question decisively influenced its outcome.*

At the Paris Congress of the Second International (1900) Connolly's Irish Socialist Republican Party (founded in 1896) achieved separate representation for Ireland in the face of opposition from the British delegates. The latter argued that Ireland was not an independent country, but part of Great Britain. At the Congress the Irish delegation gave the British a further lesson in revolutionary socialism by being one of the two delegations totally opposed to socialists entering bourgeois governments. Connolly, unable to attend the Congress, fully supported the Irish delegation's stand.[2] The ISRP unfortunately had little influence at that time in Ireland but it began the struggle to unite the cause of Irish Labour with national independence.

The Irish TUC (1894) was formed at a time when British unions were still predominant in organising Irish workers and British parties like the Independent Labour Party and the Fabians had a few branches in Ireland, especially in Dublin and Belfast. However, from 1907 onwards the process of Irish workers joining the British amalgamated unions began to receive a succession of major jolts as 'New Unionism' raised its head in Ireland. James Larkin was at the centre of this process.[3]

Larkin was born in Liverpool of Irish parents in 1876. He had to earn his living at the age of 11. By 16 he was a member of the Independent Labour Party and a socialist. During the Boer War he was arrested and fined several times for his street-corner denunciations of the War as a 'jingo-imperialist venture'. In 1901 he joined the National Union of Dock Workers and soon after leading a strike in 1905 he was elected to be the Union's general organiser. It was in that capacity that Larkin first went to Ireland in 1907 on an organisation drive for his Union.

Larkin very soon after arriving in Ireland set about organising the dock workers in Belfast (1907), Dublin (1908) and Cork (1909) in the Union. In Belfast in 1907 he led a bitter and violent strike when fifty English dockers imported through the Shipping Federation to Belfast were being used to smash the Union. During the strike troops fired on workers in the Catholic Falls Road area killing three and injuring many others. The employers and the authorities tried to sow divisions between the Catholic and Protestant workers, using the fact that Larkin was a Catholic, but due to Larkin's efforts, they did not succeed. The strike eventually went to arbitration with the dockers, although organised, having to go back on not very satisfactory terms. Nevertheless in managing to unite Protestant and Catholic workers in organising the docks in Belfast, Larkin's achievement, while not to be durable in the long run, was remarkable.

John Maclean, the Scottish revolutionary socialist, who on the invitation of Larkin had been in Belfast for a few days during the strike, on his return to Scotland, wrote articles defending the strikers and accusing the Liberal Government of murder. He was attacked by Philip Snowden, that vile reactionary Labour MP, who had defended the Government's 'employment of the military to quell disorder'.[4] The *Socialist*, the paper of the Socialist Labour Party – a left-wing split from the Social Democratic Federation – also took up the defence of the strikers, and in particular attacked the Labour MPs in parliament. 'Beyond asking a couple of questions, they did nothing... From Shackleton to Will Thorne they have become accomplices of capitalist murder'.[5] Just like the Labour MPs on Ireland today. Already the divide in the British labour movement on Ireland was becoming clear.

Larkin now concentrated his energies in organising the dockers in Dublin. In 1908 he was involved in another series of bitter strikes, with the employers again attempting to smash the Union. During this period Larkin increasingly clashed with Union Headquarters. On one occasion, the Union leadership in England settled a dispute over his head. Sexton, General Secretary of the Union, was bitterly opposed to Larkin's activities and, particularly, the sympathetic strike. The dispute soon came to a head. In 1908 Larkin appealed for assistance. Sexton sent a postcard saying 'Stew in your own juice'.[6] When Larkin warned the Executive who were intent on holding his work back that 'there was a movement on foot for organising the whole of unskilled labour in Ireland',[7] Sexton's reply was to notify Larkin and all the Union branches of his suspension from the Union on 7 December 1908. Larkin's reply was to form the Irish Transport and General Workers Union (ITGWU) decisively separating from the reactionary leadership of Sexton and Co.

The ITGWU, in its rule book, announced an end to the 'policy of grafting ourselves on the English Trade Union Movement'. The Union was unique in many respects. It embodied a political programme which included nationalisation of all means of transport, the legal eight-hours-day, provision of work for all unemployed and 'the land of Ireland for the people of Ireland'.[8] It declared its dedication to the organisation into one union of all workers – skilled and unskilled – in an industry. It argued for the use of boycotts and sympathetic strike action (a revolutionary position for trade-unions) to achieve its ends. In 1911 James Connolly, having returned from America, became the Belfast Secretary of the ITGWU. So an Irish union, having broken with the English trade-union traditions, born out of bitter struggles against the capitalist class in Ireland was now led by two revolutionary socialists – James Larkin and James Connolly.

The revolutionary potential of the British trade-union and labour movement was now to be gauged by its attitude and support for the ITGWU.

THE DUBLIN LOCK OUT

By 1911, the ITGWU had established such an organisation amongst unskilled workers in Dublin that the employers had set up their own federation to combat it. In August 1913, William Martin Murphy, owner of the Dublin United Tramways Company and the Irish Independent Group of Newspapers, took the initiative in the effort of the Dublin employers to smash the ITGWU. He told the workers in the dispatch department of his newspaper company that they must resign from the Union and sign an assurance they would not strike or they would be dismissed from the company. The Union put pickets on retailers selling Murphy's paper the *Irish Independent*. The ITGWU members were locked out on 26 August. 700 workers from Murphy's Tramways Company walked off their trams leaving them wherever they happened to be. Murphy called a meeting of the Dublin Employers Federation and on 3 September 400 employers agreed to lock out all their workers. By 22 September 25,000 workers had been locked out, involving, with their families, one third of the population of Dublin. If the same proportion of workers were locked out in London today, there would be about three quarters of a million locked out.

A meeting in support of the locked out men and the strikers was called for Sunday 31 August in O'Connell Street. It was to be addressed by Larkin. Rumours suggested that the meeting would be banned.

On the Thursday, 28 August, Larkin and other ITGWU officials were arrested for seditious libel and seditious conspiracy. They were released on bail on the understanding they would not break the law while awaiting trial. On the Friday the meeting was banned by proclamation. That evening Larkin burnt the 'Proclamation of the King' in front of a crowd of 10,000 people at Beresford Place. Announcing that 'People make Kings and people can unmake them' he said that 'we will meet in O'Connell Street, and if the police and soldiers stop the meeting let them take the responsibility'.[9] Another warrant was put out for Larkin's arrest. Larkin, however, turned up in disguise on the balcony of a hotel (owned by Murphy) in O'Connell Street at the time of the meeting. After he started to speak to the crowd he was immediately arrested. Soon after, the police indiscriminately baton charged the crowd and the result was yet another Bloody Sunday in Ireland's history. Two men were killed over the weekend of Bloody Sunday and hundreds were injured.

Connolly was also arrested with Larkin. Connolly refused to recognise the court and was sentenced to three months. He was released after a week's hunger strike. Larkin was released on bail on 12 September and decided to leave for England and Scotland to appeal for support.

The support of the British trade-union movement for the strike was to be critical. At its 1 September Congress the British TUC could not avoid discussing the Dublin events. In the debate James Sexton called for support, 'black as James Larkin might be, and James Connolly too'.[10] Very useful! The Congress did not vote support for the strike. It simply condemned the conduct of the Dublin police and decided to send a delegation to investigate the situation there. A motion demanding the release of Larkin and Connolly and calling for finance for the strikers was not put to the vote. 'Revolutionary speeches' were made by Ben Tillett and Robert Smillie, but this couldn't help the strikers.

While the TUC delegation was in Dublin it spent a great part of its time trying to patch up a dirty compromise with the employers. But the employers refused to comply, no doubt confident in the knowledge that if the TUC hadn't acted at the beginning of the strike they had little to fear. In contrast, the strength of the Dublin workers was demonstrated on 3 September when 50,000 workers marched behind the coffin of James Nolan, one of the workers murdered by the police. The funeral procession was guarded by ITGWU squads bearing makeshift arms – an embryo of the Irish Citizen Army formed the following month as an armed workers defence force against the attacks of police and scab workers. The Dublin police kept out of sight.

Soon the number of workers on strike or locked out grew. The British TUC began to send money and foodstuffs to Dublin. The Miners Federation voted to give £1,000 a week and various Labour newspapers opened subscription lists. But the bulk of this aid did not come until late September. Although the money and foodships were vital to workers whom the employers were trying to starve back to work, they could not take the place of solidarity action.

While the British TUC was as afraid of the ITGWU as the Dublin employers, the rank and file responded quickly to the example of the Dublin workers. The Liverpool railwaymen went out on strike on 9 September and began real solidarity action, which the Executive of the National Union of Railwaymen and the British TUC did their best to destroy. 3,000 in Liverpool came out one day, followed by 4,000 in Birmingham the next day. Transport strikes took place in London, Liverpool, Birmingham, and Manchester. NUR officials led by J H Thomas were trying everything they could to get the workers back. (Eventually, they did succeed.) The strike spread to other parts of the country. The rank and file wanted a national strike. The British TUC responded by announcing a fund and the first of the foodships for the strikers. The revolutionary socialist Sylvia Pankhurst's comments were well placed when she said:

'In the long-drawn misery of the Dublin lock-out its victims pleaded vainly for sympathetic action by British transport workers, and received instead a "food ship" from the Trade Union Congress – a mere handful of crumbs in the vast desert of their need'.[11]

When, at the end of October, the Dublin Strike Committee appealed for direct financial aid, the British TUC sent £2,000 to be distributed only to affiliated unions. As the ITGWU was not affiliated to the British TUC it was not able to have any of this money.[12]

On 27 October, Larkin's trial was held and he was sentenced to seven months in jail. On the following Sunday a gigantic meeting took place in the Albert Hall in London to protest against Larkin's sentence. Sylvia Pankhurst defied arrest to speak at this meeting in support of Larkin. Connolly called on everyone to work and vote against the Liberal Government until Larkin was free. Public opinion and the by-election results soon had the desired effect as the Liberals lost votes. Larkin was freed after only 17 days in gaol.

Larkin then launched his 'fiery cross' campaign of public meetings in England, Scotland and Wales. 5,000 heard him speak in the Manchester Free Trade Hall with 20,000 waiting outside. The workers called for national strike action. A few days later, mid-November, the British TUC decided to call a special Congress on the Dublin lock out for 9 December in order to head off the pressure of the rank-and-file workers for national strike action. Larkin addressed a massive meeting in the Albert Hall the next evening – 10,000 inside and 15,000 waiting outside. George Lansbury, Editor of the *Daily Herald*, and other socialists denounced the Labour Party and the reactionary trade union officials for their inaction.

A few days later Larkin decided to go over the heads of the trade-union leaders and appeal to the rank-and-file. He told them through a manifesto printed in the *Daily Herald* to tell their leaders 'for the future they must stand for Trade Unionism' and 'that they are not there as apologists for the shortcomings of the capitalist system'.[13] Larkin had issued a revolutionary appeal to the British workers to split from their treacherous leaders and unite with the Dublin workers. Attacks on Larkin now began. J H Wilson, head of the National Seamen's and Firemen's Union, issued a manifesto denouncing Larkin and the methods of the Transport Union in Dublin. Larkin was soon to reply. He told a massive meeting in London in referring to J H Wilson and Philip Snowden that 'I am not going to allow these serpents to raise their foul heads and spit out their poison any longer'. He denounced the union leaders and the Labour Party for failing to support the strike. J H Thomas was particularly singled out for forcing rank and file railwaymen back to work.

The 9 December British TUC Congress took place. Connolly presented the Irish case for holding out. Then, to everyone's amazement, Ben Tillett moved a resolution condemning Larkin's unfair attacks on British trade union officials. He was then considered one of the most militant trade unionists in Britain and had only a few weeks earlier stood on platforms with Larkin calling for armed worker squads. He went on to ask the Congress to affirm its confidence in the ability of these officials to negotiate an honourable settlement. Armed squads were one thing. Attacking the leadership of the trade union movement quite another. Larkin confronted Tillett with a choice: stand with the masses, with Larkin and against his fellow trade union leaders, or desert the workers and go over to the other side. Tillett went over. When the First Imperialist War broke out nine months later Tillett became a recruiting sergeant for imperialism.

Speaker after speaker got up and condemned Larkin. He was finally called on to reply. He began, 'Mr Chairman and human beings', and amidst continual uproar he denounced those leaders who had betrayed the strike. He told them the Dublin workers would struggle on to the end. The Congress offered nothing. After all it had only been called to stave off the pressure of the rank-and-file.[14]

The strike was eventually lost. Without British TUC support it could not be won. It revealed, as events in Britain were later to show and Ben Tillett's sell-out conclusively proved, that the revolutionary trends in the British working class were not strong enough to defeat the opportunist leadership of the British labour movement. Opportunism had triumphed.

The opportunist leaders of the British labour movement and the employers of Dublin certainly were in agreement on one vital thing. As William Martin Murphy so clearly said about his stand:

> 'It is not a question of an attack on trade unionism at all. I have been in business for nearly fifty years, and I have never before known anything like Larkinism. It is not trade unionism in the ordinary sense at all.'[15]

The Secretary of the Engineering Employers' Federation made the same point.

> 'A victory for the syndicalist leaders there would be disastrous for the employers not only in Dublin, but throughout the United Kingdom.'[16]

The revolutionary unionism of the Dublin working class had shown the way. Larkin instinctively followed what Lenin was later to call 'the essence of Marxist tactics'.[17] He went deeper and lower into the masses. The ITGWU represented the organisation of the unskilled Irish workers and exposed to the world their revolutionary strength and courage. The democracy of the ITGWU was firmly based on the masses, its organising principle proletarian solidarity. It created the first armed workers' militia – the Irish Citizen Army. It later opposed the imperialist war. It spurned 'respectability', 'compromise' and 'moderation'. The ITGWU had only one measure for its actions: the needs of the working masses. Little wonder that British imperialism, the Dublin employers and the British trade union leaders hated it.

In the years just before the lock-out the British working class had demonstrated its ability to fight in a series of bitter strikes – the transport strikes of 1911 and 1912, and the miners' strikes of 1912. But in 1913 it could not rise to the challenge of Dublin's revolutionary lead. The British working class had proved unable to prevent its leaders selling out the revolutionary Irish. As a result those same leaders were able to draw the British working class into support for the imperialist war and so lead it to political defeat. The same leaders were to betray the struggles of the British working class right up to the defeat of the General Strike.

The defeat of the Dublin workers had established one essential point. The Irish working class could only free itself as part of a revolutionary national struggle to separate Ireland from Britain. Behind the Dublin capitalists lay British imperialism and its agents in the British working class.

The lock-out had, however, also exposed the fundamentally reactionary character of the Irish (Home-Rule) Party. During the lock-out the Redmondite Nationalist newspaper *Freeman's Journal* had sided with the employers, most of whom anyway were members and supporters of the Home-Rule Party. William Martin Murphy was in fact a millionaire former Nationalist MP.

The bourgeois character of Arthur Griffith's *Sinn Fein* was also exposed. Griffith had always attacked Larkin as an 'English trade unionist'. He defended the Dublin employers.

'Not the capitalist but the policy of Larkin had raised the prise of food until the poorest in Dublin are in a state of semi-famine . . . '[18]

During the lock-out the attitude of the British TUC in substituting food-ships for solidarity action played straight into Griffith's hand. He rightly regarded the food-ships as an insult and declared 'when the Irish brother Goes Out the English Stays In'. The action of the TUC confirmed Griffith's long held position that 'whether the English call themselves Liberals or Tories, Imperialists or Socialists – they are always the English'.[19]

The revolutionary wing of the Republican movement, however, stood by the workers. The seven men who were to sign the 1916 Proclamation in fact sympathised with the workers.[20] During the lock-out *Irish Freedom* said, in attacking the employers,

'The cause of Irish liberty is more the cause of the people than the plutocrats, and the new Ireland we work for will not be governed by money-bags.'[21]

In the lock-out the alliance of the working class and the revolutionary wing of Republicanism came into existence. The strike was lost, but the ITGWU and the loyalty of the workers to trade unionism still remained. Further, the Irish workers possessed the Irish Citizen Army which in March 1914 proclaimed:

'that the first and last principle of the Irish Citizen Army is the avowal that the ownership of Ireland, moral and material, is vested of right in the people of Ireland.'

And that one of the principal objects of the Irish Citizen Army was 'to arm and train all Irishmen capable of bearing arms to enforce and defend its first principle'.[22] The Irish Citizen Army was to join with the Irish Republican Brotherhood in the next stage of the struggle – that for an Irish Republic. This alliance led by Connolly and Pearse was to carry out the Easter Rising.

HOME RULE AND THE EXCLUSION OF ULSTER

The General Election of December 1910 created a parliament in which 84 Irish (Home-Rule) Party members held the balance of power between the Liberal/Labour majority and the Conservative opposition. In August 1911 an act was passed limiting the veto of the House of Lords, so removing one major obstacle to the passage of a Home-Rule Bill. The Liberal government was forced, through pressure from the Irish Party, to introduce a Bill in April 1912 to give a very limited measure of Home Rule to Ireland. In this Bill, the British Parliament retained the sole right to make laws connected with foreign relations, defence and external trade. It retained full control over taxation. It held the power to alter or repeal any Act of the proposed Irish Parliament. While Redmond's Irish Party enthusiastically supported the Bill, many sections of the national movement denounced it.

The Ulster Unionists began a militant campaign against the Bill. They made it clear that they would ignore the British Parliament and would take over the Province of Ulster instantly Home Rule came into force. The leadership of this rebellion fell to Sir Edward Carson. Preparations for armed resistance to the British Parliament began. Following the precedent of 1886, Ulster Unionist thugs demonstrated against Home Rule by attacks upon Catholics. On 12 July 1912 two thousand Catholic workmen were driven out of the Belfast shipyards.

Under Carson's leadership, Unionist paramilitary forces, the Ulster Volunteers, began training openly in the use of arms. Carson repeatedly said that he didn't 'care two pence whether it was treason or not'. He knew he could get away with it. After all, Bonar Law, leader of the Conservative Party, in July 1912 in a speech at Blenheim in England in the presence of Carson had said:

'There are things stronger than parliamentary majorities. I can imagine no length of resistance to which Ulster will go, in which I shall not be ready to support them . . . '[23]

Although Asquith, leader of the Liberal Party, described this as a 'declaration of war against Constitutional Government', he took no action against those involved. On 28 September, Carson's infamous Covenant was drawn up which said that if Home Rule was 'forced upon us we further solemnly and mutually pledge ourselves to refuse to recognise its authority'. It was signed by nearly half a million Ulster men and women. In December 1912 all those men who had signed it were asked to enrol for either political or military service against Home Rule. The aim was to get an armed force of some 100,000 men. The Liberal Government took no action against Carson.[24]

All through 1913 arms were imported into Ulster for use by Carson's volunteers. Ex-officers and reserve officers of the British Army offered their services to train the volunteers. During March, orders were sent by the Government to the Commander-in-Chief of the armed forces in Ireland, General Gough, to move troops from the Curragh camp in the South to Ulster to protect arms depots which it thought were to be raided by the Ulster Volunteers. General Gough and other officers from the British Army said they would resign their commissions rather than serve against Ulster Unionists. The officer class of the army had mutinied. The Liberals refused to take action against them. The army officers had, after all, close links with the English landed aristocracy as well as the leaders of the Conservative Party, that is, they were linked to a significant section of the British ruling class. The Liberals, knowing where their real class interests lay, gave assurances that the armed forces would not be used to crush opposition to the Home Rule Bill. The following month, under Carson's orders, 35,000 rifles and 2,500,000 rounds of ammunition were openly landed on the Ulster coast. Parliament and the law had been overruled by the officer class of the British Army.

The lessons from this episode are important. The Liberals had no qualms in sending Tom Mann and others to prison in 1912 when they called upon soldiers not to shoot striking workers. The Liberals had, in fact, used armed soldiers against striking workers at Tonypandy in 1910 and Llanelly and Liverpool in 1911. But they refused to confront Carson, Bonar Law and the army officers who mutinied at Curragh. Why did the Liberals allow the aristocratic officers at the head of the British Army to tear the British law to shreds and give British workers, in Lenin's words, 'an excellent lesson of the class struggle'?

Essentially, because even this mild Irish Home Rule Bill challenged the
interests of a significant section of the British ruling class, and
threatened to begin the process of undermining British imperialism's
rule in Ireland. And, as Lenin argued:

> 'These aristocrats behaved like revolutionaries *of the right* and
> thereby shattered all conventions, tore aside the veil that prevented
> the people from seeing the unpleasant but undoubtedly real class
> struggle . . .
> Real class rule lay and still lies *outside* of Parliament . . . And
> Britain's petty-bourgeois Liberals, with their speeches about
> reforms and the might of Parliament designed to lull the workers,
> proved in fact to be straw men, dummies, put up to bamboozle the
> people. They were quickly *"shut up"* by the aristocracy, the men in
> *power*.'[25]

The Liberals, concerned to maintain British imperialist rule, had no
choice. In a period of the growing polarisation of class rule, they could
not appeal to the only force capable of putting down the rebellion – the
working class – they had, after all, been using the army to put down
strikes. They simply gave way to the demands of those who held real
power. And real power was *outside* Parliament.

The Home Rule Bill had been put forward to contain the growing
opposition to British rule in Ireland. It was an attempt to use the
moderate bourgeois Irish Party as the vehicle for preserving British
rule in Ireland in a more acceptable and less naked form. The Ulster
Unionists backed by a powerful section of the British ruling class protested. Even at this time to speak of Ulster as though it was overwhelmingly Loyalist was simply nonsense and everyone knew that.
After a by-election in early 1913, Ulster's elected representatives in the
House of Commons consisted of 17 Home Rulers and 16 Unionists.
Anyway, the issue for the British ruling class was not democracy –
then or today. The issue was to preserve British imperialist rule in
Ireland and democratic rights would be brushed aside when that was
threatened. Lloyd George demonstrated this when, in May 1916, he
gave Carson a written pledge that 'Ulster does not, *whether she wills it
or not*, merge in the rest of Ireland'.[26] Thirty years later this position
was repeated by the post-war Labour Government which said:

> 'So far as can be foreseen, it will never be to Great Britain's
> advantage that Northern Ireland should become part of a territory
> outside His Majesty's jurisdiction. Indeed, it seems unlikely that

Great Britain would ever be able to agree to this even if the people of Northern Ireland desired it.'[27]

The Labour Party, faithful as ever to Great Britain, that is, British imperialist rule, gives the game away. Democracy – well, that is for those prepared to be fooled. That is why British rule in the North of Ireland today is defended on the basis of 'democracy', that the people in the Six Counties want to preserve the Union with Britain.

In May 1914, the Liberals announced an amendment to their Home Rule Bill which excluded part of Ireland from the operation of Home Rule. Ireland was to be partitioned in order to preserve British rule. The Irish national movement was immediately split. Griffith's Sinn Fein, the revolutionary Republicans and Irish Labour were totally opposed to the partition of Ireland. The Irish Party accepted it. The Irish bourgeoisie, represented by the Irish Party, knew that it could only oppose partition by mobilising the revolutionary forces of the Irish people. Having experienced the revolutionary determination of the Irish working class during the Dublin lock-out, it knew that mobilising such forces would threaten its very existence as a class. Forced to choose between the struggle for national freedom and its own class interests, the Irish bourgeoisie abandoned that struggle and formed a corrupt alliance with British imperialism.

The revolutionary socialist James Connolly completely understood the real meaning of partition for the Irish working class:

'Such a scheme as that agreed to by Redmond and Devlin, the betrayal of the national democracy of industrial Ulster would mean a carnival of reaction both North and South, would set back the wheels of progress, would destroy the oncoming unity of the Irish Labour movement and paralyse all advanced movements whilst it endured.'[28]

All hopes of uniting workers irrespective of religion and sectarian divisions would be shattered if a part of Ulster were to be separated from the rest of Ireland. Connolly understood all too well how British imperialism had perpetuated divisions in the Irish working class through the union with Britain. He knew why the Protestant working class invariably sides with British imperialism against the national aspirations of the Irish people. He was able to explain why the Protestant working class supported Orange ideology, which was not only hostile to nationalism but also opposed to the interests of the working class. Connolly recognised the basis of these facts in the different social economic and political positions occupied by Protestant and Catholic workers. And it was British imperialist domination of Ireland that was the root cause of these divisions in the working class:

> '...the Orange working class are slaves in spirit because they have been reared up among a people whose conditions of servitude were more slavish than their own. In Catholic Ireland the working class are rebels in spirit and democratic in feeling because for hundreds of years they have found no class as lowly paid or as hardly treated as themselves.
>
> 'At one time in the industrial world of Great Britain and Ireland the skilled labourer looked down with contempt upon the unskilled and bitterly resented his attempt to get his children taught any of the skilled trades; the feeling of the Orangemen of Ireland towards the Catholics is but a glorified representation on a big stage of the same passions inspired by the same unworthy motives.'[29]

The Protestant working class, just like the skilled workers in Britain possessed certain privileges (better wages, better conditions, greater job security, political rights) denied the rest of the working class. The Protestant workers, therefore, feared and opposed the Irish workers' fight for equality because they thought this would undermine their own position. They likewise accepted Orange ideology and sided with British imperialism because of their privileged position in relation to the Catholic worker. That is why Connolly could argue:

> 'the doctrine that because the workers of Belfast live under the same industrial conditions as do those of Great Britain, they are therefore subject to the same passions and to be influenced by the same methods of propaganda, is a doctrine almost screamingly funny in its absurdity.'[30]

What prevented basic class interest uniting Catholic and Protestant workers was precisely the Union with Britain. While suppressing the democratic rights of the Irish people as a whole, British imperialism guaranteed certain rights and privileges to the Protestant minority in Ireland. By bolstering the Northern industrial capitalists in Ireland, it guaranteed a relatively privileged position for Protestant workers. The Protestant workers saw their privileged position as a consequence of British rule and that is why they supported that rule.

Connolly understood that independence for Ireland would result in equal rights for Catholic and Protestant workers. And only the loss of

its privileged position would allow the 'possibility of an immense spirit-
ual uplifting of the Protestant working class'. Only in such circumstances would the Protestant working class be able to recognise its real class
interests with 'its brothers and sisters of different creeds'.[31] While
British imperialism remained in Ireland such developments were not
possible. Partition would block any hopes for the unity of the Irish
working class. The Irish capitalists in the South and Orange capitalists
in the North therefore had a common interest in supporting partition.

Such was Connolly's hostility to partition that he argued that it
should be fought with armed resistance if necessary. He reminded the
workers of Belfast how during the Belfast Dock Strike (1907) none of
the officer class resigned when told to shoot down workers and shed
blood in Ulster. No Cabinet members apologised to the relatives of the
workers they had murdered. British imperialism had an interest in
supporting Carson and the Loyalists in order to maintain British
domination of Ireland. Without British backing, the Unionists could
easily be dealt with. For:

> '... were the forces of the Crown withdrawn entirely, the Unionists
> could or would put no force into the field that the Home Rulers of
> all sections combined could not protect themselves against with a
> moderate amount of ease.'[32]

It was not for nothing that the British ruling class had turned a blind
eye to the arming and drilling of the Loyalists. Indeed, it was only on 4
December 1913, nine days after the inauguration of the Irish
Volunteers, an armed force of the Irish Nationalists, that the British
Government issued a proclamation prohibiting the importation of
military arms and ammunition into Ireland. The Ulster Unionists were
reputed to have already between 50,000 – 80,000 rifles at this time.
Then, as today, behind the Protestant armed gangs and thugs were the
British imperialist forces. The Liberal Government and Ulster
capitalists had a common interest in the exclusion of Ulster, as the best
available way to prevent the 'new unionism' and the rapidly developing
Irish labour and socialist movement from uniting the Catholic and
Protestant working class. A divided working class, whilst aiding the
Ulster capitalists, also perpetuated British imperialist rule and
seriously undermined the possibility of a united socialist movement in
Ireland.

The internationalism of the British labour movement was now to be
tested. Partition of Ireland not only threatened to undermine the
struggle of the Irish working class, but was also a direct denial of the

right of the Irish people to self-determination. The working class in Britain had an internationalist duty to uphold this right and oppose the partition of Ireland. This was the only possible basis for unity of the Irish and British working class and for a united struggle against their common enemy, British imperialism.

Instead of following the lead of the revolutionary Irish working class, the British labour movement followed the Irish bourgeoisie. It followed Redmond rather than Larkin and Connolly. The British Labour Party ignored resolutions from the Irish Trade Union Congress, preferring to adopt the recommendations of the Irish Party. The British Labour Party acted like its British imperialist masters towards the Irish TUC when Irish representatives proposed to establish a separate and independent party. The Irish members requested that political contributions of Irish members of amalgamated unions (British based) be turned over to the Irish Congress to aid the formation of an Irish Labour Party. The British Party refused because, according to Arthur Henderson, the constitution of the Irish Labour Party, unlike the British, did not allow affiliation of socialist and co-operative bodies: the differences made the objectives of the two parties different. The Irish explanation that their different circumstances demanded this, did not move these Labour Party leaders like Henderson so infected with that British imperialist mentality which had such deep roots in the British labour movement. Henderson wanted the Irish Labour Party to be the tail of the British Labour Party.

The Irish Congress executive in 1914 urged the British Labour Party to oppose partition and, if necessary, to vote against the entire Home Rule Bill in order to prevent it. But the British Labour Party knew better, it followed the lead of the Irish Party – the party of Irish capitalists – in supporting partition. George Barnes, Labour MP, justified this treachery on the grounds that 'the Nationalists of Ireland have sent men to Parliament and the Labour men have not'. Connolly's reply to this will suffice: 'The love embraces which take place between the Parliamentary Labour Party and our deadliest enemies – the Home Rule Party – will not help on a better understanding between the militant proletariat of the two islands'.[33] Once again, the corrupt and privileged leadership of the British labour movement joined with British imperialism and the Irish bourgeoisie against the Irish working class. Having betrayed the revolutionary trade-unionism of Larkin and Connolly during the Dublin lock-out, it now betrayed the revolutionary nationalism of the Irish masses. It was now clear that no section of the Irish people, apart from the Irish bourgeoisie, could place any trust in the official labour movement in Britain. Once again, Connolly's stand was confirmed; the only way to defend the interests of the Irish working class was complete separation from Britain.

At this point, the First Imperialist War broke out. The Home Rule Bill was passed, but was suspended until after the end of the war.

IMPERIALIST WAR

On the declaration of war the European Socialist movement disintegrated, as socialist parties sided with their own imperialist bourgeoisie. The major exceptions were the Russian and Irish labour movements. Lenin and Connolly were among those very few who stood by the resolution on war passed at the Stuttgart Congress of the Second International (1907). This argued that it was the duty of socialists, should war break out, to use the economic and political crisis 'to rouse the people and thereby hasten the abolition of capitalist rule'. As Connolly said:

> 'Should the working class in Europe, rather than slaughter each other for the benefit of kings and financiers, proceed tomorrow to erect barricades all over Europe, to break up bridges and destroy the transport service that war might be abolished, we should be perfectly justified in following such a glorious example and contributing our aid to the final dethronement of the vulture classes that rule and rob the world.'[34]

And if this did not occur then it was 'our duty to take all possible action to save the poor from the horrors this war has in store'.

Connolly was among those in Ireland who saw the war as an opportunity to end British rule. 'England's difficulty is Ireland's opportunity.' Connolly, and then Lenin after him, both following in the tradition of Marx and Engels, saw a national revolution in Ireland as a blow delivered against the English imperialist bourgeoisie, which would sharpen the revolutionary crisis in Europe. Connolly proposed as an immediate step that the labour movement should prevent the food that ought to feed the people of Ireland from being exported in ever greater quantities so 'that the British army and navy and jingoes may be fed'. To prevent the working class in Ireland from starving, it may mean more than transport strikes, if necessary it could mean 'armed battling in the streets to keep in this country the food of our people'. He continued:

'Starting thus, Ireland may yet set the torch to a European conflagration that will not burn out until the last throne and the last capitalist bond and debenture will be shrivelled on the funeral pyre of the last war-lord'.[35]

James Larkin, leader of the Irish Transport Union, before he left for America on 24 October 1914 to collect funds for the Union, vigorously denounced the war and any Irish participation in it. 'Stop at home. Arm for Ireland. Fight for Ireland and no other land.' By the end of August 1914 he, like Connolly, saw that Ireland had now the 'finest chance she had for centuries' to free herself from British rule. Addressing 7,000 people in O'Connell Street, he told them that the Transport Union was prepared to do all it could to facilitate the landing of rifles in Ireland. He appealed for recruits to the Irish Citizen Army.[36]

In Ireland, the majority of labour and socialist organisations opposed the war. No representative labour body officially supported the British war effort, and the leading figures of the labour movement were strongly opposed to it. The Dublin Trades Council declared against Irish involvement in the war in September 1914. In Belfast, the anti-war feeling was at its weakest. Whole sections of the Protestant working class were 'loyal' to Britain. Nevertheless, Connolly and his supporters fought to win the Belfast workers to an anti-war position, often in a very hostile environment. In this development already can be seen the consequences of the forthcoming partition of Ireland. For with partition, the Protestant workers of Belfast would be completely cut off from the anti-imperialist forces of the Irish working class.

On 10 August 1914, the Irish TUC Executive issued a proclamation, 'Why should Ireland starve?', and it declared that 'a war for the aggrandisement of the capitalist class has been declared' and urged all workers 'to aid us in this struggle to save Ireland from the horrors of famine' by means of control of foodstuffs and the prevention of profiteering etc. In September 1914, the ITUC executive passed a resolution, sponsored by Larkin, condemning economic conscription. The resolution condemned 'the insidious and cowardly action of employers in dismissing men from their employment with a view to compelling such dismissed men, by a process of starvation, to enlist volunteers'.[37]

While the Irish working class had revolutionary leaders like Larkin and Connolly there would be no Irish labour movement support for Britain's imperialist war. In fact, the Irish labour movement, after

Connolly's murder by the British, and Larkin's absence in America, continued to prevent conscription of any kind until the end of the war. On 23 April 1918, with the exception of the Belfast area, there took place the first general strike in the European labour movement against the more vigorous prosecution of the war through conscription in Ireland.

This stand of Irish labour was in sharp contrast to the totally pro-imperialist response in Britain. The British TUC and Labour Party enthusiastically supported the war. On 24 August 1914, they declared that there should be an Industrial Truce for the duration of the war; and on 29 August, the Labour Party agreed to an Electoral Truce and placed the party organisation at the disposal of the recruiting campaign. In May 1915, the Labour MP Arthur Henderson, having already sided with the Irish bourgeoisie against the Irish working class, now joined a War Coalition Cabinet with the most reactionary forces in Ireland, including no less than 8 Ulster Unionists. The loyalist thug and reactionary, Sir Edward Carson, was made Attorney-General and Bonar Law, Secretary of State for the Colonies. A more calculated insult to the Irish people could not have been conceived. A more destructive blow to any hope of united struggle between the Irish and British workers against imperialism could not have been conceived. Two other Labour MPs, William Brace of the Miners, and G H Roberts of the Printers, joined in this filthy act of betrayal by taking junior offices.

The small socialist movement in Britain was not able to make any effective stand against the war. The largest organisation, the British Socialist Party, under Hyndman's control, wholeheartedly supported an allied victory in the war. It later split and after the Hyndmanites left in 1916, the new leadership, while disowning a chauvinist line on the war, did not elaborate any clear alternative. Leading labour movement figures such as Keir Hardie, George Lansbury MP (editor of the *Daily Herald*) and Ramsay MacDonald supported the war once war broke out. Only the tiny Socialist Labour Party and the Women's Suffrage Federation (later Workers Socialist Federation) developed a revolutionary opposition to the war. There were also small numbers in the ILP who opposed it on pacifist grounds. John Maclean in Glasgow and Sylvia Pankhurst in London were the revolutionary leaders in Britain who maintained the most consistent opposition to the war. It is no surprise that they also gave unwavering support to the Irish struggle for self-determination.

To return to Ireland: the anti-war forces of the labour movement were soon joined by the revolutionary wing of the national movement. Redmond's Irish Party necessarily supported the war in alliance with British imperialism. Redmond and his supporters organised recruiting meetings up and down the country in defence of Britain and the Empire. His efforts were supported by the Irish employers, who sacked workers in their thousands in order to force them, by starvation and poverty, to 'volunteer' to join the British army. Once again, the Irish bourgeoisie betrayed the national struggle to protect its own class interests. The Irish Party was as 'loyal' to Britain as the Ulster Unionists.

The revolutionary wing of the Irish Volunteers led by, among others, Padraic Pearse, opposed any support for British imperialism. On the contrary, they saw the war as an opportunity to strike a blow for Irish national freedom. 'England's difficulty is Ireland's opportunity.' Redmond's support for the war led to a split in the Irish Volunteers. A National Convention on 25 October 1914 saw a section of the Irish Volunteers, 12,000 out of 200,000, affirm their determination to maintain a defence force in Ireland, resist conscription and defend the unity of the nation and its right to self-government. Those who remained with Redmond became known as the National Volunteers. Most of the National Volunteers joined the British army.

From the outbreak of war, the Irish Citizen Army co-operated fully with the Volunteers. When Connolly made contact with the Irish Republican Brotherhood, forerunner of the IRA, secretly organised within the Irish Volunteers, the first steps towards the Easter Rising were made. The IRB had also decided on the outbreak of war that an uprising must be organised. They had, in fact, sounded out other nationalist groupings for their views. It is of note that Arthur Griffith's Sinn Fein opposed a rising and broke with the IRB and the Volunteers. Padraic Pearse was made director of the IRB in December 1914. The alliance of revolutionary nationalism and Irish labour had now been forged. Under the leadership of Pearse and Connolly it carried out the Easter Rising.

Starting from the interests of the working class, Connolly opposed the imperialist war and saw it as an opportunity to free Ireland from British rule. Starting from the interests of the Irish national struggle Padraic Pearse equally opposed the war and equally saw it as an opportunity to end British rule in Ireland. The alliance of revolutionary nationalism and Irish labour which was born in the Dublin lock-out came to fruition during the imperialist war.

We have already said that the main consideration for the socialist revolution today is a united fight against the imperialist powers, the imperialist bourgeoisie, and their bought-off agents in the working class movement. And that this requires the working class to fight in alliance with national liberation movements to destroy imperialism. In the struggle for Irish self-determination the significance of this position is clearly seen. On the one side we see the forces of revolutionary nationalism in alliance with the class-conscious workers in Ireland. On the other the forces of reaction: the Irish bourgeoisie, the British imperialist bourgeoisie, and its agents in the British working class. The defeat of the Irish struggle for national freedom and the working class struggle for socialism in both Ireland and Britain, was decisively influenced by the failure of the British working class movement to unite with the Irish national liberation movement against British imperialism.

NOTES

1   Lenin, *LCW* Volume 20 p. 150.
2   See Challinor R, *The Origins of British Bolshevism* London 1977 pp. 9–13. Also Kendall W, *The Revolutionary Movement in Britain 1900–1921* London 1971 pp. 14–15.
3   Material on Larkin, the Irish Trade Union movement, the Dublin Lock Out and the response in Britain is based on the following major sources: Larkin E, *James Larkin* London 1965; Mitchell A, *Labour in Irish Politics 1890–1930* Dublin 1974; Clarkson J D, *Labour and Nationalism in Ireland* New York 1925; and the following newspapers: *Manchester Guardian, The Socialist, Labour Leader, Daily Herald* and *Justice*.
4   Challinor R, *op cit* p. 51. See also Milton N, *John Maclean* London 1973 p. 35.
5   *The Socialist* September 1907.
6   Clarkson J D, *op cit* p. 221 fn. 1.
7   Larkin E, *op cit* p. 62.
8   *ibid* p. 63.
9   *ibid* p. 123.
10 *Manchester Guardian* 2 September 1913.
11 Pankhurst S, *The Suffragette Movement* London 1977 p. 501.
12 Moran B, '1913, Jim Larkin and the British Labour Movement' in *Saothar* 4 Dublin nd p. 41.
13 *Manchester Guardian* 22 November 1913.
14 Larkin E, *op cit* pp. 147–155.
15 *Manchester Guardian* 6 September 1913.
16 See Holton B, *British Syndicalism 1900–1914* London 1976 p. 135.
17 Lenin, 'Imperialism and the Split in Socialism' *LCW* Volume 23 p. 120.
18 Ellis P B, *A History of the Irish Working Class* London 1972 p. 191.
19 Clarkson J D, *op cit* p. 279 and p. 264.

20 Mitchell A, *op cit* p. 49.
21 Clarkson J D, *op cit* p. 286.
22 See Ellis P B, *op cit* p. 207−8.
23 Macardle D, *The Irish Republic* London 1968 p. 81.
24 *ibid* pp. 81−2.
25 Lenin, *LCW* Volume 20 p. 228.
26 Macardle D, *op cit* p. 181 (emphasis added).
27 British *Cabinet Paper* CAB 128/32 quoted in *The Guardian* 11 December 1980.
28 Connolly J, *Ireland upon the Dissecting Table* Cork 1975 p. 53.
29 *ibid* p. 40.
30 *ibid* p. 41.
31 *ibid* p. 26.
32 *ibid* p. 54. The arguments above closely follow Roy Spring's article 'Connolly and Irish Freedom' part two, *Hands Off Ireland!* No. 5 September 1978 pp. 18−20.
33 Mitchell A, *op cit* p. 44.
34 Connolly J, 'Our Duty in this Crisis' *Selected Works op cit* p. 237.
35 *ibid* p. 238.
36 Larkin E, *op cit* pp. 181−2.
37 See Mitchell A, *op cit* pp. 60−3.

CHAPTER FOUR

IRISH REVOLUTION

The First Imperialist War gave revolutionaries in Ireland the opportunity they had been waiting for. England's difficulty was again Ireland's opportunity to free itself once and for all from the stranglehold of its brutal oppressor, British imperialism. By taking decisive action in this period, the Irish national movement could begin the process which would destroy British imperialism and lay the basis for the socialist revolution in Europe.

The revolutionary socialist James Connolly had fully grasped the importance of this opportunity for the Irish working class. He became one of the driving forces advocating an armed insurrection. He prepared the Irish Citizen Army for such an eventuality. In January 1916, after secret meetings with members of the Irish Republican Brotherhood, he became part of the Military Council preparing detailed plans for an armed uprising on Easter Sunday 23 April 1916.

On 8 April 1916 Connolly announced in the *Workers Republic* that:

'The Council of the Irish Citizen Army has resolved after grave and earnest deliberation, to hoist the green flag of Ireland over Liberty Hall [headquarters of the ITGWU], as over a fortress held for Ireland by the arms of Irishmen.'[1]

The flag was to be hoisted on Palm Sunday 16 April. It symbolised the commitment of the most advanced sections of the Irish working class to the revolutionary struggle for Irish freedom.

For Connolly the participation of the working class in the national revolution offered the only guarantee that a 'free' Irish nation would be 'the guardian of the interests of the people of Ireland'.

'We are out for Ireland for the Irish. But who are the Irish? Not the rack-renting, slum-owning landlord; not the sweating, profit-grinding capitalist; not the sleek and oily lawyer; not the prostitute pressman – the hired liars of the enemy. Not these are the Irish upon whom the future depends. Not these, but the Irish working class, the only secure foundation upon which a free nation can be reared.

The cause of labour is the cause of Ireland, the cause of Ireland is the cause of labour. They cannot be dissevered. Ireland seeks freedom. Labour seeks that an Ireland free should be the sole mistress of her own destiny, supreme owner of all material things within and upon her soil. Labour seeks to make the free Irish nation the guardian of the interests of the people of Ireland, and to secure that end would vest in that free Irish nation all property rights as against the claims of the individual, with the end in view that the individual may be enriched by the nation, and not by the spoiling of his fellows.'[2]

The initial proposal to raise the green flag over Liberty Hall was defeated (7 votes to 5) by the Executive Committee of the Dublin Branch (No 1) of the ITGWU. Permission was only granted to raise the flag when, at a later meeting, Connolly threatened to sever his connections with the Union. And then, only on the understanding that the Citizen Army would shortly leave Liberty Hall and 'probably never return'. Such a promise could easily be made as the planned Rising was only ten days away.[3]

This clash of interests within the Union is of importance for later events. It pointed to a fundamental divergence of interests developing in the Irish working class movement. Already an influential layer was emerging in the Union which sought to separate 'trade union issues' from the struggle against British imperialism. The split in the international working class movement, between a reformist and revolutionary wing, which, with the victory of the reformists, had destroyed the revolutionary potential of the European working class, was starting to emerge in the Irish labour movement.

The ceremony to raise the flag over Liberty Hall took place as planned on 16 April, with the Citizen Army in formation in front of the Hall. After the ceremony, Connolly, in the presence of Irish Volunteer Officers, gave a lecture to the Citizen Army on street fighting. Later on that night he addressed the Citizen Army alone and informed them of the planned uprising. He told them that the odds were a thousand to one against them. And that:

'In the event of victory, hold onto your rifles, as those with whom we are fighting may stop before our goal is reached. We are out for economic as well as political liberty.'[4]

Members of the Citizen Army were offered the opportunity to withdraw from the planned Rising with no recriminations. No one did.

THE EASTER RISING

The Rising was planned for numerous dates before Easter Sunday 23 April 1916 was finally decided on. The plan was for simultaneous risings throughout Ireland beginning with the seizure of Dublin City Centre at 6.30pm, to be followed shortly after (7pm) by risings in the provinces.

The national movement was split over the issue of offensive action. Griffith, the leader of Sinn Fein, opposed a rising. Eoin MacNeill, the formal head of the Irish Volunteers, argued that the Volunteers and the Citizen Army should build up their forces in readiness to respond to offensive action by the British – such as the introduction of compulsory conscription or mass repression against the Volunteers. He was opposed to offensive action. Connolly and Pearse, the leader of the revolutionary wing of the Volunteers, opposed the vacillating arguments of MacNeill. They believed that any delay would not only cause demoralisation among the Volunteers but put the movement in grave danger of pre-emptive action by the British. Connolly also believed the opportunity provided by the imperialist war would be lost if the revolutionaries did not strike a blow now. The Military Council which planned the Rising, therefore, did not inform Griffith or MacNeill of their plans.

The plan for the Rising involved the mobilisation of all the Irish Volunteers as well as the much smaller Citizen Army. Orders for the Rising under the guise of 'three days of manoeuvres' beginning Easter Sunday were sent out. Close to the appointed day for the Rising things began to go wrong. An expected shipment of arms from Germany was destroyed. Roger Casement, who went to Germany to organise support and arms, was arrested on his return. On Good Friday, Eoin MacNeill discovered that the 'three days of manoeuvres' were in fact the signal for the Rising. He confronted Pearse and was told the truth. On Saturday morning MacNeill issued a countermanding order calling off all Volunteer activities over the three days. This was printed in the *Sunday Independent* and sent by messengers into the provinces. The Military Council which had planned the Rising met on Easter Sunday and decided to go ahead the next day, Easter Monday 24 April. The orders were sent out. They knew the British authorities would now be warned of the Rising and would be preparing mass arrests and internment of those likely to be involved. It was 'now or never'.

On Easter Monday at 10am the Rising began. About 1,200 answered the summons to parade in Dublin – nearly the whole of the Citizen Army and over 1,000 Volunteers. The plans which had been made required nearly twice that number. MacNeill's countermanding order and arrests of Volunteers by the British authorities had had a telling effect. Throughout the rest of Ireland there was only sporadic and short-lived action – the most significant being the seizure of Athenry in Galway by the 1,000 strong Volunteer units led by the left-wing Volunteer leader Liam Mellows.

The first act of the revolutionaries was the taking of strategic buildings in Dublin. Outside the GPO Padraic Pearse read the Proclamation of the Provisional Government. The Proclamation was a revolutionary democratic programme which united the aspirations of the revolutionary petit bourgeoisie and the Irish workers against British imperialism. It included the following:

'We declare the right of the people of Ireland to the ownership of Ireland and to the unfettered control of Irish destinies, to be sovereign and indefeasible . . .
The Republic guarantees religious and civil liberty, equal rights and equal opportunities to all its citizens, and declares its resolve to pursue the happiness and prosperity of the whole nation and of all its parts, cherishing all the children of the nation equally, and oblivious of the differences, carefully fostered by an alien government, which have divided a minority from the majority in the past.'[5]

It was a democratic secular Republic which was declared. The Proclamation was signed by Thomas J Clarke, Sean MacDiarmada, P H Pearse, James Connolly, Thomas MacDonagh, Eamonn Ceannt, and Joseph Plunkett. Thomas J Clarke was a living survivor of the Fenian movement of the nineteenth century, P H Pearse represented the revolutionary petit bourgeoisie, and James Connolly represented the most advanced sections of the Irish working class. This was the alliance which led the Easter Rising.

The battle lasted nearly one week. The revolutionaries were faced by overwhelming odds. British imperialism used straight-forward terror to destroy the Rising. Major buildings were simply blown to pieces. Heavy artillery, even warships, were used to bombard Dublin City centre. Passers-by in the street were simply shot dead by the British forces. On 25 April Francis Sheehy Skeffington – a well known Irish pacifist who took no part in the Rising – was arrested along with two journalists by Captain Bowen-Colthurst. That evening, Sheehy Skeffington, taken on a raiding party as a hostage by Bowen-Colthurst, witnessed Bowen-Colthurst shooting dead a young boy called Coade. The next day Bowen-Colthurst shot dead Sheehy Skeffington and the two journalists. There was, of course, no trial not even a court martial. These murders, like so many before and since, were simply covered up.

By the Saturday it was clear that nothing further would be gained by continuing the battle. Pearse and Connolly signed an unconditional surrender document at 3.45pm 29 April 'in order to prevent the further slaughter of Dublin citizens and in the hope of saving the lives of our followers now surrounded and hopelessly outnumbered'. Two more days went by before all the insurgent commanders surrendered.

During the Rising nearly 500 people were killed (over 250 civilians) and nearly 3,000 injured. 179 buildings in Dublin alone had been destroyed by fire or artillery. Total damage costs were in the region of £2½ million. Relief had to be given to 100,000 people, a third of the population of Dublin.

REIGN OF TERROR

Within a few weeks of the Rising, over 3,000 men and 70 women were arrested. Anyone suspected of Republican sympathies was imprisoned along with the Volunteers and Citizen Army members who had fought during the Rising. From all over Ireland they were brought to Kilmainham Prison and Richmond Barracks in Dublin. The prisoners were crowded into bare rooms, unprepared for habitation, thirty to each room. Over 1,800 men and 5 women were deported and interned in prison camps in Britain – most without any trial.

Ninety of the insurgents in the Rising, including all its leaders, were tried and sentenced to death by a secret court martial. The first the Irish people heard of this reign of terror was the announcement of the executions of Pearse, MacDonagh and Clarke on 3 May. Between that date and 12 May fifteen men were shot including all the signatories to the Proclamation. On 12 May Sean MacDiarmada and James Connolly were shot. Their courts martial had been delayed as both had been seriously injured in the fighting. Connolly had been wounded twice and his leg was shattered. On the morning of 12 May he was taken from his bed, placed on a stretcher, carried to the place of executions, tied to a chair and shot. Thus was one of the greatest socialist leaders of the working class movement murdered by British imperialism.

The number and manner of the executions caused a wave of anger and revulsion against British imperialism. Because of this, and after all the revolutionary leaders of the Rising had been shot, the executions, bar that of Roger Casement, were stopped. Those sentenced to death had their sentences commuted to life imprisonment. Among those were Constance Markievicz, Eamon de Valera, William Cosgrave, and Thomas Ashe.

At the time of the Rising it was widely argued that the executions and mass repression were 'blunders' by the British authorities. Even today the standard bourgeois history of Ireland still peddles the myth that without these 'blunders' the mass support that quickly developed for the Rising and the struggle for Irish independence would not have occurred. The real facts show, however, that British imperialism had no choice but to unleash such repression if it was to maintain its rule in Ireland. As the imperialist war dragged on, opposition to British imperialism was bound to intensify. The British ruling class knew this, and was determined to deprive the national movement in Ireland of its revolutionary leadership.[6]

The British ruling class recognised the significance of the Rising, and, in particular, the importance of its leaders, Pearse and Connolly. Connolly represented the militant working class. By uniting the armed Irish working class with the revolutionary wing of the national movement led by Pearse, Connolly had driven the national movement to the left. This alliance posed the greatest threat to British imperialism. In the middle of an imperialist war it threatened to begin the process not only of destroying British imperialism's rule in Ireland, but also of sharpening the revolutionary crisis in Britain itself.

The Rising had shown that it was possible to take action against imperialism. It had fatally undermined the Irish Party's efforts to secure a bourgeois imperialist resolution to the Irish question. Imperialism could not possibly allow Pearse and Connolly to live. It *had* to demonstrate to the Irish people that rebellion would be answered with terror. The British terror that followed the Rising was as inevitable as the support that built up for the Rising and the revolutionary struggle for Irish independence. The Rising represented the fundamental interest of the Irish people, just as the terror unleashed by British imperialism was carried out in the fundamental interests of the British ruling class.

How could the British ruling class allow Connolly – the greatest revolutionary produced within these islands – to live? Who better than Connolly was there to organise the Irish working class against the deepening crisis of imperialism in the First World War? Who but Connolly would ensure that the Irish working class united with the revolutionary wing of the national movement to fight the Home Rule charade? British imperialism had no choice but to use terror. That this terror failed to prevent the rise of a mass movement for Irish independence does not alter this fact at all.

Not only British imperialism but the Irish bourgeoisie demanded Connolly's death. On 10 May, after 12 executions had taken place, William Martin Murphy continued the campaign, begun during the Dublin lock-out, to rid his class of Connolly. His newspaper, the *Irish Independent*, published a photograph of Connolly alongside a caption: 'Still lies in Dublin Castle recovering from his wounds'. An editorial menacingly demanded: 'Let the worst of the ringleaders be singled out and dealt with as they deserve'.[7]

Not only British imperialism and the Irish bourgeoisie applauded Connolly's murder but so did the British Labour Party. The Labour MP Arthur Henderson was a member of the War Cabinet which brutally crushed the Easter Rising and ordered Connolly's execution. When news reached Parliament that the army had summarily executed James Connolly, this vile social democrat, Arthur Henderson, led other Labour MPs in spontaneous applause.[8]

The Irish bourgeoisie, British imperialism and its agents in the working class – the British Labour Party – had all united to put down with terror the Easter Rising. They were forced to crush the leadership of the revolutionary alliance of the working class with the revolutionary wing of the national movement because it threatened them all. The execution of the leaders of the Easter Rising, far from being a 'blunder', deprived the national movement of those leaders most capable of representing the interest of the Irish people in a mass struggle to totally destroy British imperialism's rule in Ireland. As later events were to show, the loss of those leaders played an important role in the devastating splits and divisions in the coming struggle for Irish independence. Nevertheless, the Easter Rising was the birth of the modern revolutionary national movement in Ireland. And the working class, having provided one of its leaders, had shared in the formulation of the Republican standpoint – the position which has always guided the revolutionary wing of the national movement to this very day.

SOCIALISTS AND THE EASTER RISING

Just before he was executed, Connolly remarked '(The Socialists) will never understand why I am here ... They will all forget I am an Irishman'.[9] How right was Connolly! The response, with very few exceptions, of the European labour and socialist movement was an almost unanimous condemnation of Connolly's action in leading a section of the working class into a national uprising.

The Easter Rising demonstrated again the thoroughly reactionary character of the British labour and socialist movement. The Scottish ILP weekly *Forward* uttered the empty abstraction, 'a man can be a nationalist or an internationalist', to criticise Connolly. *Socialist Review*, journal of the ILP, announced in September 1916, 'In no degree do we approve of the *Sinn Fein* rebellion. We do not approve of armed rebellion at all, any more than any other form of militarism or war'.[10] Pacifism in an imperialist nation oppressing the Irish people by armed force is, as Lenin remarked, 'the most pernicious opportunism'.[11]

George Lansbury's *Herald* informed its readers on 29 April that it was 'against all war – civil wars no less than wars between nations ... '. A week later it argued the reactionary consequences of that view: 'the rising was foredoomed to failure and in my (George Lansbury's) opinion was a crime against the Irish people'. For social democrats like Lansbury the question of Ireland came down to the issue of 'how are we to administer in a satisfactory manner this small country?'.[12] The *Call*, soon to be the official organ of the British Socialist Party, while understanding the efforts of the 'Irish people to throw off the alien yoke ' nevertheless argued 'to rise as the men in Dublin rose, without adequate force ... was foolish'. It then went on to support Home Rule for Ireland.[13] The *Socialist*, paper of the Socialist Labour Party left 'the merits, or demerits, of the revolt aside' and simply told its readers in June 1916 that 'armies are the force used by capitalist states to maintain their undisputed sway. Armies are not only used against "foreigners" '?[14] Very practical!

Only *The Woman's Dreadnought* of 6 May 1916 (later to become *The Workers Dreadnought*) in a full page article written by Sylvia Pankhurst opened with a clear declaration of support for the right of the Irish people to self-determination. It was the most principled statement by a British socialist at a time of great anti-Irish hysteria. She thought the Rising may have been mistaken but she understood that 'their rebellion was but a stage in the long struggle for Irish independence'. And she unreservedly joined 'in common sorrow . . . for the Rebels who have been shot'.[15]

Very few socialists were able to understand Connolly's determined action in participating in the Rising despite his very clear writings on the national question. Trotsky in an article on 4 July 1916 on the Easter Rising showed how little he understood the national question and its relation to the working class struggle for socialism when he wrote:

'An all-Ireland movement such as the *nationalist dreamers* had expected simply failed to materialise. The Irish countryside did not stir. The Irish bourgeoisie, and likewise the higher and more influential stratum of the Irish intelligentsia, held aloof. There fought and died only the workers of Dublin, together with some revolutionary enthusiasts from the petty bourgeois intelligentsia. *The basis for national revolution has disappeared even in backward Ireland* . . . The experiment of an Irish national rebellion . . . is over. But the historical role of the Irish proletariat is only beginning. Already it has brought into this revolt, even though under an archaic flag, its class indignation against militarism and imperialism. This indignation will not now subside.' (*our emphasis*)[16]

Trotsky's assessment was totally wrong. His followers, to this day, refuse to recognise this fact. They, like Trotsky, deny the vital importance of the national question for the working class today. In attacking the Irish liberation movement as 'petit bourgeois' (nationalist dreamers) they, like Trotsky, write off the real forces fighting in a revolutionary manner and substitute for them an 'ideal' movement which does not exist. That is the essence of what is called *petit bourgeois socialism*.

Lenin alone pointed to the real significance of the Rising and in so doing laid the foundation for our understanding of the Irish revolution today. In attacking those in the European socialist movement who denied the significance of the national struggle or wrote off the Rising as a 'putsch', he argued:

'The term "putsch", in its scientific sense, may be employed only when the attempt at insurrection has revealed nothing but a circle of conspirators or stupid maniacs, and has aroused no sympathy among the masses. The centuries-old Irish national movement, having passed through various stages and combinations of class interests . . . manifested itself in street fighting conducted by a section of the urban petty bourgeoisie *and a section of the workers* after a long period of mass agitation, demonstrations, suppression of newspapers, etc. Whoever calls *such* a rebellion a 'putsch' is either a hardened reactionary, or a doctrinaire hopelessly incapable of envisaging a social revolution as a living phenomenon.

'To imagine that social revolution is *conceivable* without revolts by small nations in the colonies and in Europe, without revolutionary outbursts by a section of the petty bourgeoisie *with all its prejudices*, without a movement of the politically non-conscious proletarian and semi-proletarian masses against oppression by the landowners, the church, and the monarchy, against national oppression, etc – to imagine all this is to *repudiate social revolution*. So one army lines up in one place and says, "We are for socialism", and another, somewhere else and says, "We are for imperialism", and that will be a social revolution! . . .

'Whoever expects a "pure" social revolution will *never* live to see it. Such a person pays lip-service to revolution without understanding what revolution is.'

The misfortune of the Irish was, according to Lenin, that they rose 'prematurely' before the European revolt of the proletariat had time to mature. But Lenin knew that revolutions cannot be conducted according to a time-table:

'It is only in premature, individual, sporadic and therefore unsuccessful, revolutionary movements that the masses gain experience, acquire knowledge, gather strength, and get to know their real leaders, the socialist proletarians, and in this way prepare for the general onslaught . . . '[17]

Connolly's position, endorsed by Lenin, was vindicated by history when nine months after he died Tsarism was destroyed in Russia and nine months after that the Bolsheviks triumphed and Soviet Russia was established.

REVOLUTIONARY NATIONALISM AFTER THE RISING

The Easter Rising became popularly known as the 'Sinn Fein Rebellion', despite the fact that the leader of Sinn Fein, Arthur Griffith, had played no part in the Rising, had condemned it and rejected its Republican standpoint. A new Sinn Fein movement was soon to arise on the foundations laid by the Easter Rising. The British gaols and internment camps became training schools for this new Sinn

Fein standpoint. When the interned, untried prisoners were released in December 1916, they spread the Republican position all over Ireland. The ex-prisoners were eager to build the organisations necessary for a new uprising. The IRB was reconstituted, and the Volunteers were reformed with Michael Collins, who had fought in the GPO during the Easter Rising, as Director of Organisation. They began drilling and training in secret.

Arrests of Volunteers and Republican agitators soon took place. The arrested men refused to recognise the jurisdiction of the courts. In gaol they demanded political status and answered the British refusal by going on hunger strike. In September 1917, the death after force-feeding of Thomas Ashe, a Commandant during the Easter Rising, led to massive protests. Almost all Dublin was in mourning and on 30 September 1917, 30–40,000 people took part in a funeral procession in military formation. Its advance guard were Irish Volunteers carrying rifles, and it included 9,000 Volunteers in uniform, and thousands of trade union members marching in formation. Constance Markievicz led a Citizen Army contingent wearing full uniform with a revolver in her belt. At the cemetery three volleys were fired over the grave. Collins, in a very short funeral oration, said: 'that volley we have just heard is the only speech which it is proper to make over the grave of a dead Fenian'.[18] After this massive show of strength, the British authorities conceded political status. A new mass, militant and Republican Sinn Fein had been born.

On 25 October 1917, nearly 2,000 delegates attended the Ard-Fheis (Conference) of a revitalised Sinn Fein. A new Constitution was drawn up. In the debate Griffith vigorously opposed Republicanism but was defeated. He stood down as President of Sinn Fein and was replaced by Eamon de Valera, the only surviving Commandant of the Easter Rising. Arthur Griffith became Vice-President and the executive included Eoin MacNeill, Cathal Brugha and Constance Markievicz. Sinn Fein, despite the very divergent trends in its membership, now stood firmly for Irish Republicanism.

IRISH LABOUR AFTER THE RISING

The aftermath of the Easter Rising left the Irish labour movement in disarray. With Connolly's murder, Irish labour lost its most capable leader – the only socialist leader who had really understood the importance of the national cause. Liberty Hall lay in ruins, files had been seized or destroyed, and the printing press and equipment of the

Workers Republic were destroyed. Immediately after the Rising, the government arrested all trade union leaders who had shown nationalist sympathies.

Connolly's successors to the leadership of the Irish labour movement had not supported the alliance he had created with the revolutionary nationalists. They had not taken any part in the Easter Rising. After the Rising, they concentrated on 'economic' issues and on the revival of the trade union movement. Although prepared to use their association with Connolly to rebuild and expand the movement, they did not attempt to maintain organisational ties with the revolutionary nationalists. They made no attempt to revive the Citizen Army at the time the Irish Volunteers were being rebuilt. These men believed political power could be won through an advanced social-economic programme which would appeal to the workers. The national issue played little part in their calculations. For these leaders, Connolly's revolutionary courage and leadership had gone unheeded.

The leadership of the Irish labour movement fell on two members from Belfast who were in no way involved with the Rising – Thomas Johnson and David Campbell. They disassociated the labour movement as a whole from any responsibility for the Rising. While they demanded the immediate trial or release of the imprisoned trade union leaders, they did not protest at the executions of the leaders of the Easter Rising. Neither did the Dublin Trades Council when it resumed its meetings in July 1916. The Irish TUC Executive, at its first Congress for 2 years in August 1916, announced through Johnson's opening address:

> 'This is not a place to enter into a discussion as to the right or wrong, the wisdom or the folly, of the revolt . . . as a trade-union movement, we are of varied minds on matters of historical and political development . . .'[19]

Delegates were asked to stand in memory of Connolly and others who died in the Rising, but were also asked to remember those that died fighting on the side of the British in the imperialist war 'for what they believed to be the cause of Liberty and Democracy and for love of their country'. Johnson himself gave his personal support to the 'Allied cause'. The Executive also attempted to disassociate the Transport Union from the Citizen Army stating that 'not more than half' of the army participants in the Rising were members of the Union and that the army was simply a tenant in Liberty Hall.[20] The 'unity' of the Irish labour movement – there were the Unionist members in Belfast to consider –

and the protection of its organisations became the dominant consideration. This was now put before the real interest of Irish labour which was to build an alliance with the revolutionary nationalists in the struggle to establish a democratic Irish Republic. Because of this, Irish labour's political influence continually diminished in the revolutionary struggles ahead.

Irish labour and Sinn Fein did unite in a successful mass campaign against the attempt of Lloyd George to introduce conscription in April 1918. The Irish TUC-Labour Party called a 24-hour general strike for 23 April 1918 – it was the first general strike against the war in any Western European country. It was a near total success apart from the Belfast area where Unionist workers were concentrated. It demonstrated the power Irish labour could wield in the national cause.

THE GENERAL ELECTION DECEMBER 1918

Immediately at the end of the war, Lloyd George called a General Election. This saw the destruction of the Irish (Home-Rule) Party and a massive electoral victory for Sinn Fein. Out of 105 seats returned for Ireland, Sinn Fein won 73, while the Irish Party won only six, and four of these in Ulster were due to an agreement with Sinn Fein. The Unionists won 26 seats. Of the nine counties of Ulster, the Unionists polled a majority in only four. The vast majority of the Irish people, nearly 70%, had voted for an independent Irish Republic.

The Irish TUC-Labour Party did not contest the elections. Sinn Fein had offered a pact with Labour, to stand down in certain constituencies if Labour candidates would sign a pledge, which committed them to an independent Irish Republic and to unconditional abstention from the English Parliament. The Irish Labour Party refused to accept this principled position. Its manifesto supported abstention but said that they might attend the English Parliament at some time 'if special circumstances warranted it' and a special Congress-Party meeting approved it. The Labour manifesto also said nothing about participation in an Irish national assembly that Sinn Fein proposed to establish after the election. As the election drew near, it became clear that this position of the Irish Labour Party would receive little support. Nationalist workers would now vote overwhelmingly for Sinn Fein. Most Unionist workers would not vote for any degree of Irish independence. The Irish Labour Party decided not to stand. Its executive rationalised this on the grounds it wanted to give the electorate a chance to decide on the question of self-determination.[21] But this was nothing more than the inevitable result of official Labour's bankrupt policy on the national question.

DAIL EIREANN

The extent of the Republican victory at the election was much greater than it seems. The British authorities had done everything in their power to prevent it. Sinn Fein election meetings were banned, election agents and speakers arrested, election addresses were censored or suppressed, and election literature was confiscated. More than a hundred Sinn Fein leaders were in gaol after arrests following the anti-conscription campaign, and the greater part of the country was under military rule. Of the 73 Republicans elected, 36 were in gaol, including de Valera and Griffith, and many others were 'on the run' or in the USA evading arrest. As with the election of Bobby Sands in 1981, the British would ignore the results. 'Democracy' for the British ruling class was only invoked when its effects strengthened their own class rule.

An Irish national assembly was called for 21 January 1919. Everyone elected in Ireland was invited regardless of Party. 27 Republicans eventually met in the Mansion House, Dublin. Dail Eireann (Assembly of Ireland) was declared. A declaration was adopted which affirmed Ireland as 'a sovereign and independent nation' and which ratified the 1916 Proclamation. The Dail also adopted, but not without opposition, a 'Democratic Programme' which was drawn up after advice from the leaders of Irish Labour. It was a social programme which expressed the continuing influence of Pearse and Connolly.

There were now two 'governments' in Ireland. The one, Dail Eireann, backed by the vast majority of the Irish people. The other that of the British authorities, operating from Dublin Castle possessing the forces of repression to impose their decrees. It is worthy of note that it was not the so-called 'Western Democracies', which had just fought an imperialist war under the guise of protecting small nations, that recognised the newly founded Irish Republic. The only national government to recognise Dail Eireann was the revolutionary government under Lenin in Soviet Russia.

On 6 March, all Irish political prisoners were released from gaol after a member of the Dail died in Gloucester prison. De Valera, who had escaped from prison in February, now back in Dublin, became on 1 April 1919 President of the Irish Republic. One of those freed, Constance Markievicz – the first woman elected to Parliament in a British election – became Minister of Labour in the Dail.

WAR OF INDEPENDENCE

The first phase of the war came with the actions taken by the British to prevent the Dail establishing its machinery of government. The attempt by the Dail to raise a loan of £250,000 was treated as 'seditious'. Newspapers publishing advertisements for the loan were suppressed. Warrants were issued for the arrest of many of the Ministers and Deputies of Dail Eireann. The National Arbitration Courts set up by the Dail were declared 'illegal assemblies' and finally on 10 September 1919, Dail Eireann itself was suppressed and all national movements in Ireland were banned.

Thousands of English troops were being poured into Ireland from the beginning of 1919, with tanks, armoured cars and other weapons. The Royal Irish Constabulary (RIC) with nearly 10,000 men maintained fortified barracks commanding each town and village. Clashes occurred with the Irish Volunteers – now renamed the Irish Republican Army. A clash between IRA men of Cork and the military in Fermoy on 7 September resulted in a soldier being killed. The response of the British gave some idea of the terror that was to come. 200 English regular soldiers on the following day descended on Fermoy and in an orgy of destruction sacked and looted shops and wantonly destroyed anything they could get their hands on. A guerrilla war had started.

Early in 1920 a Curfew Order was placed on the towns and the British adopted an official policy of terrorism with the introduction of the 'Black-and-Tans', named after their mixed uniforms, and the 'Auxiliaries'. Both were officially off-shoots of the RIC – the British refused to admit officially that more than extended 'police measures' were necessary to maintain law and order in Ireland. The same policy they adopt today. The 'Tans' were recruited from England and chosen from a 'tough' class of men including ex-army recruits and criminals who had had their sentences remitted if they volunteered for service. The 'Auxiliaries' were a mercenary force recruited from ex-officers of the Army, Navy and Air Force.

The struggle that developed shocked the whole world and eventually had a dramatic effect on public opinion in Britain once the truth became known. Murder, arson, torture of prisoners, systematic beatings, looting and destruction of whole areas became the routine of British inflicted terror. The British forces were seen by the Irish people in the same way as the Nazi Gestapo were viewed in Europe during the Second Imperialist War. The IRA fought back. They ambushed British forces and destroyed official British government buildings. In one weekend in April 1920 most of the income tax offices in Ireland were sent up in flames. IRA ambushes of the British forces were replied to with terror – by beatings up, looting and destruction of houses, buildings, businesses in the surrounding area. Recruits joined the IRA in larger and larger numbers and the British forces had to retreat into the larger towns from most outlying areas. In such areas Republican Courts were established which maintained basic law and order and were accepted by the people. The impotence of the British authorities in the face of the popular acceptance of the authority of the Dail increasingly became clear.

The British then as today called the popular forces of the IRA 'terrorists' and 'murderers'. Then as today the real terrorists were the British forces. A report of one of the 'Tans' atrocities gives some idea of what the British forces were like:

> 'A party of Black-and-Tans, capturing six unarmed Volunteers at Kerry Pike near Cork, cut out the tongue of one, the nose of another, the heart of another, and battered in the skull of a fourth.'[22]

In total contrast, then as today, as confirmed in non-official British army reports, the IRA were regarded as a highly trained disciplined force which 'imbibed the military spirit, the sense of military honour etc...'. Behind their organisation it was said 'there is the spirit of a nation'.[23] The secret army Document 37 captured and made public by the Provisionals in May 1979 gives a similar description of the IRA forces today.

THE PEOPLE'S WAR

In this period of the war, small-holders and landless peasants were seizing large estates mostly owned by absentee landlords and dividing them up among the workers. The Dail had set up Land Arbitration Courts in May 1920 to deal with the problem of land disputes. But these courts leant over backwards to be helpful to Unionist landowners. The majority of verdicts were in favour of the landlords and the IRA in certain areas was used as a counter-revolutionary force to put into practice what these Courts decided. However in others areas especially where the people were most active in the national struggle, eg West Cork, Co Clare, the IRA co-operated with the people in seizing, confiscating and redividing the large estates. The class divisions in the national movement, on issues like these, were bound to come to the fore.

IKBR-F

The Irish working class became increasingly militant in this period. Already, before this phase of the war, a general strike had been called by the Trades Council in Limerick in April 1919 in response to the British authorities proclaiming Limerick a special military area with special permit regulations for access to the city. The General Strike continued for 12 days. With support from the public, the local leaders of the IRA, and the IRA Chief-of-Staff, the Strike Committee organised food distribution, issued notes of exchange and controlled the operation of traffic. This strike became known as the Limerick Soviet. It achieved its aims and the British military order was soon withdrawn.

On 5 April 1920, a two-day General Strike was called by the Irish labour movement in support of 100 Irish prisoners who were on hunger strike in Mountjoy prison for Prisoner of War status or release. It was dramatically effective. The prisoners were unconditionally released and British policies towards prisoners were forcibly changed.

May 1920 saw the munitions transport strike. It followed the example of the refusal of British dock workers to load munitions on the *Jolly George* because the arms were for the Polish government, then at war with Soviet Russia. Dublin and Dun Laoghaire dockers refused to unload a British munitions ship. The Transport Union supported them. The strike soon spread. When the British used troops to unload the munitions, the railway workers refused to move them. Some railway men were threatened with shooting by British army authorities, in some cases actually having a revolver put to their heads. But they refused to move the trains. These men were members of the British based National Union of Railwaymen and they also saw the Polish case as a precedent. While the NUR had supported the Polish boycott, it did not approve the actions of its Irish branch. The NUR Executive, led by the treacherous Mr J H Thomas MP, attempted to bargain the men back to work. A special TUC Congress was called to consider the whole Irish issue in July 1920, as a bargaining measure in the hope of getting the men to call the strike off. It refused to take a principled stand. Instead it passed a militant sounding call by the miners for a general strike if Britain did not call a truce, withdraw its troops, and give Ireland self-government under Dominion status with guarantees for minorities. Even this essentially reactionary motion (the Irish wanted a Republic) could not lead to action – it was never intended to do so – because it embodied no timescale after which the strike would be called. However in spite of the lack of support from the British unions, the railwaymen continued their action for some months in defiance of the British authorities. 1,500 men were dismissed during the dispute which received wholehearted backing, including financial support, from the Irish labour movement. According to General Macready, the British Commander-in-Chief in Ireland, this action of the Transport workers created 'a serious set-back to military actions during the best season of the year'.[24]

In spring 1920, after a strike for higher wages, fifty workers took over a creamery in Knocklong owned by a prominent Unionist. The creamery was a trading centre for all farms in the district – one of the biggest in Ireland. Under the slogan 'we make butter not profits' they decided to seize control of the factory and mill as the Knocklong Soviet Creamery. The farmers continued to supply milk to the creamery which continued to process and distribute. It was eventually destroyed by British troops on 22 August as part of a systematic attack on Irish industrial life. By April 1921 British troops had destroyed some sixty-one cooperative creameries alone.

In May 1921 the Arigna coal mines in Co Leitrim were taken over by the workers, and a red flag hoisted. In September, the port of Cork was taken over and run as a Soviet.

The Irish Revolution, as the War of Independence conclusively demonstrated, involved the mass of Irish people. It not only challenged British imperialism but threatened the continuation of capitalist class rule itself.

THE RESPONSE OF THE BRITISH LABOUR MOVEMENT

The social democratic wing of the British labour movement – the Labour Party, the Independent Labour Party – did not support the struggle of the Irish people for a democratic Republic. They only raised their voice on the Irish question to condemn the Republican movement or to head off any support for that movement which might be building up in the British working class. They opposed the violence and brutality of British imperialism only because it created a revolutionary opposition to imperialism among those it oppressed. 'Repression has driven many Nationalists belonging to the Constitutional school into the arms of Sinn Fein'. And 'under such conditions it is practically impossible to bring the Irish Republican Army to bay ... Executions and torture are not deterrents; they have indeed, the opposite effect'. (Labour Party Reports, January and December 1920)

The Labour Party and its supporters wanted better management of Irish affairs under some form of non-violent neo-colonial rule – that is

Home-Rule or Dominion Status under the umbrella of the British Empire. The Irish however wanted an independent Republic and were engaged in a war against British imperialism to obtain it. The British, therefore, could only maintain their rule by atrocities and terror. Ireland had become ungovernable by British imperialism. It was in this context – and rather late in the day – that the British Labour Party started to speak on the question of Ireland. And its primary concern was to save British imperialism from its own 'excesses'.

The June 1920 Labour Party Conference narrowly passed a motion which called for 'free and absolute self-determination'; the withdrawal of British troops and an all-Ireland constituent assembly to draw up a constitution. Very good . . . except that the Irish already had an all-Ireland constituent assembly (Dail Eireann) and a constitution (the Easter Proclamation 1916 and the Dail Democratic Programme 1919). The Irish people, led by the IRA, were fighting and dying to protect *their* constitution and *their* assembly. The real question was whether or not the Labour Party would recognise Dail Eireann and the Irish Republic. This the Labour Party refused to do. In March 1920, during a by-election in Stockport, two men representing local Irish voters asked the Labour Party to recognise the Irish Republic. The Labour Party issued a lengthy, evasive statement which did not recognise the Irish Republic. The local Irish responded by standing William O'Brien, at the time a political prisoner, against the official Labour candidate.[25]

Even this position only lasted until December 1920 when the definitive Labour Party policy on Ireland was adopted following two Commissions of Enquiry in January 1920 and December 1920. It began by saying that the Labour Party was in favour of self-determination, and then went on to show that it clearly wasn't. It called for:

1. The withdrawal of all armed forces from Ireland.
2. The placing of responsibility for the maintenance of order in each locality on local authorities themselves, as in Great Britain outside the Metropolitan area.
3. An immediate election by proportional representation, of an entirely open Constituent Assembly, charged to work out at the earliest possible moment, without limitations or fetters, whatever constitution for Ireland the Irish people desire, subject only to two conditions – that it affords protection to minorities and that the Constitution should prevent Ireland from becoming a military or naval menace to Great Britain.[26]

This position might deceive some British socialists today, but it was viewed by revolutionaries with contempt at that time. As *The Workers Dreadnought* said, the question was 'are you for, or against, the Irish Republic?'. On British Labour official policy, it therefore asked, what do Labour's conditions for self-determination mean? It answered:

'*Labour Party Statement*, 'Protection to Minorities'.
Probable Meaning, The handful of people in Ulster to be given equal power with the rest of Ireland.
Labour Party Statement, 'The Constitution should prevent Ireland from becoming a naval or military menace to Britain'.
Probable Meaning, Ireland to be kept within the Empire under the control of the British Army and Navy . . . [27]

The *Communist* (successor to *The Call* as paper of the British Communist Party) offered the Labour Party what it regarded as a 'charitable' suggestion. It was to cut out from their policy all but clause 1 the withdrawal of the British forces from Ireland. It asked of the proposed Constituent Assembly etc 'By whose authority will this conclave assemble?' and answered 'that of the British Empire of which the Labour Party is a worthy pillar'. It said that the only solution to the Irish question was 'to recognise the Irish Republic as an established fact and to enter into a proper and reasonable treaty of peace with its accredited representatives'.[28] Revolutionaries then recognised that the Labour Party's policy on Ireland was only designed to protect British imperialism and maintain the British Empire.

Those very small sections of the socialist movement in Britain which took the communist side of the split in the international working class movement did consistently support the Irish people's struggle for self-determination. Revolutionaries such as John Maclean and Sylvia Pankhurst gave a lead to the movement speaking at meetings and writing articles and pamphlets commenting on the unfolding events. But they were never able to build a mass movement like that associated with the Hands Off Russia campaign. That campaign was built on an anti-war, pacifist mood in the British working class. A Hands Off Ireland campaign would have had to directly confront British imperialism. It never got off the ground. The Communist International therefore took British Communists to task:

'The International will not judge the British comrades by the articles that they write in the *Call* and *The Workers Dreadnought*, but by the number of comrades who are thrown in gaol for agitating in the colonial countries. We would point out to the British comrades that it is their duty to help the Irish movement with all their strength, that it is their duty to agitate among the British troops, that it is their duty to use all their resources to block the policy that the British transport and railway unions are at present pursuing of permitting troop transports to be shipped to Ireland. It is very easy at the moment to speak out in Britain against intervention in Russia, since even the bourgeois left is against it. It is harder for the British comrades to take up the cause of Irish independence and of anti-militarist activity. We have a right to demand this difficult work of the British comrades.' (Radek, Second Congress of Communist International July 1920)[29]

It is one of those bitter facts of British labour movement history that at the very time when the Irish struggle should have been central to communist propaganda and agitation, the communists in Britain were devoting pages and pages of their press to the question of affiliation to the Labour Party. That is, affiliation to the very Labour Party which throughout its short history had done even more to undermine the Irish people's struggle for self-determination than anything done by the British ruling class.

THE TREATY AND PARTITION

The increasing political difficulties facing the British government forced Lloyd George to introduce the Government of Ireland Act (1920) – an amended version of the old Home Rule Act (1914). It proposed two Parliaments, one for the six north-eastern counties of Ulster, the other for the remaining twenty six counties. The Parliaments would be subservient to Westminster. Only six counties of Ulster were chosen, so that the Unionists would have a large majority. The Ulster counties of Cavan, Donegal and Monaghan where the nationalists had overwhelming majorities were excluded whereas Fermanagh and Tyrone with small nationalist majorities were included. The Act included a provision that the two Parliaments might, if they chose, set up an All-Ireland Council, which could agree to a reunited Ireland. However this was mere window dressing for the benefit of Americans and the British Labour Party. Lloyd George knew that the Loyalists in the proposed Six Counties would never agree to a united Ireland.

Dail Eireann simply ignored the Act. Municipal and Urban elections in January 1920, under a proportional representation system designed by the British to severely undermine Sinn Fein, only confirmed that the majority of the Irish people wanted a Republic. In the nine counties of Ulster, 23 towns fell to Sinn Fein and only 22 to the Unionists. The June

1920 county election results strongly confirmed this result. The northern capitalists and the Orange Order began to panic. Pogroms were organised against the Catholics. All Catholic workers were driven out of the Belfast shipyards and out of factories where Loyalists predominated. Some 10,000 men and 1,000 women were expelled from their jobs by loyalist thugs wielding stones, bludgeons and revolvers. Only after four days did the military intervene. 22 civilians were killed and nearly 200 were severely injured. During August 400 Catholic families were driven out of their homes. Those responsible for this thuggery and murder received the backing of the British authorities. They were the 'loyal' friends of Britain who were there to prevent the establishment of a united Republican Ireland.

The inability of Britain to defeat the IRA, and the growing opposition in Britain to British terror in Ireland forced the Truce of July 1921. However in Belfast there was no truce. Orange mobs and the newly formed 'special police' burnt down 161 Catholic homes, killed 15 people and injured another 68. This was soon after the Northern Ireland Parliament had been elected with Craig as Prime Minister. Initial negotiations showed the Government was prepared to give the Twenty Six Counties Dominion Status within the British Commonwealth, but partition would remain as long as the Parliament of Northern Ireland wanted it. The Dail unanimously rejected these conditions on 23 August 1921 but appointed plenipotentiaries to resume negotiations.

On 6 December 1921, Collins and Griffith signed the Treaty. It gave the Twenty Six Counties of Ireland Dominion Status within the British Commonwealth in the form of a 'Free State'. The north eastern six counties were to remain partitioned and part of the United Kingdom. The agreement had been signed under the threat of 'an immediate and terrible war'. It immediately split the Republican movement. On 7 January 1922, 64 members of the Dail voted for the Treaty, 57 demanded its rejection. On 9 January, de Valera resigned as President of the Dail and Griffith was elected. The IRA's nineteen divisions had split into eleven for the Republic and eight for the Free State. The Civil War soon began.

British imperialism was determined to ensure that the anti-Treaty forces would be wiped out. In collusion with the pro-Treaty Republicans, particularly Arthur Griffith, the British government opposed all efforts to avoid civil war. For example, when Collins and de Valera agreed a Coalition Pact in May 1922 in order to avoid civil war, Lloyd George and Churchill immediately demanded that the Pact be broken. Churchill declared that the Pact was a breach of the Treaty and therefore 'the Imperial Government resumes such liberties of action . . . (as) the re-occupation of territory, as we think appropriate to the gravity of the breach'.[30] On 14 June 1922 Collins repudiated the Pact. On 23 June the British government ordered Collins to fire on the anti-Treaty HQ at the Four Courts, Dublin. Collins refused. The next day General Macready, GOC British forces in Ireland, was ordered to attack the Four Courts. Finally this pressure forced Collins to attack the Four Courts on 28 June 1922 and thus make civil war inevitable.

With the aid of British imperialist arms and weapons the reactionary 'Free State' forces eventually gained total control. A bourgeois neo-colonial state had been created. In the North pogroms and killings of Catholics continued. Connolly's all too prophetic warning in March 1914 had come true. Partition of Ireland had brought a 'carnival of reaction both North and South'.

The British labour movement must take a great deal of responsibility for these developments. Time and again – Dublin lock-out 1913, Easter Rising 1916, War of Independence 1919–21 – through its subservience to British imperialism, the British labour movement had betrayed the Irish people's struggle for self-determination.

Lloyd George could not have threatened Griffith and Collins with a 'terrible war' if the labour movement had taken a principled stand. After 'pacifying' Ireland, British imperialism could more easily take on the British working class. For it was the same leadership of the labour movement which having betrayed the revolutionary Irish, would so easily betray the struggles of the British working class up to and including the 1926 General Strike.

While the British Labour Party, the ILP, and the British TUC welcomed the reactionary 'Free State', the tiny Communist movement in Britain continued to support the anti-Treaty forces. It followed the lead of the Communist International in siding with those revolutionary forces of Republicanism still determined to fight for a united Ireland. That stand taken by the Communist movement should be our starting point today.

COMMUNISTS AND THE TREATY

After the signing of the Treaty in December 1921 the small British Communist Party made it clear that, as far as it was concerned, 'there is no Irish settlement'. In an article 'A Fresh War in Ireland Soon', *The Communist* argued:

'The war on the British Empire is therefore not over. It may be forced to assume other methods and disguises, but it will go on. Not till every trace of the British connection is wiped out will the Irish war of independence cease'.[31]

British communists then understood that the Republican struggle was not at an end. They fully supported the anti-Treaty forces. They urged Irish workers to continue the war against British imperialism. And they were critical of the Irish Labour Party's and Transport Union's neutrality in the face of the national struggle, arguing that they were seriously undermining the working-class cause.

Communists recognised that British imperialism had gained a considerable victory by splitting the Irish national movement from top to bottom. Not only had the 'Orange garrison' been supplemented by the 'Griffith garrison' but a 'deep weakness in the Imperialist structure' had 'been repaired just when the revolt of subject nations in India, Egypt and Ireland was seriously threatening it'.[32] In the Dail debate on the Treaty the Irish revolutionary Liam Mellows referred to this same point. The acceptance of the Treaty would mean that 'we are going into the British Empire now to participate in the Empire's shame, and the crucifixion of India and the degradation of Egypt. Is that what the Irish people fought for freedom for?'[33] As a result, British workers and oppressed peoples now faced in British imperialism 'a strengthened and stabilised foe'.

The Communist emphatically rejected the simplistic view held by some 'socialists' that the normal course of economic development in Ireland, by intensifying the class struggle 'North' and 'South' of the border, would reunite the Irish working class and lead to a united struggle against the Irish bourgeoisie. This was based on the false assumption that the signing of the Treaty had disposed of the national issue. The unity of the Irish working class would not be possible until British imperialism was driven out of Ireland. For this reason communists were on the side of those 'who carry on the tradition of 1916'. British and Irish workers had a common interest in the victory of the anti-Treaty forces and in the defeat of British imperialism in Ireland. *The Communist*, in July 1922, called upon British workers, not to make or send munitions to Ireland, to demand the withdrawal of British troops, and to 'do for the Irish what you did for the Russians'.[34]

The partition of Ireland had divided the Irish working class. The artificial statelet created by the British in the Six Counties was designed to maintain loyalist dominance in that part of Ireland. The loyalist

(Protestant) workers in the Six Counties were a privileged section of the working class and the maintenance of their privileges (higher wages, jobs, housing etc) depended on the union with Britain. They were the most implacable enemies of a united independent Irish Republic for this reason. Any improvement in the conditions of the nationalist (Catholic) working class in the Six Counties they regarded as a direct threat to their own interests. It was clear that as long as British imperialism remained in Ireland there could be no unity of the Irish working class.

The capitalists north and south of the border had no interests in seeing a united Ireland. The partition of Ireland had, after all, divided the Irish working class and severely weakened the opposition to capitalist rule in the whole of Ireland. Once the opposition to partition had been put down this arrangement would suit the Irish capitalists in the North and South very well.

Imperialism will never voluntarily relinquish political control over an oppressed nation because such control enormously strengthens its ability to economically exploit an oppressed nation. British imperialism, faced with a revolutionary war against its rule in Ireland, had partitioned Ireland and conceded a degree of independence to the Irish bourgeoisie in the South with the creation of the neo-colonial Twenty Six Counties 'Free State'. It would however maintain its dominance and control over the whole of Ireland through its political, economic and military presence in the northern Six Counties. *Partition of Ireland is the mechanism by which imperialist exploitation over the whole of Ireland is maintained.* And the key to the continuation of partition is the support of the loyalist working class. It would obviously have the support of the northern capitalists who would lose their main markets if left outside the British Empire. British imperialism therefore has a direct interest in maintaining the privileged condition of the loyalist working class. For these privileges are the basis of loyalty to the union with Britain and the key to imperialist control over the whole of Ireland. So both British imperialism and the Irish capitalists North and South had a direct interest in a divided Ireland and a divided working class.

It follows that a united Ireland can only be achieved by revolutionary means. The partition of Ireland can only be ended by revolutionary forces which defeat both British imperialism and the Irish ruling class. Such a struggle is a revolutionary challenge not only to British imperialism but also to its agents in the British working class.

The British Labour Party gives organised political expression to a privileged layer of the British working class. This privileged layer, as we have argued (see chapter 2), has a material interest in the continuation of imperialism because it is the source of its economic and political privileges. This is why the British Labour Party has never supported the revolutionary democratic struggle of the Irish people for self-determination. For the defeat of British imperialism in Ireland would seriously undermine those economic and social conditions which give rise to the continued domination of the British Labour Party over the British working class. It would give tremendous strength and impetus to any emerging revolutionary forces in the British working class. That is why those organisations in Britain supporting the revolutionary struggle for a united Irish Republic have always been forced to confront those reactionary sections of the British Labour and trade union movement which form the British Labour Party. The Communists in 1921 were no exception to this rule. William Paul explains:

'The Communist Party of Great Britain hails the dauntless fight of the Irish Republicans in their successful struggle against the British Government. Unlike the Labour Party, which does not desire to harass the Government during the present negotiations, we defiantly declare that it is our intention to so challenge the Government, that it will gladly yield all the demands made by the Irish Republicans. In lending every assistance to Ireland, it is not only necessary for us to attack the Government, but also to warn our Irish friends that the political and trade union leaders of the British Labour movement are as dangerous to them as even a Lloyd George or a Hamar Greenwood. The cowardly ineptitude of the Labour Party in the House of Commons, so far as Ireland is concerned, is at once humiliating and treacherous. The barefaced betrayals of Ireland and her workers by the British trade-union leaders is on a level par with that of the Labour Party. We assure our Irish friends that these elements are being exposed by the Communists.'[35]

The small Communist Party did not succeed. The barefaced betrayals of the British Labour and trade union movement allowed British imperialism to impose partition on the Irish people.

It is important to understand what this meant. Imperialism was able to impose the 'carnival of reaction' that Connolly predicted would follow partition: the creation of a police state in the Six Counties and the bloody and barbaric repression of the anti-Treaty forces in the Twenty Six Counties. By the end of the civil war the Republican movement was deeply divided and many of its best leaders had been executed by the 'Free State' forces. The Irish masses, who formed the backbone of the independence struggle, had been exhausted and demoralised by two wars – one against the British and the other against the Treatyites. These were the conditions in which the sectarian Six Counties statelet was erected and in which the revolutionary nationalists struggled to rebuild a movement.

NOTES

1   Connolly J, 'The Irish Flag' *Selected Writings op cit* p. 143.
2   *ibid* p. 145.
3   Levenson S, *James Connolly* London 1977 p. 291.
4   *ibid* p. 292.
5   See Macardle D, *op cit* p. 155–6; facsimile reproduction p. 157.
6   The main argument here is contained in Terry Marlowe's article 'Easter Rising' in *Hands Off Ireland!* No 10 April 1980 pp. 16–18.
7   Clarkson J D, *op cit* p. 313 fn. 1.
8   Challinor R, *op cit* p. 150.
9   Greaves C D, *The Life and Times of James Connolly* London 1972 p. 420. See also Levenson S, *op cit* p. 324.
10   Ellis P B, *op cit* p. 232. See also Jackson T A, *Ireland Her Own* London 1971 p. 401.
11   Lenin, *LCW* Volume 23 p. 104.
12   *The Herald*, 29 April 1916 and 6 May 1916.
13   *The Call*, 18 May 1916.
14   *The Socialist*, June 1916.
15   *The Woman's Dreadnought*, 6 May 1916.
16   Cited in *Lenin on Ireland* (pamphlet) Dublin 1970 pp. 3–4. See also *Trotsky's Writings on Britain*, Volume 3 London 1974 pp. 167–169.
17   Lenin, 'The Discussion on Self-determination Summed Up' *LCW* Volume 22 pp. 355–358.
18   Kee R, *The Green Flag* Volume 3 *Ourselves Alone* London 1976 p. 34.
19   Mitchell A, *op cit* pp. 75–6.
20   *ibid* p. 76.
21   *ibid* pp. 94–100.
22   Lord Longford (Frank Pakenham), *Peace by Ordeal* London 1972 p. 49.
23   Macardle D, *op cit* p. 317.
24   Mitchell A, *op cit* p. 121.
25   Bell G, *Troublesome Business* London 1982 pp. 49–50. See also a critical review of Bell's book by T Marlowe in *Fight Racism! Fight Imperialism!* No 26 February 1983.
26   The Labour Party, *Report of the Labour Commission to Ireland* 28 December 1920 p. 113.
27   *The Worker's Dreadnought*, 12 November 1921 and 26 November 1921.
28   *The Communist*, 13 January 1921.
29   *Second Congress of the Communist International*, Volume 1 London 1977 pp. 127–128.
30   Neeson E, *The Civil War in Ireland* Dublin 1969 pp. 102–3.

31   *The Communist*, 14 January 1922.
32   *ibid*.
33   Greaves C D, *Liam Mellows and the Irish Revolution* London 1971 p. 278.
34   *The Communist*, 8 July 1922.
35   Paul W, *The Irish Crisis* (1921) Cork 1976 p. 12.

PART THREE

REVOLUTIONARY NATIONALISM IN RETREAT

LIAM MELLOWS

CHAPTER FIVE

REPUBLICANISM UNDER SIEGE

A CARNIVAL OF REACTION

Repression and discrimination have been a permanent feature of the northern statelet from its foundation until today. These features are built into the system and are essential to maintain the loyalty of Protestant workers to British rule.

The northern statelet was formed from six of the nine counties of Ulster, carefully chosen so that the Unionists would have a large majority. This meant the large Catholic minority, who would never be reconciled to a loyalist state, had to have it forced on them. And forced on them it certainly was. In a period of Unionist orchestrated terror between July 1920 and July 1922, 453 people were killed in Belfast, 37 members of the Crown Forces and 416 civilians, including 257 Catholics and 157 Protestants. Outside Belfast more than 100 died, 45 Crown Forces and 61 civilians, including 46 Catholics and 15 Protestants. Of the 93,000 Catholics in Belfast almost 11,000 were driven from their jobs and 23,000 rendered homeless. Over 500 Catholic owned shops and businesses were burnt, looted and wrecked. The Catholics were being beaten into submission.[1]

The state set up a whole machinery of repression. The Royal Ulster Constabulary was the loyalist state's armed paramilitary police force, mainly recruited from the Orange Order and the Special Constabulary, with access to rifles, sub-machine guns, and armoured cars. This force was supplemented by a Special Constabulary originally in three categories: A, B and C. However, it was the part-time B-Specials who were to be maintained in force until they were 'disbanded' in 1969. All were recruited from the Orange Order and formed a Protestant and loyalist militia. As Major Fred Crawford said at the time, 'the more

Orangemen we have in that force, the better it will be for Protestant interests and the success of the Orange body itself'.[2] The average membership of the B-Specials was between 11,000 and 12,000. The Specials were a formidable force. They had regular drilling and weapon training. They were armed with rifles, revolvers, bayonets and later sub-machine guns which they kept in their homes. In the 1950s and 1960s they had access to Bren-guns and Shortland armoured cars. The role of this force can be judged by the fact that the pogroms against the Catholics between 1920–1922 were conducted mainly by the Ulster B-Specials side by side with Orange mobs. When Sir Oswald Mosley, the leader of fascism in England, visited Belfast with the object of extending his organisation to the Six Counties, Lord Craigavon (Northern Ireland Prime Minister honoured yet again for his service to British imperialism) assured him that it was unnecessary. Northern Ireland had already, in its armed Special Constabulary, a fascist force in being.[3]

Loyalist 'law and order' was further strengthened by an extra-ordinary piece of legislation – the Civil Authorities (Special Powers) Act (Northern Ireland) 1922. It had been pushed through the Northern parliament in April 1922 at the height of the Belfast pogroms as an emergency measure to last one year. However, it was annually renewed until 1928, then renewed for five years and finally in 1933 it was made permanent. The Act gave the civil authorities all the powers of a police state. The first section began:

'The Civil Authority (the Minister of Home Affairs) shall have power, in respect of persons, matters and things within the jurisdiction of the Government of Northern Ireland to take all such steps and issue all such orders as may be necessary for preserving the peace and maintaining order'.[4]

This measure introduced the death penalty for some firearms and explosives offences and flogging and imprisonment for others. It permitted indefinite internment without trial. It allowed the authorities to suspend at will any and all of the basic liberties, from habeas corpus to the freedom of the press. People could be arrested on suspicion, and people and buildings could be searched without warrant. The onus of proof could be reversed and the holding of inquests dispensed with. It also gave the Minister power to make any further regulations, each with the force of a new law, and to delegate his powers to any policeman. And just in case anything had been overlooked in the regu-lations, even that was provided for when it stated:

'If any person does any act of such a nature to be calculated to be prejudicial to the preservation of the peace or maintenance of order in Northern Ireland and not specifically provided for in the regulations, he shall be deemed to be guilty of an offence against the regulations.'[5]

The most effective power of the Act was internment enabling the government to jail indefinitely anyone it considered a political or military threat to it. It was used immediately until the end of 1924. It was re-introduced in 1938 and lasted until 1946. It was introduced again in December 1956 and lasted until 1961. And finally it was introduced on the largest scale ever in August 1971 – being the measure which eventually brought down the government which had introduced it.

In April 1963, J Vorster, at that time Minister of Justice of the racist South African police state, whilst introducing a new Coercion Bill in the South African parliament, could say that he 'would be willing to exchange all the legislation of that sort for one clause of the Northern Ireland Special Powers Act'.[6] An enquiry carried out by the (British) National Council of Civil Liberties in 1936 commented that the Unionists had created 'under the shadow of the British constitution a permanent machine of dictatorship'. Northern Ireland was compared with the fascist dictatorships then current in Europe.[7]

Another instrument to maintain Unionist supremacy was that of gerrymandering. The technique is a very simple one. Constituency or ward boundaries are drawn in such a way as to spread Unionist (Protestant) votes over as many seats as possible, so as just to be sure of winning the seats. Whereas nationalist (Catholic) votes are crowded into as few seats as possible. This process was aided by the ending of proportional representation, and by the restricted franchise – limited to rate-payers and their spouses – which discriminated against the poorer Catholic population. The clearest example of gerrymandering was Derry City. In 1966, the adult population of Derry was 30,376 – 20,102 Catholics and 10,274 Protestants. Restricted franchise reduced the Catholic majority substantially; 14,429 Catholics to 8,781 Protestants. Finally, after numerous boundary revisions, the city was divided into three wards (see Table 1). A large nationalist majority in this way was turned into its opposite – a Unionist majority.[8] Yet another way had been found to secure the Unionist supremacy in the northern statelet.

The Unionist alliance depended on the support of the loyalist

TABLE I

	Nationalist Voters (Catholic)	Seats	Unionist Voters (Protestant)	Seats
South Ward	10,047	8	1,138	–
North Ward	2,530	–	3,946	8
Waterside Ward	1,852	–	3,697	4
	14,429	8	8,781	12

working class. The loyalist working class were a privileged section of the working class at the foundation of the state. This privileged status has been maintained by systematic discrimination against Catholics in the areas of wages, jobs and housing. Conditions in the North of Ireland are worse than in Britain but this only serves to emphasise the importance of any discrimination in favour of the loyalist working class.

Discrimination means that Catholic workers in the Six Counties tend to be unskilled manual workers while Protestants have by far the greatest share of the skilled jobs, and therefore the higher wages and privileges associated with such jobs. This was still the case in 1971. In 1977, the Fair Employment Agency published an analysis of the 1971 Census which showed that the loyalist labour aristocracy has been preserved until this day. It said:

'. . . it is clear that the Protestant is most likely to be a skilled manual worker while the Roman Catholic will be an unskilled manual worker.'[9]

A report of wage rates since 1914 in engineering, shipbuilding and construction, published in 1957, showed that for a large part of the period the rates of wages prevailing in the Six Counties for *skilled* workers were *higher* than the corresponding average in Britain as a whole. The wage rates for *unskilled* workers were lower than for Britain. This means that the differential in favour of skilled workers over unskilled workers was greater than the corresponding differential for Britain as a whole. Protestant privilege was no small thing. The 1971 census confirmed this trend of much higher wages for loyalist workers.

The differential in wages concerns those who are able to get a job. The attitude of Unionist politicians on the question of jobs leaves no doubt as to who will be most likely to be unemployed. In July 1933, Sir Basil Brooke (later, Lord Brookeborough, Prime Minister of the Six Counties) made a speech in which he said 'I have not a Roman Catholic about my own place'. While J M Andrews, the Minister of Labour, (and Prime Minister before Brooke), responded indignantly to what he regarded as a smear:

> 'Another allegation made against the government, which is untrue, is that of 31 porters at Stormont 28 are Roman Catholic. I have investigated the matter and I have found that there are 30 Protestants and only one Roman Catholic, there only temporarily.'[10]

When the Nationalists in the Stormont Parliament proposed a motion of censure on Sir Basil Brooke for his speeches, Lord Craigavon moved an amendment saying 'the employment of disloyalists (Catholics) . . . is prejudicial to the state and takes jobs away from Loyalists'.[11] The Unionist state had a clear policy of discrimination in employment against Catholics. The results can be seen.

Catholics, while only one third of the population, provided 90,000 out of the 159,000 who emigrated looking for work between 1937 and 1961 – that is nearly 57%. In July 1961 the average figure for unemployment in the Six Counties was 7%. The highest figures were in the predominantly Catholic areas of Newry 17.2%, Newcastle 16.4%, Strabane 14.4%, and Derry 13.8%. The lowest figures were Ballyclare 2.2%, Bangor 2.7%, Lisburn 3.3% – all solidly Protestant areas. And recent figures all show that nothing has changed. The influx of multinational companies' investment and British state aid into the Six Counties over the last twenty years has altered nothing at all. Most of the new investment was overwhelmingly located in loyalist areas.

Harland and Wolff, the biggest source of employment in Belfast, has been kept alive by massive British state subsidies over the last 20 years. On numerous occasions Catholics have been driven out of employment from the yards by Unionists. In 1970 among the 10,000 workers in Harland and Wolff, only 400 were Catholics. By 1975, as a result of intimidation and assassinations, the number had been reduced to 100. In the three largest firms in Belfast in the late 1960s the proportion of Catholics employed was 3%, 1.4% and 0% respectively.

The situation in housing and health reinforces the extent of Protestant privilege. Nationalist areas suffer most from unfit housing – 40-45% in nationalist Fermanagh against only 10-20% in loyalist areas like Antrim, Lisburn and Down. In the mid-1970s a nationalist in the west of the sectarian statelet was at least twice as likely to be struck down with an infectious disease (tuberculosis, acute meningitis, scarlet fever etc) as a Protestant in the east. The infant mortality rate is again consistently higher for the nationalist areas than for loyalist areas. In the loyalist north and east of the Six Counties the figures are 18.1 and 19.7 per thousand respectively. In the nationalist west it is 24.8. This rises to 32.3 in Fermanagh.

The loyalist workers' ties to Britain and its ruling class, their refusal to unite with the nationalists in the struggle for democracy and socialism is based on the real material privileges they receive. They do not defend the sectarian statelet out of some obsession with theology. Their reactionary Unionist politics grow out of their immediate social conditions. Compared to the conditions of exploitation of the mass of Catholics beneath them, the Loyalists are a labour aristocracy. Anything that threatens British imperialist rule in Ireland, threatens their privileges. That is why the loyalist worker is so opposed to the struggle of the Republican movement for a united Ireland.

This, then, is the Six Counties statelet, a police state based on terror, repression and sectarian discrimination. It was this which the British Labour government defended when, in May 1949, it enacted the new Government of Ireland Act. This Act said 'in no event will Northern Ireland or any part thereof cease to be part of . . . the United Kingdom without the consent of the Parliament of Northern Ireland'.[12] True to its history, the British Labour government – and this one was said to be progressive – legitimised the rule of a reactionary police state in order to defend British imperialism. British governments ever since, both Labour and Conservative, have upheld this standpoint. It has nothing to do with democracy. It has everything to do with maintaining British imperialism's rule over the northern statelet and through it the protection of British imperialism's fundamental interests in the whole of Ireland.

REPUBLICANISM UNDER SIEGE

The northern statelet is clearly unreformable. If the Irish working class is ever to be united, then partition has to be destroyed and British imperialism driven out of Ireland. The revolutionary wing of the national movement has always made the unification of Ireland the major plank of its platform. This is the key to any social progress in the whole of Ireland. And it can only be achieved by revolutionary means. In the years following partition, the revolutionary Republican forces, in the face of the most difficult conditions, strove to find the means to continue the struggle for a united Irish Republic.

On 24 May 1923, the civil war ended with the IRA order to dump arms. There was no surrender, simply a recognition of the present defeat and a decision to hold back the Republican forces until a new opportunity for a successful struggle occurred. W T Cosgrave, the leader of the pro-Treaty forces and the Cumann na nGaedheal Party had, with the aid of British imperialism, crushed the Republican forces in a vicious campaign of legalised terror. During the civil war, the pro-Treaty government had executed 77 Republicans including Liam Mellows, Rory O'Connor, Joseph McKelvey and Richard Barrett, who were taken out of Mountjoy prison and shot without trial. By July 1923, the Free State government held over 11,000 prisoners.

Even after the civil war the anti-Treaty forces still had considerable support. The Republicans, organised legally as Sinn Fein, contested the elections of August 1923 on an abstentionist platform. In spite of government harassment and disruption of meetings, campaign workers being attacked, and many candidates in prison or on the run, Sinn Fein won 44 seats to Cumann na nGaedheal's 63.

As a 'concession', the Treaty had included a clause providing for a Boundary Commission to revise the border 'in accordance with the wishes of the inhabitants'. The Northern Ireland government refused to appoint a representative to the Commission. The British government – a minority Labour government under Ramsay MacDonald – eventually appointed its own representative, an imperialist judge in the South African Supreme Court, and later nominated one for the Six Counties, an Orangeman and staunch Unionist. In 1925 the Commission met and, after a charade of investigation, decided by a majority to propose minor frontier changes which included the transfer of the richest land in nationalist Donegal to the Six Counties. The 'Free State' government panicked, which was no doubt the purpose of the whole exercise, and, in December 1925, agreed to recognise the existing boundary. The partition of Ireland was now consummated. The nationalist minority in the Six Counties had been sold out by the Cosgrave government and left to face the terror of a loyalist police state.[13]

The 'Free State' government was clearly hand-in-glove with British imperialism. The Dail had become the organ of British imperialist control. This was recognised in November 1925 at the General Army Convention, when the left-wing Republican Peadar O'Donnell proposed a motion which called on the army of the Republic to:

'sever its connection with the Dail, and act under an independent Executive, such Executive be given the power to declare war when, in its opinion, a suitable opportunity arises to rid the Republic of its enemies and maintain it in accordance with the proclamation of 1916.'[14]

The motion was carried. It had the effect of forcing out into the open those sections of the IRA/Sinn Fein talking about entering the Dail. Revolutionary Republicans knew that the 'Free State' was the creation of a British imposed coup and to enter its Dail would be a recognition of the Treaty and an acceptance of partition. De Valera, on the other hand, arguing that the Republic could be achieved by constitutional means, wanted to enter the Dail. He was soon to raise the question of taking the oath of allegiance (to the King and Empire), which was part of the Treaty settlement, as *the* issue of principle in order to obscure the real issue – acceptance of the British-imposed Dail and partition. He argued that Sinn Fein should enter the Dail once the oath was removed, with a programme to achieve a Republic as rapidly as possible by constitutional means. His position was put to the test at an extraordinary Ard Fheis of Sinn Fein in March 1926 and was defeated by 233 to 218 votes.

The most visible section of opposition to de Valera was Cumann na mBan, the Republican women's organisation, which had also voted overwhelmingly to reject the Treaty. On 11 March de Valera resigned as President, withdrew from Sinn Fein, and organised his followers into a new party, Fianna Fail. This party, he said, would enter the Dail only on the removal of the oath.

The assassination of Kevin O'Higgins, a Minister in the Cosgrave government, in July 1927, was used as a pretext by Cosgrave to introduce a Bill which said that every candidate for election to the Dail must on nomination swear to take the oath. On 12 August 1927 de Valera led Fianna Fail members into the Dail where they signed the book containing the text of the oath of loyalty to the British King. De Valera maintained this was accepting the oath 'as an empty formula'. Nevertheless he admitted that 'what we did was contrary to all our former actions and to everything we stood for'.[15] In participating in the British-imposed Dail he had broken fundamentally and irrevocably with the revolutionary nationalist standpoint.

In the election of 1932, Fianna Fail obtained more seats than Cumann na nGaedheal and formed the government with Irish Labour Party support. De Valera informed the British government that he was abolishing the oath and withholding payments of land annuities due to the British government as a result of the earlier Land Acts. The British then imposed punitive tariffs on Irish imports, principally cattle, into Britain. The measure was announced by the Dominions Secretary to the National Government, the Labour traitor J H Thomas MP. The aim was to cripple the trade of the 'Free State' so it would be forced to surrender within six months. The British government hoped that the resulting hardships for the farming population would lead to the return to power of the Cosgrave party. The latter collaborated by organising itself on fascist lines and developing a campaign of violent obstruction against the new government with the object of winning small farmer support away from Fianna Fail. The Economic War with Britain, in fact, lasted six years.

Cumann na nGaedheal represented the pro-British cattle-ranching and trading interests. It was a party totally subservient to British imperialist interests. Fianna Fail, on the other hand, came to power as the champion of smaller capitalist interests and tillage farmers. Its mass support came mainly from farmers working small holdings and from rural and urban wage-earners – from the people who were the backbone of the independence movement. The acquiescence of the Irish Labour Party and ITUC in the destruction of the Republic in 1922 made it easy for Fianna Fail to gain and hold on to working class and small-farmer support. On coming to power, Fianna Fail appeared to be opposing British imperialism, and many accepted its Republicanism at face value. Fianna Fail seemed to many people to offer an alternative to war and hardship in the quest for an Irish Republic.

The bulk of Irish industry in the northern Six Counties had been lost with partition. De Valera's economic policy was to begin to build up new industry in the 'Free State' behind high tariff walls. It had a limited amount of success. Industrial employment rose from 111,000 in 1931 to 154,000 in 1936 as a number of small industries were set up.[16] But the attempt to build an independent capitalist Republic, doomed to failure in any case, could only be made by increasing the suffering of the working masses. The average income per head dropped from 61% of the British figure in 1931 to 49% in 1939. The new jobs created didn't cover the pool of unemployed. And the period of protection had a disastrous effect on trade – exports falling by 40%. Eventually the vulnerability of the Irish economy to the vastly more productive British monopoly capital, together with that of other imperialist interests would begin to tell.[17] The policy later was to be drastically changed.

In December 1937 de Valera introduced a new Constitution for the

South. It claimed the whole of Ireland – including the Six Counties – as the national territory, though specifically excluding the Six Counties from the jurisdiction of the Dublin government 'pending the re-integration of the national territory'. In 1938 the Economic War was brought to an end. The Irish 'Free State' (now Eire) paid £10 million to Britain in final settlement of all claims of a financial character. In return it received concessions including the handing back of ports and naval depots retained under British control as a result of the Treaty. But partition remained. The history of the Fianna Fail party in this period proved that the attempt to pursue the struggle for a Republic by constitutional means, could only be based on the interests of Irish cap-italists, who, sooner or later, were obliged to come to terms with British imperialism and accept partition. Once again, the standpoint of revolutionary Republicanism had been proved correct. From de Valera in the 1920s and 1930s to the Official IRA in the 1970s, those who have rejected this standpoint have ended up supporting British imperialism.

REPUBLICANISM SEARCHES FOR A MASS BASE

By the end of the 1920s, the IRA was in no position to accomplish its goal of a united Irish Republic by a military campaign having mass support. Given that partition could only be ended by revolutionary means, the IRA, while maintaining its armed organisation intact, knew it had to find the means to win mass support for a renewed offensive against British imperialism and partition. However, the masses, with the memory of the recent years of bloody and bitter fighting followed by the establishment of the reactionary Cosgrave government, were ready to believe Fianna Fail's empty promise of a united Irish Republic achieved by peaceful means. The problems which confronted the IRA in this period were to prove insurmountable.

The IRA involved itself in the social issues inevitably arising among the masses. Already in 1925, Peadar O'Donnell editor of the IRA weekly newspaper *An Phoblacht*, was using its columns to support the campaign in Donegal to withhold land annuities. An organisation init-ially called the Workers Defence Corps, later renamed the Irish Labour Defence League, was formed in 1929, and it included trade unionists and members of the IRA, including prominent ones on the left. On 13 March 1930, the Workers Revolutionary Party was organised as an avowedly communist group. Peadar O'Donnell and several other IRA men were deeply involved. On 15 February 1931, the General Army Convention committed itself to set up Saor Eire, an organisation of workers and working farmers committed to overthrow British imperialism and Irish capitalism. The organisation was committed to agitation against landlordism and for state direction of essential industries, and state monopoly of banking, credit and export services. The Cosgrave government and the Catholic Church, once they realised the extent of these developments within the IRA, began a campaign against the 'Red Menace' and 'pagan communism'. New draconian 'public safety' legislation was introduced and very quickly twelve radical and revolutionary organisations including Saor Eire, the IRA and the Workers Revolutionary Party were banned. Raids and arrests took place everywhere. After the election of de Valera, Saor Eire quickly disappeared.

In 1932, the IRA became involved in the massive demonstrations and riots which took place in Belfast. Unemployment was reaching unprecedented levels, over 28%, and in the Belfast shipyards employment had fallen by over 80% in less than 2 years. The Protestant skilled workers were as hard hit as Catholic labourers. The Unionist politicians had treated with contempt a demand for improvement in starvation-level wages paid on relief schemes. Mass demonstrations of unemployed workers took place and were met by the police and military. Within a short time the streets in every working-class district in Belfast were barricaded against armoured cars, and in some areas IRA men and Ulster Protestant Association men were standing together in armed defence against the forces of the Crown. As in the 1907 Belfast dock workers' strike (see chapter three), demonstrating workers in the nationalist areas were, on the instructions of the government, fired upon by the RUC. Two nationalist workers were shot dead and fifteen wounded. In the loyalist areas police were instructed only to use batons and not firearms.[18] It was soon over. Faced with a serious threat to the loyalist alliance, the government acknowledged defeat, and offered more money for relief schemes and increased relief rates. The trade union leaders, terrified by the involvement of the IRA and left wing groups during the demonstrations and strikes, were very quick to make a deal. The unionist ruling class did their best to blame the events on 'communist Sinn Fein' elements. They began to campaign on sectarian lines. By 1935, sectarian riots against Catholics were taking place in Belfast. The loyalist alliance might temporarily be disturbed over some single issue and under extreme economic conditions, but it can never be destroyed unless the prop of the union with Britain is taken away.

It was during this period of deep economic depression and two years after the election of de Valera that the idea of a Republican Congress was formed. A section of the Army believed that, if the IRA was to find mass support for the anti-imperialist struggle to unite Ireland, it was necessary to win industrial workers and small farmers away from the leadership of Fianna Fail. This could only be done through a revolutionary party committed to building such an anti-imperialist movement. Many of the IRA who had supported Saor Eire were in favour of a Republican Congress, but the Executive and Army Council were less enthusiastic. At the next Army Convention, the proposal for a Republican Congress fell by one vote. Those in favour of the Congress then decided to go ahead. Gilmore and O'Donnell, in order to carry out the work, left the IRA.

A group of IRA officers and others prominent in Republican and Labour organisations met at Athlone in April 1934 and issued a call for a Congress. They argued that a 'Republic of a united Ireland will never be achieved except through a struggle which uproots Capitalism on its way'.[19] They appealed to anti-imperialists to attend, including those from working-class organisations from the Six Counties urging them to take up the struggle for national freedom. The immediate response was encouraging and work for the Congress began at once. A weekly paper, the *Republican Congress*, was published.

The IRA reply to the Congress appeal was published in *An Phoblacht* on 14 April 1934. It said:

'In so far as the statement referred to is an attack on the present social and economic system, and an indictment of the policies of the Governments of the Six and Twenty Six Counties, the Army Council is in complete agreement with it.'[20]

But the Army Council objected to the Congress criticism of the IRA saying 'this attack by Republicans can only assist the campaign of the Capitalists and Imperialist elements'. The central objection, however, was the issue of forming a new political party.

'This Party will, in course of time, contest elections and enter the Free State parliament. Inevitably it will follow the road which has been travelled by other constitutional Parties, which, though setting out with good intentions, ended in failure. It is not very long ago since Fianna Fail leaders told us that they wanted to go into the Free State Parliament only for the purpose of smashing it up, but they now hold this institution and the whole Free State machine as sacred.'[21]

This had been the Republican experience and is a view which has been proved correct countless times. It is quite wrong to see the dispute between the Republican Congress and the IRA as one between socialists and militarists. Those who attempt to use the Republican Congress to justify their own attack on the IRA, slander both the Congress and the IRA.

At the Congress which met at Rathmines Town Hall on 29 and 30 September 1934, two positions emerged. The first called for the formation of a new political party – a Workers' Republican Party committed to a fight for an Irish Workers' Republic. The second called for a united front of the Republican masses – workers and small farmers – for a united Irish Republic. The second position eventually was won by 99 votes to 84. But the Congress was split and leading members holding the first position refused to be on the Congress Executive.

The work went on but with little eventual success. Besides the damaging split in the Congress, the reactionary character of the Irish trade union movement and the commitment of whole sections of workers and small farmers to Fianna Fail lay behind the failure. It was precisely because of the success of Fianna Fail in holding on to the support of large sections of workers and small farmers, that the call for a united front to fight for an Irish Republic was undoubtedly correct. This was the position Connolly took in practice in 1916. Only in this way would the sham Republicanism of Fianna Fail be exposed. To call for a Workers' Republic as an immediate demand at this stage in the struggle was to be totally out of touch with reality. Peadar O'Donnell explained why:

'We dare not jump through a stage in the fight, raising now the slogan, "Workers Republic", and leaving Fianna Fail to escape, saying they are standing for one kind of Republic, but that we stand for a different one. My quarrel with de Valera is not that he is not a Socialist, for he makes no pretence to be one. My quarrel is that he pretends to be a Republican while actually the interests for which his Party acts – Irish Capitalism – are across the road to a Republic.'[22]

After the failure of the Congress, the IRA and the Republican Congress went their own ways. The Republican Congress having detached itself from the IRA collapsed within two years.

The IRA continued its efforts to unite the national question with the social questions of the day. It led the struggle against the growing fascist movement in Ireland, the Blueshirts, suffering many arrests after clashes with the fascists. It gave support to major strikes offering armed assistance to picket lines and carrying out punishment shootings of scabs. By April 1935, 104 Republicans were in prison. In June 1936, the IRA was once again banned, this time under de Valera. Many rank-and-file IRA members went to fight on the Republican side in Spain.

All the efforts to build a mass anti-imperialist movement in this period failed. The IRA, since the defeat of the revolutionary forces during the civil war had not been able to unite a mass movement behind the military and political struggle to defeat British imperialism, and end partition. The social and political conditions required simply did not exist. But the IRA did keep alive the revolutionary tradition and did maintain an armed organisation to seize any available opportunity to renew the struggle.

NOTES

1   Farrell M, *Northern Ireland: The Orange State* London 1976. Much of the statistical information on the loyalist state is taken from this book.
2   Buckland P, *Irish Unionism* Volume 2 Dublin 1973 pp. 166−7.
3   Gilmore G, *The Irish Republican Congress* Cork n.d. p. 23.
4   Farrell M, *op cit* p. 93.
5   *ibid*.
6   *ibid* pp. 93−94.
7   *ibid* p. 97.
8   *ibid* p. 85.
9   Cited in Marlowe T and Palmer S, 'Ireland: Imperialism in Crisis 1968−78' in *Revolutionary Communist* No 8 July 1978 p. 13. The material below on wage rates, employment, housing and health is taken from this source.
10   Farrell M, *op cit* p. 136.
11   *ibid* p. 137.
12   *ibid* p. 188.
13   Macardle D, *op cit* pp. 793ff and pp. 803ff.
14   Bell J Bowyer, *The Secret Army: The IRA 1916−1979* Dublin 1979 p. 53. This book and Coogan T P, *The IRA* London 1980 have been used extensively for the history of the IRA.
15   Longford Lord and O'Neill T P, *Eamon de Valera* London 1970 p. 257.
16   Purdie B, *Ireland Unfree* London 1972 p. 23.
17   Revolutionary Communist Group, 'Britain and the Irish Revolution' in *Revolutionary Communist* No 2 May 1975 p. 6.
18   Devlin P, *Yes we have no bananas: Outdoor Relief in Belfast 1920−1939* Belfast 1981 pp. 130-1.
19   Gilmore G, *op cit* p. 34. Bell J Bowyer, *op cit* p. 113.
20   Coogan T P, *op cit* pp. 107−8.
21   *ibid*.
22   Gilmore G, *op cit* pp. 53−4.

CHAPTER SIX

THE IRA GOES ON THE OFFENSIVE

From the ending of the civil war (1923) until the late 1960s, the social and political conditions did not exist to unite a mass movement behind a military and political campaign to defeat British imperialism. Nevertheless, in its efforts to keep the revolutionary tradition alive and an armed organisation intact, the IRA was to carry out two military campaigns – the first in England (1939–40) and the second in the Six Counties (1956–62).

THE CAMPAIGN IN ENGLAND 1939–40

Towards the end of the 1930s, the IRA sought to rebuild active support for the Republican Movement and decided to resume its military offensive against British imperialism. Preparations and training for a bombing campaign in England began in 1938. It was to be accompanied by a military campaign in the North, but in November 1938 three IRA men were killed on a mission to bomb customs posts when a faulty mine exploded in a house they were in near the border. This accident and some successful demolitions of customs posts increased RUC-Special Branch activity in the North. In December, 34 IRA men in the North were arrested and interned. This was to rule out any serious campaign in the North; however, it had little effect on the English campaign.

On 12 January 1939, the IRA delivered an ultimatum to the British government demanding the withdrawal of all British armed forces and civilian representatives from every part of Ireland. If the government refused, then the IRA would be 'compelled to intervene actively in the military and commercial life of your country as your Government are now intervening in ours'.[1] The British government were given four days to respond. On 16 January 1939, the bombing campaign began with seven explosions in three centres, London, Birmingham and Manchester. The aim was sabotage of basic installations such as electricity, gas, water supplies and train services. By July, there had been 127 explosions and many Irishmen and women had been rounded up, arrested and convicted.

On 24 July, the government introduced an anti-Irish Prevention of Violence Bill with sweeping powers to demand the registration of all Irish people in Britain and to deport Irish citizens at will. The Bill was passed in five days – its modern equivalent, the Prevention of Terrorism Act, took less than three – and within a week 48 people had been expelled from Britain and five prohibited from entering Britain.

IRA volunteers were ordered to make every effort to avoid civilian casualties but in the course of the campaign civilians were injured and some were killed. On 25 August in Coventry, a bomb being taken by bike to a generating station blew up prematurely, killing 5 people and injuring over 50. The police went through every Irish home in Coventry. Two men, Peter Barnes and James McCormack, were eventually arrested, and on very slender evidence were tried, convicted and executed. Barnes and McCormack, while IRA volunteers, had no direct responsibility for the Coventry explosion. But the British, as always, when dealing with the Irish, have never been in the slightest concerned with justice.

The judicial murder of Barnes and McCormack was not the only blow struck against the IRA and its supporters during the campaign. In England, 23 men and women were sentenced to 20 years in prison for their involvement in the campaign, 34 to 10–20 years, and 14 to under 5 years. In the Twenty Six Counties of Ireland, the Fianna Fail government stepped up its repression of the IRA and its supporters. In June 1939, the Offences Against the State Act was passed and over 50 IRA men were interned. In April 1940 in Mountjoy prison, two IRA volunteers, Tony D'Arcy and Jack McNeela, died after a long hunger strike to demand treatment as political prisoners.

Faced with such blows and set-backs, in March 1940, the English campaign – the IRA's first major military effort since the Civil War – came to an end. It would take some time before the IRA would be able to rebuild its organisation and resources and gather together the necessary support to conduct another military campaign against British imperialism.

The response of the British Labour and socialist movement to the IRA campaign followed what was by now a familiar pattern. The violence, brutality and injustice of British imperialism, if opposed at all, was only opposed on the grounds that it created support for a revolutionary opposition to imperialism among the oppressed. The real hostility, however, was usually reserved for the revolutionary forces fighting British imperialism.

The argument always contained some hollow gesture of support for a united Ireland. But invariably, it condemned those actually resorting to force to obtain it. So, at the time of the debate on the Prevention of Violence Bill, Arthur Greenwood, the Labour MP, could say:

> 'Terrorist methods...would achieve nothing...Many MPs on both sides of the House would like to see a united Ireland, but the way a minority had chosen would defeat its own object...'[2]

However, if the minority uses force, the Labour Party made it clear that it must be put down:

> 'Believing that IRA terrorism must be stopped, the Labour Party will not vote against the IRA Bill which is to be debated this afternoon and rushed through all its stages by Wednesday night...'[3]

There was some concern (amendments were proposed) that measures taken against the IRA might go too far and 'do violence to the liberties of the law-abiding British subject'.[4] And that widespread repression could stir up much wider opposition to British rule in Ireland. So, Wedgwood Benn (the father of Anthony Wedgwood Benn) warned the government:

> 'If you punish an innocent man, your quarrel will not be with the IRA, it will be with Ireland, and you will stir up the hatred of Irish Americans'.[5]

That even these qualifications did not go very far in the Labour Party was shown when only 17 Labour MPs voted against the anti-Irish Prevention of Violence Bill. And Wedgwood Benn was not included among them. Their overriding concern was clearly to crush any support that existed for the IRA.

The Communist Party reported the bombing campaign with little or no comment. But an Editorial on the Prevention of Violence Bill showed a significant change of position from that held by communists at the time of partition. The Communist Party opposed the Prevention of Violence Bill on the grounds that it would be used as an excuse to attack British liberty. But they had no qualms about the police attacking the IRA:

'It is wrong to describe this measure as an anti-IRA Bill. It uses the bombing activities of the IRA as an excuse for attacking British liberty . . .

'Will they (the police) know the difference between those who support an Irish Republic and the small group who are misusing the historic name of the Irish Republican Army . . .'[6]

Later, in an Editorial opposing the forthcoming executions of Barnes and McCormack, the main features of the new position became clear. The Communist Party, while 'understanding' the motives of the IRA condemned its actual struggle to achieve a united Ireland:

'We are against terrorism in politics and we have condemned the IRA bombings. But we understand the motives and the principles which actuate these Irish patriots. They want their country to be free, independent and united'.[7]

Did this mean that the Communist Party which recognised that Ireland had been divided by the force of arms would no longer defend those committed to unite Ireland by the force of arms? What was clear was that the new position was a reactionary one. Real communists would after all have opposed, without any qualifications whatsoever, both the execution of Barnes and McCormack and the Prevention of Violence Bill. And real communists would have stated that the responsibility for any injuries and deaths during the campaign lay with British imperialism.

THE BORDER CAMPAIGN 1956–62

It took 16 years before the IRA had the resources and organisation to launch a new military campaign against British imperialism. This took place in the Six Counties and was concentrated on the border.

At Bodenstown in 1949, the IRA made a declaration that force would no longer be used against the Twenty Six Counties Irish government but only against the British forces of occupation in the Six Counties. It was thought that this position, formally incorporated into 'General Army Orders' in 1954, would induce Dublin to tolerate the campaign and the use of the Twenty Six Counties as a staging post for their actions in the Six Counties. This was to prove a major miscalculation.

Plans for a campaign were drawn up in 1951. The first steps towards getting the campaign underway consisted of raids on British military barracks and armaments depots to obtain additional supplies of arms and ammunition. A very successful raid occurred in 1951 at the Ebrington Territorial Barracks, Derry. The haul included 20 Lee Enfield rifles, twenty sten guns as well as a number of machine guns. Two raids in England failed, one at Felstead, Essex in 1953 and the other at the Arborfield Depot, Berkshire in 1955. In both cases large hauls of arms were taken but in each case the vehicle carrying the arms was stopped by police and the arms were captured before they could be got away. As a result of the Felstead raid, Sean Mac Stiofain, Cathal Goulding and Manus Canning were arrested and imprisoned for 8 years. After being sentenced, Cathal Goulding, on behalf of the other prisoners, declared:

> 'We believe that the only way to drive the British Army from our Country is by force of arms, for that purpose we think it no crime to capture arms from our enemies.'[8]

The most successful raid, which aroused considerable support and new recruits for the IRA, was that at the Gough barracks, Armagh, in June 1954. There the haul included 340 rifles and 50 sten guns. A few more, largely unsuccessful, raids were to take place before the commencement of the campaign. Eight men were arrested and given long prison sentences as a result of the raid at the Omagh military barracks in October 1954. Those imprisoned rapidly gained support amongst the nationalist population for both the daring character of the raid itself and their principled conduct during the trial.

A Westminster election was called in May 1955. The IRA, through Sinn Fein, decided to contest the elections on an abstentionist platform and show they had a popular mandate for the coming campaign. They named candidates for all twelve seats, half of them prisoners who were in jail for the Omagh raid, and made it clear that they would not stand down for anyone. The bourgeois Nationalist Party, a nominal 'opposition' in the Six Counties loyalist parliament, were faced with a dilemma – much like the SDLP in the election of Bobby Sands and Owen Carron during the 1981 hunger strike campaign. Running a candidate against Sinn Fein would split the nationalist vote and allow the Unionists to win. If that happened, and with the likelihood of them getting a much lower vote than Sinn Fein, the Nationalist Party would rapidly lose any of the support they still had. They decided it was better not to stand especially after Phil Clarke, nominated by Sinn Fein, had been selected as nationalist candidate for Fermanagh-South Tyrone in preference to Cahir Healy, the Nationalist Party MP. During the fight for the nomination, Cahir Healy had denounced the policies of 'physical force' and 'abstentionism'.

Sinn Fein obtained a total of 152,310 votes in the election and won the two nationalist seats of Mid-Ulster and Fermanagh-South Tyrone. It was the biggest anti-partition vote since 1921. Sinn Fein had won the allegiance of the nationalist population on a platform stressing only the national issue and with candidates who supported the armed struggle of the IRA. This vote reflected the growing hostility of the nationalist population to the openly repressive loyalist police state.

Since the candidates elected, Tom Mitchell for Mid-Ulster and Phil Clarke for Fermanagh-South Tyrone, were 'convicted felons', both serving sentences for the Omagh raid, under British 'democracy' they were ineligible to be elected and to hold their seats. The defeated Unionist candidate in Fermanagh-South Tyrone filed an election petition in June to have Clarke unseated and himself declared elected. This eventually occurred after the defeat of a small opposition to it in the Westminster parliament led by the Labour MP Sidney Silverman supported by some left-wing Labour MPs. So much for parliamentary democracy.

As no petition was filed, the seat in Mid-Ulster was declared vacant and a by-election called in August 1955. Tom Mitchell ran again and was elected with an increased majority over the Unionist. He was again disqualified but it was found that the Unionist candidate was ineligible to take his seat because he had held an 'office of profit under the Crown'. A third by-election was held in May 1956 and this time the Nationalist Party stood a candidate. Tom Mitchell stood again and won four times as many votes as the Nationalist Party candidate – the latter losing his deposit. But the Unionist won the seat as the nationalist vote had been split. No-one could doubt, however, where the sympathies of the nationalist population lay. British imperialism had shown time and again that it would never voluntarily heed the democratically expressed wishes of the nationalist population. British imperialism had only ever been moved when confronted by revolutionary force. The outcome of the election, therefore, showed that there would be support among the nationalist minority in the Six Counties for the military campaign planned by the IRA.

At the beginning of 1956, a plan of campaign 'Operation Harvest' was drawn up by Sean Cronin. The plan was to attack the North with the aim of destroying installations and public property on such a scale as to paralyse the Six Counties. The campaign aimed to use the methods of guerilla warfare 'within the occupied area' and as support built up to liberate large areas 'where the enemy's writ no longer runs'.[9] The plan, a version of which was captured by the security forces in January 1957 after a raid, was considerably modified in practice.

The IRA decided to avoid action in Belfast because it was felt that this might provoke a loyalist backlash and lead to attacks on the nationalist areas. There was some dispute within the IRA as to whether they would have the resources and organisation to defend the nationalist areas in Belfast. And the arrest of the Belfast organiser before the beginning of the campaign finally decided the issue. But this indicated a problem for a campaign which had the aim of paralysing the Six Counties. Belfast, the political administrative and economic centre of the loyalist state was to be left alone.

There was a great deal of pressure within the IRA to launch a military campaign in the Six Counties. In 1951, Liam Kelly had been expelled for taking unauthorised action. He took most of the eastern Tyrone organisation with him and soon set up a new armed organisation, Saor Uladh. In June 1956, Joe Christle, a militant IRA member impatient with the lack of action, was expelled from the IRA and he took most of the young Dublin activists with him. His group and Saor Uladh were to link up in September 1956 and were to carry out a number of combined attacks on customs posts on the border in November 1956. These developments no doubt enabled those in the IRA leadership wanting to launch the military campaign to win the argument over their more cautious comrades.

The campaign began on the night of 11–12 December 1956. About 150 men blew up targets in the Six Counties around or near the border area: a BBC transmitter, a barracks, a territorial army building, a magistrates court, and a number of bridges were damaged or destroyed. The response of the loyalist government was immediate. It introduced internment and more than 100 northern IRA men were rounded up. By 1958, nearly 187 were held. 'Unapproved roads' in border areas were blown up by British army sappers and bridges were destroyed. 3,000 RUC men and 12,000 B-Specials were called into action and were joined by British Army Scout cars. The North was turned into an armed camp. South of the border, the number of guards doubled and the Gardai continually harassed and arrested IRA men. On 16 December, the Gardai arrested part of the IRA Army Council and eleven other members of the IRA. They were, however, this time released the same day, but the signs were ominous.

On New Year's Eve two RUC barracks were attacked in Fermanagh, and during the attack at Brookeborough two IRA men were killed. The two men, Sean South and Fergal O'Hanlon, became national heroes in the Twenty Six Counties and thousands attended their funerals – some 50,000 following Sean South's funeral in Limerick. There was an upsurge of support for the IRA, and much resentment when the Taoiseach John Costello, head of the coalition government in the South, in January 1957, had most of the IRA Army Council rounded up and jailed for short terms under the Offences Against the State Act.

On 28 January 1957 Sean MacBride, the leader of Clann na Poblachta, a party with Republican sympathies, which had joined the coalition government, was forced by rank-and-file pressure to move a vote of no confidence in the government. This was both on economic grounds and its failure to pursue a positive policy on the reunification of Ireland. It was precipitated by the government's continual harassment of the IRA. The Government was defeated and the Dail dissolved. A new election took place on 5 March. Fianna Fail was returned with a clear majority. De Valera was now back in power.

For the election, Sinn Fein nominated 19 candidates, many of them prisoners, campaigning solely on the national issue and on an abstentionist platform. Four were elected and Sinn Fein received 65,640 votes – the highest total they had received in the South since 1927, about 6% of the total vote. However, this was to represent the high point of support for the Republican Movement during the Border Campaign.

Fianna Fail under de Valera had little or no inhibitions about suppressing the IRA. Besides, the economy was in difficulties, unemployment having reached 70,000 and emigration at its highest point since the 1880s. De Valera needed to improve trading relations with Britain and quite clearly wasn't going to let the IRA get in the way. On 6–7 July 1957, soon after an IRA ambush of a RUC patrol in Co Armagh, internment was reintroduced in the South. All the Sinn Fein Ard Comhairle (national committee) except one, most of the Army Council and GHQ staff and many IRA men in the country were soon in the Curragh internment camp. It was a crushing blow. However, the IRA infrastructure in the Six Counties, hardened by coercion, still existed and functioned. But any idea of escalating the campaign was now ruled out. The campaign never regained the momentum of the initial attack. While in the first month of the campaign, December 1956, there had been 25 operations and in 1957 a total of 341, during 1959 there were only 27 incidents and in 1960 there were 26. Support for the IRA gradually fell away. In the October 1959 Westminster elections, Sinn Fein contested twelve seats, won none of them and received less than half the votes they obtained in 1955. In October 1961, there was an election in the South and Sinn Fein lost all four seats they won in 1957, their vote dropping to 36,393. The arrests, internment, repression and increased security had taken their toll. Political backing for the campaign now was down to the hard Republican core. The campaign had to be called off.

The IRA Army Council ordered their volunteers to dump arms on 26 February 1962. In a statement on the ending of the campaign it said:

'The decision to end the Resistance Campaign has been taken in view of the general situation. Foremost among the factors motivating this course of action has been the attitude of the general public whose minds have been deliberately distracted from the supreme issue facing the Irish people – the unity and freedom of Ireland.'[10]

That is, the campaign had to be ended because of the falling away of support. During the campaign, eight IRA men and one sympathiser, two Saor Uladh members, and six RUC men had been killed. Outright damage in the Six Counties was assessed at £1 million and the cost of increased police and military patrols at £10 million. But the campaign had failed. Stormont had hardly been touched.

Why did the campaign fail? Was the IRA finished? Could the revolutionary armed struggle to drive British imperialism out of Ireland ever succeed? These were questions being asked both inside and outside the Republican Movement after this defeat. The answers given to them were to have important repercussions in the movement over the next ten years.

There were many who put down the defeat to the IRA/Sinn Fein concentration on the armed struggle and the failure of the Republican Movement to take up broader 'economic and social issues'. That is, in the terms of those who argued in this way, the failure of the IRA to become more 'political'. Those arguing this position in the Republican Movement were to become the dominant trend over the next seven years with near disastrous consequences when the next phase of armed struggle began.

A typical 'left-wing' analysis of the defeat along similar lines is expressed by Michael Farrell, a leading member of People's Democracy (now part of the Fourth International) and a Trotskyist. He argued that the IRA's explanation of the defeat was inadequate. They could not simply 'blame the people' for not supporting them. The failure of the 1956–62 campaign, according to Farrell, was due to the fact that:

'... the IRA was in possibly the most unpolitical phase of its history ...and the IRA, while despising parliamentary politicians, was deeply suspicious of left-wing politics. They had no policy other than physical force and no serious political organisation to mobilise their supporters and channel their energies into the mass resistance which is complementary to all guerilla campaigns ... '[11]

And yet it was precisely those who would be regarded as 'political' from Farrell's standpoint, who went on to betray the movement during the next decade. And it was just those who, with very good reasons, deeply distrusted 'politics' who eventually founded the Provisional IRA – an organisation that, in the latest phase of struggle has held British imperialism at bay for over 14 years on the basis of mass support of the nationalist population in the Six Counties. It is Farrell's explanation that is inadequate. There is a great deal which Farrell, because of his own political standpoint, cannot begin to explain.

The revolutionary wing of the national movement has always made the unification of Ireland its central goal. It is the key to any social progress in the whole of Ireland. It is the pre-condition of reuniting the Irish working class. And finally, it has been established, time and again, that it can only be achieved by revolutionary means – by an armed struggle to drive British imperialism out of Ireland. Those who counterpose 'political'/'economic and social' agitation to the armed struggle to reunite Ireland have not understood the centrality of the national question for the Irish revolution and the Irish working class.

The Border Campaign showed two things. The first was that the social and political conditions still did not exist to unite a mass movement behind a military and political struggle to defeat British imperialism in Ireland. The second was that the Republican Movement made a major political error in its approach to the neo-colonial government in the Twenty Six Counties. Let us examine them in turn.

The campaign aimed to bring the Six Counties to a standstill. It intended, as support built up, to liberate large areas 'where the enemy's writ no longer runs'. In attempting to do this, it faced almost insurmountable obstacles. The Six Counties was artificially created by British imperialism precisely to give the Loyalists an inbuilt majority. Two-thirds of the population of the Six Counties are Protestant, the majority of whom are opposed to a united Ireland. The IRA would not only have to face the armed paramilitary forces of the loyalist state backed by the British army, but, in many areas, a hostile Protestant population as well. Under these circumstances only the *active* support of large sections of the nationalist population for the armed struggle and determined resistance to the loyalist state could guarantee a basis for a continuing military campaign.

In fact it was only in the border areas where the IRA could count on anything like widespread popular support. The decision not to engage in any actions in the Belfast area was an expression of this reality. This was a fundamental factor behind the failure of the campaign. Conditions do not permanently exist where there is *active* support for the armed struggle to drive British imperialism out of Ireland.

By the end of the 1960s, conditions were to rapidly change. The repression directed against the Civil Rights campaign had demonstrated in practice that the loyalist state was unreformable and would have to be destroyed. The revolutionary standpoint of the IRA was vindicated. The nationalist population of Derry and Belfast were to be left with no choice. They turned to the IRA demanding that it take up arms to defend the nationalist population against the paramilitary forces of the reactionary loyalist police state.

The belief that a declaration not to engage in actions in the Twenty Six Counties would lead the Dublin government to tolerate the campaign was a major political error. Once Fianna Fail had introduced internment and rounded up most of the political and military leadership of the Republican Movement, the campaign suffered a blow from which it could not recover.

Since 1914, the Irish capitalist class has always worked hand-in-glove with British imperialism to destroy the revolutionary national struggle to unite Ireland. It has no more interest in creating the conditions for a united Irish working class than has British imperialism. The political parties of the Irish capitalist class, Cumann na nGaedheal (Fine Gael) and Fianna Fail, have, since the Civil War, taken every opportunity to crush the IRA. The capitalist neo-colonial state in the Twenty Six Counties is a barrier on the way to a united independent Irish Republic. It, just like the loyalist state in the North, will have to be destroyed if British imperialism is to be defeated in Ireland.

By 1958, Fianna Fail was about to embark on a policy of export-oriented growth through a massive influx of foreign capital, mainly British and US, into Ireland. Throughout the next two decades, Ireland's economic dependence on imperialism would grow. At the time of the Border Campaign Fianna Fail was already looking to better economic relations with Britain to stabilise the crisis-ridden Irish economy. It was in no position to tolerate a resurgence of the armed struggle of the IRA against British imperialism. The writing was on the wall. In spite of bitter experience in the past and many warnings to the contrary, the IRA ignored this. As a result, the organisation suffered a devastating blow.

COMMUNISTS AND THE BORDER CAMPAIGN

The initial raids in December 1956 were responded to with the predictable denunciations in Dublin, London and Belfast. However, the Soviet Union, through *Pravda* denied British claims that the raids were only isolated actions without popular support. It argued in defence of the campaign that 'Irish patriots cannot agree with Britain transforming the Six Counties into one of its main military bases in the Atlantic pact'.[12]

The British Communist Party's coverage of the campaign consisted on the whole of short factual reports without comment. However, a major article on the campaign by Desmond Greaves in January 1957 continued with the change of position that had come to the fore after the 1939–40 campaign.[13] But this time without *directly* condemning the IRA. In an article called 'You May Disagree with their Methods, but the IRA have Just Aims', Greaves outlined a position which is transitional to the openly reactionary standpoint of the CPGB today.

Greaves attacks press propaganda which denounced the IRA as 'bandits, thugs or murderers' and explains their methods and tactics on the basis of what he regarded as their class position:

'In its barest terms, the tactics of the IRA are those of the progressive lower-middle class continued into the period when the working class *should* be leading the struggle for national independence, but (for historical reasons) *is not*'.

The aim of the IRA, a united independent Ireland is 'progressive and should receive the support of every British worker'. However, the *method* of achieving this aim is in the hands of British workers to decide.

'The British workers could, and should insist and use their power to ensure that all effort to keep Ireland divided and dependent ceases forthwith.
If we, the working class, do not do our job, then others will conduct the struggle and, of course, they will use the methods which their class position gives rise to'.

He then goes on to make it clear that if there were no partition there would be no IRA and after arguing that British workers need neither adopt nor accept responsibility for IRA tactics he says:

'... it is the private business of the various political organisations in Ireland what tactics they choose in their struggle for their rights'.

Greaves' position is deliberately evasive on the question of armed struggle and is, therefore, open to thoroughly reactionary conclusions. The armed struggle cannot be put down to the tactics of the 'progressive lower-middle class'. The armed struggle is adopted by all classes, including the working class, as and when necessary to reach the desired goal. Has Greaves forgotten that Connolly was one of the leaders of the Easter Rising? Greaves, in fact, refuses to say whether British workers should be *for* or *against* the armed struggle that the IRA is *actually* conducting in the fight for a united independent Irish Republic. Communists cannot be evasive on this issue. They must take sides.

'National self-determination is the same as the struggle for complete national liberation, for complete independence, against annexation, and socialists *cannot* – without ceasing to be socialists – reject such a struggle in whatever form, right down to an uprising or war.'[14]

The communist standpoint is clear and it is Greaves who has broken with it.

The debate following Greaves' article showed what was at stake. A letter from John Harris opposing Greaves drew out openly reactionary consequences.

'For Desmond Greaves to describe the acts of terrorism perpetrated by the IRA as "tactics" is complete nonsense ... Who knows, the use of terror may even be extended to London, in which case Desmond Greaves would be hard put to explain them away'.[15]

Indeed he would! And when the campaign was extended to London in the 1970s the CPGB, along with most of the British Left, condemned the IRA.

Letters in the *Daily Worker* of 9 January 1957 in reply to John Harris expressed the real communist standpoint. One argued that John Harris' anger was misdirected:

'Let John Harris direct his anger against himself and his fellow-members of the British Labour and trade union movement who have been too indifferent for too long to the injustice of the British-imposed partition of Ireland . . . '.

Another pointed out that the struggle of the IRA aided the British workers' struggle for socialism:

'What Mr Harris does not realise is that any blow, whether by the IRA or anyone else, struck at British imperialism helps the British people towards socialism'.

NOTES

1   Coogan T P, *op cit* p. 164
2   *Daily Herald*, 25 July 1939.
3   *Daily Herald*, 24 July 1939.
4   *Daily Herald*, 26 July 1939.
5   *Daily Herald*, 25 July 1939.
6   *Daily Worker*, 26 July 1939.
7   *Daily Worker*, 3 February 1940.
8   Coogan T P, *op cit* p. 337.
9   Bell J Bowyer, *op cit* p. 283.
10 *ibid* p. 334.
11 Farrell M, *op cit* p. 221.
12 Coogan T P, *op cit* p. 387.
13 *Daily Worker*, 3 January 1957.
14 Lenin, *LCW* Volume 23 p. 34.
15 *Daily Worker*, 5 January 1957.

PART FOUR

REVOLUTIONARY WAR

THE BLANKET MEN

CHAPTER SEVEN

FROM CIVIL RIGHTS TO INSURRECTION

What began, in the late 1960s, as a struggle of the minority nationalist population for basic democratic rights in the six north-eastern counties of Ireland, was soon to be turned into a revolutionary war to drive Britain out of Ireland. In that period, it was to be conclusively demonstrated in practice that the northern statelet was unreformable. Basic democratic rights for the nationalist population could only be achieved by ending partition and driving British imperialism out of Ireland. They could only be achieved by revolutionary means.

UNIONISM GETS A FACE-LIFT

The Six Counties statelet could not have been brought into existence without the political support of the Protestant working class. Nor could it be maintained without that support. However, that support can only be sustained on the basis of sectarianism. That is, by maintaining the privileged status and conditions of the Protestant working class. For such privileges are the foundation of their loyalty to the Union with Britain and therefore the key to imperialist control over the whole of Ireland.

British imperialism cannot play a progressive role in Ireland. For it has no interest in eliminating sectarianism or reuniting the Irish nation and the Irish working class. This is the context in which we will examine the years immediately before the Civil Rights Movement. This is the background which is necessary to understand the role played by the so-called 'liberal' Unionist Terence O'Neill.

The economy of the Six Counties statelet was in very serious difficulties in the late 1950s. Its three traditional industries – agriculture, textiles (linen industry) and shipbuilding – were in long-term decline. Employment was rapidly dropping in all three. In agriculture, between 1950 and 1961, employment fell by nearly 40%. Between 1955 and 1965 employment in the linen industry fell by 37%, and in shipbuilding it fell by 42%. In 1961, 10,000 men were made redundant in the Belfast shipyards. Unemployment was now reaching unacceptable levels among the Protestant skilled working class. Average earnings also fell from 82% of those in Britain in 1961 to 76% in 1966. If these developments were allowed to continue unabated, the loyalty of the Protestant working class, and with it the Unionist class alliance, would come under severe strain.

The political impact of these changes soon began to show. Sections of loyalist workers began to seek an alternative to the Unionist Party to defend their interests and guarantee their privileges. The Northern Ireland Labour Party (NILP), which had split in 1949 over its recognition of the border, could now put itself forward as an alternative to the Unionist Party which could attract loyalist workers. In 1953, the NILP obtained 31,063 votes (12.1% of the total) in the Stormont elections with nine candidates winning no seats. By 1958, it had won 37,748 votes (16%) with eight candidates, winning four seats. In 1962, it obtained 76,842 votes (26%) with 14 candidates – its highest total ever – and held on to the four seats won in 1958 with substantially increased majorities. No new seats were gained but the Unionists' majority in some seats was sharply reduced. This was a protest vote which the Unionists could not ignore. If the Unionist class alliance was to survive, the Unionist Party had to ensure it found jobs for loyalist workers.

The traditional response of Unionism was discrimination pure and simple. Even in 1961, Robert Babington, a Unionist barrister (later a MP) could still say:

'Registers of unemployed Loyalists should be kept by the Unionist Party and employers invited to pick employees from them. The Unionist Party should make it quite clear that the Loyalists have first choice of jobs.'[1]

Privileged access to jobs, however, presupposed that jobs were available. Having the 'first choice of jobs', which increasingly did not exist, would find little response from loyalist workers. A new approach was clearly required. Opposition to Brookeborough built up and in March 1963 he resigned. He was replaced by Terence O'Neill.

O'Neill has been widely portrayed as a 'reformist liberal' who attempted to reduce sectarianism and discrimination but was defeated by the old guard of Unionism. This is a distortion of the truth. O'Neill's entire purpose was not to undermine Unionism but to revitalise it. As he said in April 1965:

'Let no one in Ireland, North or South, no one in Great Britain, no one anywhere make the mistake of thinking that, because there is talk of a new Ulster, the Ulster of Carson and Craig is dead. We are building, certainly; but we build upon their foundations. And from that rock, no threat, no temptation, no strategem will ever shake us. We stand four-square upon it.

But it is not enough, I would suggest to you, just to be part of the United Kingdom. We want to be a *progressive* part of that Kingdom. We want to secure for our people the full fruits of this great nation's prosperity. It must be our aim to demonstrate at all times, and beyond any possible doubt, that loyalty to Britain carries its reward in the form of a fuller, richer life.'[2]

O'Neill's intention was to strengthen the Six Counties statelet. The equation of loyalty with material privileges, and the importance of the British link for securing these privileges, was central to his approach. The task was to secure the Unionist class alliance. This could only be done by restoring the eroded privileges of the loyalist working class.

If the loyalist workers were to maintain their privileges and stay 'loyal', industry in the North had to continue to provide jobs. British subsidies to existing industries could now only slow down the pace of decline, they could not halt it altogether. To ensure new jobs were provided, O'Neill embarked on a far-reaching programme to attract capital investment from outside the Six Counties statelet.

Attracted by capital grant rates of up to 45%, together with various other direct and indirect subsidies, the 1960s saw a massive rise of firms investing in the Six Counties. While 51 firms were established with government assistance between 1950 and 1959, in the period 1960–1969 no less than 172 firms were set up. This rapid growth took off in 1963, the year Terence O'Neill took over.

The impact on employment was crucial. In 1961 the number of jobs created by government sponsored industry was 40,300 – 20.5% of all manufacturing jobs; it was 64,200 (34.4%) in 1966 and 78,680 (43.2%) in 1971. The government strategy was also successful in attracting a number of large multinational corporations such as Michelin, Good-year, Du Pont, Enkalon, ICI and Courtaulds, to invest in the Six Counties. The northern statelet became a major centre of the artificial fibre industry.

The influx of imperialist capital into the Six Counties led to a shift in the economic balance of power. The old established family firms which had been the backbone of the Unionist Party were in decline. They were being displaced by the more modern highly productive firms established by imperialist capital. However, it is totally misleading to maintain that this development represented a liberal and reforming influence which could have undermined the sectarian foundations of the Six Counties statelet. On the contrary, it was only on the basis of the influx of new British and foreign capital that the Unionist class alliance could be secured and with it the foundation of the Six Counties statelet.

Evidence of the 'reforming' influence of these new developments was said to be the fact that, in August 1964, the Unionist government under O'Neill recognised an autonomous Northern Ireland Committee of the Irish Congress of Trade Unions. Brookeborough had always refused to recognise the ICTU. He was violently opposed to trade unions and especially opposed to an all-Ireland body. However, the Unionist government under O'Neill understood the necessity for union co-operation and 'normal' labour relations, if the new investment they urgently needed was to be attracted to the Six Counties. Anyway, recognising an autonomous Northern Ireland Committee of the ICTU was far from undermining the sectarian character of the Six Counties statelet. Rather, it acknowledged it by accepting a partitionist division of the Irish trade union movement and creating what was, in fact, a loyalist dominated trade union committee.

Other evidence put forward as an example of the 'liberal' influence of O'Neill's new strategy was the meeting he had on 14 January 1965 in Belfast with Sean Lemass, Taoiseach of the Twenty Six Counties Fianna Fail government. There was also a return visit in Dublin in February 1965 and inter-departmental and inter-ministerial discussions followed.

In the 1960s, Fianna Fail had embarked on a new economic strategy of export oriented growth through massive influx of foreign capital. In 1960, Lemass had signed a trade agreement with Britain after a series of talks which had begun in July 1959. At that time, Lemass had also suggested economic co-operation between the Twenty Six Counties and the Six Counties, but Brookeborough had shown no interest. The new strategy was successful for a time in increasing employment and economic growth. By March 1965, 234 new foreign enterprises had been established in the Twenty Six Counties, 40% of them British. Trade ties with Britain became closer and an Anglo-Irish free trade area was agreed on in December 1965. This is the background which had led some to believe that the Lemass-O'Neill talks heralded a new era of North-South co-operation and possible steps towards the reunification of Ireland under British imperialist rule.

O'Neill very quickly put down such talk and made it clear that discussions were only concerned with limited economic co-operation with the Twenty Six Counties. It waʳ part of his overall strategy to revive industry in the Six Counties and make foreign investment more attractive. There was no question of discussing political or constitutional changes at all. As he said some time later to an Annual Meeting of the Ulster Unionist Council in Belfast (February 1967):

> 'Because I talk to my neighbour in a friendly way across the garden fence, and perhaps even agree that we should share some gardening tools with him, it does not mean that I intend to let him live in my house.'[3]

The overall results of O'Neill's economic programme demonstrated that, far from undermining the sectarian foundation of the loyalist state, it reinforced it. The bulk of the new investment was located in the predominantly Protestant east of the Six Counties. So that unemployment, while falling dramatically in loyalist areas, remained constant or even increased in nationalist areas during the period. In June 1970, the average unemployment level (11.3%) in the predominantly nationalist area west of the River Bann was nearly twice the Six Counties average (6.2%). In some nationalist areas of Belfast and Derry it was well over 20%.

Even where investment was located outside loyalist areas, as the following case shows, discrimination along sectarian lines was very much in evidence. It was reported in 1977 that two-thirds of the workforce at the Ford Motor Company's Autolite factory in West Belfast was Protestant. The factory was situated in the nationalist area of Andersonstown where there is massive unemployment. Protestants held the best jobs within the factory and many travelled to work from as far as Bangor and Portadown, ten or twenty miles away. A few years earlier it had been discovered that the then personnel officer was simply tearing up applications from Catholics. He was not dismissed but simply moved to another position with the same status and salary. In 1977, the personnel officer vetting applications was a sergeant in the notoriously sectarian Ulster Defence Regiment.

Following the Matthew Report (1963), the government established a new city, planned to have a population of 100,000, as an alternative to

Belfast, and proposed seven other towns as industrial growth centres. The new city included the Protestant towns of Lurgan and Portadown and the area between them. It was provocatively named Craigavon after the founder of the loyalist statelet. Six of the eight 'growth centres' were within 30 miles of Belfast in loyalist territory. Under the Benson Report on Northern Ireland Railways (1963) the rail links from Belfast to Newry, and the line to Derry through Omagh and Strabane were axed – all predominantly nationalist areas. The Lockwood Report (1965) recommended that the New University of Ulster was not sited in nationalist Derry, the second largest city in the Six Counties, where there was already an old-established University college, but in Protestant Coleraine. Under O'Neill, the economic and social revival of the Six Counties was based on sectarianism and therefore largely benefited the Loyalists.

The Unionist Party got its reward. There was a loss of support for the NILP and a return of Protestant working class votes to the Unionist Party. The NILP vote fell from 76,842 (26%) in 1962 to 66,323 (20.4%) in 1965, when it lost two of the four seats it had won in 1958, to 45,113 (8.1%) in 1969. The Unionist class alliance had been well and truly secured.

THE CIVIL RIGHTS MOVEMENT

In the course of reinforcing the Unionist class alliance, O'Neill succeeded in reactivating the latent opposition to the loyalist statelet amongst the nationalist minority. The sectarian economic and social measures implemented by the O'Neill administration could only serve to highlight the discrimination against the nationalist population.

Within the Catholic middle class a movement for civil rights emerged. In a few years this movement, under a new and more radical leadership was to turn into a mass movement intent on destroying the loyalist state.

A much larger, more ambitious Catholic middle class had been created in the Six Counties as a result of the post-war developments generally associated with the growth of the 'welfare state'. Developments in the education system, including the increase in University scholarships, were of particular significance. By the mid-1960s, a section of middle class Catholics, who did not see their interests being advanced through unity with the Twenty Six Counties, were willing to work within the institutions of the loyalist statelet to end discrimination and improve their status.

In January 1964, a group of middle-class and professional Catholics founded the Campaign for Social Justice which set about collecting and publicising information about gerrymandering and discrimination in the Six Counties. As a result of this and other agitation by middle-class Catholics together with pressure from anti-Unionist MPs in the Six Counties parliament, in June 1965, a group of back bench Labour MPs in the Westminster parliament set up the Campaign for Democracy in Ulster. Included among them was Stanley Orme, the left-wing Labour Party MP who was later to administer internment when he became Minister of State for Northern Ireland in 1974. Pressure was put on the Stormont government to introduce reforms but none were forthcoming.

Opposition to the O'Neill administration also existed within the loyalist camp and included sections of the Unionist Party. Those opponents took every opportunity to challenge O'Neill for what they regarded as his break from the traditional loyalist attitude to the nationalist minority. One of his more vociferous opponents was Ian Paisley. Paisley had set up his own violently anti-Catholic Free Presbyterian Church in 1951. As unemployment grew in the later 1950s, he built an organisation called the Ulster Protestant Action whose aim was 'to keep protestant and loyal workers in employment in times of depression, in preference to their catholic fellow workers'. His movement was built on the streets and its sectarian actions often led to violent rioting.

During the 1964 Westminster elections, the Republicans were contesting a seat in West Belfast and had placed a tricolour in the windows of their election headquarters in Divis Street on the Falls Road. The RUC had given up interfering with tricolours in nationalist areas. On 27 September, Paisley, at a meeting in the Ulster Hall, threatened to lead a march to take it down himself if it was still there in two days' time. The day after Paisley's threat, the government, needing every loyalist vote it could drum up to win the seat, sent in 50 RUC men to remove the flag. They broke down the door of the Republican headquarters and took it down. A few days later it went up again. The RUC used pick-axes to break into the office and again took it down. That night Belfast had its worst sectarian riots since 1935. The RUC had water cannon and armoured cars. The nationalist defenders replied with petrol bombs. Next evening 350 RUC men wearing military helmets and backed by armoured cars were sent into the Falls Road to smash the resistance there. Over 50 civilians were taken to hospital. In Dublin, 1,000 demonstrators marched on the British embassy in protest and stoned the Gardai on duty there.

Needless to say, the Unionist Party candidate, James Kilfedder, won the election. He thanked Paisley without whose help 'it could not have been done'.[4] O'Neill himself went so far as to accuse Republican candidates of 'using a British election to try to provoke disorder in Northern Ireland'.[5]

Paisley's challenge built up. In 1965 he accused O'Neill, after the Lemass-O'Neill talks, of entertaining at Stormont a 'Fenian Papist murderer'.[6] He staged a massive rally outside the Unionist Party headquarters and forced O'Neill to abandon a function due to take place. In February 1966 he launched a paper, the *Protestant Telegraph*, which contained hysterically anti-Catholic and anti-communist propaganda, and in April he set up the Ulster Constitution Defence Committee (UCDC) to coordinate his movement, with the Ulster Protestant Volunteers (UPV) as its vanguard.

In April 1966, Paisley's agitation led the government to mobilise the B-Specials for a month and to ban trains from the Twenty Six Counties coming to the commemorations of the 50th anniversary of the Easter Rising. On 6 June, Paisley led a demonstration through Cromac Square – a nationalist area of Belfast. Local residents tried to block the road and were attacked by the RUC. After a short battle, Paisley went on to where the Presbyterian General Assembly was meeting – where his followers tried to break through a police cordon to attack the meeting place. After pressure from the Wilson government on O'Neill, Paisley was eventually arrested and prosecuted. He went to jail for three months after refusing to be bound over for two years. His followers reacted violently and there were riots outside the prison.

In February, March and April 1966, a number of petrol bomb attacks on Catholic shops, homes and schools had taken place and one woman had been killed. On 27 May, a Catholic man, John Scullian, was shot and fatally wounded in Clonard Street off the Falls Road. On 26 June three Catholic barmen were shot as they left a pub in Malvern Street. One was killed. Three men (including 'Gusty' Spence) were arrested and charged with the murder. They were later found guilty and sentenced to life imprisonment. They belonged to the Ulster Volunteer Force – a small group of Paisley supporters who had set up an armed organisation.[7] The UVF was also responsible for the petrol bombings and the murder of John Scullian. Those responsible for the murders belonged to the Prince Albert Loyal Orange Lodge. On 12

July 1967, during its annual parade, the Lodge on passing the gates of Crumlin Road jail in Belfast stopped to pay homage to the three murderers held inside.

The government banned the UVF under the Special Powers Act and O'Neill let it be known that a leading member of the UVF was a prominent official of Paisley's UCDC. He was Noel Doherty, secretary of the UCDC, a printer who had set up the presses of the *Protestant Telegraph*, a B-Special and a Unionist candidate in the Belfast Corporation elections in 1964. It says a great deal about the nature of the sectarian statelet that Paisley's brand of loyalism now commands massive support.

O'Neill's own assessment of the UVF murders is instructive. His main concern was that the growing tide of nationalist protest might gain a hearing in Britain. It was vital if Ulster was to remain a loyalist state that an acceptable face be presented to the world whatever the reality within. In a speech to the Mid-Armagh Unionist Association in November 1966 he argued:

'The events of 1966 have turned an intense and curious scrutiny upon us. And as we stand in this spot-light it remains as true now as it was over half a century ago that we must have the understanding and support of a substantial proportion of the British people. *That is why* we must condemn recent extremist activities which would not be supported by any of the British political parties or even by a single British MP. Of course we cannot please everyone. There are certainly strong Southern Irish forces in Great Britain, with spokesmen in Parliament, who seek nothing less than the reunification of Ireland. We cannot please that section of opinion and we are not going to try.

'... If we can demonstrate that behind all the talk about "discrimination" is a warm and genuine community spirit; if we can demonstrate that we seek the advantages of British citizenship only because we bear the same burdens – then the voices of criticism will fall increasingly upon deaf ears ...

'*I do not want Ulster to change its nature*, but rather to show again its best face to the world ... ' (*our emphasis*)[8]

O'Neill was a staunch Unionist and an Orangeman who marched with his Orange Lodge every 12 July. After he became Prime Minister, he joined two other off-shoots of the Orange Order, the Apprentice Boys and the Royal Black Preceptory. While attempting to present Ulster's 'best face' to the world, he had taken no steps to end: gerrymandering of local government, sectarian discrimination against Catholics, and the existence of the Special Powers Act and the B-Specials. It was against this background that in January 1967 the Northern Ireland Civil Rights Association (NICRA) was formed.

After the defeat of the 1956–62 campaign, the IRA, under the direction of a new revisionist leadership (see page 135ff) had turned to 'economic and social agitation' within the system as the means to bring it down. They set up Republican Clubs as part of a strategy of engaging in open and legal political action. In 1967, William Craig, Minister of Home Affairs, banned the Republican Clubs saying they were front organisations for Sinn Fein and illicit recruiters for the IRA. This happened just before celebrations, planned for the 100th anniversary of the Fenian uprising, were to take place. The Republicans retaliated by having a 'banned' public meeting which was attended by civil liberties representatives, Gerry Fitt, elected in March 1966 as Republican Labour MP for West Belfast, and other interested observers. A few prominent Republicans were arrested but later released. Left-wing students and Young Socialists also held protest marches in Belfast against the banning.

The Republican Movement had also set up Wolfe Tone Societies as discussion forums for Republicans, communists, socialists and other left-wing radicals. It was through such societies in the Six Counties and the Republican Clubs that the IRA was to play a significant role in the Civil Rights Movement. NICRA's official foundation took place at a public meeting in January 1967. However, it could be said to have been formed earlier in August 1966 at a secret meeting, in Maghera Co Derry, at which Cathal Goulding, the IRA Chief of Staff supported the plans for the movement. And as a result, the IRA played a significant part in the open Civil Rights campaign.

NICRA was modelled on the National Council for Civil Liberties in Britain. A broad-based committee was founded to run the movement and included Republicans, members of the Communist Party, trade unionists and individuals from committees associated with earlier campaigns for reforms. For the first year of its existence, it carried out activities similar to its predecessor, the Campaign for Social Justice. NICRA eventually adopted a series of demands, none of them in themselves revolutionary, as the basis of the movement. They were:

1. One-man-one-vote in local elections
2. The removal of gerrymandered boundaries

3. Laws against discrimination by local government, and the provision of machinery to deal with complaints
4. Allocation of public housing on a points system
5. Repeal of the Special Powers Act
6. Disbanding of the B-Specials

The fight for these demands, however, would very soon lead the Civil Rights Movement into direct conflict with the loyalist state.

In Caledon, Co Tyrone, the local Republican Club was giving support to homeless Catholic families squatting in newly-built council houses. The Unionist-controlled Dungannon Rural Council wouldn't allocate houses to them. In June 1968, a Catholic family was evicted from a council house in which they had been squatting. A nineteen-year-old unmarried Protestant, Emily Beattie, secretary to a local Unionist politician, was allocated the house. Austin Currie, a Nationalist MP in Stormont, who had been raising the matter, occupied the house in protest and was evicted and fined.[9]

In August 1968, the Dungannon-based Campaign for Social Justice decided to hold a march from Coalisland to the Market Square, Dungannon, to protest against the sectarian housing policy. With some reluctance NICRA agreed to support the march and it was announced for 24 August. Paisley's UPV immediately called a counter-demonstration and promised violence if the march entered the Market Square, Dungannon. The RUC then rerouted the march from the centre of the town.

The march was a remarkable success. By the time it reached the barrier the RUC had erected, between 3,000 and 4,000 were present. The IRA leadership encouraged its members to support the march. The RUC in fact estimated that 70 of the stewards on the march were Republicans and 10 of them were members of the IRA.

About 1,500 UPV counter-demonstrators, many of them members of the B-Specials, were gathered in the Market Square. When the Civil Rights march reached the RUC barrier a few scuffles took place and the organisers stopped the march and held a rally. After speeches, the leaders of the march advised the marchers to go home. Instead, the marchers sat down in the road singing songs and staying there until quite late into the night.

As Sean Mac Stiofain so accurately commented seven years later, 'little did the handful of people who sponsored it, or the Republican leadership who supported it, imagine where that first civil rights march was to lead the entire nation'.[10] It took one more demonstration in

Derry on 5 October 1968 to turn the Civil Rights Campaign into a mass movement.

Derry was an obvious place to have the next Civil Rights march. It had a nationalist majority yet it was Unionist controlled. There was massive unemployment – one in five out of work. Vast inequalities in housing – a nationalist city where, in the 1960s, a council house was the gift of the Protestant mayor.

The request for the march came to NICRA from local activists, Republicans and socialists. It was planned for 5 October 1968. The proposed route was to be along business streets from the Waterside station on the east side of the Foyle, across Craigavon Bridge and to the Diamond in the centre of the city. Since the RUC had batoned the Anti-Partition League off the streets in the 1950s, no anti-Unionist demonstration had attempted to go through the walled city.

Five days before the march was due to take place, the Apprentice Boys of Derry gave notice of an 'annual' parade passing exactly over the same route as the Civil Rights march on the same day. No one had ever heard of the 'annual' parade before, but it had the desired effect. William Craig, Minister of Home Affairs, banned the march. NICRA wanted to call the march off, but after being told by Derry activists that they would march anyway, it went ahead.

On 5 October, about 2,000 marchers set off from Waterside station and got about 200 yards before they were met by a solid wall of the RUC.[11] As the march reached the police cordon, the RUC waded in. The first to be batoned was Gerry Fitt MP who was one of those leading the march. The marchers soon found out that they were caught between two lines of police in a narrow street. The police savagely batoned the marchers and hosed them at close range using water cannon. Men, women and children were clubbed to the ground. Nearly a hundred people were treated in hospital.

Later, there was fighting at the edges of the Bogside – a staunch nationalist area of Derry – which lasted until the early morning. Police cars were stoned, shop windows smashed, petrol bombs thrown, and barricades were erected.

The march had been covered by television and millions in Ireland and Britain had seen the armed thugs of the RUC smashing up a peaceful demonstration. Millions were horrified when they saw the naked facts of loyalist state violence. The nationalist minority in the Six Counties was experiencing the limitations of non-violent action in opposition to the sectarian policies of the loyalist state. A peaceful demonstration had been batoned off the streets. The 5 October 1968 proved to be another turning point in Irish history.

THE REAL FACE OF UNIONISM

Events now began to move very quickly indeed. A number of demonstrations by students took place in Belfast. People's Democracy, a loose activist body of left students committed to civil rights reforms was set up and involved in various actions including a sit-in in Stormont. On 15 October, the Nationalist Party withdrew as the official 'opposition' in Stormont. On 4 November, Harold Wilson, recognising the need to contain the Civil Rights Movement, saw O'Neill, Craig and Faulkner and demanded they introduce reforms urgently.

Another march was planned in Derry for 16 November over the original route of the earlier march. On 13 November, Craig banned all marches inside the walled city for a month. Three days later, 15,000 Civil Rights marchers assembled and attempted to march into the city centre. The march was confronted by a massive force of RUC. The organisers – the moderate broad-based Derry Citizens Action Committee led by John Hume and Ivan Cooper – prevented a violent confrontation as marchers and RUC stood face-to-face for 30 minutes. Eventually, the police barricades were breached, the RUC recognising that they were powerless to stop the marchers. Eventually thousands reached the city centre – the Diamond – and a meeting was held. It was a remarkable victory. The Unionists had got together more RUC men than ever before and they had been beaten. If the swelling tide of the Civil Rights Movement was to be contained, the government would have to grant reforms.

On 22 November, O'Neill announced a package of planned reforms. Derry Corporation would be abolished and replaced by a Development Commission. A grievance investigation machinery would be considered and an Ombudsman appointed. Local authorities would be encouraged to allot their houses on the basis of a 'points' system. The company vote would be abolished for local elections, and the government would consider suspending part of the Special Powers Act as soon as conditions allowed it to be done 'without undue hazard'. But the nationalist minority had gone beyond accepting such cosmetic change. Another demonstration was announced for Armagh on 30 November.

By this time, O'Neill was being seriously challenged by hard-line

Unionists in his party. They recognised all too clearly that granting the demands of the Civil Rights Movement and ending discrimination would destroy the privileged position of loyalist workers and the loyalist petit-bourgeoisie in the Six Counties state. Unless the Civil Rights Movement was halted then it would threaten the very existence of the sectarian statelet itself. The Unionist 'right' now turned to more direct action against the Civil Rights agitation.

On the 30 November, having failed to get the Armagh march banned, Paisley and his right-hand man, a retired Army Major, Ronald Bunting, descended on the route of the march at 1 am in the morning with 20 to 30 car loads of supporters. They set up barricades and armed themselves with sticks and other weapons, including pipes, sharpened at the ends. The RUC in fact seized two revolvers and 220 home made weapons from them. About 5,000 Civil Rights marchers arrived in the town but they were blocked at a barrier put up by the RUC. 75 yards further down behind another barrier were assembled 1,000 Paisleyites armed with sticks and clubs. 350 RUC men had made no effort to remove them and had in fact given way to an armed loyalist mob. The Paisleyites had scored a victory over the Civil Rights Movement.

O'Neill went on television and appealed for support for his policies and his intended limited reforms. He called on the Civil Rights Movement to take the heat out of the situation as their voice, he said, had been clearly heard. Following his broadcast, NICRA called a 'truce' – marches were called off for a period of a month. On 11 December, William Craig was sacked from the government by O'Neill for making a speech criticizing O'Neill's policy.

At this stage, People's Democracy announced a three-day 'long-march' of 75 miles from Belfast to Derry. They recognised that O'Neill's limited reforms amounted to very little. They wanted one man one vote in local government elections and action on unemployment and housing. The march was opposed by NICRA.

The march began on 1 January 1969 with 80 participants. Every few miles loyalist thugs blocked the route. The RUC regularly diverted the march which was frequently stoned and attacked. At the nationalist village of Brackaghreilly near Maghera, the marchers were persuaded to stay in the Gaelic Hall. Shortly after, 50 armed men – the local company of the IRA – set up roadblocks. They had heard that the march was going to be attacked and had persuaded the marchers to stay in the village. Their information, however, had not been accurate.

The major ambush was planned farther up the route at Burntollet, a few miles from Derry.

On 4 January at 8.30am about 200 loyalist thugs armed with iron bars and nail studded coshes, surrounded by heaped piles of stones, waited on a hillside for the marchers to arrive. 100 of these men were later identified as members of the Ulster B-Specials. The RUC had watched the gathering of the ambush, chatting with the B-Specials and made no attempt to stop it taking place. The march arrived led by an escort of 80 police. It was brutally attacked and marchers were beaten unconscious – one nearly drowning in a river as a result.

The battered marchers determinedly went on and eventually reached Derry. Most of the marchers were injured with many covered in blood. They were met in the Guildhall Square by thousands of angry Civil Rights supporters who were in no mood for a truce. Very soon battles broke out with the police who tried to drive those assembled back into the Bogside.

At 2am next morning a drunken mob of RUC men ran amok in the Bogside breaking down doors, smashing windows and beating up anyone in sight. Next morning the people in the Bogside organised; barricades were built, vigilante patrols carrying clubs patrolled the streets. A radio transmitter was installed in one of the flats. Free Derry was born. The RUC were kept out of the area for nearly a week. The barricades were only finally taken down after the Derry Citizens Action Committee – Hume, Cooper and others – had persuaded the people that they were no longer necessary. However, this was a foretaste of the momentous events yet to come.

Although O'Neill viciously attacked the marchers calling them hooligans he was forced by the pressure of the Civil Rights Campaign to announce on 15 January a government inquiry to investigate the disturbances and underlying causes – the Cameron Commission. It was this decision that accelerated the inevitable process which was to bring O'Neill down. On 23 January, Faulkner resigned from the government in protest. On 3 February, 12 Unionist backbenchers called for O'Neill's resignation. That evening O'Neill called an election for 24 February to try and get a mandate for his policies.

Paisley had been sentenced to three months imprisonment for the Armagh affair. He appealed and got out of jail to stand against O'Neill in the election – the first time O'Neill had not been elected unopposed since 1946. The result was inconclusive, with O'Neill back in power but having 11 anti-O'Neillite Unionists in the Parliamentary

Party. O'Neill himself barely scraped home against Paisley obtaining 7,745 votes to Paisley's 5,331, with a Civil Rights candidate holding the balance of 2,310. In Derry, McAteer, the leader of the Nationalist Party, lost to John Hume, the independent Civil Rights candidate.

The two sides were polarising. On 14 March, four of the 'Old Guard' members of NICRA – including Betty Sinclair of the so-called Communist Party – resigned in protest against the increased militancy of the Civil Rights Campaign. On 17 April a by-election for the Mid-Ulster seat at Westminster saw the election of Bernadette Devlin (McAliskey), a student member of People's Democracy, who had won the nomination as a united anti-Unionist candidate. It showed that the entire nationalist minority had swung behind the increasingly militant Civil Rights Campaign.

Two days later there was a minor battle between the RUC in Derry and the youth of the Bogside using stones and petrol bombs to hold the police off. The police burst into a house in William Street and beat everyone up. Sammy Devenny, the owner of the house, later was to die from the injuries he received. The growing anger of the Bogside eventually forced the police to withdraw. There were fierce clashes between Nationalists and Orange marchers in Belfast and Dungannon with the RUC intervening on the loyalist side.

On 20–21 April, bombs went off wrecking an electricity link-up in Portadown and a blast went off at the Silent Valley reservoir in Co Down which provides water for Belfast. It was immediately assumed to be the IRA.

On 22 April, O'Neill finally accepted the only position which might placate the nationalist minority – one man one vote, universal adult suffrage. The next day, Chichester-Clark resigned. On the following day, the Unionist Parliamentary Party accepted the change by 28 votes to 22. Faulkner voted against.

That night, just after midnight, more explosions occurred wrecking water pipelines and leaving Belfast short of water. Three days later, Terence O'Neill resigned to be replaced on 1 May 1969 by Chichester-Clark. Months later it was revealed that the series of bomb blasts were the work of the loyalist UVF attempting to simulate IRA attacks with the object of forcing the waverers in the Unionist Party to bring O'Neill down. The battle lines were firmly drawn.

INSURRECTION – THE BATTLE OF THE BOGSIDE

On 21 May, desperate to hold back the growing militancy of the nationalist minority, and after a meeting between Harold Wilson and Chichester-Clark, Wilson announced that local elections would be held under 'One Man, One Vote'. But this was much too late even though NICRA called a temporary halt to demonstrations.

In North Belfast, fierce battles took place in the Ardoyne over several weekends between the RUC and the nationalist working class. On 12 July, an Orange parade was stoned in Derry and for three days battles raged between the RUC and Bogsiders, with the RUC shooting and wounding two civilians. On 2 August an Orange march passed the nationalist Unity Flats in Belfast. The residents turned out to protest. The battles went on for three days with loyalist mobs, led by the recently formed Shankill Defence Association trying to attack the Unity Flats and Ardoyne. At one stage, serious clashes took place between the loyalist mobs and the RUC, with many being injured and arrested. The RUC eventually attacked the besieged residents of Unity Flats and an elderly Catholic, Patrick Corry, died in an RUC barracks after being beaten up by the police.

At the beginning of August, a detachment of British troops was moved into the RUC headquarters for stand-by use in Belfast. This time they were not used. But the direct involvement of British imperialism was increasing. 500 extra troops had already been flown into the Six Counties in August after the first UVF explosions to be used as guards over vital installations. On 16 July, Harold Wilson had already given Roy Hattersley, the Minister of State for Defence, the job of preparing for the intervention of British troops in the Six Counties.

The crunch was to come on 12 August, the day of the Apprentice Boys' parade in Derry, when thousands of Orangemen come to Derry and parade through the city and around the walls to commemorate the lifting of the siege of Derry in 1689. It is an annual celebration of Protestant ascendancy and serves to remind the nationalist population who was master even in the city of Derry with a nationalist majority.

The Stormont government turned down all appeals to have the march banned. The Bogside was cordoned off by the RUC. As the parade was passing one of the entrances of the Bogside, it was stoned. The RUC, closely followed by a loyalist mob, baton-charged and the battle was on.

At the end of July, the Republican Clubs had announced they had formed a Derry Citizens Defence Association and they invited other organisations to join. Most did. It was chaired by Sean Keenan, a veteran Republican. After the events in Belfast on 2 August it made plans for a defence of the area.

Barricades had gone up on 11 August in anticipation of the events to come. Once the battle was on, they were built all around the area. Open-air petrol bomb factories were established, dumpers hijacked from a building site were used to carry stones to the front line. First aid stations manned by doctors and nurses were set up. The radio transmitter used during the last major battle in January pumped out Republican music and messages to the fighters. Two-way radios taken off television crews were used for communications. The area was intensively patrolled.

The youth went on to the roof of a block of high-rise flats which dominated Rossville Street – the main entrance to the Bogside. They were continually supplied with thousands of petrol bombs – the dairy was said to have lost 43,000 bottles. This was the decisive move. As long as they were there the police could not get past the flats. Every time they tried, petrol bombs rained on them.

The RUC used armoured cars to try to break through and fired CS gas – the first time it was used in Ireland. But they failed to penetrate the barricades at the flats. The tricolour and Starry Plough (emblem of the 1916 Easter Rising) were flown from the roof of Rossville flats. The Bogside was impregnable to the police. It was an insurrection. Free Derry was now well and truly born.

As the battle went on, mass rallies were arranged for other national-ist areas to keep the RUC at full stretch. There were battles everywhere with the most serious violence taking place in Dungannon and Belfast. The government refused to pull the RUC back from the Bogside. On the 13 August, a senior army officer on the streets of Derry told General Freeland, the British Army Commander, that the police could not possibly contain the Bogside for more than 36 hours. By the 14 August, the RUC were exhausted and beaten. At 3pm, Chichester-Clark requested British troops. At 4.30pm, Wilson and Callaghan agreed. And at 5pm, the British army rumbled over Craigavon Bridge across the River Foyle into the heart of Derry. The British Labour government had sent troops to aid the 'civil power' in the Six Counties. It was intended to have one and only one effect – to support loyalist supremacy, the basis of British imperialism's continued rule in Ireland. The introduction of the troops was the recognition of the fact that the Six Counties statelet was unreformable and that the nationalist resist-ance could not be bought off.

THE BELFAST POGROM

As the British troops, armed with sub-machine guns, entered Derry, the RUC and B-Specials immediately withdrew from the Bogside. Negotiations between the Derry Citizens Defence Association and the British army led to an agreement that British troops would not attempt to enter the Bogside, and that the RUC and B-Specials would be kept behind their lines. In Derry, the nationalist people had won. In other nationalist areas, battles still raged.

John Gallagher was killed by a high velocity bullet in the back when B-Specials opened fire into a crowd after a Civil Rights meeting in Armagh. Others in the crowd were wounded. Shots were also fired in Dungannon where again B-Specials fired into a nationalist crowd wounding two men and a girl. 8,500 B-Specials had, in fact, been mobilised throughout the province on 14 August with the agreement of the Labour Home Secretary James Callaghan.

As British troops entered Derry on 14 August, the events which make up the Belfast pogrom were about to begin. The evening before had already given some indication of this. A meeting called by the Civil Rights Association took place in the courtyard of Divis Flats – a high-rise block of flats on the nationalist side of Divis Street. The meeting was called in response to appeals from Derry 'to take the heat off the Bogside' and to protest against the RUC. About 200 people turned up. The meeting decided to hand a petition to the local police headquarters in Springfield Road, in protest against the RUC brutality in Derry. The RUC District Inspector, Cushley, although in the building, refused to take the petition saying that the local headquarters had been temporarily transferred to another station in Hastings Street right back down Divis Street. Cushley proceeded to leave the building to go to the other station. With this development, the crowd became angry and a few skirmishes took place and windows were smashed. The Civil Rights protesters then moved to Hastings Street and the police station was stoned and later some petrol bombs were thrown. No real damage was done.

Cushley then ordered out Shorland armoured cars which were driven to confront the crowd, many of whom scattered into the surrounding streets. A section of the protesters, outraged by the RUC decision to loose armoured cars upon them, went back to the Springfield Road Police Station and attacked it with stones and petrol bombs. The RUC fired shots at the crowd and two youths were injured. A few shots were returned by a couple of the demonstrators who had guns. Police on the station roof opened up with rifle and sten gun fire and scattered the crowd. Remarkably, no-one was killed.

But this was nothing in view of what was yet to come. The next day, the Shorland armoured cars would go out on to the streets, this time, mounted with their usual weapons, the Browning 0.30 inch machine gun. This machine gun has a range of almost two-and-a-half miles and fires six to eight high-velocity bullets every second. It only fires bursts, never single shots. It was for many years the standard machine gun for the American army. It was now to be used, with devastating consequences, by a sectarian police force on the closely packed streets of Belfast.

After the previous night's events, the news at 3pm the next day that the hated loyalist B-Specials were being mobilised led to barricades going up at strategic points along the nationalist Falls Road. Hundreds of petrol bombs were prepared to defend the nationalist areas. By 10.30pm, barely a street in the area was unblocked and thousands of people assembled behind the barricades in the nationalist areas. The RUC once again sent out Shorland armoured cars. This time, they were armed.

On the Shankill Road, crowds of Loyalists mingled with hundreds of B-Specials armed with rifles, revolvers and sub-machine guns. At about 10.30pm, bands of loyalist civilians wearing white arm bands began moving down the Shankill Road and into streets intersecting with the Falls Road. Other groups headed north for the isolated nationalist area of the Ardoyne.

The attacking loyalist mobs were well-organised and well-equipped with petrol bombs. They moved into the 'mixed' streets between the Falls Road and Shankill Road – Percy Street and Dover Street. Hundreds of stones and petrol bombs were thrown and as the Loyalists came on they tossed petrol bombs into the Catholic homes on their way. The RUC stood behind them and looked on. By midnight, both streets were ablaze.

The Loyalists came on and shots were fired from Dover Street at the retreating nationalists. Three men in a crowd of nationalists lined across Divis Street fell under a hail of bullets. Eventually, the Loyalists broke through into Divis Street planting a Union Jack there.

Some IRA men with a few weapons, including one Thompson sub-machine gun, attempted to hold back the loyalist attackers, firing from the vicinity of Divis Flats. A Loyalist, Herbert Roy, was killed. Others were injured. At this moment, RUC armoured cars appeared on the scene and randomly fired bursts of Browning machine gun fire into the nationalist Divis Flats. Trooper Herbert McCabe, a young British soldier on leave was on his balcony and was killed instantly. Four high-velocity bullets pierced two walls before entering nine-year-old Patrick Rooney's bedroom and blowing half his head away. Thirteen flats were badly damaged.

In the Ardoyne, the loyalist attacks were even fiercer. There, the RUC, B-Specials and loyalist mobs burnt down three nationalist streets. The RUC, during the battles that raged, opened fire with sub-machine guns and one Catholic, 50-year-old Samuel McLarnon, was shot while pulling down a blind at a window of his home. Another man, Michael Lynch, was killed by the same machine gun fire. Over 20 people were wounded.

The death toll for the night of 14–15 August was six. Hundreds were injured. A scene of utter devastation lay around Divis Street and the Ardoyne. Around 150 Catholic homes had been burnt out in Belfast and Catholics from houses still unburnt in the 'mixed' streets were evacuated the next day. Over a thousand families were to leave their homes. Their houses were promptly occupied by Loyalists. Thousands of Catholics became refugees taking trains to the Republic.

Events had now gone too far for the Stormont Cabinet. It doubted the ability of the RUC to take another night of serious confrontation. The British army had to be called in. A formal request for further troops for use in Belfast came from the Stormont Cabinet at 12.25pm that day and it was given immediate approval by Callaghan. Just after 5pm on Friday 15 August, about 600 troops moved into the area around the now well barricaded Falls Road.

While the troops were taking up their positions, loyalist mobs were attacking a small nationalist enclave, the Clonard. It began after 3pm Friday afternoon. Very soon, fifteen-year-old Gerald McAuley was shot dead as he helped Catholic families evacuate their furniture in the Clonard. The Loyalists invaded the Clonard monastery grounds and were fired on and held off by two nationalist defenders of the area in the monastery. The Loyalists fired back. That evening an entire Catholic street, Bombay Street, was razed to the ground. It was after these events and later in the evening that British troops went into the Clonard area. However, they didn't go into the Ardoyne.

In the Ardoyne, another pitched battle took place this time between the nationalist defenders of the area and the Loyalists and the RUC. A Catholic street was burnt out – 23 Catholic homes were destroyed. British troops were to enter the Ardoyne the next day, Saturday 16 August. Within a week, up to 6,000 troops were available to be deployed.

NOTES

1   Farrell M, *op cit* p. 227.

2   O'Neill T, *Ulster at the Crossroads* London 1969 p. 51. For a discussion of these points see Marlowe T and Palmer S, *Revolutionary Communist* No 8 *op cit*.

3   O'Neill T, *op cit* p. 163.

4   De Paor L, *Divided Ulster* London 1973 p. 154.

5   Farrell M, *op cit* p. 234. See pp. 233–4 for a full account of this incident.

6   The Sunday Times Insight Team, *Ulster* London 1972 p. 42. This book and Farrell M, *op cit* have been used extensively for the historical background in this and later chapters.

7   For a detailed account of the Malvern Street murder and the history of the UVF 1966–1973, see Boulton D, *The UVF 1966–73* Dublin 1973.

8   O'Neill T, *op cit* pp. 54–5.

9   From this period until the end of 1974 extensive use is made of Deutsch R and Magowan V, *Northern Ireland A Chronology of Events* in 3 volumes: 1968–71, 1972–73, 1974, Belfast 1973–5. These volumes are an almost daily record of events.

10   Mac Stiofain S, *Memoirs of a Revolutionary* Edinburgh 1975 p. 108. Sean Mac Stiofain's book is a detailed revolutionary account of the birth and development of the Provisional IRA.

11   The figure of 2,000 is agreed in most accounts of the march. A notable exception is Eamonn McCann, one of the organisers of the march, who claims that there were only 400 on the march, with 200 looking on. See McCann E, *War and an Irish Town* London 1980 p. 41.

CHAPTER EIGHT

THE RISE OF THE PROVISIONAL IRA

At a press conference at Stormont on Sunday 17 August, Chichester-Clark reiterated statements he had been making earlier in the week: the real cause of the 'disorder' was to be found in the activities of extreme Republican elements – meaning the IRA – and 'others determined to overthrow our State'. Nothing could have been further from the truth. In fact, when the all-out attack on the nationalist areas took place, the IRA neither had the organisation nor the weapons to carry out an effective defence of those under siege.

> ' . . . when the inevitable happened in Belfast's beleaguered nationalist ghettos on August 14, 1969, the victims to their horror found themselves without protection from the one source they hitherto trusted – the Irish Republican Army. When the people sought the weapons they needed to defend themselves, these weapons were not available, apart from a few old guns which were quickly put to use and at least saved an even greater massacre.'[1]

Slogans such as IRA = I RAN AWAY appeared on the walls of Belfast. They were, as Mac Stiofain justifiably argues, grossly unfair to those local units in Belfast who had to take the brunt of the attacks with next to no resources.[2] Nevertheless, they were one expression of the bitterness felt in the nationalist areas at the failure of the IRA to mount an effective defence of their areas. It was this state of affairs which was to intensify the divisions already existing in the IRA and lead to a split in the Republican movement.

REVOLUTIONARY NATIONALISM V REVISIONISM

After the end of the Border Campaign the IRA was in disarray.

Disputes that had flared up among the leadership in the Curragh internment camp during the campaign created bitter divisions in the movement and led to many resignations. And there were bitter recriminations from some against those who had called off the campaign.

It is precisely in such periods of demoralisation and defeat that revisionist influences can take root in a revolutionary movement. And that is what happened. Unfortunately, these new influences were associated with 'socialist' and 'communist' politics. In fact, the 'socialism' of this new trend had little in common with the communist tradition. On the contrary, the views and positions of those involved, as later events were to conclusively confirm, put these so-called 'socialists' and 'communists' in the 'evolutionary socialist', revisionist camp of the Second International. The Communist International, in fact, was formed in opposition to this trend.[3]

When the turmoil in the movement was over, Cathal Goulding became Chief-of-Staff of the IRA, a Dublin accountant Tomas Mac Giolla became President of Sinn Fein and a computer scientist, Dr Roy Johnston, considered to be a Marxist, became the movement's education officer. All these three were to play a leading role in the creation of the Official IRA – later to become the pro-imperialist, pro-Stormont Sinn Fein the Workers Party, now known as the Workers Party.

Many on the Left have portrayed the dispute between the two trends in the Republican Movement as that between socialism and a narrow nationalism, between 'political' agitation on 'social and economic issues' and 'physical force' Republicanism. Nothing could be further from the truth. The split was over the way forward for the Republican Movement. It involved choosing between the revisionist and the revolutionary national position on the fundamental issues of the Irish revolution: can imperialism be reformed; the centrality of the national question; the question of armed struggle; the question of participation in the imperialist-imposed partitionist parliaments, Stormont and Leinster House, and the imperialist parliament itself at Westminster.

Sean Mac Stiofain, the first Chief-of-Staff of the Provisional IRA made it clear when commenting on the new trend which developed in the Republican Movement after 1962, that revolutionary nationalists were not opposed to agitation on economic and social issues as such. Only that they saw the real danger of such agitation being separated from the national question.

'By 1964, however, it was apparent that some of the new leadership were heading off in a very different direction. They were becoming

obsessed with the idea of parliamentary politics and wished to confine the movement almost entirely to social and economic agitation.
It went without saying that agitation on social and economic issues
was part of the struggle for justice. But I believed that we should not
allow ourselves to get so committed to it that we would lose sight of
the main objective, to free Ireland from British rule. It was British
domination which had led to many of the abuses and injustices that
called for social agitation'.[4]

Mac Stiofain's doubts were confirmed in 1969 when the IRA found
itself totally unprepared to defend the beleaguered nationalist population in Derry and Belfast against the B-Specials and RUC thugs.

Cathal Goulding further confirms Mac Stiofain's view in an interview he gave in 1970. After putting down the failure of the 1956–62
campaign to the people 'having no real knowledge of our objectives' he
stated how they intended to overcome this:

'Our first objective . . . was to involve ourselves in the everyday problems of people; to organise them to demand better houses, better
working conditions, better jobs, better pay, better education – to
develop agitationary activities along these lines. By doing this we felt
that we could involve the people, *not so much in supporting the
Republican Movement for our political ends*, but in supporting agitation so that they themselves would be part of a revolutionary force
demanding what the present system just couldn't produce'.[5] (*our
emphasis*)

The roots of future revisionism lie in this statement. First we will take
up the 'everyday problems of the people' and then . . . the national
question. But this is a break from the revolutionary national position.
For it separates the social and economic issues facing the people from
their source – British domination over Ireland. The centrality of the
national question for the Irish people is, in fact, put to one side, to be
taken up at a later stage.

The revisionist trends within the movement soon became embodied
into a political programme. It contained nine proposals the most
important of which was to abolish the traditional policy of parliamentary abstentionism – one of the most important foundations of the
Republican Movement. It proposed that Republican candidates if elected would take their seats in the Dublin, Stormont and Westminster
parliaments. It was this issue which directly precipitated the split. At
the heart of the division was the defence by the Provisional IRA of the
revolutionary national position.

The Provisional IRA knew that imperialism could never play a progressive role. They understood that the Stormont parliament in the North, and the Leinster House parliament in the South, creations of imperialism, had to be destroyed if a united Irish Republic was to be achieved. Finally, they recognised and proclaimed the necessity of revolutionary armed struggle if British imperialism was to be driven out of Ireland.

A great deal has been made of the 'anti-communism' of the Provisionals in the first few years of their existence. This attitude derived from their actual experience of so-called communist organisations in Britain and Ireland. These organisations had long since broken with the communist tradition. The Communist Party of Ireland after the war took what can only be regarded as a pro-Unionist position, participating in elections in the North, and opportunistically abandoning an anti-partitionist position. The CPI went so far as to organise itself on partitionist lines creating separate parties for the Six Counties and Twenty Six Counties. Many individual so-called 'communists', and associated groups, the Connolly Association, the CP of Northern Ireland, the Irish Workers' Party, were all involved in supporting or building up the revisionist trend in the Republican Movement. Also the British Communist Party had long since given up a principled position on the question of Ireland. Mac Stiofain quite clearly explained his position:

> 'Certainly as revolutionaries we were automatically anti-capitalist. But we refused to have anything to do with any communist organisation in Ireland, on the basis of their ineffectiveness, their reactionary foot-dragging on the national question and their opposition to armed struggle.'[6]

The final word on the two trends in the Republican Movement can safely be left to an article printed in the Provisional's newspaper *An Phoblacht*.

> 'Other contenders for the title of Republicanism (and there are many) will term the revolutionary as the one with the most in political jargon of the left – the pious exhortation to the people to rise to a socialist Utopia before ever attaining National Unity – freedom and independence – or the misguided idea that sitting in Leinster House is "a new weapon in the hands of the revolutionary". You don't destroy something by joining it and giving it credibility and credence. You don't break up an oil slick by swimming through it – you burn

it. The real revolutionary is the man who sees the issues clearly, preaches the alternatives and risks his neck (not his necessary popularity and Dail seat) in the destruction of imperialism.'[7]

THE SPLIT IN THE IRA

The state of the IRA throughout the Six Counties was a direct consequence of the policies pursued by the revisionist leadership of the Republican Movement after the defeat of the 1956–62 Border Campaign. This leadership had pushed the national question into the background. They concentrated on what they called 'social and economic' agitation almost to the exclusion of the military struggle to reunite Ireland. It was their political leadership that left the IRA totally unprepared to defend the nationalist minority in the Six Counties as the Civil Rights Movement was forced into confrontation with the paramilitary defenders of loyalist privilege in the loyalist state.

Sean Mac Stiofain, later to be Chief of Staff of the Provisional IRA, and many other Republicans based in the Six Counties, time and again warned the Republican leadership of the dangerous situation that was developing with the growing Civil Rights Campaign. As Mac Stiofain later wrote:

'I and others in Republican circles saw that the civil rights strategy and the Unionists' puzzled and threatening reaction to it could lead to a very dangerous situation. Therefore, it was more than ever essential to maintain the IRA at as high a standard of military efficiency as possible.

'Demanding an increase in active training, I pressed the point that some of our own members had helped to initiate the new weapon of mass civil rights protest in the North. The least we expected of the IRA was that it would be ready to meet the dangers that this development might bring about.'[8]

But the revisionist leadership of the Republican Movement, by various manoeuvres, such as increasing the size of the Army Council and packing it with their own supporters, were able to vote down all proposals to organise armed defence of the nationalist areas in the Six Counties. The degree of bankruptcy of the leadership of the Republican Movement at that time, and an indicator of the future direction those supporting that leadership would take, is well illustrated in the response to Mac Stiofain's proposals by one member of the Army Council who argued that the British army would have to protect people in the North from the excesses of the RUC![9]

After the August events, the revolutionary nationalists in the Republican Movement began to organise. The entire country was combed for arms, and arms dumps in the South were emptied and distributed to the IRA throughout the Six Counties. By September 1969, the Belfast Brigade Staff of the IRA was reorganised. Additional members opposed to the revisionist leadership were co-opted on to the Belfast command. At the same time, the Belfast Brigade decided to have nothing more to do with the Dublin leadership.

Matters came to a head at an extraordinary Army Convention in the middle of December 1969. The revisionist leadership had packed the Convention with its own supporters. Before the Convention were two crucial resolutions. The first was that the IRA should enter into a National Liberation Front (NLF) with organisations of the so-called 'communist' and 'socialist' left. In particular, with those groups which had helped to formulate the revisionist standpoint of the present leadership of the Republican Movement. The second resolution was that the Republican Movement should end its policy of abstention from the Westminster, Dublin and Stormont parliaments. The latter proposal for many delegates had the merit of being a clear-cut issue. In the words of Sean Mac Stiofain, Republicans would now have to choose between accepting the institutions of partition or upholding the basic Republican principle of Ireland's right to national unity. The Convention voted to end the traditional policy of abstentionism. At the end of the Convention, those opposed to this position went to a pre-arranged meeting-place and set into motion the necessary steps that would very soon lead to the formation of the Provisional IRA.

The new grouping quickly won nine of the thirteen Belfast units of the IRA to its ranks. At a special Convention held before Christmas 1969, a Provisional Army Executive and Provisional Army Council were elected – the Provisional IRA was born. It immediately repudiated the revisionist proposals passed at the extraordinary Army Convention. Its first public statement was put out on 22 December 1969. It declared:

'allegiance to the Thirty-Two County Irish Republic proclaimed at Easter 1916, established by the first Dail Eireann in 1919, overthrown by force of arms in 1922, and suppressed to this day by the British-imposed Six County and Twenty-Six County partitionist states'[10].

It argued that the compromising policy of the revisionist leadership of the Republican Movement was:

'the logical outcome of an obsession in recent years with parliamentary politics, with the consequent undermining of the basic military role of the Irish Republican Army'[11].

As ample evidence of this neglect it pointed to the failure to provide the maximum defence of the nationalist areas of the Six Counties 'against the forces of British imperialism'. It claimed allegiance of the majority of Army units, volunteers and Republicans generally.

On 10/11 January 1970, the Sinn Fein Ard Fheis (Conference) was held. Those supporting the principled Republican standpoint attempted to get the Ard Fheis to reject the NLF (Official IRA) proposals. On 11 January a marathon debate took place on the proposals to remove all restrictions on parliamentary participation. The revisionists failed, by 19 votes, to get the necessary two-thirds majority to alter the position. After a motion was put calling for a vote of allegiance to the Official Army Council, delegates supporting the Provisional Army Council withdrew from the hall to a pre-arranged meeting place where a Sinn Fein Caretaker Executive was formed. Its first act was to pledge allegiance to the All-Ireland Republic and give support to the Provisional Army Council. It was also agreed to publish a new Republican newspaper *An Phoblacht* (The Republic).

Representatives of (Provisional) Sinn Fein met the Executive of Cumann na mBan, the women's section of the Republican Movement. Just as it had unanimously opposed the partitionist Treaty of 1921, the Cumann na mBan Executive now unanimously decided to accept the authority of the Provisional Army Council. The split in the movement was complete.

The struggle of the nationalist population for basic democratic rights in the late 1960s had demonstrated beyond doubt that the Six Counties statelet was unreformable. The insurrection in Derry in August 1969 and the defeat of the hated RUC had shown that the nationalist resistance to the sectarian statelet could no longer be contained. When the British Labour Government sent British troops into Derry to give support to the defeated paramilitary forces of the loyalist state the truth was exposed. Behind the RUC stood the British army. Behind the loyalist state stood British imperialism.

It now became increasingly clear that basic democratic rights for the nationalist minority could only be achieved by destroying the loyalist state, ending partition and driving British imperialism out of Ireland.

The nationalist population once again was to turn to those forces which had kept alive the revolutionary struggle to reunite Ireland – the revolutionary wing of the national movement and its armed vanguard, the IRA.

The Provisional IRA was soon to become an effective modern guerilla army with growing support among the nationalist minority in the Six Counties. The conditions had at last again emerged in Ireland for a revolutionary national movement to win mass support for a renewed offensive against partition and British imperialism.

DUBLIN GOVERNMENT UNDER PRESSURE

The Dublin government came under immediate pressure as soon as the Six Counties erupted and the Battle of the Bogside began. Already in February 1969, not long after the savage attack on the Civil Rights marchers at Burntollet Bridge, an emissary from a group of Fianna Fail TDs had approached the commander of the IRA in South Derry with a proposition about arms. In view of the growing violence directed against the Civil Rights Movement they were prepared to supply arms for defence of nationalist areas on condition that a separate Northern command of the IRA was set up and political agitation in the South was given up. A group of businessmen with close relations to the Fianna Fail ministers Blaney, Haughey and Boland were prepared to finance the venture. This was reported to the Dublin HQ of the IRA and although some negotiations took place, they were interrupted by the eruption of the crisis in the Six Counties. Attempts were later made by the NLF (Official IRA) to attribute the formation of the Provisionals to Fianna Fail finance. There was no truth in this.

On Wednesday 13 August at 11am, when Lynch's Cabinet met, Blaney and Boland, supported by Haughey, called for intervention in the Six Counties by the Irish army. Lynch supported by the majority of the Cabinet totally rejected this. Compromise was reached. The government ordered the Irish army to the Border and set up army field hospitals at various crossing points for use by those wounded in the North who would face possible arrest in Six Counties hospitals.

Lynch went on television that evening and made a very strong statement. It included the following:

'The Stormont Government evidently is no longer in control of the situation, which is the inevitable outcome of policies pursued for decades by them. The Government of Ireland can no longer stand by.

'It is obvious that the RUC is no longer accepted as an impartial police force.

'The employment of British troops is unacceptable and not likely to restore peaceful conditions.'

Lynch went on to call for a UN peace-keeping force for the Six Counties and said that the Irish army had established field hospitals on the Border. He concluded:

'Recognising that the re-unification of Ireland provides the only permanent solution to the problem, the Government have made a formal request to the British Government to enter into early negotiation to review the present constitutional position of the Six Counties...'[12]

The speech cruelly raised false hopes for a while among the beleaguered nationalists in the Six Counties. It also enraged the Loyalists. Lynch, however, did not intend to do anything. He knew he had to make some gesture to control the growing anger throughout the Twenty Six Counties against the loyalist attacks on the nationalist minority in the Six Counties. He, just like the British government, was not prepared to let the events in the Six Counties spill over and destabilise the government in the Twenty Six Counties. He was prepared, when the situation called for it, to give a militant sounding speech calling for the re-unification of Ireland, but was totally opposed to ending partition in the only way possible – by revolutionary means. He made this clear when, after the terror of the Belfast pogrom, a demonstration against the British Embassy in Dublin on 16 August was baton charged by the Gardai and over 50 people were injured. He reinforced this on 19 August when, after a statement by Cathal Goulding, Chief of Staff of the IRA, saying that volunteers had been active in the Bogside and other parts of the Six Counties, Lynch declared that his Government would not tolerate 'usurpation of their power by any group whatsoever'. He also condemned what he called 'the wanton destruction of property and looting and the lawless behaviour by a small minority which has taken place in Dublin and elsewhere in recent days'.[13]

Blaney, Haughey and Boland had not resigned when Lynch rejected the call for intervention by the Irish army in the Six Counties, nor did they attempt to make a public issue of it. They were more concerned to challenge Jack Lynch's position as Taoiseach by outmanoeuvring him on the Republican issue.

As part of the compromise, the Cabinet agreed to set up a sub-committee to deal with the Six Counties. It also created a Northern 'relief' fund of £100,000 out of government funds. Officially, this money could not be used to send arms to the Six Counties as this would lead to a direct conflict with the British government. However, it came out, after British intelligence had tipped off the Fine Gael opposition party, that a large amount had been used in this way. In May 1970, Lynch dismissed Blaney and Haughey after revelations about their involvement in illegally imported arms, valued at over £30,000, which had been recently seized. Boland resigned in protest. Blaney, Haughey and the others involved including Captain James Kelly, an Irish army intelligence officer, were tried for illegal arms deals in September/October 1970 and were acquitted. Their defence had been that the arms importation had the sanction of the government. However, the major outcome of this debacle was that Lynch, in spite of everything, emerged stronger and was now free of his main rivals, without even confronting anything like a party split.

BRITISH IMPERIALISM INTERVENES

There can be no doubt that when the Six Counties erupted, it was the intention of Callaghan and Wilson only to send troops into Derry. In Derry, the RUC had been prevented from invading the Bogside, and they were a defeated and exhausted force when the British army was sent in to contain the growing insurrection. In Callaghan's own words:

'(The troops') immediate orders were to relieve the exhausted police and prevent riots breaking out in the centre of Londonderry'.[14]

In fact, what shocked the Labour-imperialist Callaghan most was not the sectarian violence of the RUC but its inability to put down the nationalist revolt. In Callaghan's view, the RUC should have carried out an 'invasion' of the Bogside 'by tackling the rioters from the rear'.[15] It failed to do this so the British army had to be called in. It was only *after* the insurrection in Derry had been contained that the Labour government found the additional troops to send into Belfast to control the dangerous situation developing there.

The role of the British army in the Six Counties was quite unambiguous. Its task was to prevent a full-scale insurrection developing which would inevitably spill over into the Twenty Six Counties and once again raise the national question throughout Ireland. In Derry, where the nationalists were in a majority, this meant replacing the defeated RUC to contain the nationalist revolt. In Belfast, where the nationalists were a minority, it was to prevent the loyalist pogrom against the nationalist minority developing to civil war proportions. It was not a concern on the part of British imperialism to prevent Catholics being butchered and driven out of their homes by loyalist thugs. For British imperialism had not prevented previous Belfast pogroms in the 1920s and 1930s. And for nearly 50 years British governments, Labour and Tory alike, had allowed sectarian discrimination and loyalist repression free rein in order to put down any nationalist opposition to the loyalist state.

On sending troops into the Six Counties, the British government was forced initially to tread carefully. Their task was to restore stability to the loyalist state. To do this, they had to take into account the extent of the nationalist rebellion against the loyalist state, the growing pressure on the Dublin government to take some action, and the widespread international coverage of events in the Six Counties after the rise of the Civil Rights Movement.

At first, the response of sections of the nationalist minority to the entry of British troops was one of relief. It was understandable that an exhausted people, having faced days of savage attack from armed loyalist forces, should see the entry of British troops into the Six Counties as a new factor in the situation.

In Derry, the appearance of the troops was clear proof that the nationalists had won. The hated RUC and B-Specials had been kept out of the Bogside and the army had made no attempt to breach the barricades. Within 24 hours, a delegation from the Defence Association had told the Army Commander that no soldier would be permitted to come through the barricades until the police were disarmed, the B-Specials disbanded and the Special Powers Act and Stormont abolished.

In Belfast, the troops had to put a halt to the loyalist pogrom against the nationalist minority. Not to have done so would have meant civil war spreading throughout the Six Counties with serious consequences also for the stability of the Twenty Six Counties state. Most of the Falls Road and Ardoyne were now behind barricades and the British army and the RUC kept outside. Conditions, put by the Defence Committee, for the barricades being removed were the same as those in Derry. Behind the barricades the IRA were bringing in arms to organise defence of the areas. Morale in the nationalist areas was high.

Together with the introduction of the troops went the necessity for reforms in order to take the steam out of the nationalist minority's rebellion. On 19 August, Chichester-Clark, Faulkner and Porter, the Home Affairs Minister, were summoned to Downing Street to see Wilson, Callaghan and Healey, the Minister for Defence. An agreement was reached that the police and B-Specials would be put under British army control with the B-Specials 'phased out' of riot control. Also the pace of reforms would have to be speeded up. A communiqué was issued, the Downing Street Declaration, which began by reaffirming the pledge that:

'... Northern Ireland should not cease to be a part of the United Kingdom without the consent of the people of Northern Ireland ... The border is not an issue'.

It also included a statement, which, given that pledge, could only be regarded as vacuous:

'... Every citizen of Northern Ireland is entitled to the same equality of treatment and freedom from discrimination as obtains in the rest of the United Kingdom, irrespective of political views or religion'.[16]

However, it would appeal to those calling for moderation. That night, Wilson said on television that the B-Specials would be phased out. The next day it was announced that Lord Hunt – chosen because of his 'police responsibilities in colonial situations'[17] – was to look into the whole structure of the police forces in the Six Counties. A few days later the Scarman Tribunal was set up to report on the 'disorders' between April and August 1969.

Callaghan came to Belfast a week later and met the Stormont cabinet. Three working parties, of Whitehall and Stormont Civil Servants, were to be set up to study ways of dealing with discrimination in housing and jobs and improving community relations. A permanent British government representative was to be sent over to keep an eye on developments. Callaghan also toured the battle areas of Belfast and Derry. He was given a friendly welcome by the Catholics in the Falls and Bogside. For them, his appearance symbolised a political defeat for the Unionist Party.

On 12 September, the Cameron Commission – appointed by O'Neill in January 1969 – reported. While attacking 'extremists' on both sides, it confirmed and documented the existence of discrimination and gerrymandering against Catholics. It pointed to 'serious breaches of discipline and acts of violence' by the RUC and it described the B-Specials as 'a partisan and paramilitary force recruited exclusively from Protestants'. It also spoke of a 'failure of leadership on all sides' which had allowed tensions to build up and eventually to explode in violence.[18]

All this talk of 'reform' and ending 'injustice', all these inquiries and reports, it should be remembered, came *after* the mass Civil Rights Campaign, *after* the insurrection in Derry and *after* the near civil war in the Six Counties. British imperialism had made no attempt to democratise the statelet in 50 years because it had no need to. It now took the steps it did in order to reconcile the nationalist minority to the Six Counties statelet *after* they had rebelled. It could not succeed. For the loyalist statelet, the key to British domination over Ireland, could only exist as long as the Unionist alliance between the loyalist workers and capitalists survived. And that alliance was based on the privileged status and conditions of the Protestant working class. That is, on the lack of civil rights and the discrimination against the nationalist minority, and with the necessary repressive apparatus to enforce such conditions. To make any real inroads into discrimination, to introduce real reforms would threaten Unionism, the loyalist statelet and therefore British domination over Ireland. Inevitably, the Loyalists would fight against such developments and British imperialism and the British army would have to back them. The nationalist minority, in the words of Sean Mac Stiofain, 'would quickly realise that a colonial power does not send its army to hurry up social reforms'.[19]

THE ROAD TO REVOLUTIONARY WAR

It is quite unacceptable to an imperialist power to have areas of its colony which are out of its control. Nationalist areas in Belfast and Derry were behind barricades. The people, not the RUC and British army, policed and controlled these areas. Behind the barricades, the IRA was organising defence of the areas and acquiring arms. One of the main concerns of the Labour government and the British army was to get these barricades taken down. It was not going to be an easy task. Republicans and others had argued, immediately the troops had been sent in, that the British army was not to be trusted and that the people could only rely on themselves to defend their areas.

All the talk of 'reforms' and 'justice' was designed to impress those waiting to be impressed, and especially the so-called 'moderates' in the nationalist community. It was to them that the British army turned when the pressure was building up to get the barricades down.

The first move came on 2 September when General Freeland, Commander of the British forces in the Six Counties, approached the Central Citizens Defence Committee (CCDC), Belfast, to ask for the barricades to be removed. The main personalities involved in negotiations were Jim Sullivan, a Republican leader in the Lower Falls and later to be a leader of the Official IRA, Paddy Devlin MP (NILP) and Tom Conaty, a Catholic businessman. The Committee refused because Freeland would not give a guarantee that the RUC would not be allowed back into the Falls Road area.

On 4 September, the army moved in at dawn and began to remove barricades from the nationalist Turf Lodge estate on the outskirts of Belfast. The residents were shocked and women formed a chain across the road to stop them. But the army succeeded.

On 6 September, with the aid of the Lower Falls priest, Father Murphy, Jim Sullivan and Paddy Devlin, some barricades in the Falls Road area came down. On 8 September, under pressure from Loyalists claiming that General Freeland was discussing with the IRA, Chichester-Clark went on television and said that the barricades were an act of defiance and must come down in 24 hours. The moderate Catholics negotiating with the army were horrified by this speech. A delegation of leading personalities from the CCDC was put together to see Callaghan. An agreement was reached that the barricades would come down and that soldiers would be at the end of the streets to prevent loyalist attacks.

The delegation then tried to sell the agreement to the CCDC. There was a great deal of dissent led by Francis Card, Billy McKee and Leo Martin, later to emerge as leaders of the Provisional IRA. In the end, Father Murphy was forced to use the power of the Church to get the deal accepted. Dr Philbin, Bishop of Down and Connor, was brought in to persuade the community to take the barricades down. He was driven round the Falls Road area in an army Land Rover. By Wednesday morning, the barricades were down. Shortly afterwards, in Derry, a mass meeting at Free Derry Corner voted to breach the main barricade in Rossville Street. However, divisions and tension were building up within the nationalist community and hostility towards the army was beginning to grow.

On 10 October, the Hunt Report was published. It recommended the disarming of the RUC and the disbandment of the B-Specials. The RUC was to have a British Chief Officer – Sir Arthur Young – chosen because of his previous colonial experience in Gold Coast (Ghana), Kenya and Malaya[20]. The report also recommended the establishment of a new, part-time military force, later called the Ulster Defence Regiment.

The following night, angry Loyalists came in their thousands down the Shankill Road and tried to attack the nationalist Unity Flats. They were halted by an RUC cordon. Loyalist gunmen opened fire and killed an RUC man, Constable Arbuckle – the first one killed since 1962. The army claimed the rioters fired more than a 1,000 rounds from weapons which included a machine-gun and several sub-machine guns. The troops opened fire and killed two Loyalists and wounded many more. 22 soldiers were injured, 14 with gunshot wounds. The army riot squad moved into the Shankill Road beating up Loyalists, searching houses and capturing guns and ammunition. 68 people were arrested.

Sir Arthur Young saw his task as winning Catholic confidence in the police and, in particular, in getting the police back into the nationalist strongholds like the Falls and the Bogside. The RUC had not patrolled the Falls area for five years except in pairs of armed Land Rovers. The police had not entered the Bogside on foot for a number of years. On the day after the Shankill riots, Callaghan brought Young into the Bogside and introduced him to a cheering crowd. Military police came in, unarmed, to patrol the area. They were to do so for the next six months. The RUC made a formal return to the Falls Road Belfast on 17 October.

In this period, the British government believed that its main troubles were over and events had now taken an upward turn. Moderate Catholic opinion shared this optimism. But fundamentally, nothing had changed. The reforms that mattered so far were merely promises of reforms and would remain so. As one liberal journalist, Henry Kelly, put it:

'Reform did not bring one new job to the North, it did not heighten the standard of living . . . it did absolutely nothing to give the working class Catholic any reason to feel identified with the system . . . '[21]

The reforms that had gone through did nothing to alter the fundamental character of political power of the loyalist statelet. Within six months this reality would be exposed.

The signs that a new conflict would soon break out could already be seen, where it mattered, on the streets, in the working class nationalist areas of Belfast and Derry. McCann's description of the situation in the Bogside conveys the resentment building up there among the working class youth:

'Reforms had filtered through on to the statute book. An Ombudsman had been appointed. Derry Corporation had been abolished and replaced by a Development Commission. A points system for the allocation of houses was in operation. Moderate Unionists could, and often did, point proudly to this record of progress. None of it, however, made any difference to the clumps of unemployed teenagers who stood, fists dug deep into their pockets, around William Street in the evenings. Briefly elevated into folk-hero status in the heady days of August, praised and patronized by local leaders for their expertise with the stone and the petrol bomb, they had now been dragged back down into the anonymous depression which had hitherto been their constant condition. For them at least, nothing had changed and they were bitterly cynical about the talk of a reformed future. "We'll get nothing out of it. The Orangemen are still in power." Occasionally they would stone the soldiers.' [22]

That the Orangemen were still in power became clear as events began to unfold. An internal RUC investigation of police action in the Bogside on 4 January 1969 recommended charges against certain RUC men. It was announced on 3 September 1969 that no action was to be taken. On 21 October 1969, an open verdict was returned on the murder of John Gallagher in Armagh on 14 August 1969. No-one was charged or disciplined. An inquest on the death of Samuel Devenny, badly beaten up in his own house by the RUC in April 1969, said his death was due to natural causes. The policemen who beat him up were never identified or charged. However, Bernadette Devlin (McAliskey) MP was charged with riotous behaviour during the siege of Derry and sentenced on 22 December to six months in prison. She was granted £250 bail pending an appeal.

The battles, however, really started again with the beginning of the loyalist marching season during April 1970. They led to the first direct conflict between British troops and Irish nationalist civilians for two generations. It took place on the nationalist Ballymurphy housing estate on the western edge of Belfast. For two hours, an Orange parade marched up and down the Springfield Road where it overlooks Ballymurphy, before leaving for a rally in Bangor. When the Orangemen returned to Belfast that night, they were attacked near Ballymurphy with bottles and stones by angry nationalist crowds. The army intervened and barricaded off the nationalist area. They were attacked by about 400 nationalist youth, and 20 soldiers were injured. The next evening, when the nationalist crowds gathered again, 600 soldiers supported by five Saracen armoured cars moved in and occupied the Ballymurphy estate. They were attacked with stones and bottles. The troops then fired 104 canisters of CS gas saturating the estate, ignoring the plight of children and old people living there. The nationalists replied with petrol bombs. Barricades went up and the confrontation lasted three days. General Freeland went on television and threatened to shoot dead anyone throwing a petrol bomb. Callaghan supported him. The way to avoid being shot was easy, he said, 'Don't go out with a petrol bomb'[23]. The army had now taken over the RUC's role as protector of the highly provocative Orange parades.

The British army, Unionist politicians and the press tried to blame the IRA for the disturbances. In fact, both sections of the IRA were attempting to limit the confrontation. The Provisional IRA were not yet fully reorganised and they did not want a confrontation with the British army at this stage. Nevertheless, they issued a warning to Freeland that if he carried out his threat to shoot petrol bombers then the Provisional IRA would take retaliatory action.

On 17 April 1970, there was a by-election in the Unionist South Antrim and Barnside seat of Terence O'Neill, who had been given a life peerage. Ian Paisley won the seat. The two sides were inevitably polarising again.

The battles recommenced during the Orange marches in June. Attempts to have them banned were rejected by the Labour government. An Orange march on 2 June was diverted away from the Ardoyne by a local army officer as it would have passed the mouth of Hooker Street full of burnt out Catholic houses. The Loyalists were furious. Two nights of vicious rioting took place in the Shankill Road area and there were clashes with troops.

Everyone knew that the Orange marches, planned to go past strong nationalist areas later in June, would lead to violent clashes. The Stormont Cabinet refused to call them off. On 26 June, Edward Heath, the new Prime Minister after the Tory election victory, was asked by Burroughs, the new British Permanent Representative, to have them banned. Heath said he would inform the new Home Secretary, Maudling, of the situation. Nothing was done and the inevitable happened.

On Saturday 27 June, Orange marches passed the nationalist Ardoyne, Clonard, Unity Flats and the isolated enclave of Short Strand in East Belfast. Battle soon commenced between loyalist and nationalist groups and nationalist youth and the army. The Provisional IRA was now to face its first major test in defending the nationalist minority.

As an Orange march passed the Ardoyne, stones were thrown and gunfire broke out. There were exchanges for roughly 35 minutes. At the end, three Loyalists lay dead. The Provisional IRA commander said that the first shots had come from the loyalist side.

The second battle took place in the Short Strand where 6,000 nationalists are surrounded by 60,000 Loyalists. In the evening after the march, loyalist mobs were trying to bomb the St Matthews Church which dominates the entrance to the area. Paddy Kennedy, a Republican Labour MP in Stormont, asked for protection for the church by the army. He was told nothing could be done as the army was overstretched. The Provisional IRA went into action to defend the area. There was a long gun battle. At the end of it, two loyalist gunmen had been killed and two fatally wounded. One Provisional IRA auxiliary, Henry McIlhone was killed and Billy McKee, the Provisional Commander in Belfast was wounded. The Loyalists were held off. The Provisional IRA had emerged as the only effective defender of the area. Its growth was now ensured.

In Derry, the Bogside had also erupted again. On Friday 26 June, Bernadette Devlin (McAliskey) lost her appeal against a six month jail sentence. The RUC agreed that she should surrender at Victoria Barracks in Derry that evening. A 'farewell' meeting was arranged for Free Derry Corner. On her way to this meeting from Belfast, her car was stopped five miles outside Derry. She was immediately arrested and taken to Armagh prison. When the crowd waiting for her heard this, they were furious. Battle with the army commenced. It was to last all weekend. The first Perspex riot shield appeared on the street – a brick hit it and it broke. Rubber bullets were fired for the first time. CS gas was fired and the nationalist youth replied with petrol bombs. On Sunday, moderate Catholics led by John Hume called a meeting of prominent people to find a peace formula. It was decided to send a deputation to the British army to ask them to withdraw their soldiers from the area. Sean Keenan, a leading figure in the Provisional IRA, refused to go. He said what they had to do was to defend themselves. When asked 'against whom', he replied 'the British army'[24]. A week later it would be conclusively shown that what he said was true.

As soon as the weekend battles were over, the Stormont Cabinet met and introduced a draconian Criminal Justice (Temporary Provisions) Act, 1970. It was rushed through Stormont on 1 July after a record 18 hours sitting. It brought in mandatory six month minimum prison terms for offences connected with rioting – 'riotous behaviour', 'disorderly behaviour', and 'behaviour likely to cause a breach of the peace'. The moderate Nationalist opposition in Stormont did not oppose it.

On the same day, the Joint Security Committee, which included Porter, Freeland, Young and Chichester-Clark met and discussed the weekend events. They decided that the trouble had spread because the army had not been tough enough when it first broke out. The 'reforms' had failed. Repression and force were now the order of the day.

On 3 July, the army raided a house in Balkan Street in the Lower Falls

–a stronghold of the Official IRA. The army had received a tip-off about arms. They found a small collection of arms including twelve pistols and a somewhat archaic sub-machine gun. As the soldiers tried to get back to their vehicles a crowd blocked their path. Having pushed their way through to their armoured personnel carriers, one of the drivers reversed and crushed a man to death against some railings. The crowd began to stone the soldiers. The army sent in more troops who fired CS gas throughout the area. Petrol bombs were thrown.

The army withdrew from the area to regroup. Immediately, barricades were built and an NLF (Official IRA) unit took up position to defend the area. Freeland had the whole area cordoned off. The army then moved in with massive force and attacked. A helicopter overhead directed the operation. The battle of the Lower Falls began. The army fired thousands of rounds of high-velocity ammunition. Three civilians were killed. The area was saturated with CS gas. Everywhere people choked. There was nowhere to escape. Inside and outside houses, choking clouds of CS gas were everywhere.

At 10.30pm, Freeland declared a curfew of the whole Falls area and did not lift it until Sunday morning 35 hours later. While the curfew lasted, a house-to-house search of the whole area took place. The army smashed doors, ripped up floors, tore out fire places, smashed furniture, stole money and left a trail of destruction behind them. Then to rub it in they took two clearly delighted Unionist ministers, John Brooke and William Long, on an excursion of the area on the back of an army Land Rover.

Freeland's curfew prevented bread and milk vans coming in to deliver. Mothers with children were at their wits end. The women of Belfast came up with an answer. Over 1,000 women and children marched into the Lower Falls carrying bread, milk and other necessities. They pushed aside the troops and distributed the food. It is said that when they came out a good many items the army was searching for came out with them, hidden in prams and under coats. The army's haul was tiny – 35 rifles, 14 shot guns, 6 automatic weapons, 52 pistols and rounds of ammunition. This should be compared with the over 100,000 guns estimated to be in loyalist hands at that time.

The people of 5,000 households had been subjected to deliberate institutionalised terror. The purpose of the operation had been to intimidate the nationalist people. It had the opposite effect. As Sean Mac Stiofain was to write later:

'Far from intimidating the Irish people, the behaviour of the British that weekend alienated them in tens of thousands. Coming on top of the successful IRA-led defence of Ballymacarret [Short Strand] and other districts, what the battle of Lower Falls did was to provide endless water for the Republican guerrilla fish to swim in.'[25]

The Provisional IRA had not at first been involved in the Lower Falls battle. However, it gradually came into engagement with British troops, carrying out diversionary actions in other parts of Belfast. A bank was also blown up in Andersonstown and the soldiers who came to investigate were fired on.

The Falls Curfew confirmed everything that the Provisional IRA had recognised from its formation. The Civil Rights Movement had inevitably come into direct conflict with the very existence of the loyalist state. And in that conflict, the real enemy, British imperialism and its troops, had emerged and would have to be fought and destroyed if there was to be any progress for the Irish people.

In the next few months, recruitment to the Provisional IRA rose dramatically. So did nationalist support. The nationalist youth that had fought the RUC and loyalist mobs on the streets of Derry and Belfast were now joining *their* Army – the Provisional IRA.

NOTES

1 Provisional IRA, *Freedom Struggle* Dublin 1973 pp. 9–10.
2 Mac Stiofain S, *op cit* p. 124.
3 See chapter 2.
4 Mac Stiofain S, *op cit* p. 92.
5 Interview with Cathal Goulding in *New Left Review* No 64 November/December 1970 p. 53.
6 Mac Stiofain S, *op cit* p. 135.
7 *An Phoblacht* June 1971.
8 Mac Stiofain S, *op cit* pp. 109–110.
9 *ibid* p. 112.
10 *ibid* p. 142.
11 *ibid* p. 143.
12 Brady S, *Arms and the Men* Wicklow 1971 pp. 38–39.
13 Deutsch R and Magowan V, *op cit* Volume 1 p. 40.
14 Callaghan J, *A House Divided* London 1973 p. 42.
15 *ibid* p. 37.
16 *ibid* pp. 191–192.
17 Wilson H, *The Labour Government 1964–1970* London 1974 p. 876.
18 See Farrell M, *op cit* p. 265 and Deutsch R and Magowan V, *op cit* Volume 1 p. 44.
19 Mac Stiofain S, *op cit* p. 123.
20 Callaghan J, *op cit* p. 112.

21   Kelly H, *How Stormont Fell* Dublin 1972 p. 93.
22   McCann E, *op cit* pp. 73−4.
23   Deutsch R and Magowan V, *op cit* Volume 1 p. 63.
24   McCann E, *op cit* p. 76.
25   Mac Stiofain S, *op cit* p. 157.

CHAPTER NINE

REVOLUTIONARY WAR

As nationalist resistance refused to subside, the intervention of British imperialism in the Six Counties more and more assumed the character of open warfare against the nationalist minority. What for the nationalist minority began as a struggle to reform the Six Counties was now to turn into a revolutionary war to smash the loyalist state, end partition and drive British imperialism out of Ireland. As British imperialism increasingly turned to institutionalised terror to break the resistance of the nationalist minority, so that minority gave greater and greater support to the army that defended it – the Provisional IRA.

Many incidents over the next six months were to confirm this trend. On 31 July 1970, in New Lodge Road Belfast, Danny O'Hagan was shot dead. Local people insisted that he was unarmed after the British army had tried to justify the shooting by saying a petrol bomb had been found on the ground by his side. All too often the nationalist minority were to hear similar British army lies to cover up cold-blooded murder.

In this period the British army made regular use of the Criminal Justice Act introduced in July 1970. This Act gave mandatory six month prison sentences for offences associated with rioting, including 'behaviour likely to cause a breach of the peace'. One of its first victims was Frank Gogarty, a former chairman of the Civil Rights Association. He was arrested when tape-recording sounds of a disturbance taking place on 1 August 1970 in Belfast. Stopped by an army patrol, he was thrown against a wall, searched, kicked, sworn at and thrown into a jeep. His offence was to shout 'Stop kicking me, you British bastard'. For that, he got a six month sentence in Crumlin Road Gaol. Another nationalist, a Belfast docker, John Benson, got six months for writing a slogan 'No tea here' on the wall of his street[1]. Between August and December 1970 a stream of nationalist youth involved in skirmishes with the army got the mandatory six months sentence under the Criminal Justice Act, many on the perjured evidence of British troops.

With the British army stepping up its attacks and harassment of the nationalist minority, anti-Unionist politicians soon began to realise that support was rapidly slipping away from them and their programme of reform through the Stormont parliament. In an attempt to contain this development, six anti-Unionist MPs came together on 21 August 1970 to form a new party, the Social Democratic and Labour Party (SDLP). The SDLP supported the eventual reunification of Ireland but argued that it could not be achieved by violent means. The names of the founding members of the SDLP read like a roll call of those who for the next 13 years were to spend most of their energy attempting to divert nationalist support away from the Provisional IRA – Gerry Fitt, Paddy Devlin, Austin Currie, John Hume, Ivan Cooper and Paddy O'Hanlon. This party, the voice of the Catholic middle class in the Six Counties, was supported by the Twenty Six Counties government and financed by southern Irish businessmen. The Dublin government not only supported this development but shared the SDLP's hatred for the Provisional IRA. By the end of 1970, the Dublin government had already rounded up and gaoled many Republicans. In December 1970, Lynch, after press rumours of plots to kidnap Dublin government ministers, even threatened to re-introduce internment without trial. This would have given great encouragement to both the SDLP and the Loyalists in the Six Counties.

The SDLP, however, did not speak for the nationalist working class. Increasingly, the Provisional IRA did, and they were rapidly recruiting the nationalist youth to their ranks. Small scale sabotage operations, striking at communications and power supplies, and retaliatory actions against British troops by the Provisional IRA built up towards the end of 1970.

In the Ballymurphy area of Belfast, where British troops were permanently stationed, skirmishes between the nationalist youth and the British army were frequent occurrences. On 11 January 1971 a major confrontation broke out.

Ballymurphy is a strong nationalist area, where the Provisionals were in the process of training hundreds of new recruits. The last thing they wanted, at this stage, was a major confrontation with the British army. The activities of the youth were, however, inviting a large scale occupation of the area by British troops. And the Provisional IRA took steps to cool down the situation. They had almost succeeded in doing this when, on 14 January, 700 troops invaded the area to carry out a house-to-house search of the Ballymurphy estate.

The situation immediately blew up again. Guns, petrol bombs and sulphuric acid were used by residents on the estate to resist the invasion of their area. One soldier was wounded. Republicans warned the army to withdraw if the situation was not to reach a point of no return. It took another two days before the Provisional IRA was able to end the confrontation and bring the situation under its control.

During the Ballymurphy confrontation an approach was made by the British army to the Belfast Brigade of the Provisional IRA. Contact had been made on a number of occasions before the latest events blew up. A meeting took place, with the consent of the Provisional leadership, during which the British army representatives agreed that there would be no activity by their own forces or the RUC in certain areas of Belfast. Control of community peace in those areas was to be left to the IRA.

Despite the fact that the British forces could not be trusted for very long, this agreement had the merit of not forcing the Provisional IRA into a premature confrontation with the British army. It also meant that nationalist areas were seen to be policed successfully by the IRA. Republican courts were set up and in many areas petty crime was significantly reduced. The Provisional IRA was beginning to emerge as a People's Army.

THE WAR BEGINS

After the Ballymurphy events, pressure on Chichester-Clark from the loyalist side began to build up. Already in August 1970 Paisley and Craig had called for the re-arming of the RUC, the re-introduction of the B-Specials and internment. And at the end of November the influential Belfast County Grand Orange Lodge passed a motion of no confidence in the government. On 18 January 1971 Chichester-Clark saw Maudling and demanded more troops, more arrests and a military offensive against the IRA. He got a declaration from Maudling, that the army 'may now take the offensive' against the IRA. On 25 January 170 delegates of the Ulster Unionist Council, the Unionist party's main body, not satisfied with the declaration, called on Chichester-Clark to resign. On 27 January Craig announced in Stormont that two RUC men had been surrounded by a nationalist crowd in the Clonard area and had been told by members of the Provisional IRA to leave if they valued their lives. They were rescued by British troops who, after escorting them out of the area, advised them to stay out. This, according to Craig, was proof of British army complicity in 'no-go' areas. Pressure was now building up for the British army to act.

On 3 February 1971, on the orders of General Farrar-Hockley, a force of the Second Royal Anglians cordoned off and searched the Ardoyne and Clonard areas. Crowds gathered and fights broke out with the troops. At lunchtime that day, in the Clonard area, the predominantly loyalist workers from the nearby Mackie's engineering works came out onto the streets and began to abuse and jeer at the nationalist crowds, throwing ball-bearings and other missiles at them. The army and the RUC deliberately turned their backs on the loyalist attackers and confronted the nationalist crowds. After the Mackie's workers had gone back to work, the army decided to clear them off the streets by roaming up and down the streets in their jeeps. At least two people were knocked down and injured. Two nights of the fiercest battles the British army had faced in Belfast followed. Eight soldiers were wounded by gun-fire and one by a gelignite bomb.

On 5 February Farrar-Hockley went on television and said that the area had been searched because of evidence that 'it harbours members of the IRA Provisionals'.[2] He proceeded to name five men who he claimed were members of the Provisional IRA. He failed to mention the fact that these were the men with whom the British army had been having talks.

There were no more talks. An agreement had been broken, and the Provisionals had publicly stated that further repression against nationalist areas would be met by force. From defence of nationalist areas and limited sabotage operations, the Provisional IRA moved onto the offensive – into a more determined phase of retaliation.

On 6 February 1971 a British army patrol was ambushed in the New Lodge Road in Belfast. Gunner Robert Curtis was shot dead and four other soldiers were wounded, one who later died. This was the first time in almost fifty years that a British soldier had been killed in action by the IRA.

That same night, in the Old Park area, UVF snipers began firing from a loyalist street into a nearby nationalist street. Residents asked British troops to take some action against the sniping. They refused. During this attack on a nationalist area Jim Saunders, a company officer of the Third Battalion IRA, was killed. When the British army did become involved it was to shoot dead an unarmed man, Barney Watt, a member of Sinn Fein.

Next day, Chichester-Clark went on television and announced that 'Northern Ireland is at war with the Irish Republican Army Provisionals'.[3]

On 9 February the funerals of the two Republicans killed took place.

After the traditional volley had been fired over Jim Saunders' coffin and a guard of honour formed round the hearse, British troops tried to enter the street and interfere. Hundreds of furious people surrounded them and drove them out of the area. The funeral of Barney Watt was attacked by Loyalists and the tricolour draping the coffin was seized. The funeral processions of both men were followed by immense crowds.

Almost every day now the British army and the RUC cordoned off and searched nationalist areas, harassing and beating up the residents. These areas also had to face sectarian attacks from Loyalists. The nationalist minority replied with stones and petrol bombs, and the IRA with bombs and guns. Some of the most blatantly corrupt judicial decisions took place in the courts in this period. When Republican supporters picketed courts, they were arrested and got mandatory gaol sentences. Loyalist counter demonstrators were left alone. A loyalist dealer in illegal guns got a suspended sentence whereas a nationalist labourer, Joseph Downey, was gaoled for a year for shouting 'You shower of bastards, up the IRA' as an Orange parade passed by.[4]

On 27 February two RUC men were shot dead after savage clashes between nationalist crowds and the police and army in the Ardoyne. On 10 March three Scottish soldiers were found dead in a ditch in unexplained circumstances. Both the Provisional and Official IRA denied having any responsibility. Loyalist pressure on Chichester-Clark increased. He again demanded more troops, greater repression including troops permanently stationed in nationalist areas. The British government could not meet his requirements and on 20 March he resigned.

On 23 March 1971 Brian Faulkner was elected leader of the Unionist Party. Faulkner had been Minister of Home Affairs during the IRA's 1956–62 Border Campaign. He believed internment was a major factor in bringing about the IRA's defeat. He immediately took steps to force Westminster to agree on internment again. The army was sceptical at this stage, believing that internment would unite the nationalist minority behind the Provisionals. Nevertheless, in April, British army intelligence and RUC Special Branch set up a joint internment working party to draw up the names and addresses of those who could usefully be interned.

During March, as Faulkner and the British government were preparing for internment, the Official IRA launched a series of criminal attacks, including torture and murder, against Provisional IRA personnel. The Provisionals kept retaliation to a minimum and took steps to bring about a truce. Even after the truce the Officials shot down Tom Cahill, a Provisional IRA volunteer. The Officials are the same people who, today, under the guise of The Workers' Party, parade themselves as 'democrats' and consciously spread pro-imperialist propaganda about so-called Provisional 'atrocities'.

In April the Provisional IRA began a bombing campaign. The aim was to bring down the Stormont regime. The immediate object of the campaign was '(1) to stretch the British army to the limits of its resources and to keep pressures off the nationalist areas; (2) to weaken the economy by sabotage operations against government and commercial property with the British taxpayer picking up the bill for damage done'. In April, 37 major explosions took place; May – 47, and June – 50 operations.[5]

The British army propaganda apparatus attempted to make out that the IRA operations were of a sectarian nature and directed against civilians. And there was no shortage of overpaid hack journalists, working for the pro-British, pro-Unionist media, prepared to spread this propaganda. The IRA, in fact, always gave warnings when bombs were placed so that civilians could be cleared from the area. The British army and the RUC have, on certain occasions, failed to pass on warnings, no doubt to sustain their anti-IRA propaganda campaign, and civilians have been killed and injured as a result.

In June, Faulkner tried to buy off middle class Catholic opinion by making a gesture to the SDLP, which he hoped might tie them more closely to the Stormont parliament and begin to take support away from the Provisionals. He offered the SDLP the chairmanship of two of the three new committees to be set up to consider government policies. At the same time, with this 'carrot' followed more and more 'stick'. Repression of the nationalist communities, which supported the Provisionals and wanted an end to Stormont, continued unabated. Faulkner had announced, on 25 May, that the troops could shoot 'with effect' anyone acting suspiciously.[6]

In July in Derry, the nationalist youth and the British army were involved in serious clashes for nearly seven days. The British army used CS gas, rubber bullets, truncheons and rifle butts to break down the resistance of the youth. They eventually used real bullets. Two unemployed Derry men, Seamus Cusack and Desmond Beattie were shot dead. Neither belonged to the Republican Movement. The British, as usual, claimed that they were armed and later said that Beattie had thrown a bomb. They could produce no evidence to substantiate this. Forensic tests proved that Beattie had had no contact with explosives and local people said that Cusack was going to remove a child from the danger zone when he was shot.

After the shootings, immense crowds attended a Provisional IRA rally and young people literally queued to join the IRA. John Hume knew he had to act if he was not to lose all support in the area for the SDLP. He held a press conference in Derry with other members of the SDLP (Fitt, however, refused to attend) and announced that, unless an 'impartial' inquiry into the killings of Cusack and Beattie was set up within four days, he and other SDLP members would leave Stormont. No inquiry was granted, in spite of the attempts of the wretched Fitt to find some compromise, and the SDLP had no alternative but to leave Stormont on 15 July. Now the 'carrot' that Faulkner had offered in June was no use – the donkeys were in no position to bite.

The Provisionals stepped up their campaign after the murder of Cusack and Beattie. There were 91 explosions in July. In Derry alone 70 troops were injured, several with gunshot wounds. Two soldiers were shot dead in Belfast and elsewhere many more soldiers were shot and wounded. On 17 July an IRA active service unit took over the *Daily Mirror* plant near Belfast and blew it up. Damage was estimated at £2 million. The plant never reopened and the compensation bill paid by the British government was said to be in the region of £10 million.

On 19 July Faulkner informed Heath that internment of Republicans and their supporters was now necessary. The army began to get prepared.

INTERNMENT WITHOUT TRIAL

The aim of internment was two-fold. It was firstly to destroy the nationalist resistance to the loyalist state by removing committed Republicans and their supporters from the struggle on the streets. And secondly, it was to terrorize the nationalist minority to such a degree that it would no longer be prepared to support the IRA.

Internment required adequate information and intelligence. On 23 July the army carried out a series of dawn raids on republican homes in the Six Counties using 1,800 troops plus RUC men. The aim was to gather information and to serve as a dry run for internment day which was set for 10 August. It is claimed by the *Sunday Times* that a list of names was then drawn up. It included no more than 120–130 said to be members or officers of either wing of the IRA, and a futher 300–500 regarded by the police as 'IRA sympathisers'. There were also 150 or so names of older Republicans who had been interned before – one of them picked up during internment was 77, blind and had been jailed in 1929. Finally, there was a small group of left-wing socialists and

NICRA activists who were included because, in Faulkner's words, 'they would have called meetings to protest against internment'.[7]

On 7 August a soldier opened fire on a van in Springfield Road killing the driver, Harry Thornton, a building worker. The army, as usual, claimed that shots had been fired at them – this 'explanation' was later changed to a soldier 'mistakenly' thinking he had been fired on when an old van backfired. A passenger in the van, Arthur Murphy, was dragged from it, assaulted by the soldiers, taken into Springfield Road RUC Station and savagely beaten up. He was reluctantly released six hours later, after a great deal of pressure and argument from local people. His face was a mass of bruises. Local people testify that when soldiers gathered round the van some were shouting gleefully 'we got one, we got one'.[8] The anger of the people soon led to major confrontations with the army. It was at this stage that the British army decided to bring internment forward by 24 hours.

At about 4 am on 9 August 1971 the internment swoops began. By the evening 342 men from all over the Six Counties had been dragged out of their beds, arrested and distributed to three holding centres. They were detained without charge or trial under Section 12 of the Special Powers Act. The whole operation was directed at the nationalist minority. Not a single Loyalist was arrested. Very few members of the Provisional IRA – 56 in all according to a Provisional IRA statement – were taken in and none from their leadership. The Provisionals had been warned by their own intelligence officers that internment was imminent. Volunteers had been told to stay away from home. Mac Stiofain says that he was able, by the use of elementary security procedures, to contact every local leadership in the Six Counties before noon of the first day of internment.[9] There can be little doubt that the vast majority of those interned had no connections with either wing of the IRA.

Of the 342 picked up, 116 were released within 48 hours and nearly all the others were taken to Crumlin Road prison or to HMS Maidstone, a prison ship moored in Belfast dock. Soon, news of systematic sadistic brutality in the interrogation of internees began to surface. Arrests had been conducted with considerable force, houses were damaged and relatives of the interned had insults and obscenities hurled at them by the arresting soldiers. Most of the detainees, throughout a period of sleeplessness and enforced hunger, were subjected to one or more forms of physical and psychological brutality. Almost everyone taken in had been beaten up. Men had been blindfolded and terrorised by being thrown out of a moving helicopter which they were told was high in the air but which was, in fact, only a few feet off the ground. Many men had been made to run the gauntlet barefoot between lines of troops with batons across an obstacle course with stumps of trees, sharp stones, broken glass and tacks. Others were forced to do exhausting exercises for hours on end. All were continually abused and made to feel that the British army were their absolute masters and had to be obeyed no matter what 'illogical' commands were given.

As news of the internment raids spread, and later of the brutality of the arrests and interrogation, the nationalist people rose up in outright defiance against the British army. In Derry, on 9 August, the people reacted with such fury that the army was prevented from completing its operation. Obstructive behaviour, from standing in a crowd and refusing to allow soldiers to pass, to petrol bomb attacks on army vehicles, took place everywhere. The IRA took on the British army in battles which in some places lasted over several days. In Belfast gunfights were raging in the Falls Road, the Markets, Ardoyne, Andersonstown and the New Lodge Road. The fiercest battle took place around the Ballymurphy estate involving paratroopers sandbagged into the nearby Henry Taggart Hall. Three civilians and a Catholic priest, who was giving last rites to one of the victims, were killed. Six people were wounded and an 11-year-old boy was castrated by a high-velocity bullet fired by one of the soldiers.

Co-operation between the people and the IRA was increasingly close especially on the big estates in Belfast. Crowds would draw troops towards them and then scatter leaving the British army as open targets for the IRA.

Believing the claims of the British army to have arrested a large proportion of the membership of the IRA, loyalist mobs used the opportunity to 'help the army' to put down the resistance in the nationalist areas. Loyalist snipers opened fire in the Ardoyne. Armed UVF members came out on to the streets. They were confronted and driven back by organised IRA units of quite unexpected strength.[10] Whole streets were soon on fire with both Protestants and Catholics leaving their homes. Over 7,000 refugees were reported to have arrived in army camps set up in the Twenty Six Counties. The death toll for 9 August was two British soldiers and ten civilians, seven of them Catholics. After four days, there were 22 dead, 19 of them civilians.

Claims by Faulkner, Maudling and the British army that internment had been a success and a high proportion of the IRA leadership had been arrested were soon made to look foolish. On the very day, 13 August, the British army claimed to have inflicted a major defeat on the IRA, killing between 20 and 30 gunmen, Joe Cahill, leader of the

Provisional IRA in Belfast, addressed an international press conference in a school behind the barricades in Ballymurphy. He announced
that their organisation was intact, that they had lost only two men
killed in action and had not been badly affected by internment.

During August, there were over 100 bomb explosions throughout the
Six Counties, many of them massive, as the Provisionals stepped up
their offensive. In Derry, the Creggan and Bogside were effectively
sealed off, protected by IRA manned barricades and beyond the reach
of not just the RUC but also the British army. Free Derry was a secure
base to launch guerrilla operations. The same was largely true for
many nationalist areas in Belfast.

The mass of the nationalist population now joined those in the working class nationalist estates who had already started a rent and rates
strike in protest against internment. Soon even government figures
showed there were 26,000 families participating in the strike. By October it was costing the government in the region of £500,000. On 16
August 8,000 workers took part in a one-day protest in Derry. On 19
August, after a demonstration in Derry had been broken up by the
army with water cannon and rubber bullets and John Hume and Ivan
Cooper had been arrested, 30 prominent Catholics in Derry announced
their resignations from positions on public bodies. On 22 August 130
councillors withdrew from local councils. Internment was now forcing
even the Catholic middle class into opposition to the state. The
nationalist minority had now united around one of the key Provisional
IRA demands – to destroy the loyalist state.

The anger of the nationalist minority intensified when news began to
filter out about a number of internees (there were 12) who had been
secretly moved from the internment holding centres to an unknown
destination (in fact, the Palace Barracks, Holywood – a few miles from
Belfast) and held there for over seven days. There they were subjected
to sophisticated psychological torture. They became 'guinea-pigs' to
test out 'sensory deprivation' techniques. The 12 internees had black
hoods placed on their heads throughout the seven days. They were
stripped of their clothes and given ill-fitting boiler suits to wear. They
had no idea where they were. Some had been told they were in England
– and they were kept in total isolation. They were forced to stand
spreadeagled against the wall, supported only by their fingertips, until
they collapsed. They were then revived and put back. This went on, in
some cases, for 2 or 3 days. They were severely beaten. During the
seven days, they were on a diet of dry bread and water – some said they
went without water for days. They were prevented from sleeping and

were subjected to a 'noise-machine' in the large cold room in which they were held, which bombarded the brain with monotonous sounds of a certain pitch. An ordinary tape recorder, out of sight, added weird cries, screams and other demented sound effects. Finally, they were regularly interrogated and then returned to the room.

The hood, the noise machine, standing at the wall for prolonged periods, sleep and food deprivation and the beatings were 'sensory deprivation' techniques – a combined torture to disorientate the mind and facilitate interrogation in depth. Pat Shivers relates part of his terrifying experience:

'Bag still over head . . . Taken into room. Noise like compressed-air engine in room. Very loud, deafening.

Hands put against wall. Legs spread apart. Head pulled back by bag and backside pushed in. Stayed there for about four hours. Could no longer hold up arms. Fell down. Arms put up again. Hands hammered until circulation restored. This happened continually for twelve or fourteen hours, until I eventually collapsed . . . Slapped back up again. This must have gone on for two or three days; I lost track of time. No sleep. No food. Knew I had gone unconscious several times, but did not know for how long. One time I thought, or imagined, I had died.'[11]

However, given the degree of disorientation involved, any 'confessions' forced out of anyone undergoing these techniques were just as likely to be false as true. No doubt, the sadistic criminals directing this torture were not terribly concerned. Their aim could only have been to strike terror into the nationalist minority as the news of the treatment of the internees gradually became known. In fact it had the opposite effect and intensified the determination of the nationalist minority to destroy the loyalist state. The Provisional IRA, by this time, had a waiting list of recruits.

As news of the brutality of the internment operations during the first 48 hours began to appear in Irish newspapers, pressure built up on the British government to hold an official inquiry. Labour MPs demanded a recall of Parliament. The government conceded an inquiry to be chaired by Sir Edmund Compton, a government hack who had served as 'ombudsman' for the Unionist government. It was to sit in secret and investigate allegations of 'physical brutality' during the first 48 hours of the internment operation. Specifically excluded was all mention of mental cruelty. 340 of the detainees refused to have anything to do with the inquiry, recognising that only a whitewash was to be expected from a secret British inquiry into British behaviour.

When the inquiry was nearly complete, the *Sunday Times* published information concerning the treatment of the 'guinea-pigs' and the reports of torture using 'sensory deprivation' techniques. This information had been in the hands of the press for some weeks. The techniques were, in fact, still being used on two more men while the committee of inquiry carried out its work. Compton was forced to broaden the inquiry to include some of the new reports.

The Compton Report was published on 17 November 1971. It was not only a whitewash but was clearly designed to hide the fact that psychological torture of an experimental kind had taken place. So the forcible exercises inflicted on the men 'were devised to counteract the cold'. Requiring detainees to stand with their arms against the wall 'provides security for detainees and guards against physical violence'. The hooding, it seems, was designed for the same purpose although it added that it 'can also in the case of some detainees, increase their sense of isolation and so be helpful to the interrogator thereafter.' The noise was a 'security measure' to prevent men overhearing each other or being overheard. Finally, while recognising that ill-treatment of some of the internees had taken place, Compton said that this did not amount to physical brutality. That was because the interrogators had not 'enjoyed' their work.

'We consider that brutality is an inhuman or savage form of cruelty, and that cruelty implies a disposition to inflict suffering, coupled with indifference to, or pleasure in, the victim's pain. We do not think that happened here.'[12]

Needless to say, most people with a scrap of honesty treated the Compton Report with the contempt it deserved. All of those who went through the sensory deprivation torture suffered permanent psychological damage. Sean McKenna, one of those subjected to the torture, died on 5 June 1975 at the age of 45. On 13 February 1974 Pat Shivers, another 'guinea-pig', was awarded £15,000 damages for 'false trespass, false imprisonment, assault and battery, torture and inhuman and degrading treatment'.[13] No defence was offered by the British government. Other internees also received compensation. Yet no member of the British army or RUC has been, or will be, charged with the torture of the internees. No international crimes tribunal has ever tried Heath, Maudling, Carrington, Whitelaw, Faulkner and many others centrally involved in directing the whole internment operation. Indeed, Lord Carrington, at that time Minister of Defence, tried to cover up the crimes by going on the radio and referring to all detainees as 'thugs and murderers'.[14]

In the wake of the scandal which the Compton Report provoked internationally, the British government made another effort to justify their interrogation methods by setting up a second official inquiry with three senior judges. It was announced on the very day when the Dublin government said it intended to place before the European Court of Human Rights at Strasbourg the allegations of brutality by British troops in the Six Counties. The report of this new inquiry (March 1972) created more of a stir than the first. The majority report by Lord Parker justified the interrogation techniques, subject to certain safeguards, on the grounds that 'new information was obtained' which included an 'identification of a further 700 members of both IRA factions', 'arms caches', 'safe houses', and so on.[15] This clearly was a lie, but it gave a justification for torture. Lord Gardiner, disturbed by such open and blatant contempt for 'law', submitted a minority report saying that the methods used were not 'morally justifiable' and were 'illegal'. He did not recommend the arrest and trial of those responsible for the crimes. The Heath government said it would no longer use the 'sensory deprivation' techniques as an aid to interrogation. Mr Harold Wilson, leader of the Labour Party, welcomed this. Both had allowed the Gardiner minority report to be used as a cover for crimes which had actually been committed. Needless to say the torture and brutality went on and 'official reports' would again be found necessary. There never has been a determined, organised opposition in Britain to the torture carried out by British imperialism in the Six Counties of Ireland, or anywhere else for that matter over the last 35 years. One paragraph in the Parker Report says it all:

> 'Some or all [of these methods of interrogation] have played an important part in counter-insurgency operations in Palestine, Malaya, Kenya and Cyprus and more recently in the British Cameroons (1960–61), Brunei (1963), British Guiana (1964), Aden (1964–67), Borneo/Malaysia (1965–66), the Persian Gulf (1970–71) and in Northern Ireland (1971).'[16]

Could anyone have any doubts what the Provisional IRA were fighting?

THE FALL OF STORMONT

On 5 September 1971, the Provisional IRA announced political conditions for a truce: immediate cessation of the British forces' campaign of violence against Irish people; abolition of Stormont; free elections to a nine county Ulster parliament as a step towards a new government structure for the entire country; release of all political prisoners, tried or untried, both in Ireland and in England; compensation for those who have suffered as a result of British violence. The British government was given until midnight 8 September to reply, otherwise the IRA would have no option but to intensify its campaign.

On 8 September Harold Wilson, however, pre-empted an official British government reply. Recognising the pressure building up in support of the legitimate demands of the nationalist minority for an end to Stormont and the reunification of Ireland, he put forward his own 12-point, Labour-imperialist plan – a 'half-way house' to hold back the inevitable fall of Stormont. It included having a British minister of Cabinet rank installed in the Six Counties on a permanent basis, elections under proportional representation and a Council of Ireland between North and South. Later in November Wilson was to develop this theme calling for the re-unification of Ireland within the British Commonwealth over a period of 15 years. The British Labour Party, as in 1918–21, only makes this kind of gesture to the Irish people's demands in order to hold back what the Irish people have fought for and so nearly won. On 23 September the Labour Party supported the government in its 'handling of the Northern Ireland situation'. However, 60 Labour MPs voted against, defying the advice of the Shadow Cabinet.[17]

Nationalist resistance to the loyalist state intensified. On 12 September 15–20,000 attended a massive anti-internment rally in Casement Park, Belfast. Civil Resistance committees were set up all over the Six Counties in protest against internment, and to organise the rent and rates strike and other forms of protest. On 26 September even the SDLP made its own gesture of opposition, by holding the first meeting of an 'Alternative Assembly' after its walk-out from Stormont.

In October, Stormont introduced a punitive measure directed at those protesting against internment. It passed legislation allowing the government to deduct arrears of rent and rates, plus 'collection charges', from the wages or social security benefits of people on rent and rates strike.

The British army kept up its offensive with raids, searches, arrests and internment. In a four-week period to mid-November, 2,500 nationalist homes had been searched – which invariably meant doors smashed in, furniture broken, houses wrecked, money and valuables stolen. In some areas, where the pressure was on, the same houses could be searched each day and, in reported cases, three or four times a day. In September a permanent concentration camp for internees had been set up at Long Kesh near Lisburn – with its Nissen huts surrounded by barbed wire cages and watch-towers. Between 9 August 1971 and 16 December 1971, 1,576 men were arrested under the internment regulations with no fewer than 934 – 60 per cent – being released. That so many had to be released says a great deal about the army's operation designed to harass and terrorise the nationalist population.

Torture of the internees continued and over the next period included electric shock treatment, drugs, injections, being placed in a small cubicle and made to stare at a white perforated wall, as well as the sadistic beatings and modified versions of the psychological torture that were going on before. The fact that by October 1975, with 567 cases outstanding and many more never brought to court, £420,823 had already been paid out in compensation to 222 claimants (220 settled out of court) who had been assaulted by the security forces, surely says it all.[18] Yet again, it needs to be said, no member of the security forces, no government ministers and/or officials have been tried and convicted for these crimes.

On 13 October the British army began blowing up and spiking the border roads. Frequent clashes with the soldiers took place as local people and organised groups filled in the craters formed by the blasts. These actions by the British army further consolidated support for the Provisional IRA.

By November 14,000 British troops were in the Six Counties and were mainly concentrated in the nationalist areas. The tendency to shoot-to-kill in these areas was growing. On 23 October soldiers shot dead two women, Dorothy Maguire and Maire Meehan, who were passengers in the back of a car touring the Lower Falls. As usual the army claimed they had been fired on, but too many witnesses had seen what really happened. After the shooting the British beat up and systematically persecuted Maire Meehan's husband for months in revenge, after their story had been proved false. On 24 October, in Newry, the British army shot three youths dead as they attempted to carry out a robbery. The nationalist minority now faced an army of occupation which was intent on terrorising it.

The IRA intensified its campaign. Sabotage operations continued daily over a wide area and ambushes and attacks on British army, RUC and UDR personnel increased. After internment the IRA had revoked an instruction that the RUC and UDR were not to be subjected to deliberate attack. In October Lord Carrington had announced that the level of the UDR would be raised from 4,500 to 10,000 men. The UDR was a sectarian force of mainly ex-B Specials and Loyalists – its Catholic membership had already dropped from 15% to 8% – and it had been used during the internment operations to allow more British troops to move into nationalist areas. The RUC had been gradually rearmed during 1971 and RUC men had participated in the brutal interrogation of the internees. Both the UDR and RUC, like the British army, were now to be treated as legitimate combatant targets at all times, whether on duty or not, armed or not, in uniform or not.

The British army and Faulkner regularly claimed that, as a result of internment and the interrogation of the internees, they had the IRA beaten. Towards the end of November the IRA responded to this with a massive weekend bombing blitz throughout the Six Counties. This involved a coordinated wave of almost 100 operations, 60 of them taking place on the first day. All the border custom huts were blown up or burned down. Explosions followed in Belfast, Derry, Dungannon and Coalisland during the night and many more took place the next day.

Before the end of the year, there were some sensational prison escapes. On 16 November nine Provisionals escaped from the top-security Crumlin Road prison. And on 2 December three more Provisionals, including the Ardoyne commander, escaped from the same place. They were able to give detailed reports on the brutal torture and interrogation techniques used on the internees.

In a war, in spite of the care taken by the IRA, not only are IRA volunteers injured and killed by accidents or mistakes, but, inevitably, so are innocent civilians. The British propaganda machine always tried to make a great deal out of such tragic events, cynically using them in an attempt to drive support away from the IRA. When 15 people died as a result of the bombing of McGurk's Bar, Belfast, as usual the British propaganda machine tried to blame the IRA. The IRA, however, was not involved. Indeed, the next day a group calling themselves 'Empire Loyalists' claimed responsibility. No-one had heard of such a group being active in Ireland. Forensic evidence and the power of the explosions indicated that plastic explosive had been used. Such explosive was only available to the British army and had not been used by the IRA. This might explain the real identity of the 'Empire Loyalists' involved. [19] There were other unexplained explosions at both Protestant and Catholic owned premises in this period which pointed to British undercover agents at work, trying to stir up sectarian confrontations.

From 1 January to 8 August 1971, before internment was introduced, 34 people had been killed in the Six Counties: eleven British soldiers, four RUC men and nineteen civilians. From 9 August 1971 to the end of the year, the number was 139 dead: 32 British soldiers, seven RUC men, five UDR men and 95 civilians. Hundreds of soldiers and civilians had been injured. British imperialism now confronted an all-out revolutionary war against its occupation of the Six Counties.

Over the Christmas period, the IRA announced a three-day truce. Faulkner responded by saying that there would be no let up whatsoever in the drive to combat the IRA.

All marches and parades had been banned in the Six Counties since internment day. Nevertheless illegal marches did take place, including a 1,000 strong protest march against internment from Belfast to Long Kesh on Christmas day – it was stopped by a massive force of troops and RUC on the main M1 Motorway. The British army was given instructions to break up future demonstrations, and in many areas fighting with the troops took place. This was the situation when an anti-internment march was called by NICRA for Derry on Sunday 30 January 1972.

About 20,000 people turned out for this march. The British army sent in the First Battalion of the Parachute Regiment to prevent the march leaving the Bogside. Inevitably there were small skirmishes between the marchers and the army, but no shots were fired. Suddenly, near the end of the march, the army opened fire repeatedly into the crowd, then at people fleeing, then at others tending to the wounded. Thirteen civilians were killed, another was to die later from his wounds. Many were wounded. Several had been shot at close range on the ground and some in the back. All were civilians. The IRA had been instructed to keep away from the march after a request from the organisers and for the safety of the marchers. The IRA had not been on the march.

The British, as usual, claimed they had been fired on first, and had shot only gunmen and nail bombers. Four of the men dead, they claimed, were on their wanted list. The Parachute Regiment is a brutal, highly disciplined, highly trained assault force. Its commanding officer, Lieutenant-Colonel Wilford, had been forward with his troops. There could have been no mistakes. This was a shoot-to-kill operation, a planned cold-blooded murder of civilians, which had the aim of drawing out the IRA into a direct confrontation with the British army. It must have had the go-ahead from the Army Command and have been approved by the British government. The result was another 'Bloody Sunday' in Irish history.

The British government instituted the inevitable inquiry under Lord

Chief Justice Widgery – he had been a senior army officer himself and was admirably suited for the job. He fully exonerated the Parachute Regiment. He said they had been fired on first although 'none of the deceased or wounded is proved to have been shot whilst handling a firearm or bomb'.[20] He did, however, admit that some soldiers fired recklessly but put this down to their temperaments. The army was not guilty of murder. No disciplinary action was ever taken against the officers and men responsible for the killings. And to cap it all, Lieutenant-Colonel W i l - ford was decorated with the OBE for his services in the Six Counties!

After Bloody Sunday nationalist Ireland exploded. The guerrilla war intensified and in the next eight or nine days nearly 300 IRA operations were carried out. By mid-February another five British soldiers had been killed and many more wounded.

Tens of thousands of workers throughout Ireland stopped work and demonstrated in protest. Lynch was forced to declare 2 February, the day of the funerals of those murdered, a day of national mourning. On that day a 30,000 strong crowd marched to the British Embassy in Dublin and burnt it down. More than 20,000 attended the funerals which took place in the Bogside, Derry. 20,000 marched in London on 5 February, including many thousands of Irish workers and their families. The march was attacked by the police and 130 were arrested. Arrests took place in Oxford, York and Edinburgh as protests against the murders took place. Bernadette Devlin (McAliskey) attacked Maudling in the Westminster parliament and punched him in the face.

On 22 February the Official IRA bombed the Parachute Regiment's base at Aldershot, England, killing an Army Chaplain and six women cleaners. By mid-March 56 British soldiers had been killed and the centres of Belfast and other towns looked as though they had been blitzed. The Six Counties was rapidly becoming ungovernable. The British would have to do something to destroy the unity of the nationalist minority, and increased repression, it was now clear, could not succeed.

On 10 March 1972 the Provisional IRA ordered a unilateral 72-hour-truce. It was to demonstrate that the IRA was under effective control and discipline. A revised three-point peace plan was put out. It called for: (1) a withdrawal of British armed forces off the streets as a prelude to eventual evacuation, and a recognition of the right of the Irish people to self-determination; (2) abolition of Stormont; and (3) a total amnesty for political prisoners. If a positive response was received, the IRA's military operations would be suspended indefinitely. The British government did not reciprocate. They, on the contrary, took advantage and moved into nationalist areas making over 20 arrests.

Harold Wilson came to Ireland again in March, meeting the Dublin government and also having secret talks with leaders of the Provisional IRA. In an interview, he argued for all-party talks without limits on the agenda and called for a 'radical decision on internment'. He said the IRA 'had a disciplined, tightly-knit organisation and that their writ did run to the extent that a truce could be honoured'.[21] His remarks greatly angered the Loyalists.

The Loyalists wanted more repression to deal with the nationalist minority. A new political movement of loyalist organisations, Vanguard, was created and led by Craig. On 18 March it organised a 60,000 strong loyalist demonstration to oppose any further reform. Craig called for a dossier to be built up 'of the men and women who are a menace to this country' and said if the politicians failed them 'it may be our job to liquidate the enemy'.[22] Thousands marched in formation wearing paramilitary uniforms. Craig threatened to form a Provisional government if an initiative expected to be announced by the British government wasn't satisfactory.

On 24 March 1972 Heath announced the suspension of Stormont for one year. The British government would take over direct rule of the Six Counties. A British Secretary of State with Cabinet powers would be installed in Belfast – it was to be William Whitelaw. Stormont was destroyed. No-one could have any doubt that the Provisional IRA's military struggle had brought it down.

The Loyalists organised protests and strike-action, but they soon fizzled out. There were, in fact, no loyalist riots or serious clashes with the British army and certainly no 'Provisional government'.

The IRA had not fought to bring Stormont down in order to have it replaced by direct rule imposed by Westminster. The Provisionals announced that their military campaign would continue until their demands had been met. The Official IRA also said it would fight on. However, the SDLP, the Catholic Church, the Dublin government saw things in quite a different light. They welcomed direct rule and called for all IRA military operations to cease. British imperialism now had some room for manoeuvre. It would do all it could to prise open the cracks which the abolition of Stormont had created in the unity of the nationalist minority.

THE IRISH REVOLUTION AND THE BRITISH LEFT

The Labour Party, strongly backed by the organised trade union movement, had begun the assault on the Irish revolution as it entered its latest phase. When the American trade union movement was about to boycott trade with Britain in protest against the Bloody Sunday murders, it was Vic Feather, General Secretary of the TUC, who persuaded them to call it off. He was subsequently thanked by the Prime Minister, Edward Heath.[23] Given this background of a totally bankrupt pro-imperialist Labour and trade union movement in Britain, a great deal of responsibility for building a movement in solidarity with the Irish revolution had to fall on those organisations which considered themselves part of the revolutionary, socialist left. British communists and socialists were faced with a major test of their revolutionary credentials.

Before we go on to examine their response to the Irish war in the period 1969–72, it is necessary to say something more about certain individuals and groups on the Irish socialist left. We do this for one reason only. On many occasions the British left groups justified essentially backward and reactionary positions by reference to what Irish socialists were arguing and doing. McCann, Farrell, Bernadette Devlin (McAliskey) and other Irish socialists regularly write for British left publications and their views are often used directly or indirectly to attack the organisation leading the Irish revolution – the Provisional IRA.

Irish socialists, mainly drawn from the educated layers of Catholics who had benefited from the growth of the welfare state during the post-war period, have had very little influence on the direction of the Irish revolution. Certain individuals and groups, such as Peoples Democracy, did play a role in the Civil Rights campaign. However, once the struggle turned into a revolutionary war against British imperialism, once the main support for the struggle came from the nationalist working class, they became irrelevant. Essentially, they could not meet the challenge and sacrifices demanded by a revolutionary war against the loyalist state and British imperialism.

McCann, in his book *War and an Irish Town*, explains this. In the Civil Rights Movement, one issue had united them all – the need to reform the loyalist state:

'Partition was irrelevant ... we were not out to destroy the state but to achieve change within it – the extent of the change desired varying according to our different tendencies'.[24]

Essential to this position was the belief that British imperialism could play a progressive role in Ireland by forcing the Unionist government to introduce reforms. But the loyalist state could not be reformed and had to be destroyed. And it was not the 'socialists' but the working class youth in the nationalist areas who followed the logic of those posters in their windows depicting a clenched fist saying 'Never Again!'. In McCann's words:

> 'Never again were mobs, whether in uniform or not, going to be allowed to rampage through our streets shooting or petrol-bombing. The logic of that demanded a physical campaign against the state'.[25]

The 'socialists' tried to organise 'the unemployed youth of areas like the Bogside' – the force that was driving the Civil Rights Movement into inevitable confrontation with the state. But they offered the youth nothing but abstract formulas, programmes and organisations for fighting 'imperialism'. The imperialists were, however, down at the street corner and the youth kept asking 'when the guns were going to be handed out'. They instinctively grasped that the state had to be smashed. They were not against organisation as such but demanded a relevant one. They turned to the only organisation that represented *their* class interests – the Provisional IRA.

> 'When raging bitterness swamped the ghettos and carried partition onto the centre of the political stage, no support flowed over into the socialist camp . . . The Provisionals are the inrush which filled the vacuum left by the *absence* of a socialist option'.[26]

McCann's explanation is incomplete and, therefore, wrong. There is no socialist option *separate* from the national liberation struggle to drive British imperialism out of Ireland and *separate* from the revolutionary war to bring this about. What McCann and his friends were looking for was the non-existent middle course, a radical reformist option between the middle class orientated Civil Rights Movement for reforms, which failed, and the political confrontation with partition and British imperialism, which, given the nature of imperialism, *necessarily* required a turn to armed struggle.

The position of the Irish socialists on every major political question stemmed from their class position, which expressed itself in a belief that British imperialism could play a progressive role in Ireland. And this is their real point of contact with the British middle class socialist left.

Our Irish 'socialists', the CPGB, Socialist Workers Party (SWP), International Marxist Group (IMG) together with most of the British left all agree on one essential thing. British imperialism has an 'economic' interest in reuniting Ireland and this goal is put in danger by the intransigence of the sectarian bigots who run the loyalist state. So, for example, *Socialist Worker* could argue:

'Britain has more money invested in the South than in the North . . .
The Ulster police state is an embarrassment and an obstacle to (the)
ultimate goal: a united capitalist Ireland subjected *as a whole* to the
domination of British capital, possibly in the context of the
Common Market'.[27]

Why the partition of Ireland, which was carried out precisely to *preserve* Britain's economic interests in Ireland and to *divide* the Irish
working class (surely an important *political* consideration), should
now be a barrier to imperialist exploitation of the 'whole of Ireland' is
never actually explained.

The logic of this so-called 'socialist' position is to support British
imperialist intervention in the Six Counties. So Bernadette Devlin
(McAliskey) sent a telegram to Harold Wilson on 5 August 1969 calling
on the British government to take over housing and police. The CPGB
called for decisive intervention from London – it called on British
imperialism to reform the loyalist police state! When the troops were
sent in, it continued with this line.[28] This was 'socialist' colonial policy
all over again (see chapter 2). The Militant Tendency, as always fully
behind Labour-imperialist policy, supported the introduction of the
troops under the guise of concern lest there be a bloodbath.

'A slaughter would have followed in comparison with which the
blood-letting in Belfast would have paled into insignificance if the
Labour Government had not intervened with British troops'.[29]

Finally, *Socialist Worker* showed the same deep concern urging the
nationalist minority to accept the troops

'Because the troops do not have the ingrained hatreds of the RUC
and Specials, they will not behave with the same viciousness . . .
    The breathing space provided by the presence of British troops is
short but vital. Those who call for the immediate withdrawal of the
troops before the men behind the barricades can defend themselves
are inviting a pogrom which will hit first and hardest at socialists . . .
To say that the *immediate* enemy in Ulster is the British troops is
incorrect . . . '[30]

This fundamental belief that the SWP has in a progressive side to
imperialism was confirmed when the demand for the withdrawal of
British troops from abroad was dropped from the 'Where We Stand'
column in *Socialist Worker*. Today the SWP still justifies this position
by taking cowardly refuge behind an 'internationalism' which, at that
time, required 'having the same position as comrades in Ireland'.[31]

When the IRA split over the recognition of the imperialist parliaments, and the need to organise armed struggle to end partition and drive British imperialism out of Ireland, most of the British left took the Official IRA's side, and began to systematically attack the Provisional IRA. So the IMG studiously informed us:

'The Official Republican Movement ... is ... the most important socialist organisation in Ireland today. We think that in the long term, they will play a much greater role in liberating Ireland than will the Provisionals.'[32]

And *Socialist Worker* tells us that although:

' ... at present the militancy of many young workers takes the form of support for the "provisional" wing of the republican movement ... this wing ... is hostile to revolutionary socialism. But the Provisionals are unable to lead the militants out of the blind alley of brave but fruitless street confrontations with the troops ... They are unable to provide a political lead.'[33]

They, of course, had criticisms of the 'Officials' and argued that although they had taken a good line in 'denouncing Catholic bigotry', their 'Dublin leadership has not been willing to follow through the logic of its position'. Well, no doubt *Socialist Worker* was relieved when later it did. However, it went much further than the British left did and *completely* drew out the reactionary logic of seeing a progressive side to British imperialism. The Official IRA was soon to give up the armed struggle, and become Sinn Fein, The Workers Party, a pro-imperialist, pro-Stormont rump of reactionaries.

Finally, when the Official IRA bombed the Aldershot barracks after Bloody Sunday, the British left showed where it really stood. IRA bombing campaigns were soon to unite them all. So the *Morning Star*:

'The real fight against those responsible for the Derry shootings will be hindered not helped by bombings such as that carried out at Aldershot yesterday ... They make more difficult the forging of unity between the working people of Britain and ... Northern Ireland.'[34]

The *Socialist Worker* agreed:

'The official wing of the IRA ... has done nothing by this act [Aldershot] to weaken the Tory government ... A policy of individual terrorism has nothing in common with the socialist aim of building a mass working-class movement'.[35]

And finally the Socialist Labour League, forerunner of the Workers Revolutionary Party:

'WE CONDEMN THE BOMBING . . . until now the Official IRA has opposed the reactionary, indiscriminate violence of the Provisionals . . . the terror of the oppressor cannot be overcome by terror from the oppressed . . . '[36]

The one exception, at this time, to the outright condemnation of the bombings was the IMG. Arguing correctly that '*all* the violence in Ireland stems from imperialist oppression', Bob Purdie then said:

'The oppressed minority, through its armed vanguard the IRA, will be forced to reply to oppression in equally, if not *more* violent terms . . . Aldershot was a legitimate military target despite the tragedy of civilian deaths.'[37]

This position was not maintained. As the revolutionary war continued, the IMG was soon to join the rest of the left in condemning the Provisional IRA.

Building an Irish solidarity movement in Britain was never an important political concern of the British left. The ones that did come into existence in the period 1969−72 reflected the essentially middle class character of the British socialist left with its ambivalent attitude to British imperialism.

The Irish Solidarity Campaign was founded on 9/10 October 1970. The main organisations involved were the IMG, International Socialists (SWP), and Clan na hEireann (an Official IRA support group). It called for self-determination for the Irish people; the release of all political prisoners; the immediate withdrawal of troops; it supported the right of the Irish people to arm and organise self-defence; and opposed those fostering religious sectarianism in Ireland and preventing working class unity. The latter two of these positions were implicit attacks on the Provisional IRA, not surprisingly since the 'Officials' were working in the organisation. The mythology has it that the Provisionals supported offensive action against British imperialism while the Officials only defensive, although Aldershot took some explaining. The Provisionals were often described as sectarian Catholic nationalists by the British left. This was nothing but an Official IRA slander.

The ISC represented very little and did even less. A dispute between the IMG and IS(SWP) dominated its existence. The IMG in those days called for 'Victory to the IRA' whereas the IS(SWP) argued for 'unconditional but not uncritical support for the IRA'. When internment came and the left had to respond in some practical way, we soon saw what this division was all about.

The IS(SWP) established the Labour Committee Against Internment (LCAI). Its first act was to betray the internees in order to build an alliance with the Labour Party 'left'. It called for the release *or trial* of the internees. The signatories to the LCAI included Frank Allaun, Sydney Bidwell (who in 1981 told Tariq Ali to go back to Pakistan), Eric Heffer, Arthur Latham, Joan Lestor, Michael Meacher (who voted for the PTA in March 1977), and Jock Stallard. This open abandonment of the internees, who wanted no trials conducted by British imperialism but only their freedom, was defended by the IS(SWP) using an argument that has become a cover for the left's reactionary positions ever since.

'The LCAI was set up at the request of socialists in Northern Ireland, who appealed to the British labour movement to arouse the maximum possible protest at conditions there . . .

'*Socialist Worker* and the International Socialists fully support the LCAI and we are willing to participate in the campaign regardless of the differences we may have with some signatories on many issues.'[38]

So hiding behind Irish socialists, IS(SWP) set up a campaign with a fundamentally reactionary demand for release or trial of the internees. This not only implies the possibility of a 'fair trial' under imperialist rule, but also allowed them to construct one of their many rotten alliances with those so-called 'progressive' imperialist forces – the British Labour Party 'left'.

The LCAI achieved nothing and was pushed into oblivion by the Anti-Internment League (AIL) which called for the release of all internees. Given its principled position, the AIL was able to organise significant support among the Irish community in Britain for this demand. However, following Bloody Sunday, and given its relative success, the British ruling class decided to smash the campaign in Britain.

The Saturday following Bloody Sunday, 5 February 1972, a massive demonstration of 20,000 people called by the AIL marched from Cricklewood to Whitehall. The march was composed mainly of Irish workers, students and the middle class socialist left. There was little support from the British working class. In Whitehall, the police reneged on an agreement to allow thirteen coffins to be carried into Downing Street. A Union Jack was burned. Immediately, a flying wedge of police smashed into the march and mounted police attacked it from both ends. Chaos ensued. Fighting with the police broke out along Whitehall, into Trafalgar Square and as far as Piccadilly. Over 100 marchers were injured and 130 arrested. The next morning, three of the organisers were arrested in dawn raids.

Faced with the need to confront the state in order to oppose British rule in Ireland, the British middle class socialist left retreated. Never again was there a march of such a siz?.

Over the next ten years, and especially after the IRA military campaign in Britain began, that retreat turned into headlong flight. Rather than confront British imperialism, the British middle class socialist left has attacked the Republican Movement, denounced the armed struggle and betrayed every later attempt to build a mass anti-imperialist movement in Britain.

NOTES

1   The Sunday Times Insight Team, *op cit* pp. 227–228.
2   *ibid* p. 244.
3   *ibid* p. 245. Also Provisional IRA, *op cit* p. 28.
4   *ibid* p. 248.
5   Provisional IRA, *op cit* p. 34.
6   Farrell M, *op cit* p. 279. Also Deutsch R and Magowan V, *op cit* Volume 1 p. 107.
7   McGuffin J, *The Guineapigs* London 1974 p.45. Also The Sunday Times Insight Team, *op cit* pp. 263–264.
8   Kelly H, *op cit* p. 66.
9   Mac Stiofain S, *op cit* p. 184.
10 *ibid* p. 187.
11 McGuffin J, *op cit* p. 61.
12 *ibid* p. 90. Much of the time material on the Compton Report is taken from this book Chapter 5.
13 *ibid* p. 159.
14 Deutsch R and Magowan V, *op cit* Volume 1 p. 139.
15 McGuffin J, *op cit* p. 105.
16 Mac Stiofain S, *op cit* p. 203.
17 Deutsch R and Magowan V, *op cit* Volume 1 p. 128.
18 Faul D and Murray R, *The Castlereagh File* Dungannon 1978 p. 9.
19 Mac Stiofain S, *op cit* pp. 221–222. Also Provisional IRA, *op cit* p. 43.
20 Deutsch R and Magowan V, *op cit* Volume 2 p. 371.
21 *ibid* pp. 161–2.
22 *ibid* p. 163.
23 Faul D and Murray R, *The Shame of Merlyn Rees* Dungannon 1975 p. 38.
24 McCann E, *op cit* p. 134.
25 *ibid*.
26 *ibid* p. 135.
27 *Socialist Worker* 18 September 1969.

28   *Morning Star* 4 August and 15 August 1969.
29   *Militant* September 1969.
30   *Socialist Worker* 21 August, 11 September, 18 September 1969.
31   Birchall I, *'The smallest mass party in the world' Building the Socialist Workers Party 1951–1979* London 1981 p. 17 (pamphlet).
32   *Red Mole* 23 March 1971.
33   *Socialist Worker* 15 August 1970.
34   *Morning Star* 23 February 1972.
35   *Socialist Worker* 26 February 1972.
36   *Workers Press* 24 February 1972.
37   *Red Mole* 13 March 1972.
38   *Socialist Worker* 4 September 1971.

CHAPTER TEN

THE LONG WAR

The fall of Stormont in March 1972 changed little. The Provisional
IRA knew that direct rule from Westminster would not satisfy the
needs of the nationalist minority. And as Sean Mac Stiofain later said:

> '... there was not an iota of difference, of course, in the behaviour
> of the British troops towards the people who were supposed to be
> receiving all the imaginary benefits of direct rule. A rifle butt in the
> stomach or an insult to passing women felt much the same along the
> Falls, whether the troops delivered it under Faulkner or the new Sec-
> retary of State, William Whitelaw . . . It was not the pundits who had
> to trek out to the concentration camp at Lisburn, taking children to
> see their fathers after long waits and humiliating jeers from the
> camp guards.'[1]

The Provisionals' military campaign would continue until Ireland was
free from British rule.

British imperialism still faced the acute problem of drawing support
away from the Provisionals. The fall of Stormont had led to a clamour
from the SDLP, the Dublin government and the Catholic Church for
the IRA to cease military operations. The British government knew it
had to build on this. It had to undermine the unity of the nationalist
minority if it was to destroy the Provisional IRA. For it was the Provisionals who posed the only serious threat to British imperialism's continued domination over the whole of Ireland.

To undermine the unity of the nationalist minority, the British
government continued with the age old imperialist technique of the
'carrot' and the 'stick'. It would attempt to buy off the bourgeois
nationalists of the SDLP and their supporters with the 'carrot' of
power-sharing and the status and privileges of office which went along

with this. The nationalist minority, however, would be 'discouraged' from continued support for the Provisional IRA by finding itself at the receiving end of a great deal of official and 'unofficial' British government directed 'stick'. Internment without trial would continue, later being replaced by judicial internment – systematic torture in police cells, long remands, Diplock courts and imprisonment in specially built concentration camps. British army and RUC terror and harassment of the nationalist minority, including the use of under-cover assassination squads, were to be regulated to the degree and extent the overall situation required. And when not facing the full force of official British state terror, the nationalist minority had to confront the 'unofficial' terror of loyalist paramilitary organisations. Finally, throughout this whole period, there was a barrage of lies and propaganda from both official and 'unofficial' British sources, directed against the Provisional IRA.

TRUCE

In April and May, the Provisional IRA campaign intensified with sabotage operations against 'the colonial economic structure' and attacks on the British army and security forces. 40 bombs were planted on 13 and 14 April, hitting car showrooms, telephone exchanges, a bus station and other business premises. The big Courtaulds factory at Carrickfergus was bombed on 1 May and the Belfast Co-op, the biggest department store in the city, was blown up and destroyed on 10 May. The use of the car bomb increased. During April and May, sixteen British soldiers were killed in the Six Counties.

Early in May, Republican prisoners in Crumlin Road gaol went on hunger strike to back up their demands for political status. Five started the strike and they were to be joined by five more each week until the issue was decided. The leaders of the strike were the popular Provisionals Billy McKee and Proinsias MacArt, who had been sentenced to three years imprisonment having been framed by the army on an arms charge. As the strike progressed, meetings and demonstrations took place throughout the Six Counties. Tension built up in Republican areas and street fights with the army and police frequently occurred.

In the South, the Fianna Fail administration went on the offensive against the IRA. After people in the Irish Republic overwhelmingly voted to join the Common Market against Republican advice, Lynch felt himself strong enough to directly attack the IRA. He introduced an Emergency Bill to enable civilian prisoners to be transferred to military custody, after Republican prisoners had taken over the inner section of the Mountjoy gaol on 18 May and released scores of prisoners in protest against prison conditions in the gaol. He followed this, at the end of May, with the reintroduction of part V of the Offences Against the State Act, which allowed the setting up of Special Courts consisting of three judges sitting without a jury. After raids by the Gardai and Special Branch, leading Provisionals, including Ruairi O'Bradaigh and Joe Cahill, were arrested. They were released after a hunger strike of thirteen and nineteen days respectively. The Provisional IRA GHQ were forced underground. Many Provisionals, however, were to be arrested and imprisoned after passing through these Special Courts.

Throughout this period, pressure for an unconditional ceasefire by the IRA came from mainly middle-class Catholics, the Dublin government and Church leaders. Speeches, meetings, protests along these lines, however insignificant, were given great publicity by the pro-British, pro-Unionist media. These protests received an enormous propaganda boost after the Official IRA executed Ranger William Best, a young local Derry man home on leave from the British army. He was stationed in Germany with the Royal Irish Rangers, one of the regiments the British could not trust for work in the Six Counties. Mac Stiofain says that the Provisional IRA had information that Ranger Best had frequently been out at night stoning British troops and that he was not going to return to his base in Germany. Mac Stiofain thought that the Official IRA must surely have been told this when they took him away.[2]

There was bitter reaction to the killing in the Bogside and angry local women took over the headquarters of the Officials and formed a 'movement for peace'. The Church, press and television used the occasion to whip up anti-IRA hysteria. The 'peace at any price' brigade was reinforced by these developments. There were, however, large counter-demonstrations against this 'peace' movement, including a very large one by Provisional volunteers and supporters, but the calls for a ceasefire by political opportunists of all kinds inevitably increased. As Mac Stiofain, with some justification later said, 'this stupid killing had given them [the political opportunists] a chance to promote division and dissension in the midst of the most successful no-go area in the entire North'.[3]

The pressure for a one-sided ceasefire by the IRA built up. Peace pickets paraded outside the Sinn Fein offices in Kevin Street, Dublin. While the Provisionals and their supporters stood firm in the face of this pressure, the Official IRA did not. On the evening of 29 May, the

Official IRA announced that it would terminate all military action. No terms were mentioned. Since ninety per cent of all operational activities were carried out by the Provisional IRA, the overall effect of the decision was insignificant. The popularity and political base of the Official IRA was not strengthened. The Provisional IRA was able to intensify its campaign and during the next four weeks casualties suffered by British troops were the biggest for any month since the start of the campaign. During May, according to British figures, there were 1,223 engagements and shooting incidents and ninety-four explosions. The sabotage operations were increasingly disrupting the day-to-day functioning of direct rule. As June began, the IRA stepped up the level of its offensive.

In the second week of June, a new and more serious peace proposal was put before the IRA leadership. It came from Republican activists in Derry and had the agreement of the local IRA military leadership. It was that the Provisional IRA should hold a press conference inside the Free Derry area and agree to suspend offensive operations for a seven-day period provided that Whitelaw agreed publicly to meet the IRA. The proposal was a good one. It gave an opportunity for the Provisionals to put their terms for a peace settlement formally to the British government. It offered a truce that was not unconditional, not one-sided and not for an indefinite period. From the military standpoint, it was a good time as the Provisional IRA were strong and were causing a great deal of damage and disruption to the economic life of the Six Counties. Finally, it shifted the whole responsibility for a peace settlement back where it belonged, in the court of the British government. For, if the British now refused, it would show millions of people that the British government was more interested in destroying Irish resistance to British rule than in a peaceful settlement.

The Provisional IRA leadership agreed to accept the proposal. On Wednesday 13 June, Sean Mac Stiofain, David O'Connell, Seamus Twomey and Martin McGuinness gave a press conference in the no-go area of Free Derry and announced their offer of a truce.

Whitelaw responded quickly. He issued a statement that same evening rejecting the truce offer on the grounds that he ruled out any meetings with 'terrorists'. However, at the time of the press conference it emerged that Whitelaw had personally received members of the Ulster Defence Association (UDA) inner council in a meeting held at their request. The men had arrived at Stormont Castle, hooded and masked, and wearing sun glasses. So Whitelaw was prepared to meet leaders of the UDA, a loyalist paramilitary organisation, which was directly responsible for the campaign of sectarian murders of Catholics which had begun in the Spring of 1972 (see chapter 11). It appeared that he was not prepared to meet the legitimate leaders of the nationalist minority.

After the failure of this public approach, two SDLP members, John Hume and Paddy Devlin, suggested to the IRA that they should approach Whitelaw and make it clear to him that the IRA were serious about a truce. This was agreed.

They came back saying that Whitelaw would like a meeting with the Provisional leadership but this was 'not possible immediately'. However, a preliminary meeting held in secret with members of Whitelaw's staff was suggested. In reply, the IRA laid down four conditions if there was to be a meeting to discuss a truce. The first was the granting of political status for Republican prisoners in the Six Counties, some of whom had been on hunger strike now for nearly five weeks. Second, there were to be no restrictions on the choice of Republican representatives – the British to accept those nominated. Third, Stormont Castle was not an acceptable venue. Finally, the meeting was to be confined to the British representatives and the Provisional IRA (the SDLP had tried to get in on the act) with a mutually acceptable third party, who would not be a politician, to act as a witness. David O'Connell and Gerry Adams were nominated as representatives – the latter being at that time under detention in Long Kesh. John Hume took the terms back to Whitelaw and he accepted them all. As Mac Stiofain later said, 'within hours of publicly refusing to treat with terrorists, the British were secretly agreeing to discuss a truce with us'.[4]

Gerry Adams was released from Long Kesh and an announcement was made that the political prisoners would be given political status – called 'Special Category' status. This included the right of political prisoners to wear their own clothes, the right to abstain from penal labour, the right to free association, the right to educational and recreational activities and the restoration of lost remission resulting from the prison protest. The hunger strike ended. The Special Category status was also given to UVF and other loyalist prisoners.

On 20 June David O'Connell and Gerry Adams met Whitelaw's two representatives Philip Woodfield and Frank Steele at a secret meeting place outside Derry. There they agreed to a bilateral truce with hostilities ceasing on both sides. The IRA were to enjoy freedom of movement on the streets and the right to bear arms, as were the British. There were to be no arrests, raids, searches of persons, homes and vehicles. After ten clear days of the truce being effective, a secret meeting between the

Provisional IRA and Whitelaw would take place to discuss the IRA's conditions for ending operations altogether.

A statement was issued on Thursday 22 June announcing that the Provisional IRA would suspend offensive operations from midnight Monday 26 June provided that a public reciprocal response was forthcoming from the Armed Forces of the British Crown. Whitelaw announced that the British forces would reciprocate.

Republican intelligence – including that from a highly effective telephone tapping operation – had reported that high-ranking RUC officers and senior British army personnel had been saying that the IRA had agreed to talks because they were on their last legs. The IRA leadership decided to make it abundantly clear to all concerned that they were not negotiating from a position of weakness. All IRA units were instructed to continue in action up to the final minute of the agreed truce. In the period leading up to the truce, four British soldiers and an RUC man were killed, the last soldier being shot at 23.55 hours on Monday, five minutes before the truce was to begin. At midnight Monday 26 June 1972, all IRA operations ceased and the truce began.

A week after the truce started, the British had still not informed the Provisional IRA of the arrangements for the meeting with Whitelaw. The IRA then contacted the British representatives by telephone, using agreed numbers, and after some haggling by the British, a meeting was arranged for Friday 7 July in London.

On that date the Provisionals' representatives Sean Mac Stiofain, David O'Connell, Seamus Twomey, Martin McGuinness, Gerry Adams and Ivor Bell were flown to London for the secret meeting with William Whitelaw and other British government officials. Two of the Provisional IRA carried arms. Myles Shelvin, a Dublin lawyer, joined the meeting acting as secretary to the delegation.

They met Whitelaw in a private house in Chelsea belonging to Paul Channon, heir to the Guinness fortunes and one of Whitelaw's junior ministers. This was the first time that representatives of the IRA had fought their way to a conference with the British for over fifty years. This fact alone confirms that the imperialist propaganda about 'isolated gunmen' was, and is, a straightforward lie. The fact that the British felt obliged to negotiate with the IRA was proof that the IRA had the volunteers, the equipment and the mass support to wage war for as long as necessary.

At the meeting, the Provisionals' delegation placed a number of demands before the British government for negotiation. They were that:

1. The British government recognise publicly that it is the right of the people of Ireland acting as a unit to decide the future of Ireland.
2. The British government declare its intention to withdraw all British forces from Irish soil, such withdrawal to be completed on or before the first day of January 1975. Pending such withdrawal, the British forces must be withdrawn immediately from sensitive areas.
3. A call for a general amnesty for all political prisoners in Irish and British jails, for all internees and detainees and for all persons on the wanted list. In this regard, dissatisfaction was expressed that internment had not ended in response to the IRA initiative in declaring a suspension of offensive operations.

There were two clashes between the two sides at the meeting. The first was when Whitelaw had the effrontery to say that British troops would never open fire on unarmed civilians. He was promptly and forcefully reminded of Bloody Sunday, and told of several other occasions when this had occurred. The second concerned all-Ireland elections to decide the future of Ireland. Whitelaw brought up the 'constitutional guarantees to the majority in Northern Ireland'. He was told that it was the Government of Ireland Act 1949, passed in the British House of Commons, which guaranteed the constitutional position. And any Act of Parliament could be set aside by another through a simple majority in the same House of Commons.

Whitelaw was given a week to raise the demands with the Tory Cabinet and give an answer to them at a meeting planned for 14 July. The truce was now open-ended with each side to give 24 hours' notice of intention to break it. Whitelaw agreed. He was told that the Ulster Defence Regiment (UDR) had already violated the truce agreement by setting up roadblocks and searches. He agreed to do something about this. Whitelaw also said that the sectarian assassinations and intimidation of Catholics by loyalist paramilitary organisations – there were to be 18 sectarian murders by loyalist organisations during the fourteen days of the truce – would be brought to an end and Catholics in UDA 'no-go' areas would be protected by the British army. Finally, further contact was to be made through his officials and the meeting was to remain secret.

An off the cuff remark by one of Whitelaw's officials on the flight back to Belfast exposed the attitude of the British ruling class to the lives of British soldiers. Frank Steele, when discussing a possible resumption of the war, said 'Don't think you're worrying us with the casualties you're causing our troops at the moment . . . we lose more men through road accidents in Germany in any one year than the losses you fellows are inflicting on us'.[5] That twenty British soldiers had been killed and many injured in the last three weeks was of little concern to him and the ruling class he represented.

BRITISH IMPERIALISM BREAKS THE TRUCE

The truce was to last only two more days. The British did nothing about the sectarian assassinations and allowed the UDA to put up barricades in parts of Belfast while bulldozing nationalist ones down in Portadown. Two British army captains who had been detained by IRA volunteers after penetrating Free Derry the night before the London meeting, had been released the next day. However, two IRA volunteers from Belfast who had been arrested, in spite of telephone calls to the British representatives, were still detained two days later. The matter finally came to a head on the Lenadoon housing estate in West Belfast.

A few Catholic families who had lost their homes or had been forced to move through intimidation were allocated empty houses on the Lenadoon estate – a mixed estate. The UDA brought reinforcements into Lenadoon from outside areas and informed the British army that if Catholics moved into the houses, they would be burned out. The British army commander gave into UDA threats not allowing any more Catholic families to take up the homes allocated and so overriding the civilian authority – the Northern Ireland Housing Executive. The British army then barricaded the area. People and cars in the area were stopped and roughly searched while UDA men, some carrying arms, stood behind the British troops and looked on and jeered. When on Sunday 9 July a ten-ton British armoured car rammed a lorry containing the furniture of some of the families – the incident was televised – an angry crowd of Catholics gathered. They were attacked by troops who fired rubber bullets, water-cannon and CS gas at them. Shots were soon fired. The truce had been broken by the actions of the British army.

Efforts were made throughout the weekend to contact the British representatives and finally Whitelaw himself. When Whitelaw was eventually contacted early on Sunday evening, he said he would look into the crisis. Nothing further was heard from him. The Provisional IRA had no choice. That evening, they announced the termination of the truce and instructions were sent out to all areas to resume operations at once.

An attempt was made by Harold Wilson, then leader of the Labour opposition, to try and get the truce going again. Three representatives of the Provisionals including Joe Cahill, flew to a private air field near Wilson's home in Buckinghamshire in a chartered plane on 18 July 1972.[6] The talks came to nothing when it became clear that Wilson was not speaking on behalf of Whitelaw or the British government. Wilson never made any attempt to negotiate with the Provisionals again. No doubt when he had the power and authority to do so, his real intentions would have easily been exposed.

An imperialist government will not negotiate with representatives of a revolutionary movement without being under enormous pressure to do so. The IRA had been inflicting serious casualties on the British army and substantial damage to the Six Counties economy. Until the truce, the British had been using the people's desire for peace for their own propaganda campaign against the IRA. When this was exposed with a serious offer of a truce and peace negotiations by the Provisional IRA, the British had little choice but to go through the motions of acting on it. The Provisional IRA had also distributed their democratic programme *Eire Nua* just after the truce began. They had nearly 300,000 copies printed in English and Irish. This programme included religious and political guarantees and rights for the Protestant minority in a united Ireland and proposed four regional Parliaments including one for the nine counties of Ulster. It amounted to a serious peace proposal which could not simply be ignored.

The ending of the truce by the British government was deliberate. They needed only some pretext to do so. The dispute at the Lenadoon housing estate served their purpose. The British government built up the hopes of the nationalist minority only to smash them down again. The nationalist people wanted peace. The British wanted only to destroy the IRA – the only force to challenge their rule over the whole of Ireland. The British refused to take on the UDA and curb the loyalist assassination squads because it served their purpose not to do so.

Within a day of the truce ending, the British shot six civilians dead. In Ballymurphy this included a boy and a girl of thirteen. As the boy lay dying in the road, an elderly priest went out to him and was also shot dead. The UDA and other armed loyalists joined behind British troops in attacking nationalist areas. Many Catholic women and children fled to the South as refugees. And all the while the loyalist assassination squads continued their brutal work murdering another 13 Catholics before the end of July.

The IRA hit back hard and the British paid very dearly for destroying the truce. In the first eight days after the truce ended, the British lost at least 15 soldiers killed and over a hundred injured. In the next two weeks, they lost another ten dead. The sabotage offensive was renewed. One of its principal aims was to tie down as many British troops as possible on guard duties in the cities and towns, keeping them off the backs of the nationalist population and from being used against IRA units in rural areas. On Friday 21 July a major bombing offensive took place with 22 operations in Belfast in a period of 45 minutes within a one-mile radius of the city centre. There were 13 operations elsewhere in the Six Counties. In all cases warnings were given. But in two places in Belfast, Cavehill Road and Oxford Street, they were ignored. Nine people were killed – two were British soldiers, of the other seven one was a RUC reserve policeman, another a member of a militant loyalist organisation and five were civilians. Many people were injured.

Statements were immediately put out by the Belfast Brigade IRA accepting responsibility for the bombs, saying that warnings had been given in all cases, and that responsibility for loss of life rested with the British who failed to pass the warnings on. At first the British put out a statement, and Whitelaw stated on television, that in the two cases no warnings were given. Later this was retracted when undeniable evidence to the contrary was produced. The Samaritans, the Public Protection Agency and the Press were informed of the bomb positions at least 30 minutes before the explosions. The *Irish News* later said that they had confirmed with the agencies concerned that the warning of a bomb in Cavehill Road was given an hour and 13 minutes before the blast, and in Oxford Street 30 minutes before it happened. In both cases, the information had been immediately passed on to the security forces. The Republican Movement was convinced that the British had deliberately disregarded these two warnings in order to weaken support for the IRA among the nationalist population. In a pamphlet 'Friday – the Facts', put out by Sinn Fein a week after the bombings, after explaining what had happened they then reminded the nationalist minority,

'The Republican Movement, unlike the British, always admits the truth whether it is distasteful or not. We do not cloud the issue by false reports based on half-truths. For years now English politicians have told lie after lie about events in Northern Ireland. These run in a long list – the Widgery report, the Compton report and now "the Whitelaw Report", a report of events as distorted as all the others.

No one who has studied the situation in the last three years can deny that the British are liars, with the intention of splitting the people. When has the Republican Movement lied to the people? Why should they lie to the people? The people are the Republican Movement. We extend sincere sympathy to the relatives of those who died so needlessly.'[7]

Over the next few days, British troops launched attacks on five nationalist areas in Belfast and gun battles took place. On 27 July an increase in the number of British troops in the Six Counties of 4,000 to 21,000 was announced. On the 30 July, Whitelaw issued a statement that there would be 'substantial activity' by security forces in various parts of the Six Counties and he advised people to keep off the streets.[8]

There had been a great deal of British and Unionist propaganda about the unacceptability of the no-go areas in Derry and Belfast over recent weeks. It was clear that the aftermath of the tragedy of the bombings in Belfast was going to be used by the British as an opportunity to launch an attack on these areas. No doubt the British hoped that the Provisional IRA would come out into the open to defend them.

The Provisional IRA had no intention of a static defence of these areas against what would be a strong armoured British force. As Mac Stiofain later made clear, it 'would have been completely contrary to all the principles of guerrilla warfare'.[9] So that when 'Operation Motorman' began and thousands of extra troops and many hundreds of armoured vehicles moved at 4.30am on 31 July into Free Derry and the Belfast no-go areas, they met with no resistance from the IRA. In fact, the troops were often sitting targets as their huge heavy tanks and other vehicles got stuck in the tiny streets and British officers ran up and down shouting at the drivers. But, given the troop concentrations, to start a shooting match could only have led to serious casualties among the civilian population. As it was, the British killed two young men as they came into Derry and showed typical imperialist arrogance by commandeering schools and community centres and using them as barracks. The no-go areas were down but the IRA remained intact.

The same day, three car bombs exploded in the village of Claudy, Co Derry, killing six local people and injuring many more. The IRA were, of course, blamed but they completely disclaimed responsibility. In a statement on the bombings, the IRA pointed out that 'such actions can only suit the British Military to divert attention away from their mass invasion of nationalist Derry, Belfast and other towns'.[10] Later, information which came out concerning the under-cover activities of the Littlejohn brothers for the British security forces, showed only too clearly how the British were using *agents provocateurs* and other free-lance groups for their own propaganda ends.

The events since the truce ended – the casualties inflicted in Belfast when the bomb warnings were not passed on – allowed the British to go on the offensive. From now on, there would be no discussions with the IRA.

The British government now began a period of political manoeuvring to isolate the IRA and undermine its support in the nationalist minority. But to do this, it needed to offer the anti-IRA sections of the minority a viable alternative. However, such an alternative, promising once again to reform the Six Counties statelet, would meet the inevitable opposition from the organised loyalist forces which were determined to defend the privileges and status of the Protestant majority.

THE RISE AND FALL OF POWER-SHARING

The SDLP had been pushed off the political stage ever since they were forced to leave Stormont in July 1971. Since the fall of Stormont they had been using every opportunity to worm their way back again. On the 25 May 1972, an 'Advisory Commission' was announced consisting of 11 persons 'fully representative of opinion' in Northern Ireland (ie middle class opinion) to assist the Secretary of State in his duties. Next day, the SDLP offered a 'positive response' to what Mac Stiofain aptly termed 'Whitelaw's latest colonial reform stunt'.[11] The SDLP urged those who had withdrawn their support from public bodies after internment to return to their positions 'to demonstrate their determination to bring about community reconciliation'.[12] However, conditions were still not ripe for the SDLP to have formal negotiations with William Whitelaw and the British imperialist administration. Some more bait would be necessary and some move on internment before the craven opportunists of the SDLP would feel safe to conduct their betrayal of the nationalist minority more publicly.

On 15 June, two days after the Provisionals' press conference in Free Derry offering a truce, Whitelaw announced he proposed to hold a 'Conference of the People of Northern Ireland' on the future of the province and further that local government elections would be held on the basis of proportional representation.[13] The imperialists were dangling their bait. After the truce was over, and after the effects of the tragic deaths in Belfast on 21 July, the SDLP began to bite.

On 7 August after consultations with Dublin, the SDLP held their first meeting with Whitelaw. Internment, security, army searches, and the occupation by troops of schools in nationalist areas were some of the topics raised. After the meeting, the SDLP issued a statement saying that the release that day of another 47 men from Long Kesh camp was not adequate and they called for a complete end to internment. There were still 283 men interned. In the meantime they urged their constituents to continue with their 'admirable restraint in the present situation'.[14] Two days later, during demonstrations and protests on the first anniversary of the introduction of internment, effigies of SDLP members Gerry Fitt and Paddy Devlin were burned on the Falls Road.

On 3 August Whitelaw had had talks in London with the Irish Foreign Minister. On 4 September Lynch met Heath at the Munich Olympic Games. During the talks, Heath raised the matter of 'IRA bases' in the Twenty Six Counties 'from which raids into Northern Ireland could be mounted'.[15] It would not be long before Fianna Fail would comply with their colonial masters' demands to remove them. On 12 September the SDLP met Heath and Whitelaw in London and during discussions they informed him that they could not attend the planned 'Conference of the People of Northern Ireland', scheduled for 25 September in Darlington, Co Durham, as no agreement had been reached on the ending of internment. The conference took place and predictably produced nothing since the SDLP did not attend. The British government would need to offer a tiny bit more before the SDLP would feel able to do its bidding. More secret meetings between the collaborating parties took place and negotiating positions were laid down. On 20 September, the SDLP produced a policy document *Towards a New Ireland* which called for dual British-Irish sovereignty over the Six Counties and a British declaration in favour of eventual unity of Ireland.

On 30 October 1972 the British government produced a Green Paper – *The Future of Northern Ireland*, a paper for discussion. They also announced that the border poll – promised when Stormont was suspended – would take place in Spring 1973. The Green Paper contained the usual and fundamental commitment to maintaining the existence of the sectarian statelet:

'The guarantee to the people of Northern Ireland that the status of Northern Ireland as part of the United Kingdom will not be changed without their consent is an absolute: this pledge cannot and will not be set aside.'[16]

But the Green Paper warned with a cynical frankness that:

'...there is no hope of binding the minority to the support of new political arrangements in Northern Ireland unless they are admitted to active participation in any new structures.'[17]

At last, this offered the 'carrot' the SDLP had been longing to bite. For the Green Paper went on to say that there were:

'...strong arguments that the objective of real participation should be achieved by giving minority interests a share in the exercise of executive power.'[18]

The Dublin government was also given a cover for its collaboration with British imperialism. The Green Paper, with typical imperialist arrogance, made a gesture towards recognising the 'Irish dimension' in the Six Counties problem:

'A settlement must also recognise Northern Ireland's position within Ireland as a whole ... It is therefore clearly desirable that any new arrangements for Northern Ireland should, whilst meeting the wishes of Northern Ireland and Great Britain, be so far as possible, acceptable to and accepted by the Republic of Ireland.'[19]

For, as the Green Paper went on to say, and in this it expressed a fundamental interest which British imperialism, the Dublin government and the SDLP shared in common, such a settlement would:

'provide a firm basis for concerted governmental and community action against those terrorist organisations which represent a threat to free democratic institutions in Ireland as a whole.'[20]

This was the key factor in the whole strategy. The Green Paper recognised that the political and military struggle of the Provisional IRA not only threatened the stability of the neo-colonial and colonial regimes in the Twenty Six Counties and Six Counties respectively, and therefore British imperialist rule over Ireland, but also the capitalist system – 'free democratic institutions' – in Ireland as a whole.

The aim of British imperialism was to destroy the IRA. In an attempt to isolate the IRA, British imperialism was prepared to offer a share of political power, status and privilege to the Catholic middle class through its political mouthpiece, the SDLP. While less immediate, the IRA also represented the only serious threat to the neo-colonial government in the Twenty Six Counties. The Green Paper allowed the Dublin government to put across its collaboration with British imperialism as a realistic step towards reunification of Ireland. On 24

November Lynch met Heath in London and spoke of a 'closer meeting of minds than he had ever experienced before',[21] clearly indicating his agreement with the Green Paper. The next day the SDLP annual conference voted overwhelmingly to enter into talks with William Whitelaw on the future of the Six Counties – so breaking their pledge not to talk until internment was ended. The stage was now set to implement this latest phase of British policy.

Towards the end of September 1972 there were a number of petrol bomb attacks by unknown men on Gardai (police) stations in the Twenty Six Counties near the border. A large bomb was also found in Dundalk Town Hall and defused amidst a barrage of publicity. There were also a series of bank robberies. All these activities were immediately blamed on the IRA and intensive police and Special Branch activity against Republicans followed. In early October a group of armed men raided a branch of Allied Irish Banks in Grafton Street, Dublin. They got away with £67,000. At their trial in July 1973, the Littlejohn brothers claimed they had committed the robbery to bring about legislation in the Twenty Six Counties against subversive movements. They also later claimed that all their work, including the bomb attacks, had been carried out with the full consent of the Ministry of Defence. They had been acting as *agents provocateurs* for British intelligence. Other British agents were also at work in the Twenty Six Counties and one of them, John Wyman, was later tried in an Irish court in February 1973.

Lynch's Fianna Fail government was all too ready to play a central role in 'governmental and community action against those terrorist organisations' considered a threat to it. The background of bombings and bank raids offered the excuse. Already on 6 October, the Dublin government had closed down without warning the Provisional Sinn Fein headquarters in Kevin Street, Dublin and another building in Blessington Street housing northern refugees.

On 5 November Maire Drumm, Vice-President of Sinn Fein, was arrested and given a short prison sentence. On 19 November Sean Mac Stiofain was arrested and charged with being a member of an illegal organisation. He immediately went on hunger and thirst strike demanding his release. After a farcical trial, during which a Radio Telefis Eireann (RTE) journalist was sentenced to three months imprisonment for refusing to identify Sean Mac Stiofain's voice on a tape being used as evidence, Sean Mac Stiofain was sentenced to six months imprisonment. During his arrest, trial and subsequent imprisonment, there were massive demonstrations and one attempt to free him. After ten days and very close to death he gave up his thirst strike to avoid the inevitable bloody conflicts in the Twenty Six Counties which would follow his death. In a message sent out he argued that the fight is centred in the Six Counties and must be kept there. After 59 days he gave up his hunger strike having been ordered off by the leadership of the IRA and in Spring 1973 he was released. Seamus Twomey replaced him as Chief of Staff of the IRA.

On 24 November the Dublin government dismissed the entire governing body of RTE for broadcasting the interview with Mac Stiofain. Another bomb went off in the centre of Dublin on 25 November causing serious damage and injuring 40 people. The Provisional IRA denied responsibility for the explosion. On 27 November the Dublin government announced details of a new draconian amendment to the Offences Against the State Act under which the evidence of a Gardai Superintendent that he believed someone to be a member of the IRA or any illegal organisation would be sufficient to convict. There was widespread opposition to the Bill even from Labour and Fine Gael. It looked as if the Bill would not be passed when two huge bombs exploded in the centre of Dublin on Friday 1 December killing two men and injuring nearly 100. In a wave of anti-IRA hysteria, the Bill was passed on Saturday morning 2 December at 4am by 70 votes to 23. Fine Gael deputies voted in favour.

The Provisional IRA categorically denied responsibility for the explosions and it was widely thought that the bombs were planted by Loyalists or British agents to influence the vote in the Dail. With a system of judicial internment now in force, the gaols in the Twenty Six Counties rapidly filled up with revolutionary Republicans, including Ruairi O'Bradaigh and Martin McGuinness.

The Provisional IRA and their supporters were hard hit by repression and arrests both sides of the border. In the Six Counties sectarian assassinations increased with the vast majority of them carried out by Loyalist paramilitary organisations such as the UDA and various offshoots of that same organisation. These loyalist groups instituted a campaign of random and brutal terror directed at Catholics, involving particularly ghastly murders after the sadistic torture of the victims. There were 40 sectarian killings in the last four months of 1972 and 31 of the victims were Catholics. A number of these killings were later found to have been carried out by the British army. Hardly any of the Catholics murdered in this way had any connections with the Republican Movement.

It was only after Operation Motorman was over and the British government was trying to create a political settlement acceptable both to the Catholic middle class in the Six Counties and the Dublin government, that the British showed a little less toleration of the activities of loyalist paramilitary organisations. A gun battle between the British army and the UDA took place in September 1972 and a UDA gunman – who was also a member of the UDR – was killed. Other clashes took place in October. In February 1973, after more brutal murders of Catholics – 5 in two days – 2 Loyalists were arrested and interned. They were the first loyalist internees for 50 years. The UDA reacted with fury and a number of heavy gun battles with the army took place. However, in spite of all this, the UDA was never banned by the British government. The number of loyalist internees in Long Kesh did, however, increase to 60 by mid-1974, compared with 600 Republicans. All were released by April 1975 when there were still over 350 Republicans interned, some having been there since 1971.

The nationalist population in the Six Counties was becoming more and more divided along class lines. The Catholic middle class desperately wanted peace and clutched at the Green Paper as offering real prospects for progress – their progress. The working class in the nationalist areas, still at the receiving end of internment, British army brutality and loyalist terror squads, knew that progress for them was not possible until loyalist supremacy, and therefore British rule in Ireland, was ended. They supported the Provisional IRA. So, despite the harassment and arrests on both sides of the border, the Provisional IRA had the support necessary to continue their campaign.

In the four months since Operation Motorman, British government statistics said there had been 393 explosions and 2,833 shooting incidents. In December 1972, there were 48 explosions and 506 shooting incidents including rocket and mortar attacks. At the end of November, the IRA had begun using new Soviet RPG 7 rocket launchers with devastating effect. All this was happening in spite of army claims to have arrested 500 people including '200 Provisional IRA officers' since Operation Motorman at the end of July 1972.[22]

On Monday 25 September 1972, the day of the Darlington Conference, the Provisional IRA blew up Belfast's newest luxury hotel, the Russell Court, causing over £2 million damage. On 2 October, on the Twinbrook Estate in Belfast, an IRA unit executed three members of a British army undercover squad, who were operating in Republican districts disguised as laundry service employees and travelling in a Four Square laundry van. Two others were killed in a flat on the Antrim Road, a massage parlour used by the 'laundry men' as their HQ. The British only admitted one of their agents had been killed on that day.

These squads were a practical application of Brigadier (now General) Kitson's theory of counter-insurgency operations. It was already known that SAS type undercover squads had been in operation in the Six Counties for some time. Their operations were stepped up in September 1972, and using unmarked cars, they were involved in attempts to assassinate not only Republicans on a 'hit-list' but Catholic civilians as well. They often carried guns likely to be used by IRA units, so that having killed someone they could lay the blame on the IRA. No doubt they saw this as a means to create inter-Republican clashes and sectarian feuds. These Military Reconnaissance Force (MRF) squads hit problems early in 1974 when an RUC patrol shot two MRF men dead in an old van in South Armagh because they were acting suspiciously.

The Provisional IRA called a Christmas truce and ceased all but defensive actions for three days. The year 1972 had seen 10,628 shootings, 1,495 explosions, 103 British soldiers killed, 43 RUC/UDR men killed and 321 civilians killed. Since December 1969, the Provisional IRA had lost 75 volunteers killed while thousands had suffered torture and imprisonment. The New Year Statement from the IRA pledged that the struggle would continue 'as long as the British government persists in its policy of military repression'.[23]

The British government had another weapon in its armoury of repression. On 20 December 1972, the Report of the Diplock Commission was published and its recommendations accepted by the British government. It was set up in October 1972 to consider:

'... what arrangements for the administration of justice in Northern Ireland could be made in order to deal more effectively with terrorist organisations by bringing to book, otherwise than by internment by the Executive, individuals involved in terrorist activities, particularly those who plan and direct, but do not necessarily take part in, terrorist acts; and to make recommendations.'[24]

Diplock's recommendations were a fundamental assault on basic civil liberties. They removed trial by jury for scheduled offences – ie those associated with 'terrorist' activities, a very broad category in the Six Counties. These would be heard by a judge sitting without a jury. Most judges in the Six Counties were openly associated with the Unionist Party. The onus of proof as to the possession of firearms and explosives was changed so that the accused had to prove he/she was innocent. A confession made by the accused should be admissible as evidence provided the court was satisfied that on balance of probability they were not obtained by torture or inhuman or degrading treatment. Bail for scheduled offences should not be granted except by the High Court and only then if stringent requirements were met. And finally soldiers should have the power to arrest and detain people for up to four hours 'in order to establish their identity'.[25]

The recommendations were incorporated in the Northern Ireland (Emergency Provisions) Act 1973 which became law on 25 July 1973 and came into force on 8 August 1973. They became the basis of judicial internment – the 'conveyor belt' system that was designed to give internment a thin veneer of 'respectability' – systematic torture in police cells to obtain 'voluntary' confessions, long remands, Diplock courts, imprisonment in the H-Blocks and Armagh prison. With the Gardiner Report 1975 removing 'Special Category' status, the basis was laid for the 'criminalisation' policy administered by the Labour government. But all that was to come later.

The British government pushed ahead with its plans. On 8 March 1973 the referendum on the border was held. It was boycotted by all anti-Unionist groups including the SDLP. The boycott was remarkably effective; 41% of the electorate abstained. The result of the poll was a foregone conclusion. 591,820 votes or 57% of the electorate voted to remain part of the UK and only 6,463 voted for the alternative of unity with the Twenty Six Counties. The IRA reinforced its attitude to the border poll when it carried its campaign to England. Car bombs went off outside that symbol of imperialist justice, the Old Bailey, and outside Great Scotland Yard. One person died and 180 people were injured. Poll or no poll, the Republican movement wanted a united Ireland. The political impact of the explosions was dramatic in that they, together with the successful boycott campaign, destroyed the propaganda value of the Border poll for British imperialism.

On 20 March 1973 the British government published a White Paper on the Constitutional Proposals for governing the Six Counties. They were based on the criteria laid out in the earlier Green Paper of October 1972. The Stormont parliament and government were to be replaced by an Assembly to consist of about 80 members elected by proportional representation. The Assembly would have committees whose chairmen formed the Executive. The Executive was not to be drawn from a single party but would embody the idea of power-sharing. There would continue to be a Secretary of State for Northern Ireland at Westminster and control of security matters would remain with the British government. A Charter of Human Rights was proposed in the White Paper.

There would be a Council of Ireland for North/South discussion on relevant matters and its form and function would be decided at a conference between London, Dublin and the Northern parties after the election. The White Paper is typically vague and empty on the purpose of the Council of Ireland and the most it offers is a repetition about forms of practical economic cooperation such as tourism, regional development, electricity and transport. But it is very precise on two other aspects of the 'Irish dimension'. That is the acceptance of all parties, and particularly the Dublin government, of 'the present status of Northern Ireland' and 'the provision of a firm basis for concerted governmental and community action against terrorist organisations'. The last all-Ireland dimension of repression was *the* one vital element in the Irish dimension which the British government wanted to secure. As the White Paper put it, 'the Government has no higher priority than to defeat terrorism'.[26] The Catholic middle class had been offered a share in power, the Dublin government given an 'Irish dimension' in return for support in the campaign against the IRA and the acceptance of the present constitutional position of the Six Counties as part of the United Kingdom. The IRA put out a statement which summed up the White Paper as:

> '... a skilful application of Britain's age old policy of "divide and conquer"... Having failed by military means to break the will of the northern people to be free citizens in a free country, Britain now presents a set of political proposals which is designed to confuse and fragment the nationally-minded community and insult and provoke those who believed in maintaining the connection with England.'[27]

The White Paper led to a split in the loyalist camp. The Grand Orange Lodge condemned the White Paper at the end of April. Craig rejected it as well, and announced on 30 March the formation of a new party, the Vanguard Unionist Progressive Party (VUPP) backed by the UDA and the Loyalist Association of Workers (LAW). This party would fight the Assembly elections in alliance with Paisley's DUP and in opposition to the White Paper.

The Assembly election took place on 28 June 1973. The Provisional IRA called for a boycott but with little effect. The SDLP put up 28 candidates and got 159,773 votes and nineteen seats, making it the largest anti-Unionist parliamentary group in the history of the sectarian statelet. The anti-White Paper Unionists got 28 seats with Vanguard getting seven seats, the DUP eight seats, the West-Taylor group of Unionists ten seats, and other independent Loyalists three seats. The Faulkner Official Unionists obtained only 22 seats and the Faulkner group itself was very unstable. The anti-White Paper Loyalists had a majority and were totally committed to pressing their case home.

The 'centre' of the Six Counties politics almost collapsed. The NILP with 18 candidates won one seat and the Alliance Party – a moderate pro-British unionist party with Westerminster backing committed to reforming the Northern state – got only eight seats.

The Assembly met for the first time on 31 July and after heated wrangles and numerous procedural motions most of the members except the followers of Paisley and Craig walked out. The latter remained to carry out impromptu business and ended proceedings by singing 'God Save the Queen'.

Meanwhile the Provisional IRA campaign went on with repeated rocket and mortar attacks on British positions and camps. In the first six months of 1973, Provisional IRA operations had expended 48,000 pounds of explosives. In July and August, there were 167 bombs detonated and sniping, cross-border raids, ambushes and other operations continued into the autumn. In August and September 1973, the English bombing campaign took off again with a more extensive use of incendiary devices and small bombs. 1973 saw 58 British soldiers and 22 RUC/UDR men killed.

Repression in the Six Counties continued with the number of Republican internees climbing back towards the pre-direct rule figures. In December 1973 662 men were detained in Long Kesh. In January 1973 women were interned for the first time. Between Operation Motorman, 31 July 1972 and August 1973, the British government claimed that 1,456 people had been charged with 'terrorist type' offences, 925 since 1 January 1973. There were now nearly 1,000 sentenced political prisoners in Six Counties gaols. Assassination figures in October 1973 showed 71 had taken place, the vast majority would have been carried out by Loyalists.

In the Twenty Six Counties a new coalition government of Fine Gael and Labour had come to power after Fianna Fail lost the General Election in February 1973. Repression and harassment of Republicans continued. In March 1973, the Provisionals lost five tons of arms that had come from President Ghadaffi's Libya. The ship *Claudia* with Joe Cahill aboard was picked up in Irish territorial waters and six men were arrested and charged with smuggling arms. There were some victories. On 3 October, the sixty Republican prisoners won 'special status' after a hunger strike of 20 days. On 31 October a spectacular prison escape took place when a hijacked helicopter landed in the exercise yard of Mountjoy gaol and rescued three leading Provisionals, including Seamus Twomey.

After the June Assembly elections in the Six Counties, Whitelaw and the British spent months trying to persuade the Unionists around Faulkner and the SDLP to share power in a coalition government. But the middle ground was inevitably slipping away. Heath came to Belfast at the end of August and warned the party leaders to form an Executive very quickly. In September Whitelaw had separate talks with the three parties who broadly supported the White Paper – SDLP, Faulkner Unionists and the Alliance. Heath also met the new Twenty Six Counties Taoiseach Cosgrave and urged the Dublin government to put pressure on the SDLP to reach an agreement.

On 5 October 1973 an agreement in principle was made by the three parties to form an Executive. The SDLP accepted that there would be no change in the status of Northern Ireland until a further border poll in ten years' time. On 20 November, an anti-power sharing motion was narrowly defeated by only ten votes at the 750-strong Ulster Unionist Council. Things didn't look very promising. Yet on 22 November 1973 a definite agreement to form an Executive was made. Faulkner was to be Chief Executive, Fitt his deputy and there would be six Unionists, four SDLP and one Alliance in the 11 person Executive. There would also be a London-Dublin-Belfast conference as soon as possible to settle details for a Council of Ireland.

The anti-White Paper Loyalists were furious with these developments and they broke up the Assembly session on 28 November shouting at the Faulknerites 'Traitors; Traitors, Out, Out'.[28] On 6 December, DUP and VUPP members of the Assembly attacked the Faulknerites and the RUC had to be called to eject DUP and VUPP members from the Chamber. That evening, the DUP, VUPP and the West-Taylor Unionists united to form the United Ulster Unionist Council (UUUC) to bring down the Executive.

On 6 December the London-Dublin-Belfast Conference began at Sunningdale in England and lasted four days. A two-tier Council of Ireland and a fourteen-men Council of Ministers, seven from each side, was set up with unspecified executive powers, and a 60-member Consultative Assembly elected half by the Dail and half by the Northern Assembly. The Council's functions would be mainly in the field of economic and social cooperation. To make the RUC more acceptable to the nationalist minority in the Six Counties, the Council of Ministers was to be consulted on appointments to the Northern and Southern police authorities. In return for all this, the Dublin government agreed to accept the constitutional status of Northern Ireland, and to step up the offensive against the IRA, increasing the cooperation between the Gardai and RUC. It was clear that the Sunningdale agreement was designed to hold the Northern Ireland Executive together and increase repression of Republicans. It was in no sense designed to take steps to unite Ireland, but, on the contrary, to make sure it remained divided.

The new Executive took office on 1 January 1974. Three days earlier, the SDLP had called for an end to the rent and rates strike against internment. The SDLP was ready and willing to play the role allotted to it by British imperialism. They were prepared to serve in government while internment continued and under the very man who introduced it – Brian Faulkner. And Austin Currie (SDLP) was responsible for one of the first acts of the Executive – legislation for deductions from benefit payments to people on rent and rates strike with a punitive 25p a week collection charge.[29] The SDLP had supported and helped to organise the rent and rates strike. Now, as part of the Executive, they turned against the strikers.

As the Executive took office, Faulkner's following was steadily disintegrating. On 4 January 1974 a motion rejecting the Sunningdale agreement was carried by a majority of 80 at the Ulster Unionist Council. Faulkner resigned as Unionist leader to be replaced by Harry West, but he remained head of the Assembly group – effectively a new party. Faulkner's days were numbered and with them the whole power-sharing arrangement.

On 28 February there was a Westminster election. It had the effect of driving home what was already clear. The Protestant population and particularly the working class would not support power-sharing. The election result was a disaster for Faulkner. The United Ulster Unionist Council (UUUC) won 366,703 votes and eleven seats. The Faulknerites won none with 94,331 votes. The SDLP won one. The Labour Party won the election and Harold Wilson became Prime Minister, and Merlyn Rees Secretary of State for Northern Ireland.

On 23 April 1974 the UUUC held a conference at Portrush Co Antrim to work out an agreed policy. It was attended by representatives of the UDA and also by Enoch Powell – showing the support of a section of the British ruling class. The conference called for the scrapping of Sunningdale, the Executive and the 1973 Northern Ireland Constitution Act based on the White Paper 1973. It demanded a return of Stormont with full security powers and a new election.

THE ULSTER WORKERS COUNCIL STRIKE

After the collapse of the Loyalist Association of Workers (LAW) in 1973, a new body, the Ulster Workers Council (UWC) was set up by some LAW members. This new organisation concentrated on recruiting loyalist workers, in particular shop stewards and other key workers especially in the power stations. Loyalists had a firm grip on shop stewards' and works committees in the power stations and throughout the engineering industry. LAW had been campaigning since 1971 to oust communists, Catholics and even Labour supporters from union positions in the industry.

On 14 May the Assembly was faced with a Loyalist motion opposing Sunningdale. The UWC announced if the motion was defeated they would call a general strike. The call was backed by the Ulster Army Council which coordinated Loyalist paramilitary organisations. The motion was defeated by 48 votes to 28 and that evening, the UWC strike began. Although intimidation was used by supporters of the UWC, the fundamental reason for the strike's dramatic success was the mass support it had amongst the loyalist working class. The key weapon was control of the power stations and the UWC were able to reduce power output to a couple of hours a day. Industry was not able to operate and if workers turned up they were soon sent away. Shops and businesses closed down everywhere. UDA road blocks were set up all over Belfast and the RUC and British army made no attempt to intervene. By Monday 20 May the shut down was almost total.

On Friday 17 May car bombs exploded during the evening rush hour in Dublin and Monaghan in the Republic. There were no warnings given and 33 people were killed with over a hundred injured. The bombs were planted by the UVF. The UDA press officer, Sammy Smyth, said 'I am very happy about the bombings in Dublin'.[30]

On 19 May, Rees declared a state of emergency taking power to use troops to maintain essential services. But the troops did nothing where it mattered on the ground.

There were pathetic attempts made by the Irish Congress of Trade Unions on 21 May to lead workers back to work. One was a march led by Len Murray, British TUC leader, which had less than 150 marchers — many not workers — who were attacked and jeered at by Loyalists and had to be protected by the British army throughout. The ICTU represented no-one but themselves.

The next day, the UWC banned petrol supplies to all but essential users — the latter being determined by the UWC. The economy was in chaos, the Executive was desperate.

The Provisional IRA set up emergency committees to distribute food, fuel and cash throughout the nationalist areas, ignoring the massive British army presence still being maintained in those areas.

On 23 May Faulkner, Fitt and Napier, the leader of the Alliance Party, flew to London and begged Wilson to use his troops. On 25 May Wilson went on television and in a vitriolic speech called the strike leaders 'thugs and bullies' and referred to them as 'people who spend their lives sponging on Westminster and British democracy . . . '.[31] There was still no action.

The SDLP, having lost almost all credibility among the nationalist minority, threatened to resign by 27 May if Wilson did not use troops. On 27 May the troops moved in and occupied petrol stations throughout the Six Counties to supply essential workers like doctors and nurses. It was an empty gesture. The Loyalists threatened to close power stations down completely if troops went near them, together with water and sewage plants.

The Faulknerites came to terms with reality. They called on Rees to negotiate with the UWC. He refused and they resigned on 28 May 1974, bringing the Executive down with them. The UWC called off its stoppage and the Assembly was suspended for four months and then indefinitely. That was the end of power-sharing.

A British army officer writing in the Monday Club magazine — *Monday World* — in the Summer of 1974 claimed that the Labour government had actually decided to use troops to end the stoppage on 24 May, but the Army refused. The writer said 'For the first time, the Army decided that it was right and that it knew best and the politicians had better toe the line'.[32] The Labour-imperialist government did toe the line just as the Liberal-imperialist government had done in March 1913 during the Curragh mutiny (see chapter 3). Again, it was clear that real power lies outside parliament.

Power-sharing could only have worked if some improvement in the social position of the Catholic working class could be achieved. This was not possible in the context of the Six Counties — a sectarian statelet based on loyalist privilege and loyalist supremacy. The Loyalists understood that the Executive could only work if it offered something tangible to Catholic workers. And it was precisely their fear that it might which led them to bring it down.

The British state now recognised that there was no longer any other way than outright repression to defeat the real threat to its interests in Ireland — that from the nationalist masses led by their vanguard, the IRA.

NOTES

1   Mac Stiofain S, *op cit* p. 242.
2   *ibid* p. 250.
3   *ibid* pp. 250–1.
4   *ibid* p. 265.
5   *ibid* p. 285.
6   Haines J, *The Politics of Power* London 1977 p. 129.
7   Provisional IRA, *op cit* p. 72.
8   Deutsch R and Magowan V, *op cit* Volume 2 p. 202.
9   Mac Stiofain S, *op cit* p. 298.
10   Provisional IRA, *op cit* p. 79.
11   Mac Stiofain S, *op cit* p. 248.
12   Deutsch R and Magowan V, *op cit* Volume 2 p. 180.
13   *ibid* p. 186.
14   *ibid* p. 205.
15   *ibid* p. 213.
16   Northern Ireland Office, *The Future of Northern Ireland* London 1972 p. 33.
17   *ibid* p. 27.
18   *ibid* p. 36.
19   *ibid* pp. 33–34.
20   *ibid* p. 34.
21   Deutsch R and Magowan V, *op cit* Volume 2 p. 244.
22   Bell J Bowyer, *op cit* p. 397.
23   Provisional IRA, *op cit* p. 84.
24   Diplock Lord, *Report of the Commission to consider legal procedures to deal with terrorist activity in Northern Ireland* London 1972 p. 1.
25   *ibid* pp. 3–4.
26   *Northern Ireland Constitutional Proposals* London 1973 p. 30 and p. 32.
27   Provisional IRA, *op cit* p. 90.
28   Deutsch R and Magowan V, *op cit* Volume 2 p. 358.
29   Farrell M, *op cit* p. 316.
30   Deutsch R and Magowan V, *op cit* Volume 3 p. 59.
31   Fisk R, *The Point of No Return* London 1975 p. 253. This book gives the definitive account of the UWC strike.
32   *ibid* p. 154.

CHAPTER ELEVEN

ULSTERISATION

The fall of the power-sharing Executive in May 1974 showed, yet again, that the Six Counties statelet was unreformable. The attempt to isolate the IRA and undermine its support in the nationalist minority by offering a share of power to the anti-IRA sections of that minority had failed. No viable alternative could be created, no overall improvement in the social position of the nationalist minority was possible in the sectarian statelet that had been created to preserve British imperialist rule in Ireland. The Ulster Workers Council strike had forcefully reminded the British government that the price of 'loyalty' to British imperialism was the preservation of loyalist privileges and loyalist supremacy in the Six Counties of Ireland. It was a price which the British Labour government was quite prepared to pay.

The power-sharing policy had been used by British imperialism as part of an overall strategy to isolate and defeat the IRA. It did not succeed. On the contrary the actions of the SDLP, in attacking the rent and rates strikers during its brief taste of political power, only undermined the SDLP's support among the nationalist minority. And finally the collaboration of the RUC, UDR and British army with the UWC strikers in bringing down the power-sharing Executive demonstrated all too clearly that behind the loyalist statelet stood British imperialism. No social progress would be possible until British imperialism was driven out of Ireland. The failure of power-sharing had in fact vindicated the political standpoint of the Provisional IRA.

The emphasis of British policy had to change. There was no longer any way other than outright repression to defeat the nationalist threat to British imperialism's interests in Ireland. And, as had happened time and again in such circumstances, it was left to a British Labour government to take the new path and demonstrate British imperialism's resolute commitment to maintain the sectarian loyalist statelet in the Six Counties of Ireland. In 1949 it was a British Labour government which introduced the Government of Ireland Act offering constitutional guarantees to maintain loyalist supremacy in the Six Counties statelet. In 1969 it was a British Labour government which sent British troops into the Six Counties of Ireland to support loyalist supremacy and prop up the increasingly unstable loyalist statelet. And in 1974 it was a British Labour government which laid the basis for, and later administered, the regime of terror known as 'Ulsterisation' – yet another attempt to destroy the IRA and break the back of its support in the nationalist minority.

FIRST STEPS TO 'ULSTERISATION'

There was a great deal of confusion about British strategy in the period following the UWC strike until the appointment of Roy Mason as Secretary of State for Northern Ireland. With the failure of power-sharing the ruling class openly discussed its options. There was talk of a new round of constitutional initiatives, of phased withdrawal, and of open and direct repression to defeat the IRA. Events during this period until mid-1976 encouraged all sides to make confused and wrong assumptions about what was taking place. In particular, the truce in February 1975, the lowering of troop levels in 1975 and the impact of the economic crisis in the Six Counties in the form of closures, redundancies and rising unemployment, led many to believe that withdrawal was being given serious consideration.

One important factor which allowed the British ruling class to openly review its options in this way was the complete absence of any pressure from the British working class movement on the issue of Ireland. There was no movement in Britain which was able and prepared to seize the opportunity to argue that the fall of power-sharing conclusively demonstrated that the loyalist statelet was unreformable. There was no movement able to use the fall of power-sharing as the basis of a major campaign for British withdrawal from Ireland. Further, by passing the Prevention of Terrorism Act in November 1974, the British Labour government provided a legal cover for the systematic harassment of the Irish community in Britain. In so doing it effectively blocked a politically conscious section of the working class from playing a central role in a campaign for the withdrawal of British troops from Ireland. Finally, while appearing to review its options, the British Labour government did in fact throughout its term of office gradually increase repression in the Six Counties until it became a daily onslaught against the nationalist minority. And it was able to do this without any serious interference from within Britain.

Important components of the new policy were already being prepared before the fall of the power-sharing Executive. However the significance of such developments was not immediately clear. In April 1974 Merlyn Rees, the Secretary of State for Northern Ireland, outlined some new proposals. They included a phased programme for the release of detainees, structural changes in the RUC to increase its efficiency, greater flexibility of troop movements with a smaller Army 'to make way for normal policing', and the setting up of a committee, under the chairmanship of Lord Gardiner, to review the working of the Northern Ireland (Emergency Provisions) Act, 1973. Significantly, on security Rees said that the community in Northern Ireland must help itself to 'return to normality' and not believe law and order was a matter for the United Kingdom 'rather than for them'.[1]

All this talk of a 'return to normality', of 'normal policing' was preparing the way for 'Ulsterisation' – for the 'primacy of the police' in fighting the IRA and for 'criminalisation' of the revolutionary national struggle led by the IRA to free Ireland from British rule. When the Gardiner Report appeared after the fall of the power-sharing Executive, this emphasis became much sharper. One of its most important recommendations was to remove Special Category status from Irish political prisoners. That is, to deny the political legitimacy of the IRA's military campaign to free Ireland from British rule.

With these April proposals Merlyn Rees announced that he intended to lift the ban on Sinn Fein and the Ulster Volunteer Force. This occurred in May 1974. That Rees was prepared to lift the ban on the UVF, a known loyalist paramilitary organisation centrally involved in the sectarian assassinations of Catholics shows the totally cynical direction of British government policy. As justification for this move it was said that the UVF had ceased terrorist activity by forming a political organisation called the Volunteer Political Party. However, it soon became embarrassingly clear that the activity of the UVF was much the same as before – including the assassinations of Catholics – and the UVF had to be banned again in 1975.

The lifting of the ban on Sinn Fein was clearly an attempt to suck revolutionary Republicans into the 'political' sphere of electioneering and ineffectual peaceful protest. It was part of the overall effort by the British to undermine support for the armed anti-imperialist struggle. Legitimate 'political' activity was to be defined in such a way as to exclude the armed struggle against British imperialism. Those engaged in that struggle were to be regarded and treated as 'criminals'. So while the legalisation of Sinn Fein offered revolutionary Republicans a legal platform for anti-imperialist propaganda and protest, the British would continually attempt to use it to depoliticise the armed anti-imperialist struggle. It was a danger that had to be continually borne in mind.

REES AND INTERNMENT

No one should be deceived by Rees's term of office. If anything his record was as bad as, if not worse than, Whitelaw's. And he was just as committed to defeating the nationalist threat to British rule in Ireland. When he was opposition spokesman on Northern Ireland Rees visited Long Kesh and spoke to James Moyne, a Republican internee in Cage 8. Rees told him he was disgusted with internment and would end it within six weeks of Labour returning to office. James Moyne died in Long Kesh as a result of medical neglect on 13 January 1975, nearly 11 months after the Labour Party had won the election.[2] In fact, in the first three full months of Labour's term of office March-May 1974 there were 134 new internees, a net *increase* of 64 after 69 releases and one escape. Only three of the releases were the direct result of powers held by the Secretary of State, Rees. The rest were due to the reviews and appeals machinery set up before Rees was in office. It was Merlyn Rees who stepped up the internment of women – a punitive measure against the nationalist community. All the women interned were Catholics and of the 31 interned up to 1 February 1975, 20 occurred while Rees was Secretary of State.

During the first six weeks of the truce from 10 February to 24 March 1975 at least 11 Catholics were brutally murdered and over 30 Catholic premises and buildings were bombed by loyalist paramilitaries – the UVF/UDA operating under various flags of convenience. During this period not only were no loyalist assassins and bombers interned but Rees released *all* the remaining UVF/UDA internees. At the same time only 24% of internees alleged to be members of the Provisional IRA had been released despite the truce. On 17 April 1975 – again during the truce – Rees made a statement in the House of Commons to the effect that if internment were ended 'at a stroke' there would be civil war in the North by morning. This led to a bitter comment by Fr Dennis Faul and Fr Raymond Murray – reproduced in their pamphlet *The Shame of Merlyn Rees* – that Mr Rees' statement 'confirms our opinion that he has no intention of ending it [internment]. He never had.'[3]

Essentially they were right. Internment without trial would be ended only to be replaced by judicial internment – a vicious process of incarcerating Republicans. The legal and political foundations for judicial internment had been systematically prepared during Merlyn Rees's term of office.

The conditions that internees and other political prisoners were subjected to in Long Kesh were appalling. The following gives some idea of what they had to endure:

'Here in Cage Six, 67 men live in accommodation meant for 35. Maybe we should be grateful in a way because it used to house 80 men, but due to the very rare releases the numbers have shrunk slightly.

Six months ago, during a British Army raid on the cages one of the huts was so badly damaged by soldiers that the authorities deemed it unlivable and demolished it completely. This meant that the men from this hut had to move into the other two huts which were already at this time overcrowded.

Subsequent raids have rendered the canteen and the study hut useless. In the shower house we are left with three showers, three WCs and six wash-hand basins. The rest have been wrecked and smashed by some sick Brits. The health hazard from the conditions in this cage are obvious, but the authorities refuse to move on the subject and will not let any man transfer to another cage.

We are left now that confessions are heard, Masses celebrated, food is eaten and all studying is done in one of the living huts.' (PRO, Internees, Cage 6, 21 August 1974)[4]

There had been a great deal of organised protest by both Republicans and Loyalists to improve the quality of the food and living conditions in Long Kesh. The medical treatment was also appalling. The authorities refused to act. When the prisoners went on strike and increased their protests in September and October 1974 refusing prison meals etc, they were penalised by having food parcels, cigarettes and visits stopped. Even Paddy Devlin (SDLP), an inveterate enemy of the Republican movement, was forced to say that 'after this the burning down of Long Kesh was inevitable'.[5] On Tuesday 15 October 1974 Republican prisoners attacked prison officers and set fire to most of the huts in the camp. The flames could be seen for miles. Soldiers were brought in. They attacked the prisoners brutally beating them up. Helicopters flew over the cages spraying CS gas into the compounds. Next day Republican women prisoners in Armagh gaol seized the Governor and three prison officers and held them as hostages in an attic. The women demanded assurances that none of the political prisoners (including Loyalists) would be maltreated. Troops and police surrounded the prison. The Governor and the prison officers were released the next morning after reassurances were given by two clergymen. Clashes took place between prisoners and prison officers in Crumlin Road gaol, Belfast, in the afternoon. And that same evening prisoners at Magilligan Prison, Co Derry, set fire to their huts. On Thursday 500 more British troops were brought into the Six Counties bringing the total to 15,600.

The morning after the events in Long Kesh the Northern Ireland Office (NIO) put out a statement saying that three prison officers had been injured. It also said that no prisoners had been hurt and there had been no contact between the security forces and prisoners. At midday Rees issued a statement saying nine prisoners were in hospital and a number had been treated at the prison. Rees lied. In one hospital alone out of the three used to treat prison casualties, 16 prisoners were suffering from severe injuries and many more were treated elsewhere. Paddy Devlin maintains that he had a photostat copy of a document issued by the NIO saying 21 prisoners were in hospital receiving treatment for injuries.[6]

When a protest was made about the discrepancies, all hospitals were cleared except for eight prisoners – no doubt to bring the figures in line with Rees's first public statement. Of those excluded from hospitals were prisoners suffering multiple and major injuries like bone fractures, concussion, bruises and abrasions. They were returned to the prison to lie on concrete slabs and amidst ashes and dirt were exposed to outdoor conditions. The Provisionals claimed that a hundred prisoners were injured. The NIO eventually said that 29 had been injured together with 23 soldiers and 14 prison officers.

Immediately after the events at Long Kesh, Rees announced that 'such demonstrations will not influence me in any degree to change the policy . . . in relation to detention'.[7] The same day Austin Currie (SDLP) felt it necessary to say that the Secretary of State should be recalled as he had no credibility left. And even a member of the pro-unionist Alliance Party argued that 'the whole credibility of British Ministers has suffered to such an extent that it is difficult to see how any of them can ever be believed again'.[8] Quite!

CONSTITUTIONAL CONVENTION

The totally cynical disregard which the Labour government has for the legitimate interests and grievances of the nationalist minority was demonstrated afresh on 4 July 1974. The government issued a White

Paper calling for elections to a Constitutional Convention so that the people of Northern Ireland could play 'a crucial part in determining their own future'. The functions of the Northern Ireland Convention were mainly 'to consider what provisions for the Government of Northern Ireland would be likely to command the most widespread acceptance throughout the whole community there'.[9] There was never the slightest doubt about its outcome. The Labour government simply required a breathing space. It was biding its time as it prepared the next stage of its policy of repression. Since the February 1974 General Election it was clear that the United Ulster Unionist Council (the bloc of anti-power-sharing Loyalists) would win crushing majorities in all forms of elections. The October 1974 General Election only confirmed that with the UUUC winning 58% of the total vote on a platform of uncompromising opposition to power-sharing or a Council of Ireland. The Faulknerites were almost annihilated, with even the Officials' Republican Clubs getting more votes.

The Convention elections took place on 1 May 1975. Revolutionary nationalists called for a boycott and the total poll of 64% was fai-' low. The result was a massive victory for the UUUC which won 46 out of the 78 seats: together with the seat of an independent Loyalist associated with the UVF, the anti-power-sharing Unionists had an overall majority of 16. Faulkner's party won a mere five seats with Faulkner himself just scraping in on the ninth count in South Down. The SDLP lost two seats leaving a total of 17, the Alliance Party had eight and the almost defunct NILP got one. The Officials' Republican Clubs now more and more in alliance with British imperialism, did disastrously with none of their candidates coming near to winning a seat.

The Constitutional Convention inevitably called for the restoration of Stormont, that is, for devolved government without power-sharing. It rejected any Irish dimension and called for increased security measures and the defeat of 'terrorism', by which it meant the IRA.[10] The Convention Report was discussed in the House of Commons on 12 January 1976. Before the debate Harold Wilson made a statement on security in Northern Ireland. After announcing that the Spearhead Battalion had been moved from Great Britain to Armagh and was being joined by troops of the notorious Special Air Service Regiment (SAS) he said:

'Without a solution of the formidable security problems, the necessary conditions will not exist for constitutional advance and reconciliation'.[11]

In the debate on the Convention Report Merlyn Rees made it clear that the government had no intention of withdrawing from the Six Counties of Ireland since it would threaten the stability of British imperialist rule both sides of the border.

'The Government are in no doubt that this would be a grave mistake. It would solve nothing. I have no doubt that withdrawal and abandonment of our responsibilities towards citizens of the United Kingdom would precipitate violence on an even greater scale than we have seen so far. And we must not assume that violence could be confined to Northern Ireland. It would spread to Great Britain and also to the Republic of Ireland.'[12]

In the debate 'power-sharing' was replaced by much vaguer talk of 'participation' and John Biggs-Davidson dispensed with the much talked of Irish dimension when he said:

'Combined border operations, action by the Republic and the United Kingdom to deny equipment, respite or hiding place to those who have been rejected at the ballot in Northern Ireland and the Republic and who resort to the bullet and the bomb, the speedy enactment of the Criminal Law Jurisdiction Bill as a second best to extradition – that is the Irish dimension that matters today . . . '[13]

The so-called Irish Republic was only too happy to oblige with a series of vicious anti-Republican laws passed during 1976. It was clear by early 1976 that the British ruling class through its faithful servant the British Labour Party was now ready to concentrate its energies on its primary task of repression, that is, of defeating the nationalist threat to its rule in Ireland led by the IRA.

THE SECOND TRUCE

A second truce occurred within the period between the White Paper on elections to the Constitutional Convention in May 1974 and the Convention Report of November 1975. The Provisional IRA wanted a truce not only because they shared the nationalist minority's desire for an end to the six-year old war but also because they believed that the British intended to withdraw quite soon from the Six Counties of Ireland. The British wanted a truce primarily because they needed to take pressure off the security forces while the reorganisation of the RUC into an effective 'anti-terrorist' force was taking place. They were also concerned about the effects on the British public of the Provisional IRA's bombing campaign in England. An additional consideration for sections of the British administration in the Six Counties was that a truce might create a more conducive response to the Constitutional Convention elections to take place in May 1975.

There can be little doubt that an influential section of the Provisional IRA leadership believed that a phased withdrawal of British troops was a real possibility. In May 1974 *Republican News* carried a front page headline 'English Withdrawal Date? 31 Dec 1974.' It spoke of the call of Liberal MP John Pardoe for a withdrawal of troops by that date, and went on to argue:

> 'As England totters towards economic collapse and bankruptcy she must cut every conceivable cost. The last outposts of Empire are to be abandoned and with Cyprus, Malta and Singapore, Ireland is also to be evacuated. But Mason's terms are: when the RUC and UDR are ready to take over.'[14]

Mason was at that time Secretary of State for Defence. The kind of withdrawal he had in mind was that associated with 'Ulsterisation' and not a united Ireland. Nevertheless, the Provisional IRA felt that the pressure on the security forces in the Six Counties and most importantly the bombing campaign in England were having a significant impact on the British ability and determination to continue the war. According to the *Sunday Times* Commander Huntley of the Bomb Squad went some way to acknowledging as much in relation to the bombing campaign in England. In a secret report he said:

> 'If the campaign is accentuated even marginally . . . it is extremely doubtful as to whether there are sufficient trained investigators to successfully combat it, in manpower or technical support terms'.[15]

The threat was significant. The security forces in the Six Counties numbered over 30,000 and they were unable to seriously impair the IRA's ability to wage war against the British forces. The equivalent figure for Britain would be over a million. It was therefore not unreasonable to assume that the British could be bombed to the negotiating table. It was after all the *only* way it had happened in the past.

On the British side their political initiatives were in disarray. No one could seriously entertain any useful outcome from the Constitutional Convention. The British were under quite severe pressure to take some action. They had not managed to undermine in any serious way the Provisional IRA's ability to continue its military campaign. Their programme of 'Ulsterisation' required a wholesale reorganisation of the RUC. It still needed more time. This reorganisation, it should be remembered, was one of the key elements in Merlyn Rees's proposal of April 1974. Kenneth Newman, an ex-detective of the Palestine Police 1946–8 and an ex-Commander in the Metropolitan Police, had been brought to the Six Counties in September 1973 and was playing a central role in this reorganisation. He was concerned with the investigative and detective work of the RUC. The aim was to make the RUC into a force capable of gathering and using information of the kind needed to defeat the IRA and break the back of its support in the nationalist community. This reorganisation still had some way to go if it was to be effective. A truce would take the pressure off the security forces while it was completed. Newman was promoted to Chief Constable of the RUC in 1976. Together with Roy Mason he was to sanction a system of brutality and torture carried out in specially constructed interrogation centres. That system, a vicious assault on the nationalist minority, was the central component of British imperialist policy to defeat the IRA between 1976–1979. Newman gained a great deal of experience for the British ruling class during this period in the Six Counties of Ireland. That experience is now to be used in England. Less than one year after the uprisings in British cities in the summer of 1981, Newman was made Commissioner of the Metropolitan Police.

Steps towards a truce began when a Protestant clergyman Rev William Arlow made contact through Maire Drumm with the Provisional Army Council. The Provisionals knew that Rev Arlow was informally in touch with Sir Frank Cooper, Permanent Secretary and a key policy maker at the Northern Ireland Office at Stormont. Very soon a meeting was arranged at a small inconspicuous hotel at Feakle, Co Clare, on 10 December 1974. The Provisionals took the meeting very seriously. Rev Arlow, a number of Protestant clergymen and a retired Methodist headmaster, Stanley Worrall who had recently been in touch with Frank Cooper, met Ruairi O'Bradaigh, Maire Drumm, Seamus Loughran, Billy McKee, David O'Connell, Seamus Twomey, Kevin Mallon and J B O'Hagan – all key figures in the Provisional movement. Frank Cooper was informed that the meeting was to take place and although he declined to send an observer he asked to be kept informed. The meeting was however interrupted by a tip off from Dublin Castle that the Irish Special Branch was on its way. The members of the Provisional IRA on the run quickly disappeared, the others from Sinn Fein and the clergymen remained and waited for the Irish Special Branch to arrive. Discussions however had got under way despite the interruptions.

Secret and discreet negotiations continued around the possibility of a truce. Speculation was widespread. Provisional IRA sources in Dublin made it clear they had been offered nothing. They had made three demands: the withdrawal of British troops to barracks, an immediate end to internment and an acknowledgement of the right of the people of Ireland to control their own destiny. No ceasefire would take place while internment lasted and British troops continued to occupy Republican areas in the North. The Provisionals also demanded an increased opportunity to express their views both through negotiations with the British and through local political activity. The issue of the Price sisters was also raised. In June 1974 they had ended a hunger strike of 206 days – for 167 days of that period they had been forcibly fed – to demand transfer from Britain to a prison in the Six Counties. Roy Jenkins, Labour Home Secretary, had agreed when under pressure that they would serve the 'bulk of their long sentences near their homes in Northern Ireland'.[16] So far no change had occurred.

On 15 December the Price sisters were moved from Brixton prison to Durham. Three months later they were transferred to Armagh gaol in the Six Counties. Negotiations continued with Rev Arlow acting as intermediary between the Provisional IRA Army Council and the British Northern Ireland Office. On 19 December the Ministry of Defence announced it would pay £41,717 to the relatives of the 13 people murdered by British soldiers on Bloody Sunday 30 January 1972, 'in a spirit of goodwill and conciliation'.[17] The next day the Provisional Army Council announced a Christmas 'suspension of operations' from midnight Sunday 22 December to Thursday 2 January 1975. In a statement it said that the suspension of operations had been ordered on the 'clear understanding' that a positive response would be forthcoming from the British government.[18] It was designed to give the British government an opportunity to consider proposals for a permanent ceasefire.

Rees offered nothing tangible in response to the ceasefire. In a statement on the same day he said that 'the actions of the security forces will be related to the level of any activity which may occur. No specific undertakings will be given'. However he ended by saying that 'a genuine and sustained cessation of violence over a period would create a new situation'.[19] The Northern Ireland Office said it would not be pushed into releasing large numbers of detainees because of the unilateral ceasefire but promised a 'more relaxed atmosphere' over detention if the ceasefire were to be extended. The Provisional IRA continued with its military campaign right up to the ceasefire. Three hours before midnight 22 December a bomb was thrown at the London home of

Edward Heath in Belgravia, blowing out the windows on the first floor balcony. At midnight the Provisional IRA ceasefire came into effect.

Not unexpectedly the loyalist politicians condemned the British government, which they accused of having negotiations with the IRA. Harry West, leader of the Official Unionist Party said that the IRA was on its last legs militarily. It desperately needed a breathing space to re-form and re-group. It had now been given one and 'it would set the cause of peace back many years if the security forces adopted a low profile'. Inevitably the Rev Ian Paisley, leader of the DUP, accused the British government of accepting IRA 'conditions' for a truce.[20] The Loyalists only wanted peace on their terms, that is, through a return of a Stormont government that would sustain loyalist supremacy. A little pressure came from the other side. On 27 December the *New Statesman* in an editorial 'An Ultimatum for Ulster' urged a start to the withdrawal of troops from Northern Ireland by 30 June 1975, coupled with the resignation of Merlyn Rees.

On 31 December Merlyn Rees announced the release of 20 detainees and offered a three day New Year parole to 50 others. This was hardly significant given that there were still well over 500 detainees. However he also said that 'if a genuine and sustained cessation of violence' occurred the government 'would not be found wanting in response', that he would give further details of how the army could make a planned, orderly and progressive reduction in its present commitment and that once violence had ceased it would become possible to release detainees progressively.[21] On 1 January 1975 the Provisional IRA announced a two-week extension of the Christmas ceasefire.

On 9 January Rees rejected direct or indirect negotiations with the Provisional IRA. The IRA Army Council had no choice, it ended the ceasefire on 16 January saying there had been no response to the peace proposals and also an increase in British army activity. The Army Council also mentioned the fact that Rees had only released three detainees at Christmas, whereas the previous year (under a Tory administration) 65 had been released. The military campaign began again.

Very quickly Rees and Cooper agreed to secret talks. On 19 January the Rev Arlow drove two Provisionals to a secret meeting with two British Foreign and Commonwealth Office officials, James Allan and Michael Oatly. Further pressure was applied on the British when more bombs went off in Belfast and a blast at Walthamstow pumping station left thousands of London homes without water. This was the first bomb in England for a month. Another meeting took place.

In the continuing talks the British negotiators said they believed the IRA was unable to control its Active Service Units in England. The IRA replied by stating that there would be a spate of bombings in Britain ending at midnight 27 January 1975. On 27 January six bombs went off in Manchester and London – after that there were no more explosions. The Provisionals had made it clear to the British that they could turn the bombs on or off as they wished and unless they were offered something tangible the talks would get nowhere. When Allan next met the two Provisionals he was authorised to offer terms. On 9 February 1975 the Provisional IRA Army Council announced an indefinite truce for 6pm the following day, 10 February.

A substantial agreement drawn up between the Provisional IRA and British government representatives lay behind the truce.[22] There was no jointly signed document but both sides kept minutes of the discussion. The agreement included:

1.   Detainees being progressively released over the next period. Internment without trial in fact ended in December 1975 – it was however to be replaced by judicial internment. Many of the internees were found jobs in government sponsored schemes in West Belfast.
2.   British soldiers adopting a much lower profile in the Six Counties with large scale army searches in nationalist areas being abandoned. Specified Provisional IRA leaders were given immunity from arrest.
3.   'Incident centres' were set up with government money to monitor the ceasefire. Provisional Sinn Fein would run their own centres reporting breaches of the truce to the Northern Ireland Office. They would also use them to run community advice centres for local people. These advice centres angered the politicians of the SDLP who furiously complained that local control had been handed over to the Provisionals.
4.   The Provisionals were given a verbal commitment of a planned and orderly British withdrawal from the Six Counties over a period of years. There was never to be a public commitment but there can be little doubt that a private assurance was given by the British representatives. The grounds for refusing a public commitment were the difficulties associated with the British commitment to the Unionists and the consequences for the British government of the dangers of a 'bloodbath' should they withdraw. The promise of withdrawal clearly did not have Cabinet sanction and did not come up at any meeting where Wilson was present. During further discussions between the two sides, evidence of the intention to withdraw was said to be the exclusion of Harland and Wolff, the Belfast shipyard, from the Aircraft and Shipbuilding Industries Bill to be

presented to parliament by Tony Benn. It was already known that Short Brothers and Harland, the Belfast planemakers, were not to be included – together these were two of the biggest British firms in the Six Counties. The same period was also to see the closure of five government bases in Northern Ireland – an air traffic control centre, an FCO radio station, two RAF establishments and a Royal Navy depot. There was also the closure of the Belfast and Heysham ferry. The British government almost certainly intended these developments to be seen as symptoms of withdrawal.

On the basis of these and other commitments the truce went ahead and deaths and injuries on both sides dropped dramatically. The truce in fact never officially ended. It ultimately petered out in November 1975 with the closure of the 'incident centres'. Discussions between British representatives and the Provisionals however were to continue intermittently until July 1976. However, while these talks were taking place, the British were actively implementing the recommendations of the Gardiner Report – a crucial component of Ulsterisation.

THE GARDINER REPORT

The Gardiner Report was published on 30 January 1975. The committee was set up by Merlyn Rees, under the chairmanship of the Labour Peer, Lord Gardiner, to consider measures to deal with terrorism in Northern Ireland and to review the Northern Ireland (Emergency Provisions) Act, 1973. The first meeting took place on 19 June 1974 *after* the fall of the power-sharing Executive. Its meetings were held in private and it did not publish the evidence it received. It began by making its political assumptions clear. This was necessary, the Report said, because the work was being undertaken 'in something of a political vacuum' and at 'a time of growing questioning in Britain on the future relationship of Northern Ireland to the rest of the United Kingdom'. The first and most important was that:

> 'Northern Ireland will remain part of the United Kingdom for the foreseeable future, whatever form of political devolution from Westminster to Stormont may eventually command consensus. It follows that the Government at Westminster and the people of Great Britain cannot divorce themselves from responsibility for the political, social and economic development of Northern Ireland.'[23]

This assumption was not new. It was contained in all British reports on events in the Six Counties of Ireland. However it surely has added weight at a time when a truce was about to start based on a verbal commitment from representatives of the British government of 'a planned and orderly British withdrawal from Ireland over a period of years'. Something quite definitely concerned with 'the foreseeable future'. Other assumptions included security remaining the responsibility of the British government and the need for some form of power-sharing arrangement. The Constitutional Convention elections were to take place in May.

The Report gets down to business very quickly and is very precise where it matters. On 'Terrorism and Subversion' it states:

> '...terrorists who break the law...are not heroes but criminals; not the pioneers of political change but its direst enemies'.[24]

The Report was published at a time when the British government was in the process of conducting serious political negotiations with the so-called 'terrorists' and 'criminals'. This is typical of imperialist hypocrisy and the lies which the British government reserves for the British public.

Gardiner strongly argued for continuing to use most of the important recommendations of the Diplock Commission embodied in the Northern Ireland (Emergency Provisions) Act, 1973. These recommendations have already been discussed and are a fundamental assault on basic civil liberties (see chapter 10). On Diplock courts the Report had the effrontery to say:

> 'But for the fact that there is no jury, the non-jury courts are ordinary courts, sitting in public with variations in the law of evidence which, on the whole, are not major ones'.[25]

In a language only the British ruling class are capable of, Gardiner recommended these 'ordinary' courts, typical of imperialist justice, should continue. The Report also said that the 'increased success of the RUC in bringing prosecutions against alleged terrorists' had resulted in the average time spent in custody before trial increasing from 25 weeks in October 1973 to 35.5 weeks in September 1974.[26] This was an official indication of the first stages of 'judicial internment'. A RUC prosecution meant at least nine months in custody before even being brought before a Diplock court.

Gardiner recommended the continuation of Section 6 of the 1973 Act. This allowed a confession made by the accused to be admissible as evidence provided the court was satisfied that in all probability it was not obtained by torture or inhuman or degrading treatment. Given the 'court' amounted to a loyalist judge appointed and paid for by the British, it explains the so-called 'success' rate of the RUC. It was also the recommendation that led to the systematic torture of those arrested and brought to interrogation centres like Castlereagh from 1976–1979 for the purpose of obtaining confessions.

The main new recommendation from Gardiner was the ending of Special Category status for political prisoners. This was a central feature of 'Ulsterisation'.

'Although recognising the pressures on those responsible at the time, we have come to the conclusion that the introduction of special category status was a serious mistake . . . We can see no justification for granting privileges to a large number of criminals convicted of very serious crimes, in many cases murder, merely because they claim political motivation. It supports their own view, which society must reject, that their political motivation in some way justifies their crimes . . . We recommend that the earliest practicable opportunity should be taken to end the special category.'[27]

While the British government was recognising the political legitimacy of the IRA's struggle for national liberation through the truce negotiations, the Gardiner Report was recommending far-reaching steps to take that political legitimacy away.

Finally in line with the ending of Special Category status, Gardiner advocated the building of the H-Blocks – a cellular system of prison accommodation, rather than the compound type which now housed some 71% of prisoners.

'Prisons of the compound type, each compound holding up to 90 prisoners, are thoroughly unsatisfactory from every point of view; their major disadvantage is that there is virtually a total loss of disciplinary control by the prison authorities inside the compounds . . .'.[28]

In the compounds, political prisoners wear their own clothes, receive extra visits, etc and are segregated according to the political organisations to which they belong. In the compounds the political prisoners through their leaders direct a great deal of the day to day activities in the prison. It was this that Gardiner wished to end. For it was a clear acknowledgement of the political character of the offences for which those inside had been detained. Those inside the compounds acted and were treated as 'prisoners of war' – for that was what they were and still are.

Gardiner reported that the prison population had risen from 727 at the beginning of 1968 to 2,848 in November 1974. It was clear that this fourfold rise in the number of prisoners was directly associated with the political conflict and therefore was primarily of a political character. Yet this was what Gardiner wished to deny. New prison accommodation was soon being built as the Labour government took active steps to implement the fundamental recommendations of Gardiner.

Gardiner did not recommend the ending of internment without trial because of the 'risks of increased violence', although he did say that internment could not 'remain as a long-term policy'. The decision to end internment, the Report said, had to be made by the government.[29] Much of the public debate centred around this aspect of the Report so obscuring its essential recommendation – the 'criminalisation' of the revolutionary national struggle to free Ireland from British rule.

THE TRUCE BREAKS DOWN

The Provisionals' representatives who were negotiating with the British at the time of the Gardiner Report told them that any attempt to remove Special Category status would be resisted by all means possible including the shooting of warders. Nevertheless the talks went on presumably because of the private assurances from the British representatives of an 'orderly and planned withdrawal' from Ireland. And they continued to the sound of building work progressing apace on the new cellular prisons. Tim Pat Coogan claims that the leaders of the different political organisations in the compounds were even allowed out of the prison to inspect the H-Blocks while they were being built.[30] As a 'concession' in an attempt to make the abolition of Special Category status more acceptable, the British offered fifty per cent remission of sentence to all prisoners. There could be little doubt what the British had in mind. The only 'withdrawal' they were considering was 'Ulsterisation', the 'primacy' of the paramilitary RUC and the UDR in maintaining the loyalist statelet.

During the truce deaths and injuries continued but seldom involved the Provisionals or the security forces. There was a feud between loyalist paramilitary organisations in this period and just before the main truce was declared Charles Harding-Smith of the West Belfast Brigade of the UDA was shot. As during the first truce in 1972, the loyalist assassination and bombing squads moved into action during the period of the truce, and in the first five months of 1975, 35 Catholics were murdered. The greatest number of sectarian killings have always occurred when IRA activity has been low. And they mostly result from the activities of loyalist assassination and bombing squads.

At the end of 1974 a split occurred in the Official IRA and the Irish Republican Socialist Party was formed. The IRSP had been formed mainly by those who had left the Officials in protest against the organisation's ceasefire and increasing collaboration with British imperialism. Derry Officials went over to the IRSP en bloc. The military wing of the IRSP, the Irish National Liberation Army, arose out of a bloody feud with the Official IRA in Belfast just after the truce began. When the Belfast IRSP members left the Officials they took their weapons with them to supply the armoury of INLA. The Officials attempted to wipe out IRSP/INLA before it got off the ground, pistol-whipping and kneecapping its members and, on 20 February, shooting dead Hugh Ferguson. The Official IRA, while refusing to take up arms against British imperialism, were however quite prepared to use their arms against the IRSP and INLA. After Ferguson's death INLA hit back. The battles went on until May as the Officials tried unsuccessfully to put down what they regarded as a mutiny. In October and November 1975 the Officials through a series of provocations in Belfast caused another feud this time with the Provisional IRA. Before this came to an end eleven people had been killed and fifty wounded. Little wonder that in 1977 Long Lartin POWs, in a debate on socialism and nationalism, described the Official IRA as 'a bunch of mixed-up left-wing social democrats who happen to have arms which occasionally they use against Republicans'.[31]

From January to April 1975 according to David O'Connell there was a conscious effort on the part of the military to observe the truce but on the part of the police there was a conscious effort to wreck it. RUC Chief Constable Flanagan refused to adopt a low profile and far from making his men less visible, he pulled them in from all over the Six Counties to send them into the nationalist West Belfast.[32] Violations of the truce increased and the Provisionals began to retaliate although both sides continued to insist they would observe the truce. By October 1975 the Provisionals had logged over 1,500 violations of the truce in Belfast alone.

'Apart from raids, arrests, searches, harassment of the local population in nationalist areas, the British Army committed several murders'.[33]

The Convention elections in May 1975 had made it clear, to even the most optimistic liberal dreamers, that no political compromise was achievable. After this and the Gardiner Report, the British declaration of an intent to withdraw was rapidly being exposed for the cynical deceit it always was. The bombing campaign in England was reactivated in September to remind the British of the price of refusing to withdraw. It was to no avail. The war began again. The truce was now more nominal than real.

In the first fortnight of November the incident centres were closed down. The Provisionals continued to use theirs as advice centres. The same month Merlyn Rees made a key announcement in the House of Commons. After 1 March 1976 Special Category status would no longer apply to anyone convicted of offences committed after that date. There would be no further flow of new prisoners to the compounds but existing prisoners would retain most of the privileges associated with Special Category. On 5 December 1975 the last internees were released from Long Kesh. By the end of 1975 a new legal and judicial framework existed for putting Republicans away. Judicial internment replaced detention without trial. Diplock together with Gardiner was to make the struggle in the prisons the central political issue over the next six years.

Even as late as the end of October 1975 there were those in the Republican Movement who believed that British disengagement from Northern Ireland was 'now inevitable'.[34] This was based on an underestimation of the *political* importance for British imperialism of its occupation of the Six Counties of Ireland. The 'economic cost' to British imperialism was not the ultimate consideration. The revolution in Ireland, as Marx and Engels argued over 100 years before, posed a critical threat to the stability of British imperialism not only in Ireland but also in Britain. The Irish revolution is the key to the British revolution.

Merlyn Rees instinctively recognised this fact when he said during the Constitutional Convention debate in the House of Commons in the speech already quoted, that British withdrawal would lead to the violence spreading to Great Britain and the Republic of Ireland. A J Beith, then Northern Ireland spokesman for the Liberal Party blurted out something along the same lines in the same debate when he said:

> 'I do not see how we can contemplate creating something akin to Angola 20 miles off our own shores . . . '[35]

T E Utley at the time a leader writer for the *Daily Telegraph* gave expression to the nightmare that haunts the ruling class in relation to Ireland:

' . . . The instant withdrawal of British troops . . . would plunge the whole of Ireland into anarchy on a scale hitherto unimagined. Whatever side emerged victorious would almost certainly be anti-British and would tend to look for support to Britain's enemies.

' . . . British security is hardly compatible with the existence of a Cuba a few miles from her Western shores . . . '[36]

Finally John Biggs-Davidson has often voiced the essential connection:

'What happens in Londonderry is very relevant to what can happen in London, and if we lose in Belfast, we may have to fight in Brixton or Birmingham. Just as Spain in the thirties was a rehearsal for a wider European conflict so perhaps what is happening in Northern Ireland is a rehearsal for urban guerrilla war more widely in Europe, particularly in Britain.'[37]

The Republican movement itself later recognised that the belief in a British withdrawal, which was the main factor in the lengthy truce, was a mistake. In 1977, delivering the keynote Bodenstown oration, Jimmy Drumm stated:

'The British government is NOT withdrawing from the Six Counties and the substantial pull-out of businesses and closing down of factories in 1975 and 1976 [the period of the truce] were due to world economic recession though mistakenly attributed to symptoms of withdrawal.

'Indeed the British government is committed to stabilising the Six Counties and is pouring in vast sums of money to improve the area and assure loyalists' support for a long haul against the Irish Republican Army.'[38]

That the truce was a mistake was strongly hinted at in 1978 in an interview given by a senior member of the IRA leadership on behalf of the Army Council:

'There is absolutely no question of another ceasefire or truce. In my opinion the last one went on far too long and it would be almost impossible for anybody to persuade the volunteers that another one would be in the interests of the movement or its objectives.'[39]

The objective effect of the truce for the British was to give them valuable breathing space in which to re-organise RUC/British army intelligence gathering. This resulted in significant damage to the IRA. To such an extent that the IRA in 1977–8 were obliged to carry out a major, and successful re-organisation establishing the present cell structure. As the Army Council spokesman said in the same interview:

'The reason for this was that the British were penetrating the old structure, which was too susceptible to good intelligence work.'[40]

ULSTERISATION AND LOYALIST TERROR

The transferring of responsibility for 'security' to the loyalist 'security forces' involved not only an increase of their numbers but also an increase and an improvement in the weaponry supplied to them. Total British army numbers declined from a maximum of 21,000 (lowest level 16,500) in 1973 to 12,000 by 1980. However, in the same period the RUC (90% Protestant) increased from 4,500 to 7,000, the RUC Reserve from 2,500 to 4,500 (1,000 were full-time) and the UDR (97% Protestant) had 8,000 members by 1980 (of whom 2,500 were full-time). The size of the UDR was approximately the same as the part-time paramilitary loyalist force the B-Specials 'disbanded' in 1969 on the recommendation of the Hunt Report. However that Report had also recommended that the UDR should number no more than 4,000 and be entirely part-time. Thus by 1980 there were altogether 19,500 members of the loyalist 'security forces' in the North of Ireland, bringing the total together with the British army to 31,500.

Along with the increase in numbers in the RUC and UDR has gone an increase and improvement in their weapons. The UDR is equipped with British army self-loading rifles (SLRs), machine-guns and armoured cars. The RUC not only has pistols but has also been armed with Sterling sub-machine guns, M1 carbines and SLRs. It has been given heavy armoured personnel carriers. So the RUC has not only fully returned to being the paramilitary force which it was before the Hunt Report in 1969 but is now much better armed.

The RUC plays an essential role in the other component of the 'Ulsterisation' strategy. That is, in the attempt to 'criminalise' the struggle against British imperialist rule in Ireland. This 'criminalisation' of the revolutionary national struggle followed on from the recommendations of the Diplock (1972) and Gardiner (1975) Reports. It included the ending of Special Category status for political prisoners, together with the arrest and systematic torture of Republicans directed by the RUC in special interrogation centres, in order to obtain 'confessions' and thereby convictions in non-jury Diplock courts. The RUC was increasingly to take over from the British army in attempting to suppress demonstrations in support of political status for Republican POWs. And in many police divisions the UDR – rather than the British army – became the 'back-up' force for the RUC, just as the B-Specials were until 1969. In all this we can see that the return to 'normality' the British Labour government had in mind as part of its 'Ulsterisation' strategy, was the attempt to lay the basis for restoring loyalist rule in the Six Counties without the massive presence of British troops.

Disputes between the Loyalists and the British government in this period – such as the loyalist strike of May 1977 – were simply concerned about the *pace* at which the strategy of 'Ulsterisation' was being implemented. The Labour government had undertaken a policy of repression directed against the nationalist minority to lay the basis for the restoration of loyalist rule. The Loyalists were constantly demanding greater repression and the immediate restoration of Stormont. However British imperialism was not prepared to have the pace of increased repression determined by the Loyalists. The difference was about means not ends. When the Loyalists felt too little repression was being directed against the Republican areas by the official 'security forces' increased activity by loyalist paramilitary organisations and loyalist bombing and assassination squads – the unofficial 'security forces' – would take place.

The official and unofficial 'security forces' have performed complementary roles in terrorising the nationalist minority in the Six Counties.[41] The link between them was established with the tacit agreement of the British government at the very foundation of the loyalist statelet. Entire units of the murderous UVF as well as other smaller loyalist paramilitary groups were recruited into the newly established Ulster Special Constabulary in 1920 and helped establish the state of 'Northern Ireland' by armed force. In a period of loyalist orchestrated terror between 1920 and 1922 over 300 Catholics were killed many of them by the USC. In response to the Civil Rights movement in 1969 the Ulster B Specials joined loyalist mobs in burning out entire streets of Catholic homes, while the RUC attacked nationalist areas with armoured cars and heavy machine guns. Several people were killed and hundreds more were injured. Although the B Specials were disbanded in 1969, many simply joined the RUC Reserve and the UDR. About 50% of the UDR was initially recruited from ex-B Specials and it soon became clear that the UDR was simply the B Specials under another name. Since the fall of Stormont in 1972 the hundreds of Catholics murdered by both the unofficial and official 'security forces' are witness to the continuity between the present system of repression and that established at the foundation of the state.

LOYALIST PARAMILITARY ORGANISATIONS

The main loyalist paramilitary organisations – the unofficial 'security forces' – are the UVF and UDA. The UVF has roots in the initial stages of the Irish conflict. In the 1960s it re-emerged as a small underground terrorist group centred on the loyalist Shankill Road in Belfast. It had an essentially working class membership and a high proportion of shipyard workers. It was said to consist of supporters of Ian Paisley. The UVF carried out the Malvern Street murders in 1966 and was banned. Since that time it has carried out bombings of Catholic premises and been deeply involved in sectarian murders of Catholics. It was legalised briefly in 1974 (with Sinn Fein) and the ban was reimposed in 1975.

The UDA was formed at the end of 1971 out of existing loyalist 'defence' groups. It was heavily armed and staged a series of mass rallies of masked and uniformed men early in 1972. It openly engaged in drilling and other paramilitary operations in May 1972. Its membership comes mainly from the loyalist working class. It has, with the UVF, been mainly responsible for assassination campaigns against Catholic civilians. It was also heavily involved in gangsterism and protection rackets, and various feuds to gain control of the organisation have led to leading members being killed or injured. The UDA played a crucial role in the UWC strike which brought down the power-sharing Executive. It has never been made unlawful in spite of its known involvement in brutal murders of Catholics. A letter in the UDA's newspaper in February 1972 carried a call to suppress the nationalist minority in the following terms:

'Why have they not started to hit back in the only way these nationalist bastards understand? That is ruthless, indiscriminate killing... If I had a flame-thrower, I would roast the slimy excreta that pass for human beings...'[42]

In less emotionally disturbed terms a member of the Protestant Action Force (a pseudonym for the UVF) in the September 1976 issue of the UVF journal *Combat* expressed the rationale behind the random sectarian murders of Catholics when he said:

'There is only one means of defeating an insurgent people who will not surrender, and that is to subject them to a greater force and degree of terrorism than they are able to give or receive. There is only one way to control an area or ghetto that harbours terrorists and insurgents, and that is to reduce its population to fear by inflicting upon them all the horrors of terrorist warfare. Where these means cannot, for whatever reason, be used, the war is lost.'[43]

One does not need to look far for more 'respectable' exponents of such views. In 1971 Brigadier Frank Kitson the British army's 'counter-insurgency' expert, who served in the Six Counties from September 1970 to April 1972, made the threat that he would 'squeeze the Catholic population until they vomit the gunmen out of their system'.[44] Internment, Bloody Sunday, torture and assassinations have all been used by British imperialism in its attempt to terrorise the nationalist minority into submission. However there are political and propaganda limits to the use of such measures by the official 'security forces', as is shown by the numerous attempts by British governments to cover up for them. They must be acceptable to both public opinion in Britain and more significantly to that abroad. However, such methods of terrorising the nationalist minority into giving up its struggle for freedom can be pursued without any such limitations by the unofficial 'security forces' – the UDA, UVF etc.

The loyalist paramilitary organisations and death squads regard themselves in a support capacity to the official 'security forces':

'. . . There is no essential moral difference between official Government action and unofficial loyalist action in the struggle against terrorism and subversion . . . the prime objective of the Ulster Volunteer Force is to train, equip and discipline a dedicated force of loyalist volunteers capable of supporting the Civil and Military Authorities in protecting the people of Northern Ireland in the face of armed aggression from foes foreign and domestic . . . '

They also see themselves as an assurance against any possible decline in the official terror directed against the nationalist minority:

'. . . in the event of political weakness on the part of the Government leading to ineffective security measures, the Ulster Volunteer Force upholds the right to take such effective measures as it may, from time to time, consider necessary for the defeat of terrorism, aggression and insurrection'.[45]

This it should be remembered only repeats the threat made in 1972 by

William Craig, the ex-minister of Home Affairs in the Stormont Parliament, to a Vanguard rally before the fall of Stormont that 'if the politicians fail it will be our job to liquidate the enemy'. A month later in a speech to the Conservative Party's Monday Club in London, Craig said he was prepared to 'shoot to kill' to keep Ulster British and continued:

> ' . . . When we say force we mean force. We will only assassinate our enemies as a last desperate resort when we are denied our democratic rights'.[46]

Finally when confronted with the consequences of his speeches – the sectarian murders of Catholics – he said in a BBC radio interview in December 1972 that although he was not happy with what was happening:

> ' . . . if it is impossible to win our democratic rights without this sort of thing happening then I am prepared to tolerate it'.[47]

So were the British government and the official 'security forces'. In practical terms this has meant the brutal killing of hundreds of Catholics in random assassinations.

ASSASSINATIONS

Apologists for loyalist terror have attempted to explain such assassinations as the last resort of Loyalists provoked beyond endurance by the IRA. Nothing could be further from the truth. The years which have seen the greatest number of sectarian killings have been those years in which a truce has existed between the British army and the IRA or IRA military activity has been low. In 1972 there were 122 sectarian assassinations. During the fourteen days of the 1972 truce which began on 26 June, there were 18 sectarian killings, by 31 July this had risen to 39. The bulk of the assassinations were the result of an organised and concerted campaign carried out by loyalist assassination squads which began in the spring of 1972 and carried on into 1973. The years 1975 (150 killings) and 1976 (175 killings) saw the highest number of sectarian killings and were years in which IRA military activity was low. For most of 1975 a ceasefire existed between the IRA and the British army and discussions between the Provisionals and British government representatives continued until July 1976. The real reason for the assassinations was to terrorise the nationalist minority into submission at a time when the loyalist groups felt that too little repression was being directed by the official 'security forces' against Republican areas. This is the significance of the rise in assassinations during periods of cease-fire or when talks are taking place between the British government and the IRA. When the Ulsterisation campaign began in earnest towards the end of 1976 the number of sectarian killings dropped dramatically to 25 in 1977 and even fewer in 1978. The Loyalists were satisfied after the massive increase in arrests and systematic torture of Republican supporters in Castlereagh etc that the repression of the nationalist minority could be safely left once more to the official loyalist 'security forces' – the UDR, RUC backed by the British army.

That the loyalist assassination squads were concerned to terrorise the nationalist minority can be seen from the brutal character of their killings of Catholic civilians. Their victims were very seldom members of the IRA, and they were very often tortured before being killed. Gerard McCusker, a 25 year old Catholic, was found shot through the head on 14 May 1972. His body had lacerations and bruises consistent with a heavy beating, hair had been pulled out and both his wrists had been broken. A few days after the 1972 truce broke down a loyalist terror squad carried out a particularly brutal killing. On 12 July 1972, at about 3am in the morning, four men broke into the house of Mrs McClenaghan, a Catholic widow with three children. The McClenaghans were a Catholic family living in a Protestant street. The men raped Mrs McClenaghan in front of her mentally retarded 15 year old son David – the other two children were staying with friends. Then they took them both into a bedroom and murdered her son in front of her eyes. She was then shot three times. However she survived and was able to identify and convict the murderers. In her evidence she said one of the men wearing a balaclava helmet had 'UDA' written in ink on one of his hands.

The trial of the 'Shankill Butchers' in early 1979 showed the systematic sadism of the loyalist assassination gangs in their sectarian murders of Catholics. It was also one of the many examples of the involvement of a member of the official 'security forces' in a loyalist death squad and pointed to a clear toleration of their activities by the RUC.

The 'Shankill Butchers' gang killed with impunity for a year and a half (from November 1975 to March 1977), killing altogether 19 people despite clear evidence known to the police pointing to the identity of the killers. Over the period they killed 12 Catholics and 7 Protestants. Of the 7 Protestants murdered, four were shot dead in situations where the gang believed their victims would be Catholics, and three were killed in feuding and brawling incidents. Over the eighteen months, six Catholics had their throats cut, some from ear to ear cutting the flesh right back to the spine. A seventh was bludgeoned to death with a hatchet.

The 'Shankill Butchers', members of the Lawnbrook unit of the UVF, used the same vehicles time after time when they went out on their gruesome killing expeditions. There were repeated reports from witnesses that they had heard a vehicle which sounded like a heavy black taxi engine. Telephone calls claiming some of the killings were made in the name of Captain Long — there is a Long Bar in the Shankill Road. William Moore, the killer most aptly described as the 'Butcher', was a barman in the Long Bar, he owned and drove a black taxi and he was a former butcher's assistant! The 'Shankill Butchers' were responsible for the fatal bombings of the Officials' Easter Parade in 1977, which led to an inter-Republican feud as the Officials stupidly blamed the IRA for the bombing and in response fired into a crowd at an IRA parade at Milltown Cemetery. The RUC would have known it was a loyalist bombing from forensic tests but chose to remain silent. The RUC also tried to cover up for the fact that one of the convicted 'Shankill Butchers' was a serving member of the UDR at the time of his involvement and arrest.

The gang was only eventually arrested because one of its victims who was tortured, slashed with knives, strangled and left for dead, miraculously survived and was, therefore, able positively to identify the members of the gang and thus force the police to arrest them. A great deal was made about RUC 'impartiality' after the trial but this simply was a British propaganda lie. An important element in the campaign of terror against the nationalist minority has been the knowledge by loyalist death squads that they are virtually immune from arrest and prosecution. The fact is that the vast majority of the hundreds of loyalist murders which have taken place since 1972 remain 'unsolved'.

The active involvement by members of the official 'security forces' in loyalist terror attacks takes a number of forms. It includes participation in the attacks, the supply of information, training in the use of weapons and the supply of guns.

Many members of the 'security forces' are members of loyalist paramilitary organisations. Towards the end of 1976 a spokesman for the UDA said that 61 out of the 180 UDA prisoners in Long Kesh were members or ex-members of the 'security forces'. The spokesman estimated that altogether nearly 200 of the Loyalists in prison for political offences at that time were members or ex-members of the 'security forces'. By the beginning of 1979 about 100 members of the UDR had been convicted of offences involving loyalist paramilitary activities — the number who are guilty of similar offences but have never been convicted remains a matter for speculation.

That the official and unofficial 'security forces' see themselves carrying out complementary roles in terrorising the nationalist minority into submitting to loyalist rule is openly acknowledged. In July 1975, at the height of the sectarian murders of Catholics, the UVF issued a statement which included the following:

> 'Many of our contacts within "Charlie" and "Delta" RUC Divisions have reported that the vast majority of grass roots constables, together with several [Special] Branch and CID personnel, were overjoyed at the results of certain PAF operations in recent weeks'.[48]

The 'operations' referred to were a series of sectarian killings, including the killing of two Catholic brothers and their pregnant sister in Tyrone. Members of the 'security forces', especially the UDR, have also themselves carried out many terror attacks on Catholics. UDR members were heavily involved in a series of loyalist murders in Co Tyrone and Co Armagh in 1974 and 1975. In May 1974 a member of the 8th Battalion of the UDR machine-gunned a Catholic man and his wife to death at their home in Co Tyrone. In August 1975 members of the UDR carried out the massacre of three members of the Miami Showband, a southern group whose members were ambushed when returning to the Twenty Six Counties. The three were killed and two wounded after the five band members had been lined up and machine gunned down. Two of the loyalist gang were killed in a premature explosion when they attempted to blow up the Showband's van. The death notices in the UVF's journal *Combat* came not only from the UVF but also from members of the UDR, who expressed their deep regret at the death of their 'colleagues-in-arms' who had been 'killed in action'.[49]

The passing of information to loyalist gangs is important. Often UDR check-points have been noticeably absent when loyalist killings have taken place suggesting either active cooperation or precise information relating to the movement of the 'security forces' being passed to the loyalist gangs. The British army and the RUC have openly cooperated with the UDA in allowing the UDA to set up checkpoints, particularly in Belfast. Many victims of loyalist killings have been picked up at such checkpoints.

It is well known that copies of many files on suspected Republican sympathisers have been passed from the RUC, UDR, and British army to loyalist groups. These files contain not only the names, addresses and photographs of such suspected sympathisers but also detailed information about them, such as their place of work and car registration numbers. In 1975 an organisation called the Ulster Central Intelligence

Agency consisting mainly of members of the RUC, UDR and UVF was set up to coordinate all this information for the benefit of loyalist paramilitary groups.

The UDR provides an ideal training ground for loyalist paramilitary groups. Many join the UDR, receive their weapons training, and then leave after a year or two – the turnover in the UDR is extremely high, nearly 50%. The easy access by the UDR to British army weapons is particularly helpful to loyalist gangs. Since 1972 hundreds of guns have been stolen with the cooperation of members of the UDR. There were two raids in 1972, when the UVF emptied the armouries of the UDR in Lurgan and West Belfast despite the presence of armed sentries and elaborate alarm systems. In 1975 the UDA – with the help of members of the 5th Battalion of the UDR – stole over 200 guns from the UDR armoury at Magherafelt. Guns stolen in such raids – particularly Sterling sub-machine guns – are known to have subsequently been used in killings by loyalist paramilitary groups.

There are those apologists for loyalist terror who attempt to equate it with the IRA's military struggle to free Ireland from British rule. The IRA is fighting a war. It carries out military actions against the 'security forces' and sabotage operations against commercial and economic targets in pursuance of this war. Unlike the loyalist terror gangs the IRA does everything possible to avoid civilian casualties. Inevitably in a war innocent civilians will be killed or injured. The responsibility for this rests solely with the British government and is the result of British imperialism's occupation of the Six Counties of Ireland.

There have been very few cases of IRA units retaliating against the gruesome killings carried out by loyalist murder gangs. The IRA is conducting a military campaign against British imperialism not against Protestants. The IRA Army Council has consistently resisted demands to take retaliatory action. However one case is repeatedly brought up and is used to attack the IRA. It occurred in Bessbrook South Armagh on 5 January 1976. Ten Protestant workmen were machine-gunned to death after they had been ordered out of their mini-bus. This was a retaliatory killing. Five Catholics had been murdered in two attacks on the previous day in South Armagh in the same area. There was bound to be a response. The loyalist terror gangs clearly got the message. Sectarian killings in the area stopped immediately.

The hypocrisy of the British left was exposed as soon as they commented on the killings. They used them to condemn the IRA. The *Morning Star* carried a small article on 5 January 1976 which had the headline '5 Catholics shot dead'. There was no editorial. After the shooting of the

Protestants the lead article screamed out on 6 January 1976 '10 workers massacred in South Armagh' and an editorial stated that 'there must be outright condemnation of retaliatory murders and of recent threats by the Provisional IRA to resume a full-scale campaign of violence . . . '. *Socialist Worker* condemned the killing at Bessbrook 'without reservation' and *Workers Press* (paper of the Workers Revolutionary Party) said that 'such indiscriminate slaughter' far from being a deterrent 'can only play into the hands of the ultra-right gangsters'. The day before this occurred *Workers Press* condemned the military campaign of the IRA.[50]

The loyalist terror gangs such as the UDA and UVF see sectarian assassinations as a *strategy* to terrorise into submission what they regard as the treacherous and rebellious members of an inferior community – the nationalist minority. The British government and official 'security forces', like the governments and security forces in El Salvador and Guatemala, tolerate the activities of the loyalist death squads because they share the identical aim of crushing a rebellious people. In that they have also the support of the cowardly British media. When Maire Drumm was murdered in a hospital bed by a loyalist death squad a few weeks after she had given up the vice-presidency of Sinn Fein the British press rejoiced. 'Grandma Venom Assassinated' screamed the *Daily Express* and they subheaded their story 'A female Hitler: she died by the gun she loved so much'. And the *Daily Telegraph* showed the criminal subservience of the British media to British terror in Ireland. In an editorial it stated:

> 'No normal person could suppress one moment of exultation at the death of Mrs Drumm. She died as she lived by violence and hatred. Justice is done.'[51]

Behind the loyalist death squads stands British imperialism supported by a bought and paid-for press that openly justifies sectarian assassinations.

NOTES

1   Deutsch R and Magowan V, *op cit* Volume 3 p. 37.
2   Faul D and Murray R, *The Shame of Merlyn Rees op cit* p. 13. Much of the information below on Rees and internment is taken from this pamphlet.
3   *ibid* p. 42.
4   *ibid* pp. 26–27.
5   Devlin P, *The Fall of the NI Executive* Belfast 1975 p. 91.
6   *ibid*.

7   Deutsch R and Magowan V, *op cit* Volume 3 p. 154.
8   *ibid*.
9   Secretary of State for Northern Ireland, *The Northern Ireland Constitution* London 1974 pp. 16–17.
10 See Northern Ireland Constitutional Convention, *Report* London 1975.
11 *Hansard* 12 January 1976 Columns 28 and 30.
12 *ibid* column 51.
13 *ibid* column 151.
14 *Republican News* 4 May 1974.
15 *Sunday Times* 18 June 1978.
16 Deutsch R and Magowan V, *op cit* Volume 3 p. 87.
17 *ibid* p. 178.
18 *ibid*.
19 *ibid*.
20 *ibid* pp. 180–181.
21 *ibid* p. 182.
22 See *Sunday Times* 18 June 1978 for details of the truce agreement.
23 Gardiner Lord, *Report of a Committee to consider, in the context of civil liberties and human rights, measures to deal with terrorism in Northern Ireland* London 1975 pp. 3–4.
24 *ibid* p. 5.
25 *ibid* p. 9.
26 *ibid* p. 10.
27 *ibid* pp. 34–5.
28 *ibid* p. 33.
29 *ibid* p. 43.
30 Coogan T P, *On the Blanket* Dublin 1980 p. 61.
31 *An Phoblacht* 17 August 1977.
32 *Sunday Times* 18 June 1978.
33 *Republican News* 3 January 1976 and 31 January 1976.
34 *Republican News* 25 October 1975.
35 *Hansard* 12 January 1976 Column 127.
36 Utley T E, *Lessons of Ulster* London 1975 p. 134.
37 Cited in Troops Out Movement, *No British Solution* London nd (pamphlet) p. 22. Faligot states that Biggs-Davidson said this at a seminar organised by the Royal Institute for Defence Studies in April 1973. See Faligot R, *Britain's Military Strategy in Ireland The Kitson Experiment* London 1983 pp. 2–3.
38 *An Phoblacht* 15 June 1977.
39 *Republican News* 5 August 1978.
40 *ibid*.
41 See John D W, 'Ulsterisation and Loyalist Terror' in *Hands Off Ireland!* No 7 London April 1979.
42 Cited in Dillon M and Lehane D, *Political Murder in Northern Ireland* London 1973 pp. 56–7. This book gives details of sectarian assassinations up to 1973.
43 Cited in John D W, *op cit* p. 5.
44 *ibid*.
45 From *Combat* Volume 1 No 33 1974 cited in *ibid*.
46 Deutsch R and Magowan V, *op cit* Volume 2 p. 173.
47 *ibid* p. 252.

48   From *Combat* July 1975 cited in John D W, *op cit* p. 6.
49   *ibid*.
50   *Morning Star* 5 and 6 January 1976, *Socialist Worker* 17 January 1976 and *Workers Press* 6 and 7 January 1976.
51   *Daily Express* 29 October 1976 and *Daily Telegraph* 30 October 1976.

CHAPTER TWELVE

INSTITUTIONALISED TORTURE
1976–79

Nothing has exposed the moral and political bankruptcy of the British Labour and trade union movement more sharply than its collaboration with the regime of terror administered by the British Labour government in the Six Counties of Ireland from 1976–1979. The Labour government's 'Ulsterisation' strategy required that side by side with responsibility for 'security' being passed to the loyalist 'security forces', the RUC and UDR, went the attempt to 'criminalise' the revolutionary national struggle to free Ireland from British rule. It was this latter aspect of British imperialist strategy which was to institutionalise torture and make the fight against 'criminalisation' the dominant political issue for nearly six years.

Merlyn Rees' term of office as Secretary of State for Northern Ireland had laid the basis for 'Ulsterisation'. Judicial internment replaced detention without trial after the last internees were released from Long Kesh in December 1975. Special interrogation centres were being constructed at Castlereagh, Belfast (operating last half of 1976) and Gough Barracks, Armagh (opened November 1977). New cellular prisons – the H-Blocks – were being built and the first two blocks were completed by the time Rees left office. Four more were completed in 1977. In May 1976 Kenneth Newman became Chief Constable of the RUC. In August 1976 Roy Mason replaced Merlyn Rees as Secretary of State for Northern Ireland. And in October 1977 Roy Mason appointed Major General Timothy Creasey as Commanding Officer of British troops in the Six Counties of Ireland. The backgrounds of Mason, Newman and Creasey show clearly that the British Labour government was now prepared to sanction a regime of terror directed at the nationalist minority.

The Labour Prime Minister, Callaghan, sent Roy Mason to the Six

Counties of Ireland because the failure of the 'power sharing' strategy to isolate the IRA left him with no other policy than outright repression to defeat the nationalist threat to British imperialism's interests in Ireland. Roy Mason was the man for the job. As Minister of Defence in the Labour government he had close links with the military. Mason was typical of the racist-imperialist element in the Labour Party – privileged labour aristocracy – which had come up through the ranks of the working class. Arrogant, ambitious, full of his own self-importance and obviously totally ignorant of Irish history, he was sent to Ireland to defeat 'terrorism'. The Labour Party has a long history of brutalising oppressed peoples and Roy Mason would get on with the job. And he was soon to be working with two men eminently suitable for the task in hand.

Chief Constable Kenneth Newman began his colonial experience as a detective in the Palestine Police from 1946–1948 – the period in which the racist Zionist Israeli state was established on the backs of the dispossessed Palestinian people. He returned to join the Metropolitan police and as a young Chief Superintendent was in charge of organising police tactics to contain the huge anti-Vietnam War demonstration outside the US Embassy in Grosvenor Square in 1968. He was then put in charge of 'Community Relations'. He became an expert in the new police technology of repression aimed at controlling urban unrest. In 1973 he was sent to the Six Counties as Deputy Chief Constable and given the major responsibility for reorganising the detective and intelligence gathering work of the RUC.

Major General Timothy Creasey had impeccable credentials for commanding the British army of occupation in the Six Counties of Ireland. He had a long record of colonial repression against guerrilla armies fighting for self-determination. He was briefly involved in fighting the IRA during the border campaign in 1956. He was a brigade major during Britain's brutal war against the Mau Mau – Land and Freedom Army – in Kenya. He commanded a battalion in the war in Aden. And from 1972–1975 in Oman he had been 'on contract' as Commander-in-Chief of the army of the British imperialist puppet, the Sultan of Oman. There he led a mixed force of SAS men, regular British soldiers, 'contract' officers and locally recruited mercenaries and temporarily defeated the guerrilla army of the Popular Front for the Liberation of Oman. The PFLO complained to Amnesty International that during Creasey's period as Commander torture had been used against prisoners. They gave examples: plucking out hair, teeth and nails; burning with cigarettes and gas torches; electric shock treatment;

persons being put in sacks and dipped alternately in very hot and very cold water; keeping prisoners in shackles; and deprivation of sleep. This then was the man Mason and the British Labour government chose to command the British army during a period of systematic brutality and repression directed against the nationalist minority.

Mason, Newman and Creasey were to use torture in order to get results. While torture was nothing new in this latest phase of the war in Ireland, in the period 1976−9 it became a crucial component of judicial internment − the 'conveyor belt' process of arrest, systematic torture in police cells, forced 'confessions', long remands, Diplock courts, and imprisonment in specially built concentration camps, the H-Blocks.

NEWMAN'S REORGANISATION OF THE RUC

Newman was responsible for reorganising the detective and intelligence-gathering work of the RUC. By the time he was Chief Constable this work was complete. He instituted three major changes.

First, he centralised intelligence by establishing a Criminal Intelligence Section at RUC headquarters, Knock, near Belfast. Three new intelligence units − North, South and Belfast − were set up, subdivided into 16 Divisions, each with similar units. All units fed information into the central system at Criminal Intelligence Headquarters with each unit having access to it. In addition, the RUC had access to the central army computer at Thiepval Barracks Lisburn with details of over half the population of the Six Counties and the Metropolitan Police's Special Branch computer, believed to have records of 1.3 million people.

Second, he reorganised the CID adding four Regional Crime Squads to the existing Divisional CID − one at RUC Headquarters, the other three based at Derry, Armagh and Castlereagh. These Squads with nearly ninety detectives were Newman's torture squads for smashing the Provisional IRA. Their task, in Newman's words, was 'to target the most active members of terrorist organisations'. They carried out most of the interrogations − the majority of which took place at Castlereagh.

Third, a change of the utmost importance which was never announced as such. Newman made Castlereagh a full-time, centralised, specialist interrogation centre. What Peter Taylor, in his important book on interrogation in the Six Counties, *Beating the Terrorists?*, called 'the synthesis of his reorganisation of Intelligence and the CID'. Castlereagh became the critical link in the 'conveyor belt' process that made up judicial internment. Peter Taylor describes the process in the following passage:

'The Criminal Intelligence Unit collated the information, passed it on to the Regional Crime Squads, who interrogated terrorist suspects detained at Castlereagh under the emergency legislation for two to seven days. Here, held incommunicado, without access to solicitors or relatives, suspects made the confessions and signed the statements which were the only evidence offered by the prosecution in the majority of cases that came before the new Diplock Courts. Castlereagh was to be the cutting edge of the government's new policy'.[1]

There can be little doubt that the effectiveness of the 'criminalisation' strategy would decisively rest on 'confessions' made by suspects at the specialist interrogation centre at Castlereagh. In other words the torture of suspects was no aberration but a vital component of the Labour government's 'Ulsterisation' strategy.

ARREST

Under the emergency legislation in the Six Counties the 'security forces' have a totally unrestrained right to detain and arrest someone for questioning. The main legislation used is the Northern Ireland (Emergency Provisions) Act (EPA) 1973, 1978 (we refer to sections of the 1978 Act).[2]

Section 14 of the Act allows a soldier to arrest without warrant and detain for up to four hours anyone suspected of committing, having committed or being about to commit any offence. Section 18 allows someone to be held for up to four hours 'for the purpose of establishing his identity' and makes it an offence to refuse or fail to answer questions about identity, movements or knowledge of any recent life-endangering incident. The main purpose of the four hour detention is mass intelligence-gathering, 'screening' and harassment of the nationalist population.

Section 11 of the Act allows any constable to 'arrest without warrant any person who he suspects of being a terrorist'. The constable may enter any place to make the arrest and the person arrested can be held for up to 72 hours. The decision to arrest depends on the subjective opinion of an RUC constable and no grounds of 'reasonableness' are required. Section 11 is used to make most arrests as it gives the RUC an unrestrained right to arrest for questioning any person for up to 72 hours.

Further provision for arrest exists under the Prevention of Terrorism Act. It has the advantage of allowing the RUC up to seven days, when granted a 5 day 'extension', to force a 'confession' out of a suspect. Of the 955 arrested in the Six Counties under the PTA between 29 November 1974 and 31 December 1980, 786 extended detentions (82%) were allowed.[3] Only two applications were refused. The RUC have total control.

In the Six Counties the percentage of those arrested under the PTA and charged with an offence is 46% (November 1974 to September 1979) compared with less than 7% in Britain. The reason for this contrast is clear. In Britain the PTA is primarily used as a means of harassment and political censorship directed at the Irish community and others in Britain active in support of the Irish people's struggle for freedom. In the Six Counties most arrests are made under the EPA – over 90% between 1 September 1977 and 31 August 1978, but the PTA is seen as a more powerful instrument to put Republicans and their supporters behind prison bars. The extra time of detention permitted – seven days as opposed to three under the EPA – gives the RUC a greater opportunity to force a 'confession' out of those arrested. The *Bennett Report* (see below) went some way to acknowledging this when it said that one clear advantage to the police of arrests under the PTA is 'to give them more time in which to carry out their investigations' and that it is expected that the PTA 'should be used primarily for cases in which detention for a longer period is likely to be thought necessary'.[4]

The PTA is also used to remove key political figures out of circulation in crucial periods of political conflict. 30 H-Block activists for example, were rounded up under the PTA at the end of April 1981, just one week before the death of Bobby Sands MP on hunger strike. No charges were brought in spite of the 'extended' detentions.

The arrest and questioning procedure allowed by the emergency legislation is used both as an oppressive instrument for gathering intelligence and also as a means to harass and terrorise the nationalist minority into giving up their struggle for freedom. When the Ballymurphy priest Father Desmond Wilson claimed damages for false imprisonment by the British army in October 1979 it was thrown out of a Belfast court. The claim failed in spite of the fact that the British army admitted the arrest was a 'mistake' and he had received a letter of apology from the Army. The judge ruled that the law required only that the 'arresting officer' should have 'an honest suspicion, however unreasonable'.[5] This makes clear that the practical effect of the EPA is to give the RUC and British army a totally unrestrained right to arrest for questioning. No 'reasonable' grounds for arrest are necessary.

The statistics reflect this. The great majority of those arrested are never charged. Between 1 September 1977 and 31 August 1978 of the 2,960 held for more than four hours only 1,029 or 35% were charged with an offence. The main police centres where 'suspects' were held were Castlereagh, Gough and Strand Road.

TABLE 2

Arrests 1 September 1977–31 August 1978,
Main Police Centres[6]

Centre	Held under EPA/PTA	Number charged	% charged
Castlereagh	1,619	601	37
Gough	375	103	27
Strand Road	502	122	24

The scale on which interrogations take place in the Six Counties is shown by the number of arrests from 1975 to 1978 under section 11 EPA 1978 (or corresponding section EPA 1973), section 12 PTA 1976, or for a 'scheduled offence' under section 2 of the Criminal Law Act (NI) 1967 (those punishable by 5 or more years imprisonment). In this period there were 12,605 people arrested and questioned by the RUC for serious offences, most of them related to the struggle of the nationalist minority to free Ireland from British rule. The equivalent figure for arrests in Britain would be nearly 450,000. Nothing has changed. The loyalist statelet in the Six Counties of Ireland under British occupation always has been and still is a police state.

TORTURE

The torture of prisoners has been a continual feature of the latest phase of the war conducted by British imperialism in the Six Counties of Ireland. On 16 December 1971 the Twenty Six Counties government took the British government to the European Commission of Human Rights at Strasbourg for violations during the internment operation of Article 3 of the European Convention on Human Rights. After a case which dragged on for five years, with little cooperation and at times wilful obstruction by the British government, the Commission found Britain guilty of torture, inhuman and degrading treatment. This was modified later on appeal to the European Court of Human Rights when the 'torture' verdict was dropped. Both the Commission and Court had found that the ill-treatment of suspects constituted an 'administrative practice', that is to say, the authorities knew about it and condoned it.

Despite assurances to both the British Parliament (Heath in March 1972) and the European Court (Labour Attorney-General Sam Silkin in February 1977) that the 'five techniques' used during the internment operation would not be used again as an aid to interrogation, the torture and ill-treatment of suspects went on. Between August 1971 and November 1974 there were 1,105 complaints of assault and maltreatment lodged against the RUC and 1,078 against the Army. Nearly 800 civil court actions alleging assault by members of the 'security forces' were started between August 1971 and September 1975. By October 1975 over £420,000 had been paid out in compensation by the British government with 567 cases still outstanding. The European Commission and Court were to publish their findings in 1976 and 1978 respectively in a period when the British government was again attempting to deny irrefutable new evidence of torture and ill-treatment of suspects.

It is important to note that with the ending of internment in December 1975 the torture of suspects took on a much more organised and systematic character. Torture was to become an integral part of the 'conveyor belt' process of judicial internment. There could be no question of random brutality here. The torture of suspects was aimed at getting specific results – either a 'confession' of guilt or an agreement to sign a statement already prepared by the police. Something that could be added to the police statistics of 'solved' crimes.

Following a weekend of successful IRA operations in May 1976, during which 4 RUC men and a reserve policeman were killed and a number of others injured, wholesale arrests were made. Merlyn Rees signed seven-day detention orders on eighteen of the men arrested. One of them was the 21-year-old Terry Magill.[7]

Terry Magill was arrested at 4am by the police and army at his mother's council house in Belfast's Turf Lodge district. Magill was interrogated at Castlereagh by a team of 12 detectives working in teams of six for more than 19 hours during the 80 hours he was held in police custody. He signed four statements, two admitting murders and two involving the bombing of hotels. Magill admitted nothing until the last two-hour interview. During the interrogations he had his hair pulled and had been slapped about the face. He was burned with a cigarette on the wrist, between the fingers, on his arms, on his back and on his private parts. He was threatened with electric shocks and told he would be handed over to the UVF. The doctor who examined him when he was being charged at Townhall Street police station noted burn marks on his body. His case came to court a year later. On 8 June 1977 Judge McGrath acquitted him on the grounds that the prosecution had not proved beyond reasonable doubt that inhuman and degrading treatment had not been used and that the statements made were voluntary. What happened to Terry Magill during interrogation was soon to set the pattern for the treatment of the vast majority of so-called 'terrorist' suspects.

Terry Magill's case however was unusual in one respect only – he was acquitted on the basis of statements ruled inadmissible by the judge. According to the *Bennett Report* from 1 July 1976 to 1 July 1978, 2,293 persons appeared at the Belfast City Commission charged with 'terrorist' offences. In that period statements made by only 15 persons were ruled inadmissible in court and a further 11 statements were suspect enough for the Director of Public Prosecutions not to proceed with a prosecution. Once charged and brought before a Diplock court (non-jury court) there is a near certainty of conviction. From 1975 to 1979 between 93% and 96% of cases brought before Diplock courts resulted in convictions. And most significantly between 70% and 90% of the convictions are based wholly or mainly on an admission of guilt – 'confessions' made to the police during interrogation. For the period January to April 1979 the actual figure was 86%. All the available evidence therefore suggests that statements forced out of suspects during interrogation were all that was needed to bring about an almost certain conviction and often a long prison sentence.

The Diplock Report (1972) opened the way for this development. Its main recommendations were incorporated in the EPA 1973 (1978). It was concerned to find a method of putting so-called 'terrorists' behind prison bars other than by internment without trial. Diplock recommended not only non-jury courts for 'terrorist' offences and changing the onus of proof in the case of possession of firearms and explosives so that the accused had to prove his/her innocence, but significantly called for the admissibility of confessions unless obtained by torture, inhuman or degrading treatment. This latter recommendation is incorporated in Section 6 of the EPA 1973 (section 8 EPA 1978). It throws aside the common law principle that statements admitted as evidence should be 'voluntary', that is made as a result of free will and not as a result of undue police pressure. Secondly it breaks with guidelines laid out by the so-called Judges Rules:

'That it is a fundamental condition of the admissibility in evidence against any person, equally of any oral answer given by that person to a question put by a police officer and of any statement made by that person, that it shall have been voluntary, in the sense that it has not been obtained from him by fear of prejudice or hope of advantage, exercised or held out by a person in authority or by oppression.

'... Non-conformity with these Rules may render answers and statements liable to be excluded from evidence in subsequent criminal proceedings.'[8]

The Diplock Report made a fundamental attack on the way the Judges Rules were interpreted in the Six Counties:

'We consider that the detailed technical rules and practice as to the "admissibility" of inculpatory statements by the accused as they are currently applied in Northern Ireland are hampering the course of justice in the case of terrorist crimes . . .'[9]

Diplock then went on to recommend the suspension of the current technical rules etc on the admissibility of confessions 'for the duration of the emergency' and argued they should be replaced by a simple legislative provision that a confession would be admissible unless 'it is proved on a balance of probabilities that it was obtained by subjecting the accused to torture or to inhuman or degrading treatment . . .'. He then went on to spell out clearly what that would mean:

'It would not render inadmissible statements obtained as a result of building up a psychological atmosphere in which the initial desire of the person being questioned to remain silent is replaced by an urge to confide in the questioner, or statements preceded by promises of favours or indications of the consequences which might follow if the person questioned persisted in refusing to answer.'[10]

Any methods short of those coming under the category torture, inhuman and degrading treatment – the definition of which would be left to the unionist judiciary – were now acceptable to get suspects to confess. Methods permissible would presumably also include *threats* of torture so long as they were not carried out. By raising the threshold of 'admissibility' in this way Diplock had opened the way for the actual torture of suspects in interrogation centres like Castlereagh. As soon as the Labour government embarked on its 'criminalisation' strategy the torture of suspects necessarily became a systematic 'administrative practice'. Newman and Mason sanctioned it precisely because it was the only way they could achieve the results demanded by the Labour government.

GETTING RESULTS

On 26 July 1976 Chief Constable Newman issued a new directive to all Divisional Commanders. It was coded SB16/13 and marked 'secret'. It made it clear that from then on responsibility for the command and control of the interrogation system lay with the Chief Constable himself. Peter Taylor argues that the importance of the directive was the distinction it made between an 'interview' – the result of which criminal charges were to be preferred – and an 'interrogation' conducted for the purpose of gaining intelligence.[11] The directive, while stipulating that Judges Rules applied to an 'interview', clearly implied that they did not apply to an 'interrogation'. CID and Special Branch officers were ordered to decide whether a suspect should be interviewed or interrogated on entering police custody. Section 6 of the EPA 1973 had already given the RUC much greater latitude on the questioning of suspects. And as far as access to solicitors was concerned, a right which the Judges Rules give prisoners 'as long as no unreasonable delay or hindrance is caused', the Rules did not apply to either an 'interview' or an 'interrogation'. At Castlereagh and Gough – the main interrogation centres – solicitors were denied access to their clients as a matter of practice. The significance of the directive is that it shows that Newman took direct responsibility for the interrogation system and that he had given his detectives even more reason to assume that the 'maltreatment' of suspects during 'interrogation' had been given the go-ahead.

Of more significance are a number of meetings Newman had with members of the New Regional Crime Squads. Peter Taylor reports on one meeting held in the early summer of 1976 at Castlereagh, Belfast. There were around 100 CID and Special Branch men present of all ranks. At this meeting Newman outlined the significance of his reorganisation of the RUC. He told his men that the only way to defeat the IRA was the rigorous application of the law to put them behind bars. He said he wanted results within the law and said that those who got them would enhance their chances of promotion. At other meetings he made the same point. The pressure was on to get the results, which meant getting 'confessions' and the latitude which both the emergency laws and Newman's directives gave his men would necessarily lead to the torture of suspects during interrogation.

Every month the RUC compiled statistics which they used to

demonstrate their progress in the fight against 'terrorism'. At the end of 1976 Newman announced that the new Regional Crime Squads had successfully eliminated complete 'terrorist' units in various parts of the Six Counties. Charges against the Provisional IRA were more than double those in 1975; charges for murder and attempted murder increased by 7 per cent, use and possession of explosives by 115 per cent; miscellaneous charges – hijacking, arson and membership of illegal organisations – by 187 per cent. However complaints of assault during interview also more than doubled from 180 in 1975 to 384 in 1976. By the end of 1977 they had doubled again to 671.

TORTURERS' CHARTER

In May 1977, Lord Justice McGonigal, a former Second World War commando and founder member of the SAS, made a notorious decision which clearly removed any remaining protection suspects might still have had from maltreatment by the police.

In a judgement after a lengthy trial he stated that Parliament had taken the wordings and standards of section 6 of the EPA from Article 3 of the European Convention on Human Rights. He then went on to define the terms, torture, inhuman and degrading treatment according to the definitions given in a case brought against the Greek Colonels. Having done this he said that the Commission distinguished between acts prohibited in Article 3 and what was called 'a certain roughness of treatment'. He cited as example 'slaps or blows of the hand on the head or face'. He then gave his interpretation of section 6 of the EPA:

'. . . it appears to accept a degree of physical violence which could never be tolerated by the courts under the common law test and, if the words in section 6 are to be construed in the same sense as the words used in Article 3, it leaves an interviewer open to use a moderate degree of physical maltreatment for the purpose of inducing a person to make a statement'.

Using devious legal jargon, no doubt to conceal the fact that he had given a judicial go-ahead for torture, he then goes on to say:

'That does not mean, however, that these courts will tolerate or permit physical maltreatment of a lesser degree deliberately carried out for the purpose of or which has the effect of inducing a person interviewed to make a statement'.

and points to judges' 'discretionary powers' which provide an extra statutory control over the way in which statements are induced and obtained. However he made it clear that such powers should not be used 'so as to defeat the will of Parliament' as expressed in section 6. That is, if a degree of ill-treatment falling short of that required by section 6 (which had to be *gross*) was used to induce a statement, the judge did not automatically have to use his 'discretion' to exclude it. Judicial niceties aside, in the words of Amnesty International, 'the interpretation of section 6 given by McGonigal LJ erodes the protection of suspects from maltreatment by the police'.[12] For one of the Six Counties most senior judges had stated clearly that interrogators could ill-treat suspects within the framework of section 6. Among some sections of the legal profession the McGonigal judgement became known as the torturers' charter. McGonigal had served his masters well. He had interpreted the law in the spirit of the Labour government's 'criminalisation' strategy.

A CATALOGUE OF HORRORS

Mason took over from Rees in Autumn 1976 and the pace of RUC brutality quickened. Two priests Fr Denis Faul and Fr Raymond Murray were soon to produce a closely-typed 200 page catalogue of horrors, *The Castlereagh File*, with example after example of brutal torture carried out at Castlereagh interrogation centre. From July 1976 to November 1979 5,067 suspects were questioned at Castlereagh – 1,964 were charged and 3,103 were released. The brutal interrogation of suspects was normal practice at Castlereagh. Fr Faul and Fr Murray have listed 20 methods of brutality used in Castlereagh and other RUC interrogation centres in 1976–77 – mainly designed not to leave marks:

☆ Hair pulling ☆ Punching to back of head. Heavy slaps across the face and head. ☆ Simultaneous slapping of ears with both hands sometimes perforating eardrums. ☆ Strangling neck. Chops to the throat. Gripping and pulling of Adam's apple. Pushing fingers into pressure points of neck. ☆ Punches and kicks to stomach, buttocks, kidneys, spine. Stiff finger prodding to ribs. ☆ Manual squeezing of testicles, punching and kicking testicles; lifting naked prisoner by placing stick between his legs. ☆ Arm twisting. Bending wrist backwards both above and below arm. Finger twisting. ☆ Positions of stress-search position against wall, sitting on non-existent chair, squatting on hunkers. ☆ Press-ups to point of exhaustion; super press-ups; legs on chair, hands on ground.

Running on the spot to point of exhaustion. ☆ Wrestling holds until prisoner vomits. ☆ Strangling neck and forcing head down to the point of asphyxiation. ☆ Trailing along floor; prone on floor while personnel stand and jump on back riding prisoner like a horse. ☆ Made to lie centre back across a table or chair face upwards. Interrogators then jump on legs causing intense pain to back. ☆ Placing plastic bag, hood, jacket, or underpants, over head to restrict flow of air. ☆ Throwing prisoner from one interrogator to another. ☆ Simulated execution by clicking gun behind the head; simulated electrocution by putting plug into mouth and putting on switch. ☆ Singeing skin with matches and cigarettes. ☆ Degradations – making prisoner lick water or vomit off floor; behave like a dog; spitting in the face; stripping prisoner naked and making obscene remarks about his body, his wife, his children. ☆ Pouring liquid into ears. ☆ Threats to shoot prisoner in lonely place, hand over to UVF, threats to parents.[13]

Additionally statements in *The Castlereagh File* show that women were also sexually abused and threatened with rape.

Bernard O'Connor a middle-class schoolteacher and scoutmaster from Enniskillen was arrested at 5.30am on the morning of Thursday, 20 January 1977 by an Army/RUC patrol. His experiences at Castlereagh became widely known because on 2 March 1977 the BBC 'Tonight' programme broadcast an interview in which Bernard O'Connor told his story.

He was arrested under section 12 of the PTA which meant he could be interrogated for seven days. He was taken to Castlereagh on Thursday morning. He refused a full medical examination but signed a report written by the police doctor from his appearance. The first session of interrogation by two detectives lasted 3½ to 4 hours. He was forced to stand on his toes, bend his knees and hold his hands out in front of him. When his heels touched the ground, or he lost balance, or he tried to wipe the sweat off his forehead he was struck in the face. They tried to get him to admit to taking part in bombings and shooting in Enniskillen. Every time he denied his involvement he was struck in the face. After an hour's break and some food the next session began. This time there were three detectives and they took a 'soft' approach trying to get him to agree to lesser charges to avoid 35 years in gaol. They questioned him for 4 hours but got nowhere. Back to the cell for tea and then another session with interrogators who made out they were very angry with him for not accepting help from the previous interrogators. They said that he was a top man in the Provisional IRA and he was going to be cracked.

With the next session the brutality and torture really began. It lasted well into the next morning. He was beaten up, forced to do strenuous exercises, press-ups and sit-ups, stripped naked and made to continue with the exercises. His track-suit top was placed over his head and his nose and mouth were blocked off. He heard a detective say 'choke the bastard' and he thinks he might have fainted. At one stage he was made to strip and his underpants, severely soiled with sweat and excretion, were placed over his head and he was made to run round the room while the detectives mocked him about his private parts. He was made to pick up the contents of a wastepaper basket the detectives had thrown on the floor. The cigarette butts had to be picked up with his mouth one by one while the interrogators kicked him. He was made to lick water up off the floor. Finally he was threatened with being driven to the top of the Shankill Road and handed over to the UVF.

Bernard O'Connor admitted nothing. He was again assaulted during interrogation on the Friday. On Saturday he underwent intense questioning and was asked by a senior detective to sign a written statement admitting murder of a police constable. He refused. At tea time on Saturday he saw his own doctor and had a medical examination. After the examination his interrogators continued with different teams of detectives until 5am Sunday morning. It began again at 3pm Sunday and continued until 3am Monday morning. Interrogation continued Monday late morning until tea when he was released. No charges were made.

The TV programme with the interview went out in spite of pressure to delay it. It stirred a hornet's nest of defenders of RUC torture. Roy Mason accused the programme of being one-sided. Airey Neave, then Conservative spokesman for Northern Ireland, later to be assassinated by INLA, accused the BBC of losing sight of its responsibilities in Northern Ireland and said that the programme had damaged the morale of the RUC. The truth clearly did not matter. The Senior Deputy Chief Constable Harry Baillie said:

'It is quite clear that there is a renewed and orchestrated campaign to blacken the RUC in the eyes of the local community and the world at large. I believe, however, that a sufficiently large number of people are now wise enough to recognise the terrorist lie and to see the RUC for what it truly is'.[14]

Bernard O'Connor filled in a complaint form against the police. The Complaints and Discipline Branch of the RUC investigated the complaint and submitted the papers to the Director of Public Prosecutions as was the practice. The DPP directed no prosecution. O'Connor took out a civil action for damages against the Chief Constable, Sir Kenneth Newman. It finally came to court in June 1980. The hearing lasted 21 days. Mr Justice Murray awarded O'Connor 'exemplary' damages of £5,000 and cited a previous case in which Lord Devlin had awarded 'exemplary' damages because of 'oppressive, arbitrary or unconstitutional acts by a servant of the Government'.[15] The case did show 'the RUC for what it truly is' however the 'servant of the Government' has never been prosecuted for his crimes.

The catalogue of horror on RUC interrogation in the Six Counties grew and grew as Newman and Mason more and more vigorously denied torture was taking place. Attempts by the RUC to explain suspects' severe injuries and in one case death as a result of interrogation began to resemble those 'explanations' so frequently used by the police in the racist South African police state.

Eddie Rooney was arrested on Monday morning 28 February 1977 after a dawn swoop on his flat. He was taken to Springfield Road RUC Barracks, processed, and handed over to the RUC Special Branch for interrogation. The next thing that was heard was that a serious 'accident' had taken place at the Barracks on Monday evening. In an official statement the RUC claimed that Eddie Rooney had taken 'two detectives completely by surprise by leaping from his seat and diving through a glass window'. The window was in the top floor of the barracks. Eddie was taken to the Royal Victoria Hospital where he lay unconscious for several days in intensive care. His injuries included a fractured skull, a collapsed lung, a bad eye injury, a busted nose, severe chest and arm bruising and knuckles on one hand badly damaged.

The injuries sustained suggest a quite different version of events than that given by the RUC. In a statement *Republican News* said 'We believe that twenty-five year old Eddie Rooney ... after being beaten unconscious and his face left a bloody pulp, was thrown out of the top storey window at the back of Springfield Road RUC Barracks late last Monday night in a fake "suicide" attempt.' Eddie miraculously survived. He told his father during a hospital visit that he had been beaten for 12 hours before being taken to a window and threatened. His father said that he had passed out and could not remember anything else after the beating.[16]

Brian Maguire was a 27 year old electronics engineer who worked at Strathearn Audio plant in Andersonstown. He was secretary of his factory branch of the Technical and Supervisory section of the AUEW and an activist in the Trade Union Campaign Against Repression. Brian was arrested at 6am on Tuesday 9 May 1978 and taken to Castlereagh. He was interrogated in connection with the shooting of an RUC man. According to the police he made a statement on the same afternoon confessing to hiding a gun assumed to have killed the RUC man. Next morning, according to the police, he was found dead, hanging in his cell at 7.30am. Between 7.15am when the electric light above his cell door had been switched on from the outside and 7.30am when breakfast was brought to his cell he was supposed to have torn a strip from the sheet on his bed fastened one end to the ventilation grille, the other round his neck and hanged himself – and have done this undetected. Family and friends of Brian Maguire, needless to say, didn't believe the story. *Republican News* said 'all pointers indicate that the RUC Special Branch had, this time, gone so far with the "mock" strangulation of one of their victims that they killed him'. As in the case of the supposed 'suicide' of trade union leader Dr Neil Aggett in a South African police cell in February 1982 no one could have any doubts that responsibility for his death lay directly with his police interrogators. Brian Maguire was murdered. His death was the result of institutionalised torture in interrogation centres like Castlereagh.[17]

Buried on the same day as Brian Maguire was an IRA volunteer Jake McMahon. He was last seen alive at Musgrave Street RUC barracks on 18 January 1978. His badly decomposed body was recovered from the River Lagan at York Dock at the beginning of May – some four months later.[18]

Peter McGrath, aged 64, was arrested at his home on 6 June 1977. This elderly man was taken to Castlereagh for interrogation. He attempted to defend himself after being physically assaulted by his interrogators. He ended up spending six weeks in a psychiatric hospital after his experience in Castlereagh.[19] Many of those interrogated suffered severe mental damage and required psychiatric treatment sometimes for a number of years.

TORTURERS EXPOSED

By autumn 1977 allegations of torture were becoming so widespread that many outside the nationalist minority were no longer prepared to regard them as mere 'Provisional IRA propaganda'. On 27 October 1977 ITV's 'This Week' programme under the title 'Inhuman and Degrading Treatment' investigated ten cases whose complaints and medical reports were summarised. A Catholic GP, two men tortured at Castlereagh, a solicitor, a legal expert and a councillor on the Police Authority's Complaints Committee were interviewed. Newman refused to be interviewed. A few hours before the programme went out, Newman said he was placing his men 'on red alert' as he believed the programme likely to put their lives at risk. In a prerecorded statement on the programme – a management condition for its transmission – Newman said:

> 'Finally let me make it quite clear, there is no policy or toleration of ill-treatment in this Force. Quite the contrary. And this Force is vitally concerned with human rights. In fact, it is very concerned with the most fundamental right of all, the right to live.'[20]

Tell that to Brian Maguire's family!

The programme raised a storm of protest especially from politicians at Westminster. These well-known defenders of 'democracy' were concerned not with the torture but its exposure. Roy Mason had the nerve to accuse the programme of being 'riddled with unsubstantiated allegations' and the programme makers of 'cheque-book television' and of making a series of programmes unhelpful to the security forces.[21] That he could go on the offensive in this way, says a great deal about the corrupt character of the Labour government and Labour Party to which he belonged.

The programme however did force people to take notice. In the week following its transmission Amnesty International announced that it was sending a mission to investigate the allegations. Roy Mason announced that Amnesty would be afforded every facility, but said that no individual cases could be discussed as they were *sub judice* – the excuse everyone in authority conveniently uses to try to prevent people investigating or commenting on police crimes. The degree to which the RUC were confident that Mason, Newman et al would sanction their crimes and cover up for them is measured by the fact that even now, with public concern increasing, the complaints of assault during interview also *increased*. They only dropped significantly in the month when Amnesty International arrived in the Six Counties to carry out its investigations. The other times when they were very low were the month the *Amnesty Report* was published and the month following the *Bennett Report*. Torture could be turned on and off like a tap.

Amnesty International visited the Six Counties from 28 November to 6 December 1977 and examined 78 cases (41 had been released without charge). Besides direct testimony from 52 complainants, they interviewed many people in authority, including the Chief Constable, the DPP, members of the Police Federation, Police Authority, doctors under the Authority, head of RUC Complaints branch and so on. They met civil rights organisations, lawyers, GPs and politicians at the local and national level. The mission was not however 'afforded every facility' by the Secretary of State, Roy Mason. It was denied access to the most important information of all: the medical reports compiled by the Police Surgeons and the Senior Medical Officers at Castlereagh and Gough. The Police Authority, which employed all the doctors, had instructions from the Secretary of State not to make them available to the mission. The Police Surgeons had no objections to Amnesty seeing their reports but the Secretary of State stood firm. Roy Mason had something to hide. The official medical reports contained the most damaging testimony of all – they confirmed local GPs' findings and showed there was systematic maltreatment of suspects interrogated at Castlereagh and other police centres.

Amnesty International sent its report to Roy Mason on 2 May 1978. It had found the allegations of what it called 'maltreatment' to be substantiated:

'Amnesty International believes that maltreatment of suspected terrorists by the RUC has taken place with sufficient frequency to warrant the establishment of a public inquiry to investigate it.'[22]

Amnesty's findings confirmed the use of the torture techniques listed by Fr Faul and Fr Murray (see above). On 26 May 1978 Roy Mason wrote to Amnesty International asking its International Executive to postpone publication. He asked Amnesty to identify its 78 cases so they could be investigated. This delaying tactic however did not work.

On 30 May a picket called by the Prisoners Aid Committee, and supported by Sinn Fein, Revolutionary Communist Group (RCG), Release, Harringay United Troops Out Movement (UTOM) took place outside Amnesty International's London office. It drew attention to the inordinate delay over the publication of its Report and to the failure of Amnesty to investigate torture in the H-Blocks and English prisons.

Other forces were also at work. The report was soon leaked and on 5 June the *Irish Times* carried a brief résumé of the Report, and on 7 June BBC-TV's 'Tonight' programme gave details of it. ITV's 'This Week' planned to put out a programme on the Report which included an interview with councillor Jack Hassard of the Police Authority's Complaints Committee in which he said that the Chief Constable and the Secretary of State had known all along what was happening. The programme was banned by the IBA. Extracts of it were however shown on the BBC-TV's 'Nationwide' programme.

There was now a widespread call for a public inquiry to examine the allegations. Roy Mason and the Labour government resisted this, and instead, to cover up for their crimes, set up 'an independent and impartial' inquiry to 'examine police procedures and practice' in relation to interrogation. There was no mention of investigating the allegations in the terms of reference. The Chairman of the inquiry was Judge Harry Bennett, and it was to investigate, in *private*, the police procedures. It was not empowered to take evidence on oath or enforce attendance of witnesses or the production of documents. So much, or so little, for the much vaunted British 'democracy'. Many individuals and organisations who had given evidence to Amnesty boycotted the Bennett Inquiry on the grounds it was a private inquiry and did not address itself to the specific question of ill-treatment.

A week before the *Bennett Report* was published LWT's 'Weekend World' carried a dramatic interview by Mary Holland with Dr Irwin one of the main police surgeons responsible for medically examining 'suspects' before and after 'interrogation'. For over two years Dr Irwin had with other colleagues informed the Police Authority, the Chief Medical Officer at the DHSS and Chief Constable Newman of their concern at the 'ill-treatment' taking place but to no avail. Now he decided to speak out. On the programme he said that over the past three years he had seen roughly between 150 and 160 cases in which he was not satisfied that the injuries were self-inflicted. This reference to injuries not being 'self-inflicted' was in answer to the propaganda put out by Newman and Mason that prisoners were injuring themselves as part of an IRA propaganda campaign against the police. Indeed, as accusations of torture mounted, Newman, far from telling his police thugs to stop the torture, issued instructions to them to 'take precautions to prevent self-inflicted injuries by prisoners'.[23]

The television programme caused the predictable form of protest – again not against torture but against its exposure. A particularly nasty smear campaign was directed at Dr Irwin. The Northern Ireland Office and the RUC leaked the fact that his wife had been raped, possibly by a soldier, and suggested that Dr Irwin had harboured a grudge against the RUC ever since for failing to catch the assailant. The aim of the 'leak' was to question Dr Irwin's motives in order to undermine his damaging accusations. However it backfired. Such a tactic was not even acceptable to the Fleet Street gutter press.

The *Bennett Report* was published on 16 March 1979. Among much talk of a 'campaign to discredit the police', 'inventing allegations against the police', 'tragedies inflicted on the RUC' it was forced to admit that in the case of certain injuries on 'suspects':

> 'There can, however, whatever the precise explanation, be no doubt that the injuries in this last class of cases were not self-inflicted and were sustained during the period of detention at a police office'.[24]

The *Bennett Report* made certain recommendations for future procedures as regards interrogation on the understanding that they did not impair 'the efficiency of the interrogation in obtaining evidence leading to the conviction of criminals'.[25] These included access to solicitors every 48 hours, a medical examination offered every 24 hours, closed circuit television in the interview rooms so uniformed members of the RUC could monitor interrogations etc. All this however was clearly 'cosmetic'. The RUC is a sectarian force, an indigenous arm of British repression in Ireland. The British government sanctioned torture. Public 'concern' might force the RUC to reduce the ill-treatment and torture of prisoners for a period of time but it will inevitably return. Indeed only the week after the *Bennett Report* was published one of the Senior Medical Officers based at Gough Barracks, Dr Elliot, finally resigned after a dispute with detectives about the interrogation of two youths whose mental condition Dr Elliot was very concerned about. In his letter of resignation he said that his experiences had shown him two things: that results were expected and were to be obtained even if a certain degree of ill-treatment were necessary, and that a degree of ill-treatment was condoned at a high level.

TORTURE – AN 'ADMINISTRATIVE PRACTICE'

In 1978 more than 1,000 complaints files, covering all police activities, were submitted to the DPP. In the 826 cases in which a decision was made the DPP ordered that no proceedings be instituted against the police officers concerned in no less than 787 cases (95%). The *Bennett Report* found that between 1972 and the end of 1979 no final conviction of a police officer was recorded in any case of ill-treatment during interrogation. This in spite of the fact that compensation has been paid out to victims of torture and ill-treatment in a whole number of cases during that period. The police complaints machinery gives almost 100% protection to police officers torturing 'suspects'.

However, in addition to this, torture was condoned by the Labour government, Secretary of State Mason and Chief Constable Newman.

There is ample evidence to show they were aware of what was going on, and from their numerous crude attempts to cover up for it, it becomes obvious that they clearly sanctioned it.

The Police Surgeons had offered evidence to their Association concerning the ill-treatment of suspects as early as March 1977. The Police Authority were informed of this in April 1977. Dr Irwin had also written to the Chief Medical Officer at the DHSS about an increasing number of persons alleging assault in custody in April 1977. He also said that clinical evidence showed various degrees of injuries.[26] The Chief Constable was almost certainly informed by summer 1977 of Dr Irwin's concern and asked for an explanation of the injuries. A letter had been sent to the Police Authority in July 1977 by the Police Surgeons requesting a meeting with the Chief Constable. In October 1977 the Police Surgeons were forced to issue a press statement saying they had requested a meeting with the Chief Constable but he had not replied after Newman had denied receiving a communication from them. On 11 October 1977 the Police Surgeons finally met the Chief Constable at RUC headquarters. He said he would investigate the cases. In November 1977 the Police Complaints Committee saw Newman. Nothing was done.

By March 1978 after the visit of Amnesty International, the Police Surgeons told a secret meeting of the Complaints Committee that they would speak out publicly if things didn't improve. On 21 March 1978 a meeting between the Chief Constable, the Complaints Committee and the doctors was finally held. There was a blazing row but Newman refused to yield ground and did nothing. And so it went on.

Amnesty reports that a group of solicitors doing over 90% of all cases, after a meeting in November 1977, approached Mason and told him of their conviction that 'ill-treatment of suspects by police officers, with the object of obtaining confessions, is now common practice'.[27] The solicitors in fact considered a total withdrawal from practice in non-jury courts.

The Labour government was also made aware of what was going on. As early as November 1977 the DPP put in writing to the Chief Constable his concern at the increasing number of complaints alleging assault in police custody. He gave the Chief Constable all the necessary statistics and, in 30 cases, medical evidence showing assault had taken place. Newman was told that the courts were not the place to deal with the matter as prosecutions would not be successful. As usual he promised he would investigate. In the same month the Labour Attorney-General Sam Silkin sent a confidential minute to the Prime Minister,

James Callaghan, describing the contents of the DPP's letter to the Chief Constable. So before the Amnesty mission set foot in the Six Counties the British Labour government knew that suspects had been tortured during interrogation.

Newman left the Six Counties in December 1979. British strategy was by this time in disarray and fully exposed. Nevertheless he received a knighthood for he had served British imperialism well and consistently covered up for its crimes. It is no coincidence that this man, who sanctioned torture in the Six Counties, was, one year after the uprisings in British cities, made Commissioner of the Metropolitan Police. But, needless to say, the Labour and trade union movement which refused to oppose torture in Ireland has also refused to protest against Newman's appointment.

The Labour government's 'criminalisation' strategy demanded torture. Faithful as ever to British imperialism the Labour government sanctioned it. But it did not end in the interrogation centres. The torture and brutalisation of prisoners carried on in the prisons.

NOTES

1 Taylor P, *Beating the Terrorists?* London 1980 p. 63. Much of the detail in this chapter comes from this excellent book.

2 The detail of this legislation given below is taken from Harvey R, *Diplock and the Assault on Civil Liberties* London 1981 (pamphlet) especially pp. 11–17. See also Boyle K, Hadden T and Hillyard P, *Ten Years on in Northern Ireland* London 1980. Statistics on arrests etc are taken from both the above and Bennett H, *Report of the Committee of Inquiry into Police Interrogation Procedures in Northern Ireland* London 1979.

3 Harvey R, *op cit* p. 15.

4 Bennett H, *op cit* p. 24.

5 Harvey R, *op cit* p. 14.

6 *ibid* p. 14. The full list is in Bennett H, *op cit* p. 141.

7 See Taylor P, *op cit* pp. 65–6 and Faul D and Murray R, *The Castlereagh File op cit* pp. 9–10.

8 Cited in Amnesty International, *Report of an Amnesty International Mission to Northern Ireland* London 1978 pp. 58–59.

9 Diplock Lord, *op cit* p. 31.

10 *ibid* p. 32.

11 Taylor P, *op cit* pp. 68–9.

12 Amnesty International, *op cit* pp. 62–63 and Taylor P, *op cit* pp. 72–77.

13 See Faul D and Murray R, *op cit* p. 43.

14 Taylor P, *op cit* p. 162.

15 The case of Bernard O'Connor is given in detail in chapter 8 of Taylor P, *op cit* and Faul D and Murray R *op cit* pp. 20–41.

16 Faul D and Murray R, *op cit* pp. 116–122 and *Republican News* 5 and 12 March 1977.
17 Taylor P, *op cit* pp. 281–284 and *Republican News* 20 May 1978.
18 *Republican News* 20 May 1978.
19 Faul D and Murray R, *op cit* pp. 190–192 and Taylor P, *op cit* pp. 186–187.
20 Taylor P, *op cit* p. 222.
21 *ibid*.
22 Amnesty International, *op cit* p. 70.
23 *The Guardian* 25 June 1977.
24 Bennett H, *op cit* p. 55.
25 *ibid* p. 14.
26 Taylor P, *op cit* pp. 179–180. The information below is taken from this book.
27 Amnesty International, *op cit* p. 4.

CHAPTER THIRTEEN

THE WAR IS TAKEN TO BRITAIN

The attempt by British imperialism to remove the political legitimacy of the revolutionary national struggle to free Ireland from British rule has nowhere been more clearly demonstrated than in Britain itself. The repression directed at Republican supporters, the arrests, torture, frame-ups, and trials together with Republican resistance in the prisons have their counterparts here in Britain. While on nothing like the same scale as that in the Six Counties, the essential features have been the same.

THE BOMBING CAMPAIGN IN BRITAIN

The Republican Movement has always reserved the right to extend its war against British imperialism into Britain itself. The campaign in Britain has been sustained over the last eleven years. Numerous bomb attacks, shootings and letter bomb campaigns have taken place. While imperialist propaganda has attempted to present the campaign as 'mindless' and 'desperate' acts 'directed against civilians', in fact the campaign in Britain has always been an integral part of the overall war against British rule in Ireland.

The first bombings by the Provisionals took place in London on the day of the Border Poll in the Six Counties on 8 March 1973, with car bombs exploding outside the Old Bailey and Great Scotland Yard. They were a forceful reminder to the British people of Republican opposition to the British-imposed border. The next phase of the campaign took place after the elections to the Northern Ireland Assembly in June 1973 and during the period of wheeling and dealing to set up a power-sharing Executive, finally achieved in November 1973. Incendiary devices and small bombs were used and placed in shops and prestige targets. On 18 August fire bombs set fire to parts of Harrods. On 20 August shops were destroyed in Hampstead and fire bombs were found in Liberty's Regent Street. Bookbombs and more fire bombs followed. Two people were injured when a letter bomb went off at the Stock Exchange. The campaign ended on 12 September with two quite large bombs in London injuring six people. While the SDLP was negotiating a crooked deal with British imperialism and the Twenty Six Counties government, the IRA was making it clear that this attempt to isolate and destroy it was failing.

The next phase of the campaign opened in January 1974 after the Sunningdale agreement had been signed. There were bombs at Madame Tussauds and at the Earls Court Boat Show on 5 January. Warnings were given and no-one was injured. Next day a 30lb bomb exploded outside the home of British army Adjutant General Sir Cecil Blacker. On 4 February a 50lb bomb exploded on a coach travelling along the M62 which was carrying British army personnel from Manchester to Catterick Camp. Eight soldiers and three others were killed. Judith Ward was framed and sentenced to life imprisonment (30 years) for this bombing. The IRA said that one of their units had carried out the bombing and that Judith Ward was not a member of the IRA. On 26 March Claro-Deverell Barracks, Ripon, was bombed. The targets in this phase of the campaign were prestige tourist areas and military targets. Throughout the summer various explosions took place including one in June which extensively damaged Westminster Hall, Houses of Parliament. It came a fortnight after the murder of Michael Gaughan, an Irish prisoner who had been on hunger strike in Parkhurst prison. On 17 July a satchel bomb went off in the Tower of London killing one woman and injuring many tourists. No organisation claimed responsibility.

The next major explosions occurred in October and November 1974 when pubs used by army personnel in Guildford and Woolwich were bombed. In the Guildford explosion which occurred a few days before the October General Election, five people were killed, four of them army personnel. Paul Hill, Carole Richardson, Patrick Armstrong and Gerry Conlon were framed and sentenced to life, indefinite detention, 35 years and 30 years respectively for the Guildford and Woolwich bombings. Both bombings were later claimed by the Balcombe Street IRA Active Service Unit.

The 1974 bombing campaign in Britain created a rising demand for 'tough measures' against 'terrorism'. On 21 November 1974 the Labour government got its excuse to introduce them. Bombs exploded in two pubs in Birmingham killing 21 people and injuring over 160 others. Immediately after the bombings, the Provisional IRA issued a statement pointing out that it was not IRA policy 'to bomb non-military targets without giving adequate warning to ensure the safety of civilians'. The statement disclaimed responsibility for the bombings. Five men from the Six Counties living in Birmingham were arrested as they boarded the Heysham-Belfast ferry a few hours after the explosions. Another was arrested in Birmingham. They were beaten up by the police, forced to sign 'confessions' and framed for carrying out the Birmingham bombings. A wave of anti-Irish hysteria spread through Britain whipped up by the British press. Roy Jenkins, the Labour Home Secretary, rushed through Parliament the obviously previously prepared anti-Irish Prevention of Terrorism Act.

The Prevention of Terrorism (Temporary Provisions) Bill was presented to Parliament on Wednesday 27 November 1974. It was given an unopposed third reading at 8.46am on Friday 29 November after an all night sitting lasting nearly 17 hours. By 9.25am the Bill had been taken through all stages in the House of Lords and at 9.35am it received the Royal Assent. This draconian Act proscribed the IRA; made membership or support for it an offence; empowered the Home Secretary to expel Irish people from Britain (including people of Irish origin who had lived in Britain for less than 20 years) or to prevent their entry into Britain; gave the police draconian powers to arrest suspects without warrant and to hold them without charges for up to 7 days.

Not a single one of the so-called 'defenders of freedom' on the Labour 'left' voted against the Act. While the British 'left' opposed the PTA it put most of its energy into condemning the Provisional IRA. The *Morning Star* 'condemned terror bombings' which it said 'only play into the hands of the right wing'. It opposed the PTA – 'Jenkins' Law' – on the grounds that such measures have been tried in Northern Ireland and only end up deepening divisions in the community and increasing sympathy for 'extremists' such as the Provisional IRA.[1] *Socialist Worker* carried *five* pages on the Birmingham bombings mostly given over to attacking the Provisional IRA. It opposed the PTA because it would not stop the bombings here. On the contrary it is the history of repression that 'drives young people to the desperate planting of bombs'. Its headlines on page one sum up its priorities in the order given. 'All socialists must condemn these senseless killings; Stop the bombings; Troops out of Ireland; Fight repression in Britain and Ireland'.[2] *Workers Press*, *Militant*, *Red Weekly* (IMG) all condemned the bombings claiming that they alienated the British working class and prevented the mobilisation of British workers against British imperialism. *Militant* said the IRA bore a 'moral responsibility' for the Birmingham bombs 'even if not directly implicated'.[3] Finally the IMG felt it necessary to tell the police, in case they had any ideas of using the PTA against them, that 'the IMG has never, and does not now, support the IRA by material, financial or by any other such means . . . nor do we support them politically'.[4] The bombing campaign in England had soon terrified these middle class 'revolutionaries' into very quickly reconsidering their earlier 'Victory to the IRA' position. Not guilty M'Lord.

The PTA had not the slightest effect on the military campaign in Britain – nor was it ever intended to. Its purpose was to provide a legal cover for the systematic harassment of the Irish community in Britain in general and for all, in particular, who were prepared to fight for a united Ireland. After the Bloody Sunday murders of January 1972, the British police broke up what was to prove to be, during the present campaign, the largest demonstration in Britain against British rule in Ireland. The British government was not prepared to tolerate any serious opposition here in Britain to its rule of terror in the Six Counties of Ireland. Given both the cowardice and anti-Republican standpoint of much of the British 'left', the PTA therefore effectively blocked large-scale organised campaigning, particularly by Irish people in Britain, against British rule in Ireland. The threat of deportation, interrogation and surveillance has become part of everyday life for Irish workers in this country. The passing of the PTA indicated to those who could recognise reality that British imperialism was preparing itself for a long war against the Irish people.

Immediately following the passing of the PTA, the campaign in Britain continued in December with bombs going off in Bath, Bristol, Aldershot and in London at Piccadilly, South Kensington, Soho, Tottenham Court Road and Oxford Street. On 22 December a bomb was thrown into the London home of Edward Heath just three hours before the IRA began a unilateral ceasefire during Christmas 1974. The December bombings were not only a reply to the PTA but importantly were connected with the truce negotiations opened at Feakle on 10 December 1974. During the negotiations the British had accused the IRA of being unable to control its Active Service Units in England. The IRA replied by stating that a spate of bombings would take place in Britain ending at midnight 27 January 1975. On 27 January six bombs went off in Manchester and London. There were no more bombs in Britain until the second truce broke down.

The bombing campaign was restarted in August and September 1975 to remind the British government of the price it would have to pay if the British refused to withdraw from Ireland and the truce broke down. On 29 August a bomb went off in Kensington Church Street killing a bomb disposal expert. On 2 September, despite a 23 minute warning, a bomb placed in the London Hilton hotel detonated killing two and injuring seven. Other bombs went off in Caterham in Surrey and Oxford Street in London at the end of September. Bombs were placed in restaurants frequented by the rich, under cars and at tube stations. On 27 November 1975 the arch-reactionary Ross McWhirter, who had announced a £100,000 reward for information against the IRA, was executed.

It is clear that every phase of the bombing campaign in Britain was tied to the development of the war against British imperialism in Ireland. The IRA have always been aware that bombs in Britain have a much greater impact than similar bombs in Ireland. The British ruling class cares little or nothing about Irish people or, indeed, about its own soldiers dying in Ireland.

Despite the show trials (see below), framings, torture, lengthy sentences, deportations and the PTA, the IRA's ability to conduct military campaigns in Britain has never been undermined. Those campaigns will clearly continue until Britain finally gets out of Ireland. In a historic speech from the dock before the jury retired on 7 February 1977, Joe O'Connell, one of the Balcombe Street four, defended the IRA's position on the bombings in Britain:

'These incidents have been put completely outside the context in which they occurred in a way that is neither just nor consistent with the truth. The true context is that of the relationship between this country and our country – Ireland. That relationship is one of a state of war against the occupation of Ireland by Britain. No mention has been made in this court of the violence suffered by the Irish people: of the use of internment without charge or trial in the Six Counties; of the conviction before the European Court of Human Rights of the British Government for the torture of Irish people; nor of the many brutalities of British colonial rule. The judge has attempted to restrict the reference to bombings and shootings to 'terrorist' offences. We would like to ask the judge whether the bombing of Hiroshima and Dresden were terrorist offences? Whether the torture carried out by British soldiers in Aden and Cyprus and Hola Camp Kenya were acts of terrorism? . . .

'This government carried out acts of terrorism in order to defend British Imperialism and continues to do so in Ireland. We have struggled to free our country from British rule . . .

'We admit to no "crimes" and to no "guilt" for the real crimes and guilt are those of British Imperialism committed against our people. The war against imperialism is a just war and it will go on, for true peace can only come about when a nation is free from oppression and injustice. Whether we are imprisoned or not is irrelevant for our whole nation is the prisoner of British Imperialism. The British people who choose to ignore this or to swallow the lies of the British gutter press are responsible for the actions of their government unless they stand out against them.

'As volunteers of the Irish Republican Army we have fought to free our oppressed nation from its bondage to British Imperialism of which this court is an integral part.'[5]

SHOW TRIALS AND IMPRISONMENT

Contrary to the claims of opportunists, in the last period of the Irish war imperialist repression directed at Irish people in Britain began before a bomb went off in Britain.[6]

In February 1970 Eamonn Smullen and Gerry Doherty were sentenced to eight years and five years (reduced to five and three years on appeal) at Leeds Crown Court. They were set up by Reginald Gee, a gun dealer in Huddersfield who claimed that Smullen, Doherty and John Meehan, all members of Clann na h'Eireann at the time, had approached him for guns. With the co-operation of the Huddersfield police a conversation between Gee and the three at Gee's gunshop was secretly taped. When the three left the shop they, and a friend called John Brankin, waiting in a car nearby, were arrested by 20 police. Mysteriously the tape ran out *before* the alleged request for arms was made! Most of the talking on the tape was done by Gee himself. John Meehan and John Brankin were acquitted. Smullen and Doherty went to gaol on the unsupported evidence of the police tout Gee. Gee's later career included having his gun licence taken away in December 1974, being fined £4,000 for smuggling ivory figures into France in June 1976 and being charged with the theft of £210,000 worth of Japanese Art in Manchester in February 1977.

Michael Gaughan, who was murdered in Parkhurst prison on 3 June 1974 after being force-fed on hunger strike, was sentenced to seven years at the Old Bailey in December 1971 for a bank robbery which netted only £530 for the Republican Movement. This was two months before the first explosion on the mainland – the Aldershot bombing – took place.

As always imperialist repression preceded revolutionary resistance. The political trials of Irish men and women began with the framing of Smullen and Doherty in 1970 and continued through to the gaoling of John McComb in 1983.

However it was the military campaigns in Britain which provided the background for a massive onslaught against Irish people in Britain. Over 100 have been arrested and gaoled. The PTA has been used to harass and terrorise Irish people in Britain. The statistics of arrests make this clear. Up to the end of November 1981 – 7 years after this 'temporary provisions' Act had been passed – 5,251 persons had been arrested under the Act. Of these 4,639, 88 per cent, were neither charged with an offence nor excluded from Britain. Only 85, 1.6 per cent, were charged under the Act and of these 69, 1.3 per cent, were found guilty under its provisions. 280 people were charged with offences under other Acts. And 247 people were deported from Britain having their families split up and losing jobs and livelihood. Irish people in their thousands are subject to detention, questioning, isolation and deportation under this racist legislation. Finally conspiracy charges, forced confessions and *agents provocateurs* have been used in show trials to gaol Irish men and women.

Police agents have been used in many cases. The Luton Three – Phil Sheridan, Sean Campbell and Gerry Mealey, all members of Luton Sinn Fein – were convicted in November 1973 of 'conspiring to rob persons unknown in Bletchley'. They had been set up by a police *agent provocateur* Kenneth Lennon.[7] Lennon's role was concealed in the trial. All three got 10 years. Lennon then went on to set up 18 year old Pat O'Brien in an 'escape plot'. On 8 April 1974 O'Brien was sentenced to three years imprisonment while Lennon was acquitted. On 13 April 1974, 5 days later, Kenneth Lennon was found dead in Chipstead Surrey having been shot in the head. Three days earlier, on 10 April he had gone to the NCCL and confessed that he was a police agent whose task had been to incite Sinn Fein members. The NCCL released Lennon's statement on 16 April.

The Home Office was forced to set up an enquiry. Roy Jenkins the Labour Home Secretary gave the job to the Deputy Commissioner of Scotland Yard, Mr James Starritt. He was well chosen for the cover-up that was necessary. Starritt was of Irish Protestant origin being the son of an RUC constable with two brothers in the RUC. The *Starritt*

Report was ready on 26 April eight days after it had been commissioned and was leaked to the *Daily Express* before he signed it. The Home Secretary said that on the basis of the evidence presented 'there are no grounds for a further investigation into the actions of any of the police officers involved'.[8] The report was in fact not published for seven months on the grounds that the Luton Three and Pat O'Brien were appealing against their convictions and sentences. Pat O'Brien was acquitted on 5 June after 5 months in prison on the technical grounds that Lennon's acquittal of the charge removed the only named party to the conspiracy. Who then did O'Brien conspire with? The Court of Appeal found the use of *agents provocateurs* to infiltrate organisations and incite members to 'illegal' activities was justified. The appeal of the Luton Three was therefore turned down by the man who covered up for the Bloody Sunday murders – Lord Widgery. What would you expect? Irish men and women have never found even the pretence of justice in British imperialist courts.

In the trial of the Birmingham Six a key prosecution witness was self-confessed National Front supporter, Thomas Watt, who was harbouring the *agent provocateur* Kenneth Littlejohn at the time the Birmingham explosions took place. Littlejohn had escaped from Mountjoy prison in March 1974 and was supposedly the subject of a massive police hunt in Ireland and Britain.

In April 1977 John Higgins, the National Organiser of Sinn Fein was convicted of soliciting arms from John Banks and receiving walkie-talkie radios for 'use in connection with terrorism'. The prosecution case rested solely on the word of the notorious John Banks, ex-paratrooper and mercenary recruiter for the CIA-backed FNLA in Angola – a man with contacts with SAS, British military intelligence and Special Branch. John Higgins was given ten years – reduced to four years on appeal.

One of the earliest of the show trials was that of the Coventry seven in Birmingham October 1973. Fr Patrick Fell, Frank Stagg, and five others were charged with conspiring to cause explosions. On remand all were held in solitary. The trial was conducted with massive 'security' precautions designed to prejudice the jury. The evidence against the seven included a street map and a Barnes and MacCormack banner. (Barnes and MacCormack were IRA volunteers, framed and hanged in 1940 for an explosion in Coventry). No explosives were produced nor any trace of explosives found. Frank Stagg was sentenced to 10 years and was later murdered on hunger strike.

The most notorious framings concern the Guildford/Woolwich

bombings and the Birmingham bombings. In October 1975 Paul Hill, Patrick Armstrong, Carole Richardson and Gerry Conlon were gaoled for the Guildford and Woolwich bombings. They were gaoled on the basis of 'confessions' made after beatings, sleep deprivation and denial of food. They were convicted despite the many inconsistencies and contradictions in the police 'evidence' and particularly despite Carole Richardson's cast-iron alibi for the time of the Guildford bombings. Their appeal, following the Balcombe Street Active Service Unit's claiming of the Guildford and Woolwich bombings, was rejected. At the Balcombe Street trial the police forensic 'expert' Higgs was shown to have concealed vital evidence about these bombings at the instigation of the Bomb Squad.

After the Birmingham explosions 6 men – John Walker, Patrick Hill, Robert Hunter, Noel McIlkenny, William Power and Hugh Callaghan – were arrested and brutally beaten. Not surprisingly four of them 'confessed' after mental and physical torture including mock executions and threats against their families. The Prison Medical Officer Dr Harwood testified that the six were 'black, blue, battered and bleeding' when they arrived at Winson Green prison. The screws at the prison then beat them up to cover up the evidence of the police beating. All six were convicted and sentenced to life imprisonment mainly on the basis of 'confessions' beaten out of them. Later their appeals were rejected and their attempt to bring charges of assault against the police were stopped by Lord Denning who regarded exposure of police brutality as 'an appalling vista'.[9] The Winson Green screws, needless to say, were acquitted of assault.

This is imperialist 'justice' for Irish prisoners: lies, beatings, framings, conspiracy charges, perjured evidence, and *agents provocateurs*. All this has been openly used against the Irish without a whisper of protest from the so-called Labour and trade union movement or their 'critical' allies, the CPGB, SWP, etc on the British 'left'. It is little surprise that after the uprisings by black youth in the summer of 1981, conspiracy charges were used in the Bradford 12 case. The Bradford 12, however, were acquitted.

Irish Republican volunteers have not meekly accepted British 'justice'. They have resisted. Nowhere more so than in the case of the Balcombe Street four. Joe O'Connell, Eddie Butler, Harry Duggan and Hugh Doherty – along with Brendan Dowd – were responsible for many of the most successful IRA operations in Britain in 1974 and 1975. They formed a courageous, dedicated and highly professional Active Service Unit.

On 6 December 1975 they were surprised by the police while raking Scotts Restaurant Mayfair with bullets. Knowing the fate that awaited them – beatings or indeed murder – they decided to surround their arrest with maximum publicity by entering a house in Balcombe Street and taking a married couple hostage. On 12 December having achieved their purpose they surrendered.

At the trial, true to the revolutionary traditions of the IRA, they refused to plead and only recognised the court in so far as it was necessary to expose the Guildford/Woolwich frame-up by making it clear they had carried out the operations. They used their right to challenge the jury to produce a working class jury including five women and four blacks. The original 'randomly selected' jury panel included one man who attended church with Ross McWhirter, some nurses who attended those injured after the explosions and others who had relatives in the British army.

The four conducted the trial with such skill that the Guildford/Woolwich frame-up was decisively exposed and the political character of their actions made clear. This can be seen from Joe O'Connell's speech from the dock to the jury from which we have already given extracts above. So successful were the Balcombe Street four that the jury found them not guilty of 26 out of the 100 charges against them. Some of the jurors were reported to have been in favour of complete acquittal on the grounds that the actions of the four had been justified. So outraged were the police that they attempted to question the jury about why they had acquitted on some charges. This is completely illegal interference. The police even arrested the whole jury in a local pub where they had gone after the sentencing and where they were volubly expressing indignation at the vicious life sentences Judge Cantley handed down. They had however to release them almost immediately.

In the Six Counties British imperialism has abolished jury courts for so-called 'terrorist' offences. They have not yet done so here in Britain, maybe because they feel that even the corrupt and bankrupt British Labour and trade union movement would be forced to protest. Instead they try and influence juries by their 'security' measures or 'vet' juries to suit their own requirements. The Balcombe Street case shows that the police and judiciary cannot always have their own way when faced with an unprejudiced working class jury. A few months after this case the Labour government secretly reduced the right of challenge of jurors from seven to three.

RESISTANCE IN PRISON

Dolours and Marion Price, Hugh Feeney and Gerard Kelly went on hunger strike in 1973 to demand the right to serve their sentences in the Six Counties of Ireland. All four – part of the Belfast 10 – had been sentenced to life imprisonment having been tried for causing explosions and conspiracy. British soldiers found guilty of offences in the Six Counties of Ireland are almost automatically repatriated to serve their sentences in Britain. By 1976 statistics showed that 12 UDA prisoners sentenced in England had been transferred to the Six Counties to serve their sentences. However this right is denied Irish prisoners of war.

The Price sisters, Kelly and Feeney endured 167 days of force-feeding out of the 206 days spent on hunger strike. Force-feeding, the ramming of a tube down the throat and into the stomach, is a form of torture. It is not designed to save the health of a hunger striker but to break their spirit. They ended their hunger strike four days after the murder of Michael Gaughan after a promise of repatriation to the Six Counties by the 'end of the year'. Throughout the spring and into early summer Roy Jenkins had played dice with the lives and health of the prisoners. The death of Michael Gaughan exposed to the world the viciously reactionary character of this Labour Home Secretary and the Labour government to which he belonged. Roy Jenkins has a 'liberal' reputation. This is lying propaganda. Jenkins allowed the torture and murder of Irish prisoners in British gaols, he set up the Starritt enquiry to cover up for the Special Branch framing of Irish Republicans, and he introduced the draconian anti-Irish Prevention of Terrorism Act.

The Price Sisters were finally repatriated to Armagh on 18 March 1975 having first been transferred to Durham. Kelly and Feeney were repatriated a month later – four months after the expiry of Jenkins' 'end of the year' deadline. No other Irish prisoners have been granted this right.

Five Irish POWs have been murdered in British prisons since 1974. Michael Gaughan joined the hunger strike on 31 March 1974. On 3 June he died after the force-feeding tube had been shoved through his lung. Frank Stagg joined Michael Gaughan on the hunger strike and ended his strike on an unfulfilled promise of repatriation. After transfer to Long Lartin he again went on hunger strike and only came off after being promised he would not have to do prison work nor would he, his wife, sisters and friends have to undergo humiliating strip searches on the occasion of visits. He was transferred to Wakefield in a very weak state. Work was again demanded of him. He refused and was put down in the block on solitary confinement. On 14 December 1975 he went on hunger strike for the third time. On 12 February 1976 he died, another Irish prisoner murdered by the British prison system. In his last message he wrote:

'We are a risen people, this time we will not be driven into the gutter, even if this should mean dying for justice. The fight must go on. I want my memorial to be Peace with Justice.'[10]

Noel Jenkinson was framed for the Aldershot bombing in 1972. Held in top security units and frequently beaten he was found dead in Leicester Special Security Block on 9 October 1976. An independent autopsy was refused. Sean O'Conaill was sentenced to life imprisonment on 27 April 1974 for shooting the commander of a British Army Camp in Otterburn, Northumberland. He contracted cancer and despite this being known he was given no treatment other than indigestion tablets and ointment to rub on his chest. On 1 October 1977 he died after eighteen months of agony. Giuseppe Conlon was framed with the Maguire family in a show trial at the Old Bailey between January and March 1976. He was arrested in England while travelling to visit his son Gerard Conlon, one of the Guildford four. He went into prison, frail and suffering from TB. Denied adequate medical treatment, put into the woodwork shop and then the paint-shop at Wakefield where the dust and fumes caused him agony, he died on 23 January 1980 – the fifth Irish prisoner to be murdered in a British prison during the present campaign. And all these five brutal murders were carried out with little or no protest from the British Labour and trade union movement.

Irish POWs have always, because of their organised revolutionary resistance, been picked out for special brutality. In August 1976 Irish POWs took part in the Hull prison rising. After the rising Gerry Cunningham, Ray McLaughlin, John Walker, Paul Hill, Martin Brady, and Joe Duffy were forced to walk a gauntlet of screws who kicked, punched and batoned them. In September 1976 six Irish POWs in Albany, protesting against the solitary confinement of Brendan Dowd, were brutally beaten by a mob of screws. Fr Fell, framed in the Coventry seven trial, got a broken nose and had stitches to the head. Sean Campbell suffered a broken arm, broken leg, broken ribs, broken fingers, a punctured lung, extensive bruising and abrasions.

In August 1979 a peaceful protest of prisoners in Wormwood Scrubs was attacked by a 300 strong MUFTI squad of screws wielding batons.

Irish POW Roland Lynch suffered a badly bleeding head wound and extensive painful bruising to the head and body. 69 others had to be treated for head injuries. Four Irish POWs were moved to other prisons along with many other prisoners.

Every means is deployed to stamp out the revolutionary resistance of Irish POWs. Not only murder and beatings but also isolation. In 1977 86 out of 92 Irish POWs were in top security Category A. Of 12 prisoners held in Special Security Blocks in Parkhurst and Leicester, six are Irish POWs who are held in total isolation from the rest of the prison population.

Solitary confinement, either as punishment or under the infamous Rule 43 (for good order and discipline), is a major weapon used against Irish POWs. Hugh Doherty and Eddie Butler were held in solitary confinement for two years and four months. Patrick Hackett has been in solitary for over four years. After the Hull rising Joe Duffy spent 18 months and Ray McLaughlin 12 months in solitary confinement. Liam McLarnon spent two years in solitary under rule 43.

To break up resistance, solidarity and organisation Irish POWs are subjected to constant transfers. Between July 1975 and October 1977 Brendan Dowd was transferred ten times! Transfers are frequently timed to coincide with visits so that relatives, after long and expensive journeys, arrive at the prison to be informed that the prisoner concerned has been transferred to another prison 200 miles or more away. Families are subjected to harassment and visits interfered with in a further effort to isolate the POWs.

Despite all this brutality – unchanging under Labour and Tory governments – Irish POWs have earned a justified reputation as leaders of resistance in the prisons. Patrick Hackett, who lost an arm and a leg in a premature explosion, has refused to wear prison uniform since 1976. Despite failing eyesight and poor heath – a result of years in solitary confinement – his resistance continues.

Irish POWs have used rooftop protests, hunger strikes, blanket protests, work strikes to defend their rights as prisoners and promote their demands for political status and repatriation. All these protests are followed by beatings, solitary confinement and loss of remission. Yet the fight continues.

Paul Hill was one of those who released Artie Clifford from the punishment block during the Hull rising of August 1976. Artie Clifford's barbaric treatment was the immediate cause of the rising. The leading role which Irish POWs have played in the prison resistance movement has forged strong bonds of solidarity between the Irish prisoners and other prisoners especially the black prisoners. So that when Irish POWs took to the roof at Long Lartin from 4 May to 10 May 1981 in protest at the murder of Bobby Sands, the other prisoners united to prevent any attack on the POWs.

The unceasing brutality against Irish POWs exposes the real character of British 'democracy' – a 'democracy' of the rich founded on imperialist repression, murder, beatings and torture. The resistance of Irish POWs not only sharply exposes the abject failure of the British Labour and trade union movement to defend fundamental democratic rights, but has demonstrated time and again that the real defenders of democracy, the real fighters for justice are the heroic captured Irish freedom fighters incarcerated in British gaols.

NOTES

1 *Morning Star* 30 November 1974.
2 *Socialist Worker* 30 November 1974.
3 *Militant* 29 November 1974.
4 *Red Weekly* 5 December 1974. *Workers Press* 22 November and 25 November 1974 condemn the bombings as 'terrorism'.
5 The full speech is in *The Irish Prisoner* No 3 London nd. Also reprinted in *Hands Off Ireland!* No 4 May 1978.
6 Material for this section is taken from a number of sources, particularly the following: *The Irish Prisoner/PAC News, Hands Off Ireland, Fight Racism! Fight Imperialism!* Also the following pamphlets: Prisoners Aid Committee, *Irish Political Prisoners in English Jails* London 1980, and Sinn Fein, *Special Category A* Dublin 1980.
7 See Robertson G, *Reluctant Judas* London 1976.
8 *ibid* p. 161.
9 See *Hands Off Ireland!* No 10 April 1980.
10 *Irish Prisoner* No 2 London nd.

CHAPTER FOURTEEN

THE FIGHT AGAINST 'CRIMINALISATION'

The Labour government's attempt to remove political legitimacy from the revolutionary national struggle to free Ireland from British rule had led to the systematic torture of 'suspects' in the Six Counties of Ireland from 1976-1979. The torture and brutalisation of political prisoners however did not end with the 'confessions' forced out of prisoners in the interrogation centres. It continued in the specially built cellular prisons – the H-Blocks.

As part of its 'criminalisation' strategy the Labour government had ended Special Category status for Irish political prisoners. Those political prisoners convicted of offences after 1 March 1976 would no longer be placed in the compound-type prisons together with their comrades, but would serve their sentences in the cells of the H-Blocks. In the compounds political prisoners through their leaders direct a great deal of the day-to-day activities in the prison. They wear their own clothes, organise educational and recreational activities, receive extra visits etc and are segregated according to their political organisations. In July 1982 there were still over 150 political prisoners in the compounds. In the compounds the political character of the offences for which those inside have been detained is clearly acknowledged.

In the H-Blocks the prisoners had to wear prison clothes, do prison work, and their day-to-day activities were under the control of the prison authorities. Political prisoners who had been arrested under *special* emergency laws, tortured in *specially* built interrogation centres, tried in *special* non-jury courts under *special* rules of evidence were no longer to be granted *Special* Category status for the duration of their prison sentences. In the H-Blocks the political status of the political prisoners was to be denied.

THE BLANKET PROTEST

After the publication of the Gardiner Report the ending of Special Category status was discussed during the truce 'negotiations' between the IRA and British government representatives in 1975 and early 1976. The British government offered to increase remission from one-third to one-half as a 'concession' to make the ending of Special Category status more acceptable. The Provisional IRA representatives in rejecting this warned that any attempt to remove Special Category status would be resisted by all means possible including the shooting of prison officers.

The British government went ahead. In November 1975 it announced the ending of Special Category status from 1 March 1976. On 25 January 1976 remission for all prisoners was increased to one-half. The Republican Movement responded. A letter from a Republican Prisoner of War on remand at Crumlin Road gaol said:

'Rees will find it easier to walk on water than he will break our morale by trying to convince people that the Liberation struggle is not a political war. How does he propose to coerce us into wearing criminal overalls? He hasn't clarified that point yet. I can state now, and I am talking on behalf of every remand prisoner here, that the only way Rees will get prison garb on to my back is to nail it on.'[1]

A statement from the Belfast Brigade IRA, reported in *Republican News* 20 March 1976, announced that 'members of the British Prison Service' were now to be regarded as legitimate targets for IRA active service units. A policy statement from political prisoners in the compounds at Long Kesh followed a few days later. It announced that all negotiations within the prison on Special Category status were at an end and that Republican prisoners would not engage in any institutional schemes under the control of the prison administration. IRA volunteers were instructed not to wear any clothing provided by the prison service. They would only respond to the commands and directives of their superior officers, regardless of the consequences. In approving and supporting the policy statement of the Belfast Brigade IRA the prisoners made it clear:

'We are prepared to die for the right to retain political status. Those who try to take it away must be fully prepared to pay the same price'.[2]

In April 1976 two prison officers were shot dead.

The Belfast Brigade IRA statement had referred to prison officers as 'mercenaries'. There is little doubt that huge 'bounties' are paid to them to serve in the gaols and prison camps of occupied Ireland. *Republican News* reported at the time (1976) that some prison officers could earn over £200 in a normal week. By 1980 a prison officer, ordinary class, was earning £8,500 plus overtime, a senior officer £13,000, a prison governor £16,000, plus substantial fringe benefits such as holidays, canteen service, pensions and life insurance benefits. Average pay is well over £10,000.

There are no qualifications for becoming a prison officer in the Six Counties unless basic literacy is seen as one. Training is minimal. After four to six weeks recruits come into contact with prisoners directly. A further period of training of about six weeks 'on the job' then takes place. Prison officers are mainly recruited from the existing 'security forces' and are ex-British Army, UDR and RUC. Those joining without any background in the 'security forces' are almost certainly from the loyalist population. The increase in recruitment of prison officers over the years closely reflects the policy of British imperialism to put larger and larger numbers from the nationalist minority behind prison bars. In 1969 the total number of prison officers in the Six Counties was 292, in 1974 it was 1,124, by 1978 it had risen to 2,339 and in 1980 it was 2,996, over ten times the 1969 total. 'Mercenaries' is indeed an apt label for the well paid thugs working in British gaols and prison camps in the service of British imperialism's war effort against the Irish people in the Six Counties of Ireland.

On 14 September 1976 18 year old Kieran Nugent became the first political prisoner to be denied Special Category status. He had been sentenced to three years imprisonment for hijacking a van and had pledged that the British would have to nail the uniform to his back if an attempt was made to criminalise him after he had been sentenced. In an interview given to *Hands Off Ireland* soon after his release in May 1979 he described how the blanket protest began:

'It all started when I went into the reception and the screw asked me "what size clothes do you take?". I refused to answer. I said "I'm not wearing your gear". He said "You can't do this here" – he was astonished. So he went to get the Principal Officer. I was manhandled a bit and then he put the prison clothes in a brown bag and said "Right, carry it". I refused to lift it so he had to carry it himself. They drove us up to H-Block. When we arrived in the H-Block there were about nine or ten screws there. This was in the main administration part of H-Block. They stood me against the wall and punched me about a bit, and then they grabbed me and ran me about twenty or thirty yards into one of the wings – D Wing. They pushed me into one of the cells and told me to put the uniform on. I said "No, I'm not putting that gear on". So they said "Right, take your own clothes off". I refused, so then they jumped on me and forcibly removed my clothes, and held me down and punched me about. One of them then threw a blanket at me – so in fact he started the protest.'[3]

Immediately the screws tried to break him. During the day he was taken out of the cell with a bed and mattress in it and from 7.30am until 8pm at night he was placed in a completely empty cell. If he tried to sit on the floor in the empty cell two screws would come in and force him to stand up. The food he was given was very bad – tiny amounts, cold and often inedible. At first he was allowed to go outside for exercise with only the blanket on and walk around for about an hour in the mornings. He said he did this in spite of the cold, rainy weather because two screws had to go out with him and he knew they hated it. But after about six to eight weeks this was stopped when the screws told him 'we won't exercise you until you wear prison uniform'.

As more prisoners joined the blanket protest the prison authorities stepped up their harassment. An order came from them in November 1976 forbidding political prisoners on protest to wear a blanket outside their cells. It took the evasive form of a rule not allowing prisoners 'to remove bedding from their cells'.[4] Young prisoners were particularly selected for humiliation by the prison authorities. Older prisoners had food brought to them and they washed in their cells. They did not go out to the toilet but used a pot in their cells. However young prisoners held in H-Block 2, in the 18 year old group, were compelled to go to the canteen naked to collect their food in front of non-protesting prisoners. They also had to go to the toilet and washhouse naked, being mocked, abused and often assaulted by perverted sadistic screws. All prisoners were severely beaten as brutal prison warders tried to force them to accept prison clothes and coerce them to conform to 'criminal' status. The beatings usually began in the H-Block administration area when the political prisoners refused to wear prison uniform. It continued in the cells. Failure to say 'Sir' to a prison officer was the excuse for particularly vicious beatings. Many injuries were also inflicted on prisoners during often repeated sadistic and degrading internal body searches carried out whilst prisoners were forcibly held naked, face downwards across a table.

At fortnightly intervals political prisoners 'on the blanket' were charged with 'refusing to co-operate...'. For this 'hearing' the prisoner was forcibly brought to his feet by several screws and made to stand up in front of the prison governor. Refusal to address him as 'Sir' resulted in blows to the face and body. The prisoner was automatically sentenced to 14 days loss of remission and loss of all privileges. As further punishment their bedding was removed out of their cells during the day for three days. A day never passed in the H-Blocks without someone being sent to the punishment block – P-Block – on a very petty or false charge. P-Block consisted of 28 punishment cells where the men were put 'on the boards' with no bedding at all during the day. These cells were bare except for a wooden board (a bed), a concrete block to sit on and a concrete slab cemented in the wall to serve as a table. These 'concrete tombs' could not be seen out of, were heated by a small pipe and were totally sound-proofed. The prisoner was placed on a starvation diet of two rounds of dry bread and a mug of black tea for breakfast, 'lunch' of potatoes and watery soup and 'tea' the same as breakfast. The prisoners with only a blanket round them had to continally exercise to keep warm. Total silence was maintained and frequent beatings were handed out to the men by 3 or 4 screws invading the cell. The conditions and beatings were so bad that some men went on hunger and thirst strike in protest against them. Prisoners were kept in the punishment block anything from six to 30 days.

All this harassment and brutality did not break the blanket protest. In October 1976 another prison officer was shot dead and the women political prisoners in Armagh prison began a no-work protest against the withdrawal of political status. All women prisoners in the Six Counties are allowed to wear their own clothes. By May 1977 there were nearly 80 political prisoners 'on the blanket' in the H-Blocks. At this time they were all moved from H-Blocks 1 and 2 to H-Block 5. There, much less isolated from each other, they were able to reorganise and set up their own staff structure. Each wing had an officer-in-charge (O/C) and the men in that wing took their orders from him and did what he told them to do. There was a Battalion O/C – a Block O/C – who controlled the whole block. The resistance of the men was considerably strengthened. On 14 September 1977, one year after the protest began, a statement from the IRA pledged 'continual support' for the 197 comrades on protest – the vast majority 'on the blanket' in the H-Blocks, the eight shorter-term and remand prisoners 'on the blanket' in Crumlin Road gaol, and the 13 women on the no-work protest in Armagh prison.[5] By March 1978, 18 months after the protest started there were nearly 300 men 'on the blanket' and 24 women on protest in Armagh prison. The British authorities were no longer issuing weekly figures of those prisoners 'refusing to obey prison rules'. To have done so would have exposed the growing failure of the 'criminalisation' strategy.

In the first phase of the 'blanket' protest political prisoners in the H-Blocks had been subjected to barbaric and inhumane conditions for refusing to accept criminal status. The list of outrages imposed by the British government on the prisoners had led to the H-Blocks being rightly called 'Britain's concrete monument of shame'.

☆ No clothes: only a blanket to clutch around them with bare feet on concrete floor.

☆ No association or recreation: either kept in solitary confinement or two-to-a-cell built for one; these men left their cells for only 45 minutes per week to go to Mass. Many refused to go because of humiliating body searches.

☆ No exercise period: those who tried physical exercises in their cells were exhausted very quickly due to lack of proper food, lack of fresh air, lack of normal exercise.

☆ No proper food: no food parcels allowed; all food was served stale and cold in small revolting portions.

☆ No cigarettes, no newspapers, no books, no TV, no radio, no pens or writing material, no games: only two religious magazines were allowed, plus the Bible. Religious magazines were stopped after men had been forced to use the pages for sanitary purposes. Prisoners were only allowed three sheets of toilet paper a day and this ration was often reduced by sadistic screws.

☆ No proper medical treatment: every man suffered a variety of muscular aches, persistent colds, skin rashes and dandruff, and also eyesight complaints due to the bright neon lights continuously glaring on the white cell walls. To see a doctor you had to wear prison uniform.

☆ One visit and one letter a month: to have a visit a political prisoner had to wear prison uniform. He was subjected to degrading and brutal body searches both before and after visits. These conditions led to many prisoners refusing to take visits.

☆ No protection: political prisoners were regularly beaten with batons and boots by 'prison officers'.

☆ No bedding for three days: every fortnight their bedding was removed from their cells during the day for three days and the men were sentenced to 14 days loss of remission.

☆ Punishment Block: long spells in punishment cells on trivial and false charges. Prisoners were totally isolated in silence in cold cells on starvation diets. They were regularly assaulted by screws while in punishment cells.[6]

In March 1978 the men in the H-Blocks were forced to escalate their protest. Prisoners, at this time, were being sent to punishment blocks to undergo the savage conditions and brutal beatings for the most trivial thing. Harassment by the screws was intensifying. Once a week political prisoners were allowed a shower for five minutes. When they went out of their cells to walk the few feet to and from the showers they were put up against the wall and searched. During this process they were kicked and assaulted. Getting permission to go down a corridor to the toilet became a 'privilege' which was regularly withdrawn as a form of punishment and harassment. As a direct result of this increased harassment the prisoners refused to leave their cells. The warders then brought stinking plastic bowls with about half an inch of water in them for washing. The prisoners refused to use them. They now refused to brush and mop out their cells.

Slopping out of faeces and urine in the cells was not done by the prisoners but by the warders. The routine was that a trolley came round with the food for the prisoners' meals, followed by another for their slops. The food was given to the prisoners and then the slops were poured into a large plastic bin. However now the screws started returning the prisoners' pots half full, often kicking them over the floors. In many cases they refused to allow the men to slop out for a period of days. The cells were soon in a disgusting state with faeces and urine all over the floor, mattresses and blankets. The prisoners then decided to throw the slops out of the windows in an attempt to save their mattresses and blankets from being soaked. But the screws 'dressed up like spacemen with bloody big gloves' started throwing it all back through the windows again.[7] The prisoners were left with no alternative but to put it on the walls. It was either that or on the floor, their beds and blankets. This was the origin of the so-called 'dirt strike'. Far from being 'self-inflicted' as the British propaganda machine claimed, it was forced on the political prisoners by perverted, sadistic screws who had the full backing of the British government. It was aimed at breaking the prisoners' protest, and forcing them to accept criminal status. It totally failed.

The conditions in the H-Blocks rapidly deteriorated. Maggots infested the cells and prisoners would wake up with them in their hair, nose and ears. Skin and eye infections, dysentery and diarrhoea became widespread among the political prisoners. To add to this torture the sadistic screws would turn the heat fully on in the middle of summer and turn it down and sometimes completely off in the bitter cold of winter. Cardinal O'Fiaich visited the H-Blocks in July 1978 and issued a statement on the atrocious conditions he found there.

'Having spent the whole of Sunday in the prison I was shocked by the inhuman conditions prevailing in the H Blocks 3, 4 and 5, where over 300 prisoners are incarcerated. One would hardly allow an animal to remain in such conditions, let alone a human being. The nearest approach to it that I have seen was the spectacle of hundreds of homeless people living in the sewer-pipes in the slums of Calcutta. The stench and filth in some of the cells, with the remains of rotten food and human excreta scattered round the walls, was almost unbearable. In two of them I was unable to speak for fear of vomiting . . .

'The fact that a man refuses to wear prison uniform or to do prison work should not entail the loss of physical exercise, association with his fellow prisoners or contact with the outside world. These are basic human needs for physical and mental health, not privileges to be granted or withheld as rewards or punishments. To deprive anyone of them over a long period – irrespective of what led to the deprivation in the first place – is surely a grave injustice and cannot be justified in any circumstances . . .'[8]

The 'inhuman conditions' existing in the H-Blocks, conditions which could not be justified 'in any circumstances', were being inflicted on the political prisoners by a British Labour government. Yet even after the publicity generated by Cardinal O'Fiaich's statement the brutality in the H-Blocks not only continued but reached new extremes. The men were subjected to painful drenchings with high-powered water hoses being turned upon them in their cells. They suffered near-suffocation from forcible baths of boiling hot or freezing cold water. And the 'blanket men's' haggard bodies were further cut and bruised when they were forcibly dragged from their cells, scrubbed with deck scrubbers, and had their faces forcibly shaved and their hair forcibly cropped. This torture of political prisoners was to go on for more than four years. There appeared to be no limit to the depths of depravity and barbarity to which the British Labour government was prepared to sink in its treatment of naked defenceless prisoners in order to achieve British imperialism's political objective of 'criminalising' Irish Republicanism.

However they would not break the protest. Cardinal O'Fiaich in his statement noted with surprise the high morale of the prisoners.

'In isolation and perpetual boredom they maintain their sanity by studying Irish. It was an indication of the triumph of the human spirit over adverse material surroundings to notice Irish words, phrases and songs being shouted from cell to cell and then written on each cell wall with the remnants of toothpaste tubes.'[9]

The prisoners not only ran Gaelic classes but organised concerts, quizzes, political discussions on republicanism and socialism – all this carried out by shouting through quarter-inch gaps between the walls and their cell doors. News of IRA successes, or street protests passed round the prison also helped to keep up their morale. By early 1979 the first political prisoners were being released from the H-Blocks having served their sentences and having remained unbroken by the regime, more than ever sure of the justice and ultimate victory of their cause.

THE 'PEACE PEOPLE'

The attempt to isolate the IRA and undermine its support in the nationalist minority was a primary concern of the British government. Just before Mason arrived in the Six Counties a tragic event occurred which he and his propagandists believed they could exploit to drive support away from the IRA. They were aided and abetted in this task by the British media which uncritically reproduced the lies put out by the British government and army propaganda machine.

On 10 August 1976 in Andersonstown, West Belfast, the British army fired on a car driven by IRA volunteer Danny Lennon. Danny Lennon died instantly. The car went out of control and ploughed into a crowd of civilians hitting three children who died and injuring their mother Mrs Maguire. As Danny Lennon's companion climbed from the car he was hit three times by shots fired by British soldiers – despite the fact he was directly in front of the injured Maguire family. The army, instead of immediately calling an ambulance, hauled Danny Lennon's body from the car and having searched it seized a *dismantled* Armalite rifle from the back seat. The ambulance only arrived after 25 minutes.

The army claimed that shots had been fired from the car and they themselves had fired only in response to this. However it was the *Irish Times* (14 August 1976) which revealed that the Armalite in the car was dismantled and therefore no shots could have been fired from the car.

Lennon was deliberately shot dead and the Army was responsible for his death and that of the Maguire children. Indeed evidence suggests that the Maguire children were hit by British army SLR bullets before the car crashed into them.[10] Nonetheless this was the incident which gave rise to the formation of the so-called 'Peace People' and led to a number of quite large marches for 'peace' throughout the Six Counties.

This was not the spontaneous movement many made it out to be. Many of its supporters were involved with the middle-class Andersons-town-based Women Together movement which existed before the tragic deaths of the Maguire children. It also immediately received organised support from the Official IRA, the SDLP and the Catholic clergy – all concerned to drive support away from the Provisional IRA. The media turned the leaders of the movement – Mairead Corrigan, an aunt of the Maguire children, Betty Williams and a Belfast journalist, Ciaran McKeown – into well known figures. Mairead Corrigan was given paid leave by Guinness Brewery 'in order to carry out her work' and Betty Williams was a member of the middle class unionist Alliance Party.[11] They were interviewed seventeen times on Northern Ireland BBC in the first three months of the 'Peace People's' existence. However all this propaganda was in vain. While the 'Peace People' were able for a short period to exploit a deeply felt yearning for peace in the Six Counties, the day-to-day realities of British terror directed at the nationalist minority very quickly led to the collapse of this so-called 'peace movement'.

The decline in fact began only four days after the Maguire children died. At 11.45am on 14 August 1976 12 year old Majella O'Hare was killed by a paratrooper's bullet while on her way to confession in South Armagh. It was a straightforward murder. At 12.15pm the Army issued a press statement saying that gunmen had opened fire on an army patrol and a 12 year old girl had been hit; the army patrol had not returned fire. Betty Williams immediately denounced the IRA using the Army account of the shooting to call for support for 'peace marches'. However, the fact that there were too many witnesses to the murder, including Majella's father, destroyed the Army's attempt to create a new 'victim' for the 'Peace People' to exploit. At 2pm the Army issued its second statement saying that a gunman had opened fire on the army patrol and it was 'believed' that it may have returned fire. At 3.30pm the Army issued a third statement admitting it had fired. Finally a soldier was charged with manslaughter (acquitted 2 May 1977). No one had in fact fired on the army patrol.

The 'Peace People' failed to attend the 2,000 strong protest march that followed Majella's death. Catholic anger increased when Majella's death received very little press coverage compared with the deaths of the Maguire children. And what coverage there was simply repeated the lies put out by army press officers.

On 4 October 13 year old Brian Stewart was shot in the face by a plastic bullet in the Turf Lodge area of Belfast. He died on 10 October. Press coverage was again minimal and was influenced by army press statements. The army tried to make out that Brian had been 'a leading stone-thrower' in a riot – in fact there was no rioting in the area at the time. Brian Stewart's mother Kathleen was bitterly angry at the army lies. She was bitter, too, that the 'Peace People' had not sent the customary mass card after his death. Kathleen Stewart had attended some of the early 'peace marches'. She never did again. When Mairead Corrigan and Betty Williams arrived unannounced at a meeting in Turf Lodge called to protest at Brian's death, they were attacked by women enraged at their 'low profile' on British army violence.

Sinn Fein finally challenged the 'Peace People' by calling a 'Peace with Justice' march, to coincide with one planned by the 'Peace People' for 23 October 1976 in the Falls Road area of Belfast. Ciaran McKeown for the 'Peace People' boasted 'we will have 30,000 marching on our side, we will outnumber the Provisionals at least 10 to 1'. He was to regret these words. While a massive crowd of 10,000 from the Republican areas of Belfast marched behind the Sinn Fein 'Peace with Justice' banner, the 'Peace People' could muster only 5-6,000 from many parts of the country. The myth of the 'Peace People' had been very easily exploded.

The 'Peace People' claimed that their aim was to unite the community on a non-sectarian basis. But a Catholic-Protestant mass movement for peace is impossible as long as it accepts British imperialism's presence in the Six Counties of Ireland. The nationalist section of the working class cannot and will not support a movement which supports the role of the British army and the RUC in the Six Counties. The Loyalists will not support a movement which does not support the British army and the RUC. Their loyalist supporters were horrified after Mairead Corrigan and Betty Williams attempted to win back lost ground with the nationalist minority by attending the Turf Lodge meeting to protest at Brian Stewart's murder by the British army; and by their subsequent statement that army activities in areas like Turf Lodge were provocative and drove people into sympathy with the IRA. They were forced to appease their loyalist supporters by insisting that they did support the 'security forces', merely deploring their 'occasional' breaches of law. A movement for peace can only be built on an anti-imperialist basis. Anything short of this, as the 'Peace People' demonstrated in practice, means ending up on the side of British imperialism.

After this the 'Peace People' rapidly lost support in the Six Counties. Their popularity rose only overseas. They were kept alive by the media interest alone. In Britain in November 1976 they were allowed to hold a rally in Trafalgar Square – the first time a demonstration on Northern Ireland had been allowed there for four years. They were supporting British imperialism's interests after all. They collected vast sums of money, estimated at over £250,000 in 2 years, from multinational firms and other imperialist institutions in Europe. In 1977 they met the Queen on her yacht during the Jubilee visit to the Six Counties. In the same year Mairead Corrigan and Betty Williams were awarded the Nobel Peace Prize of £80,000. However by the end of 1979 the 'Peace People' had little money left and their leadership had fallen out. Ciaran McKeown was quoted as saying 'The Nobel prize damaged our credibility . . . And the fact that Betty and Mairead kept the money made it even worse'.[12] The 'Peace People' achieved nothing in the Six Counties. Their leaders had momentarily achieved international 'fame' and two of them, a little fortune.

THE LOYALIST STRIKE MAY 1977

In January 1977 Mason had sanctioned an agreement whereby the prime responsibility for security had shifted over to the RUC. Over the next few months Mason became increasingly confident that the 'security forces' were winning. Provisional IRA activity was low in this period. The 'conveyor belt' process, the reorganisation of RUC intelligence gathering procedures, and the torturing of suspects to force 'confessions' and gain intelligence had damaged the operational capacity of the IRA. As a result at the time of the Loyalist Strike the IRA were about to embark on a major reorganisation to establish the present 'cell' structure – a structure much less vulnerable to RUC/British army intelligence.

A loyalist coalition, the United Unionist Action Council (UUAC), led by Ian Paisley and backed by the main loyalist paramilitary organisations, however, was not at all satisfied with the activity of the 'security forces'. Mason's confident assurances for them were no substitute for RUC/British army assaults on nationalist areas. The UUAC threatened a general strike to begin on 2 May unless tougher action was taken against the Provisional IRA. They also demanded a return of Stormont. They hoped to stage a repeat performance of the UWC strike of May 1974. But this time the strike failed, petering out after a few days. The RUC and British army this time took action against the strikers and loyalist paramilitaries, removing barricades and preventing intimidation. The strike was never allowed to build up support.

Had not the RUC/British army stood up to the Loyalists and demonstrated their impartiality? Were not the 'extremists' on the loyalist side now isolated and defeated as the bourgeois media tried to tell us? A closer look reveals that the failure of the strike was not a defeat for Loyalism at all. On the contrary, in the course of the strike the British government moved in the direction of the demands of the strikers.[13]

On the eve of the strike, 3,000 extra troops were flown into the Six Counties. Not in fact to deal with the strike but, in the words of an Army spokesman 'to make sure the Provisional IRA does not take advantage of the situation'.[14] On the third day of the strike Roy Mason personally told the Ballylumford power workers – the key to the strike's success – that security had been stepped up and would continue to be stepped up. He stated that the RUC would be expanded to 6,500 and re-equipped, the full-time section of the UDR would be expanded to 1,800, that covert SAS operations would be increased, that the mobile anti-terrorist RUC units were being established and that the anti-terrorist laws would be reviewed. The power workers did not come out on strike. The day before the strike ended the Minister of State for Northern Ireland, Concannon, announced in Parliament that limited devolution for the Six Counties was being considered. The plan under consideration did not contain even a formal commitment to power-sharing. In short the first demand of the strike was being carried out and talk of limited devolution was a concession to the second.

The main point about the Loyalist Strike is that it was not even necessary. As Mason was able to explain on local television every night during the strike, there already was a very tough line on law-and-order. He was after all arresting, torturing and gaoling Republicans on a massive scale. But he was not prepared to have the *pace* of increased repression determined by the Loyalists. The aim of British strategy was, as far as possible, to isolate the IRA by undermining support for it among the nationalist minority. To increase repression in response to strike action by a section of Loyalists would not only generate a resurgence of support for the Provisional IRA but would also force the SDLP and other Catholic collaborators into publicly voicing opposition to the actions of the British government. This is the tactical consideration which explains the British government's decision to take action against the strike. It worked. Soon after, the SDLP, under the cover of the British government's 'refusal to capitulate' to the UUAC, came out openly in support of Mason and the RUC. Paisley's defeat was only temporary. A few weeks later his Democratic Unionist Party made unprecedented gains in the district council elections. Security was the theme he hammered.

Mason was now very pleased with himself and very confident. In August 1977, in what can only be regarded as a calculated insult to the nationalist minority, he brought the Queen on a two-day visit to the Six Counties of Ireland. She arrived in the royal yacht and 'Mason met her on deck like a proconsul, directed her progress through Protestant Ulster from a command post on board, and made sure that journalists knew of it by telephoning them individually'.[15]

Security was massive. There were hundreds of dawn raids, as repression was stepped up in nationalist areas in the week before the visit. 33,000 'security forces' were mobilised as West Belfast was combed and a submarine and two destroyers protected the royal yacht in Belfast Lough. All this so the Queen could visit a few acres of Irish soil. She could not enter Belfast but remained at Hillsborough Castle 12 miles away, and she visited Coleraine University in Co Derry.

On the first day of the visit 20,000 people took part in a Relatives Action Committee (RAC)/Sinn Fein anti-Jubilee march from the nationalist areas into Belfast city centre. The city centre was ringed with barbed wire and armoured cars and the world's press witnessed the British army and the paramilitary RUC attack the demonstrators with plastic bullets, batons, rifle butts and later live bullets. The attack on the march was resisted, led by the militant youth. It was the biggest march seen in Republican Belfast for three or four years. Despite the massive security operation a bomb exploded at Coleraine University shortly after the Queen had left. During the visit two soldiers were killed, three were seriously wounded and many others injured. The IRA had made its point. That the British media chose to ignore all this and proclaim a 'Royal Ulster Triumph' was beside the point.[16]

The political effects of Mason's insult to the nationalist minority were soon demonstrated. Late 1977 Mason unfolded a scheme for a new devolved assembly. Power was to be wielded by committees with the majority party having a majority on each committee and a majority of the committees' chairmanships. Power-sharing was no longer being seriously considered. However once or twice a year, no doubt as a concession to the SDLP, the assembly would have to approve the work of the committees by a margin which indicated 'a good measure of minority support'. The scheme got nowhere. After Mason's performance during the Queen's visit not even the SDLP dared touch this plan for a gradual return to Stormont and loyalist rule.

SAS ASSASSINATION SQUADS

On 13 September 1977, one year after his appointment as Secretary of State, Mason announced that 'the myth of British withdrawal is dead for ever'. He also said that the 'administrative devolution which has been widely discussed recently . . . is also a dead letter'.[17] Although Mason was forced a little later in the year to try (and fail) with another 'political' initiative (see above) after pressure resulting from the Lynch/Callaghan talks on 28 September it was clear that British imperialism could only prop up the loyalist statelet by repression and terror. The Labour government had sanctioned torture and murder in Castlereagh and degradation and torture in the H-Blocks. It now gave the Special Air Services regiment (SAS) the go ahead to carry out the summary execution of suspected Republicans. Ten people were to be executed in this way between December 1977 and November 1978.

The SAS have been deployed in the Six Counties almost certainly since the entry of British troops in August 1969. Their presence was admitted on two occasions after incidents involving them. The first was on 22 June 1972 when Captain James McGregor and Sergeant Clive Williams fired on three taxi drivers in Andersonstown. They were charged and appeared in court in February 1973. Both were acquitted. The other occasion was in a Lisburn Court House. Following a drunken brawl at a hotel two soldiers were charged with assault. Their regiment was given as the SAS.

Many murders have taken place in Ireland in which SAS killers have been involved. In 1972 Pat McVeigh and Daniel Rooney in different incidents were murdered by a plainclothes Army patrol, almost certainly from the SAS, shooting at them from a passing car. Many unexplained bombings were the work of British Army undercover squads, most probably the SAS.

On 12 January 1976 Harold Wilson announced that the SAS was to be deployed in South Armagh. The aim was to placate the Loyalists as well as to strike fear into the nationalist population in the area. On 12

March 1976 at 2am Sean McKenna was kidnapped by SAS men from a cottage in the Twenty Six Counties just over the border. He was asked 'which way do you want to come – dead or alive?'.[18] He was taken at gunpoint to the Six Counties and arrested. After being tortured into signing a confession he was charged. 14 months later he was sentenced to 25 years imprisonment on 'attempted murder' charges. Convicted of IRA membership up to the day of arrest he was denied political status. Soon after, on 15 April 1976, Peter Cleary an IRA volunteer was murdered by the SAS. He was dragged from his home stripped and brutally beaten by the armed SAS men. A witness said he was later dragged away apparently unconscious by two SAS men. He was taken into a field and moments later three shots were heard. Peter Cleary was shot dead with three bullet wounds in his chest. The Army said he tried to escape and in the ensuing struggle was shot dead. Mrs Cleary took the Ministry of Defence to court over the murder of her son.

The main period of the SAS 'shoot-to-kill' operations began in December 1977. The date is significant. It is less than one month after Major General Tim Creasey arrived to take over as Commanding Officer of British troops in the Six Counties. While in Oman in 1972–5 as Commander of the Sultan of Oman's army, Creasey had a large contingent of SAS men in his army. As Minister of Defence in the 1974 Labour government Mason spent some time in Oman overseeing SAS and other counter-insurgency operations. The two had now linked up again with murderous results.

Colm McNutt from the Creggan, aged 18, an IRSP member was shot dead by SAS men in plain clothes in a car park in William Street on 12 December. Paul Duffy, 20, an IRA volunteer was shot dead on 26 February 1978 after the SAS had staked out the area around an isolated hayshed which contained an IRA bomb cache. Paul Duffy was unarmed and raised his hands above his head when challenged. He was shot at close range. Denis Heaney, an IRA volunteer, was shot dead on 10 June 1978 by an SAS unit at the bottom of Harvey Street on the edge of the Bogside. Denis had recently been arrested and tortured. On his release on 19 May he said in a statement published in the *Derry Journal* that a British Army Officer had told him this was not the end of it, and that 'we will pick our time' and shoot him.[19] Three Ardoyne IRA volunteers Jim Mulvenna, Dennis Brown and Jackie Mealey were ambushed and killed while on the way to plant a bomb at a GPO depot in North Belfast on 21 June. They had surrendered on being challenged. The SAS fired over 200 rounds. Mealey had 63 bullet wounds.

Also shot were two passers-by, one fatally – he was a local Protestant, Billy Hanna, on his way home.

Sixteen year old schoolboy John Boyle was killed on 11 July. He had discovered an arms cache in Dunloy graveyard, and his father had reported it to the RUC. The SAS staked out the graveyard. John Boyle, out of curiosity, returned to the graveyard to look at the bag containing the arms and was shot dead from behind. This piece of bungling was a major set-back for the SAS stake-out policy, whose continued use depended on it wiping out IRA men, not civilians, without too much fuss. There was a trial and a lot of embarrassing publicity. Two SAS men were acquitted of the murder of John Boyle in July 1979.

On 30 September, James Taylor, a civilian, was the next victim. He, his cousin and a friend had spent the day shooting wild fowl at Lough Neagh near Ballygoney. When they returned to their car they found the tyres let down. They went to a house nearby to get a pump and on returning noticed two cars following them. James Taylor asked the occupants of one of the cars if they had let the tyres down. He was met with a hail of bullets and died instantly. The soldiers were never charged on the grounds they believed they were in a 'terrorist situation'.[20]

The final assassination victim of 1978 was 50 year old Patrick Duffy, an auxiliary IRA volunteer from Derry. He was shot dead, as he entered a derelict house in the Bogside, by soldiers lying in wait in the house for someone to collect arms from a cupboard inside. There were 18 bullet wounds in his body.

FIGHTBACK . . . ON THE STREETS

Repression breeds resistance. Torture in Castlereagh, degradation in the H-Blocks, repression and murder on the streets only served to strengthen the determination of the nationalist minority to free Ireland from British rule. The heroic fight of the prisoners against 'criminalisation' gave heart and courage to thousands of nationalist people who now began to organise. The fight against 'criminalisation' took to the streets.

The resistance on the streets began with the formation of the Relatives Action Committees (RACs) in Easter 1976 shortly after the withdrawal of Special Category status. The strongest base of the RACs from the beginning was West Belfast, particularly Turf Lodge. It took some time before the RACs really spread outside Belfast. Over the next three years it was the RACs, at first composed overwhelmingly of working class women, which carried out the day-to-day campaigning on the prisoners' struggle. They staged pickets of courts, embassies, government buildings, and British army forts in West Belfast. They occupied newspaper offices, they blocked roads and they held rallies, street meetings and marches. They took the case to the ordinary working class people on the streets.

The RACs played a central role in building the 'Peace with Justice' marches that were very important in destroying the influence of the British backed 'Peace People'. In September 1976 the 'Peace People' called a march in Derry. Sinn Fein at first decided that the best way to deal with the march was to ignore it. But at a public meeting organised by Creggan RAC the week before the march the women insisted that a 'Peace with Justice' contingent be organised to confront the 'Peace People'. The women won and the contingent was a great success. *An Phoblacht* reported at the time:

> 'Originally, the plan was to ignore the Williams/Corrigan debut in Derry, as such theatrical, highly political puppetry deserves. But at a rally in Creggan on Wednesday night . . . a groundswell of public feeling demanded a change of plan. Creggan people were angry that the peace-at-any-price people monopolise the TV screens, while people undergoing a summer of savage battering and abuse aren't allowed television time to highlight and protest'.[21]

It was the women of Turf Lodge (RAC) who chased Mairead Corrigan and Betty Williams out of a protest meeting to discuss the murder of Brian Stewart (see above) and who justified it politically on the grounds that the 'Peace People' were British agents. Lily Fitzsimons, a leading RAC campaigner, wrote at the time:

> 'Certain people will say they should have been allowed freedom of speech. Well we are sick and disgusted listening to their freedom of pro-British speeches seven days a week, on TV and radio. Which by the way is not open to our point of view or freedom of speech . . .
>   . . . true they the "Peace Women" or British agents as I class them were driven out of Turf Lodge and their car wrecked. We the Irish mothers of Irish children do not want or need them. A small price they paid in comparison to the heartache and suffering, we the true Irish people of the Six Counties, have suffered these past seven years at the hands, batons and rifles of Mason's British thugs'.[22]

It was the RAC women who led the fightback against the 'Peace People' combining two slogans: Political Status! Peace with Justice!

At the time when there were only 14 political prisoners on the blanket in November 1976 it was the women of Turf Lodge who carried out their own 'blanket protest' for five days in Turf Lodge to highlight the plight of the prisoners. A 2,000 strong torchlight procession took place in cold, wet conditions in solidarity with the women's courageous stand. It was this work and determination of ordinary working class women, relatives of the prisoners, which laid the basis for the massive protest marches in 1978 and 1979.

By the end of 1978 there were RACs all over the Six Counties with 12 in Belfast alone. No longer were they mainly confined to relatives of prisoners but involved the thousands who supported the prisoners' struggle for political status. There began a massive upsurge in the Republican Movement as the 1975/6 truce and negotiations were pushed well into the background. The heroic and courageous stand of the political prisoners, the lead in support of their struggle given by the RACs, was to bring many thousands on the streets. 35,000 attended the funeral of the revolutionary Republican Maire Drumm who had been murdered in her hospital bed at the end of October 1976 by British-backed loyalist thugs. There were 15,000 on the 1978 Bloody Sunday Commemoration march in Derry during which IRA volunteers dis-played the newly acquired M60 machine gun to massive enthusiasm from the crowds. During 1978 mobilisations of over 10,000 regularly took place. And 1978 ended with massive tenth anniversary marches. 15-20,000 marched from Coalisland to Dungannon on 27 August. In October 12,000 marched to Derry under the slogan '1968 Civil Rights. 1978 National Rights'. The hard day-to-day work of the RACs had enabled these massive protest marches to be built. As *Republican News* made clear at the time in reporting on the huge turnout for the Coal-island-Dungannon march:

'The huge turn out on the day pays tribute to the consistent agitational work carried out by RAC committees and Republicans over the last two years . . .

'Every drop of publicity has been hard won. It has been wrung out of the mass media by protest after protest by 'blanket-clad' women occupying buildings, blocking roads, and carrying out token hunger-strikes, and by foot slogging the streets in cities, towns and villages from one end of Ireland to the other, handing out leaflets detailing the horrific conditions Republican prisoners are held in . . .'[23]

The same article then went on to make the important political point

that the movement on the streets is complimentary to the armed struggle to free Ireland from British rule.

'Hand in hand with the armed struggle today's street resistance
movement is organised around clear anti-imperialist demands'.

The struggle for political status is part of the struggle to drive British
imperialism out of Ireland. From the very beginning the Relatives
Action Committees stressed the intimate connection between the issue
of political status and the war of national liberation. At a conference in
Ballymurphy concerned to discuss 'Political Status – the way forward', the RAC speaker's concluding remarks were: 'The legitimacy of
their claim to political status is based on their participation in a War of
National Liberation'.[24]

The statement from the central Relatives Action Committee in
Republican News in December 1977 made the same crucial point:

'We have always maintained a firm line that our campaign is to
establish that a War of National Liberation is being waged in Ireland. While in the past we have publicised the inhumane conditions
of the POWs...we have not allowed ourselves to be sidetracked
into seeing the prisoners as a civil rights issue, rather than a political
issue. The political prisoners fighting to defend their status know
only too well that they are being subjected to degrading and inhuman treatment by the British Government, because the Government wants the Political Prisoners to accept Criminal Status. It
would be a mockery of the ideals of the Republican Socialist POWs
if we did not recognise the Political motivation of these POWs.'[25]

What of those then who opposed the torture and degradation of the
prisoners on a 'humanitarian' or 'civil rights' basis but who did not
support the IRA's armed struggle for national liberation? Were they to
be drawn into the campaign and if so on what basis? After the so-called
'dirt strike' began in the H-Blocks, an event took place at an emergency
meeting called by Turf Lodge RAC in April 1978 which was a pointer
to future problems. Father Faul made a divisive intervention from the
platform which many regarded as an insult to the 'blanket men'. He
used the RAC platform to make a call for a Republican ceasefire.

'He claimed that "while violence goes on men will not get better
conditions" and only a ceasefire will bring improvements.

'Further he suggested that those "connected with violence"
(meaning the Republican Movement) should not be seen to be involved in the protests outside. For it would discredit the protests if
"murderers or their brothers" (!!!) were seen to be the protesters'.[26]

Before this event occurred a number of conferences had taken place which had led to the involvement of 'wider' forces in the prisoner campaign. The Coalisland Conference held on 22 January 1978 included left-wing groups such as Peoples Democracy, representatives from trade unions, and influential campaigners such as Bernadette McAliskey (via Tyrone RAC). 1,000 people attended this conference. A proposal from the Belfast Central RAC was passed unanimously. It called for a committee to be set up to 'establish activity on a 32 County basis'. Each organisation, Central RAC, Coalisland RAC, and others who supported and participated in protests, pickets, demonstrations etc would have representation on this committee. And each organisation would retain the right to its autonomy and the right to campaign on its own demands. It should be noted that among these 'wider' forces were those opposed to the armed struggle of the IRA to drive British imperialism out of Ireland.[27] However this conference and an anti-repression delegate Conference held three weeks later called for 'the immediate granting of political status to Republican Socialist Prisoners pending a general amnesty to all prisoners convicted as a result of the Irish war of National Liberation'.[28] In commenting on the Coalisland Conference *Republican News* wrote:

'The clock cannot simply be turned back [to the Civil Rights marches] . . . much as Peoples Democracy and Bernadette McAliskey might wish it to be . . .

. . . organised protests on "limited" demands against torture and in defence of status need not become the diversion from the liberation struggle that some Republicans might fear.

. . . a fightback against "criminalisation" is certainly necessary. But the humanitarian approach of Father Faul and the polite parliamentary-type protests of Frank Maguire . . . are not enough to win our aims in the short term, let alone the long term.

Instead any public campaign against torture and for political status needs to be pointed firmly in the direction of "Brits Out" and needs to recognise the necessary methods for this aim. For status and torture in reality cannot be isolated from the Brit presence; a presence which cannot be removed without armed struggle.

But this does not mean that all united fronts or joint platforms must be on the basis of everyone openly supporting the IRA's armed struggle; or that the call for "Brits Out" should swamp out the specific campaign against criminalisation. What it does mean is that the sharp end of the campaign should be directly cutting against criminalisation while the rudder is steering for "Brits Out".'[29]

Running such 'united fronts' was not going to be that easy. The real problems lay ahead. What was to be at issue was the political basis of those united fronts. For the moment however support for the armed struggle and the fight for political status were intimately connected.

FIGHTBACK ... THE MILITARY CAMPAIGN

From the beginning of the prison campaign the IRA had made it clear that it would use armed force in the fight for political status. The IRA had announced that once political status was removed then prison officers would become legitimate targets. Between 8 April 1976 and 18 January 1980, 18 prison officers and others closely connected with the prison service were killed. In December 1976 the IRA mounted over 120 operations 'in a co-ordinated strike to highlight conditions for those denied political status'[30] – there were at that time 14 men in the H-Blocks and two women in Armagh prison. Railway lines and roads were blocked at crucial points in the Six Counties, a hotel was destroyed and a bus depot attacked in Belfast. Army and RUC bases came under attack and a soldier was killed, another was injured, and 2 RUC men were injured in different parts of the Six Counties. The bombing campaign again spread to England. At the end of January 1977 the West End of London was hit by a spate of bombings – 11 explosions in the space of four hours.

At the end of 1977 Roy Mason was boasting of his own successes. The IRA he said were 'reeling'.

> 'It would have been a brave, or perhaps a rash, man who would have forecast a year ago that 1977 would see a very marked fall in the level of violence, the number of deaths, the number of bombings and the number of shootings'.[31]

There is little doubt that IRA activity was significantly reduced over 1977 due to the reorganisation that was taking place to establish the present highly efficient cell structure. There was also a shortage of explosives. But this should not be exaggerated. While the number of explosions and shootings were down 50%, the year's losses to the 'security forces' had been similar to the previous year: 15 British army compared to 14 a year earlier, 28 UDR/RUC to 38 a year earlier. Civilian deaths had however plummeted from 245 to 69. One major factor in explaining this fall in civilian casualties was the very large reduction in sectarian killings due to British army/RUC curbs on the activities of loyalist paramilitary organisations. This was in line with the attitude the British government took to the loyalist strike. British terror and repression had reached new heights so that the activities of the unofficial loyalist 'security forces' was considered both unfruitful and unnecessary.

There were however some notable successes in 1977. The IRA captured SAS Captain Robert Nairac in May. He was interrogated and then executed. During the Queen's Jubilee visit in August they breached the massive security ring at Coleraine University setting off a bomb using a long delay timing device. On the 2 November the IRA began a series of firebomb and bombing attacks – 93 operations in all – on commercial business property across the Six Counties. These operations were significantly reduced in mid-November with the beginning of the firemen's strike. The IRA recognised that the strike represented unique opportunities to massively inflict material damage on business property. They chose not to take advantage of the situation because:

'. . . such actions would be used by the ruling class to weaken the Fireman's legitimate case, opening them up to reactionary appeals to return to work on "security grounds".'[32]

This remarkable working-class solidarity, needless to say, was neither acknowledged nor reported by the British Labour and trade union movement or by the IRA's 'critics' on the British left.

In spite of the low activity of the IRA in this period Alan Wright, chairman of the Police Federation, found it necessary in September 1977 at the Police Federation Annual Conference to attack Roy Mason for issuing provocative statements.

'On a number of occasions in the past statements have been made on behalf of the government that the IRA is beaten, defeated or on the run'.[33]

Such statements, he said, invited retaliation . . . 'words can be as lethal as bullets'. Mason ignored his warning. At the same Conference he continued to speak of 'police successes' against the IRA. By early 1979 he was going to regret these words.

With the struggle on the streets building up and the reports of torture in Castlereagh and the H-Blocks starting to have a significant political effect, Mason tried to close down *Republican News*. In December 1977 British army/RUC raids took place on the press centre and two issues of *Republican News* were seized. *Republican News* fought back – it produced a single-sheet emergency issue. The same month saw raids on the homes of 36 members of Sinn Fein and sellers and distributors of *Republican News* were harassed, raided and arrested. In March 1978 leading Sinn Fein member Gerry Adams was arrested and charged with IRA membership. In April 330 RUC men backed up by the British army raided *Republican News* offices and over 20 houses seizing *Republican News* and arresting 15 Belfast Sinn Fein leaders. The printer of *Republican News*, SDLP member Gary Kennedy, was also arrested. *Republican News* continued to print and eventually the courts had to release those arrested, including Gerry Adams, after international publicity and concern, and on the grounds that Sinn Fein was a recognised legal political party.

1978 began well for the IRA with the capture and execution of a British army intelligence officer, Paul Harman, who was engaged in SAS activities in West Belfast. He was captured carrying the photos of 73 prominent Republicans together with their names and addresses. This information would obviously be lethal in the hands of British army and loyalist assassination squads. Assassination attempts on some of those on Harman's list did in fact take place later.

In February 1978 the bombing of the La Mon restaurant went tragically wrong due to a bungled warning and 12 people died. The IRA immediately put out a statement admitting responsibility which stated:

'We accept condemnation and criticism from only two sources: from the relatives and friends of those who were accidentally killed, and from our supporters, who have rightly and severely criticised us . . .

It has been the disastrous presence of British interference in Ireland and that continuing armed presence in the Six Counties which is the root cause of unrest in our country. All killings and tragedies stem from British interference and their denial of Irish sovereignty . . . '[34]

Until November 1978 IRA activity remained low. Then the full force of the successful reorganisation hit the Six Counties. Mid-November saw a massive IRA bomb blitz across the Six Counties. The total estimated damage was £10 million. The next week another wave of bombings took place. On 26 November Albert Miles Deputy Governor of Long Kesh was executed by the IRA. The IRA put out a statement which said 'This man was fully aware of the beatings and torture of the men "on the blanket" . . . we justly executed Miles for his responsibility over H-Block'.[35] At the beginning of December a third major bombing blitz took place hitting 16 towns in one hour. In December the IRA claimed the bombing of British army barracks in West Germany which had occurred in August.

1979 began with bombing and sniper attacks in many areas of the Six Counties. Four British soldiers were killed, one soldier and 6 RUC men were injured. In January 1979 bombs went off in England blowing up a gasometer in Greenwich and blowing a hole in a fuel storage tank at Canvey Island. It was Mason who was now 'reeling'.

Mason however arrogantly continued to claim the IRA were isolated. In a Panorama programme on 12 February, Mason claimed that only a couple of hundred people would be prepared to support the 'blanket men' on the street. Six days later, on Sunday 18 February 1979 10,000 people marched in defiance of Mason's claim. The lead banner on this march called by Sinn Fein proclaimed 'Smash Mason's Lie'. Mason received another blow the same month. Three assistant governors from the H-Blocks resigned and informed the IRA of their resignation in order to be taken off the death list.

The 'criminalisation' policy was now in tatters. The IRA was on the offensive. Reports of torture in Castlereagh and other police interrogation centres, of the torture and degradation in the H-Blocks resounded around the world. The Labour government which had agreed to give extra parliamentary seats to Loyalists to keep the Labour Party in power was finally turfed out of office on 26 March 1979. Gerry Fitt and Frank Maguire could not support the Labour Party on a vote of confidence because of its record of torture in the Six Counties of Ireland.

Mason left the Six Counties with his reputation destroyed. One of the most reactionary imperialist governments had been forced out of office. After the election the Tory Party would carry on where the Labour government left off. Within two years the prison struggle was to come to a head.

NOTES

1   Cited in *Republican News* 25 September 1976.
2   *Republican News* 3 April 1976.
3   *Hands Off Ireland!* No 8 August 1979.
4   *Republican News* 17 September 1977.
5   *ibid.*
6   *Republican News* supplement 27 April 1978.
7   Coogan T P, *On the Blanket op cit* p. 7 and also p. 80.

8 Cited in *ibid* pp. 158–59.
9 *ibid* p.159.
10 Faligot R, *op cit* p. 191.
11 *Hands Off Ireland!* No 1 December 1976.
12 Cited in *Troops Out* March 1980. See Campaign for Free Speech on Ireland, *The British Media and Ireland* London nd (pamphlet) for an informative article on the press treatment of the Peace People.
13 The main political points in this section come from Fitzgerald J, 'The Loyalist Strike – Whose Defeat?' in *Hands Off Ireland!* No 2 June 1977.
14 *ibid* p. 7
15 *Sunday Times* 25 June 1978.
16 *Republican News* 6 and 13 August 1977.
17 Cited in *Financial Times* 14 September 1977.
18 *Republican News* 13 December 1980. This issue contains a biography of Sean McKenna giving the details of this incident.
19 McCann E, *op cit* p. 164.
20 *An Phoblacht/Republican News* 14 July 1979. Details of other murders in this period are given in this issue.
21 *An Phoblacht* 13 September 1976.
22 *Republican News* 16 October 1976.
23 *Republican News* 2 September 1978.
24 *Republican News* 12 November 1977.
25 *Republican News* 10 December 1977.
26 *Republican News* 15 April 1978.
27 *Republican News* 28 January 1978.
28 *Republican News* 18 February 1978.
29 *Republican News* 4 February 1978.
30 *Republican News* 18 December 1976.
31 *Republican News* 7 January 1978.
32 *Republican News* 19 November 1977.
33 *Republican News* 10 September 1977.
34 *Republican News* 25 February 1978.
35 *Republican News* 2 December 1978.

CHAPTER FIFTEEN

THE PRISON STRUGGLE

POLITICAL FORCES PREPARE FOR CONFRONTATION

The history of the Irish national liberation struggle since the civil war 1922–23 has demonstrated, time and again, that the neo-colonial state in the Twenty Six Counties is a fundamental barrier to a united independent Irish Republic. The political parties of the Irish capitalist class, Fine Gael and Fianna Fail, have lost no opportunity in their efforts to crush and destroy the IRA. Just like the loyalist state in the Six Counties, the Twenty Six Counties neo-colonial state will have to be destroyed if British imperialism is to be defeated in Ireland.

That the Irish liberation struggle cannot be won if confined to the Six Counties alone was forcefully stated in the Bodenstown oration given by Jimmy Drumm in June 1977:

'We find that a successful war of liberation cannot be fought on the backs of the oppressed in the Six Counties, nor around the physical presence of the British army.

Hatred and resentment of this army cannot sustain the war; and the isolation of the socialist Republicans around the armed struggle is dangerous and has produced, at least in some circles, the reformist notion that "Ulster" is the issue, without the mobilisation of the working class in the 26 Counties . . .

The forging of strong links between the Republican Movement and the workers of Ireland and radical trade unionists will create an irrepressible mass movement and will ensure mass support for the continuing armed struggle in the North and will make for a competent force in the event of serious conflict . . . '[1]

An article by Peter Dowling in *An Phoblacht/Republican News*, after

British imperialism's war to retake the Malvinas/Falkland Islands, further reinforced this important point:

'No guerrilla war of national liberation anywhere has ever been, nor ever will be, won on the basis of military success alone. It is a question of favourably changing the balance of *political forces*, not just in Ireland, North and South, but also in Britain.

'The IRA can never hope to militarily beat the British army. What it must eventually do is break the will of the British – their army, people and government – to remain in Ireland. A necessary part of this process will, of course, be *military successes*, but that is far from being sufficient.'[2]

The war of national liberation in early 1979 had reached a crucial stage. After a major reorganisation, the IRA had returned to the military offensive in the Six Counties, and the defeat of British imperialism's 'criminalisation' strategy now centred on the prisons. The conditions in the prisons were rapidly deteriorating as the political prisoners were forced to escalate their protest against the barbaric prison regime. Although massive demonstrations in support of the prisoners regularly took place they were having little impact on the British government's determination to deny Irish political prisoners political status.

The Republican Movement and its supporters were now to face a decisive test. Could the balance of political forces in Ireland, North and South, and also in Britain be favourably changed to break the will of the British government and force it to give the political prisoners political status? What forces in Ireland and Britain could be relied upon to follow the courageous lead of the political prisoners and fight a determined struggle to force Britain to recognise their legitimate political demands? How could these forces be organised and on what political basis?

POLITICAL FORCES IN THE SOUTH

The only all-Ireland dimension which the British government was determined to secure was the cooperation of the Twenty Six Counties government in joint action to defeat and isolate the IRA. Fianna Fail and Fine Gael were only too willing to oblige. Both these collaborationist parties are far more opposed to an Ireland united under the banner of revolutionary nationalism than they are to a divided Ireland under the domination of British imperialism.

During the 1970s both these collaborationist parties took measures to curb the activities of Sinn Fein and the IRA introducing increasingly more repressive legislation to imprison Republicans. In 1972 the Lynch Fianna Fail government reintroduced the Special Criminal (non-jury) Courts and passed draconian legislation which allowed for conviction on a charge of membership of an illegal organisation on the basis of a statement of a Chief Superintendent of the Gardai. Many leading Republicans were arrested and imprisoned in 1972 and the Radio Telefis Eireann Authority were dismissed after allowing an interview with Sean Mac Stiofain to be broadcast. Republican prisoners were kept under the most appalling conditions in prison. In May 1972 the Lynch government introduced new prison legislation allowing the military detention of prisoners after Republican prisoners had taken over the inner section of Mountjoy prison in a protest against prison conditions.

The Fine Gael-Irish Labour Party Coalition government 1973–1977 carried on where the Lynch government left off. After the dramatic escape in August 1973 of Seamus Twomey (IRA Chief of Staff), J B O'Hagan and Kevin Mallon from Mountjoy prison using a hijacked helicopter, Republican political prisoners were transferred to Portlaoise prison. In November 1973 there was a mass sit-down strike in Portlaoise's recreation hall in protest against conditions there. In August 1974 food parcels were banned and association severely restricted after 19 prisoners escaped from the prison using 25 pounds of explosives. In December the same year there was a major prison protest during which 27 warders were taken hostage. The Gardai and Army were called in and rubber bullets and water cannon were used to suppress the protest. In July 1976 the political prisoners attempted to burn down the security block at Portlaoise and as a result association was withdrawn and security was tightened. Strip searches and restricted visits with screens erected in the visiting area followed. No education classes were available in Portlaoise 'for security reasons' and there were frequent cell searches and regular punishments of long periods in solitary confinement and other losses of 'privileges' for the most trivial offences. In 1977 in protest against these appalling conditions twenty Republican prisoners went on hunger strike. There were protest marches in the Twenty Six Counties. One demonstration outside the prison was brutally attacked by Gardai liberally using their batons. The strike lasted 47 days ending on 22 April 1977 in apparent failure after the intervention of a Catholic bishop. However it later emerged that a number of concessions had been made. And the hunger strike was one of the factors which led to the downfall of the Coalition government in the general election of June 1977.

1976 was the year when the Coalition government significantly increased repression and harassment of Republicans and Republican supporters. In February 1976 after the murder of hunger striker Frank Stagg in Wakefield Prison, the coalition government refused to allow him a Republican funeral. The plane carrying his body from England was diverted from Dublin to Shannon airport and the Gardai buried him in a grave prepared on the government's instructions. The grave was concreted over to a depth of eighteen inches and guarded round the clock by armed Gardai. Nine months later, after the guard had been withdrawn, Frank Stagg's remains were removed by Republicans in the presence of a priest and reburied in a Republican plot.

On 31 March 1976 at Sallins in County Kildare the Cork-Dublin train was robbed of registered packets worth nearly a quarter of a million pounds. The government used the robbery as an excuse to launch a vicious political attack on the IRSP. About 40 people were arrested – mainly members of the IRSP – and many reported that they were tortured, being deprived of sleep and food and brutally kicked and beaten. Doctors later confirmed their injuries. Six IRSP members were eventually charged and three sentenced to long terms of imprisonment by the Special Criminal Court in December 1978 (under a Fianna Fail government). Two, Osgur Breathnach and Bernard McNally, were subsequently released in 1980 after an appeal on the grounds of illegal detention, assault and battery. The third, Nicky Kelly, had his appeal turned down and remains in prison. All three had been framed. The Provisional IRA say they carried out the train robbery.

1976 saw the introduction of new emergency legislation designed to curb the activities of Republicans. The *Criminal Law Act* (introduced September 1976) increased the sentences which the Special Criminal Court could impose for membership of an 'unlawful organisation' from 2 to 7 years. It increased the penalties for other offences covered by the Offences Against the State Act. It gave the Army the right to arrest and detain suspects. The *Emergency Powers Act* (October 1976) allowed the Gardai to detain suspects without charge or reference to a court for 7 days on the word of a Gardai Chief Superintendent. The *Broadcasting Authority (Amendment) Act* allowed a minister to prevent broadcasts that might incite crime or undermine the state. It was under this authority that interviews with members of proscribed organisations were forbidden – this included Sinn Fein even though it is not a proscribed organisation. Finally in May 1976 the *Criminal Law Jurisdiction Act* had underlined the Coalition government's determination to collaborate with Britain. It allowed for the trial in the Twenty Six

Counties for offences allegedly committed in 'Northern Ireland'. This was further extended, in the case of 'Irish citizens', to offences committed 'outside the state' if they involved explosive substances. It is this legislation which led to six political prisoners being sentenced to 10 years imprisonment in the Twenty Six Counties for escaping from Crumlin Road prison in June 1981. And later the unprecedented imprisonment of Gerard Tuite for 10 years (under a Fianna Fail government) for actions which took place in London.

The torture of IRSP members in 1976 highlighted the existence under the Coalition government of what was known as the 'Heavy Gang' – a flying squad of Gardai who conducted interrogations of Republicans. There were many reports of brutality and torture at the hands of these thugs in this period. The new legislation must have given these police thugs great encouragement to pursue their activities more vigorously.

In June 1977 the viciously anti-Republican activities of the Coalition government, its disregard for civil rights, its treatment of Republican prisoners, and the freedom given to the 'Heavy Gang', led to its downfall. Fianna Fail won a landslide victory after opportunistically mouthing 'Republican' sentiments. It received 84 seats to Fine Gael/Labour's 59. However the collaboration with British imperialism continued unabated involving the use of all the emergency legislation, increased cooperation with the British over border security, radio contact between the British and Irish 'security forces', an air corridor so British and Irish helicopters could fly into each other's territory (news of this forced Lynch's resignation), RUC interrogations of suspects in the Twenty Six Counties and so on.

The neo-colonial governments in the Twenty Six Counties, whether Fianna Fail or a Fine Gael-Labour coalition, are a barrier to any progress in the struggle for a united Ireland. No reliance whatsoever can be placed on them in the struggle against British imperialism. Their primary concern is to sabotage such a struggle. Only the defeat and isolation of such collaborationist forces could change the balance of political forces in the South.

The Irish labour movement

Neither can the official Irish labour movement be regarded as a potential ally in the struggle against British imperialism. Immediately after the Easter Rising 1916 and the murder of James Connolly, the official Irish trade union movement distanced itself from the national struggle and adopted a 'facing both ways' stance which it has maintained ever since. By 1921–22, after previously passing resolutions against the partition of Ireland, it accepted partition and remained 'neutral' in the civil war: neutral that is between imperialist domination and national liberation. The logical consequence of accepting partition was the establishment of a Northern Ireland Committee (NIC) of the Irish TUC in 1944. This arose out of a subcommittee of the ITUC set up in 1942 to deal with Northern Ireland affairs. Although formally a subsidiary body of the ITUC, during the 1950s the NIC/ITUC became totally autonomous in relation to matters in the Six Counties.

In 1945 a number of Irish-based unions broke away from the Irish TUC because of the growing influence of British-based unions (British unions with branches in Ireland) on the national executive of the ITUC. In 1944 the British-based unions had a majority on the national executive. The ITGWU and ten other Irish-based unions left the ITUC and formed the Congress of Irish Unions (CIU) in 1945. They argued that the Irish trade union movement had to be reorganised on national lines with only those unions having their headquarters in Ireland being eligible for membership. Nevertheless, the urge to restore the institutional unity of the trade union movement in Ireland led to the merger of the ITUC and CIU in 1959 with the formation of the Irish Congress of Trade Unions (ICTU). To preserve that 'unity' and maintain the allegiance of loyalist trade unionists the ICTU, like the ITUC before it, has recognised the partition of Ireland by giving complete autonomy to its Northern Ireland Committee. The NIC/ICTU was recognised in 1964 by the Unionist government under O'Neill as part of a programme of attracting new investment to the Six Counties. Until that time Unionist governments had refused to recognise Irish trade union congresses and their Northern Ireland committees. However recognising the NIC/ICTU far from undermining the sectarian character of the Six Counties statelet was in fact acknowledging it by accepting a partitionist division of the Irish trade union movement. The NIC/ICTU is a loyalist dominated trade union committee. 78% of NIC-affiliated trade unionists are in British-based unions, 14% in unions based in the Six Counties and only 8% based in the Twenty Six Counties.

The official Irish trade union movement is therefore organised along partitionist lines and is limited even in the fight for basic trade union principles (such as equality in employment and housing) by its overall concern to preserve the formal 'unity' of nationalist and loyalist trade unionists. It cannot preserve this 'unity' and seriously fight against the repression and terror directed at the nationalist minority by British imperialism in the Six Counties of Ireland. Even when a trade unionist, Brian Maguire of AUEW/TASS, was found hanging in a police cell after interrogation at Castlereagh in May 1978, it was not the official trade union movement which led the protests but a small group of trade unionists in TUCAR – the Trade Union Campaign Against Repression. TUCAR was dismissed as a Republican front organisation by the official trade union movement. Similarly in April 1980 an unofficial strike of NUPE members over British army presence and surveillance in the Royal Victoria Hospital, Belfast, was condemned by NUPE officials and the NIC/ICTU as being motivated by sectarianism! Finally none other than Roy Mason, then Secretary of State for Northern Ireland, recognised the vital collaborationist role of the ICTU when he wrote to the ICTU annual conference in 1977 that he was:

'very conscious that we [British imperialism] have been well served by the trade union leadership at all levels'.[3]

Imperialism and the collaborationist Twenty Six Counties capitalist class have succeeded in creating an official trade union movement in Ireland whose material, social and political conditions of existence depend on the continuation of partition. This trend was further consolidated by the massive influx of imperialist investment in the Twenty Six Counties in the 1960s and early 1970s which provided a temporary rise in wages and employment for organised labour. At that time the official trade union movement cared nothing for the inevitable disastrous consequences that growing imperialist domination of the Twenty Six Counties would have. These consequences are now being driven home to the Irish working class as the world-wide crisis of imperialism deepens and massive redundancies and wage cuts are forced on Irish workers. The mass of Irish workers under the impact of this crisis will be driven into opposition to imperialism. But whilst individual trade union leaders may be forced to fight, the official trade union movement, which has been nourished and sustained by its collaboration with imperialism, can never be won to the revolutionary national struggle to free Ireland from imperialist domination.

The record of the Irish Labour Party in coalition governments since 1973 further demonstrates the reactionary character of the official Irish Labour movement. And it is no surprise that today, as support for the Irish Labour Party declines, it is the pro-partition, pro-imperialist Workers Party (formerly Sinn Fein – The Workers Party, formerly the Official IRA) which is gaining influence in the official trade union movement and now holds leading positions in the once revolutionary ITGWU. The Irish working class will only be won to an anti-imperialist standpoint in opposition to, and outside of the structures of the official Irish trade union movement.

A survey by the Economic and Social Research Institute of Ireland published in October 1979 showed that a majority of Irish people in the Twenty Six Counties wanted a united Ireland. Further, 42% approved of the IRA's motivation and 21% supported the IRA's activities. A poll carried out by *Aspect* magazine at the beginning of 1982 showed that no less than 23% of unemployed youth in Dublin between 16 and 24 thought the IRA a good organisation – the figure was 16% for the Twenty Six Counties overall.[4] These figures show that a significant reservoir of political support for the struggle of the Republican Movement does exist in the Irish working class. It can be built upon as the crisis of imperialism and Irish capitalism deepens. But only if a resolute stand against the pro-imperialist forces of Fianna Fail, Fine Gael, and the official Irish labour movement is taken by the Republican Movement.

THE POLITICAL FORCES IN THE SIX COUNTIES

By Easter 1979 the Labour government's 'criminalisation' policy was in disarray – destroyed by the prisoners' courage and determination, the massive street protests resulting from the painstaking work of the Relatives Action Committees and the IRA's successful military and propaganda offensive. Mason was to quietly resign shortly before the 3 May General Election. Newman and Creasey were to be removed by the end of the year. The IRA with some justification could state in its Easter statement:

> 'Roy Mason who came here with so much confidence and so many boasts departs very soon as a defeated man, and we will grind the next British War-Lord into the ground as we have done with Mason! It matters little who rules at Westminster; they'll still send their gunmen and tanks and SAS murderers to repress the Irish people. But by a combination of political work, street resistance and uncompromising revolutionary guerrilla warfare we will inflict a political defeat on the British government's will to stay in Ireland ... '[5]

However the political prisoners' struggle for political status was still to be resolved. The prisoners were putting pressure on the Republican Movement to step up its protest to force the British government to restore political status. By mid-1979 the prisoners were beginning to argue for a hunger strike to force the British government's hand. The IRA leadership was strongly opposed to a hunger strike and although it could not persuade the prisoners to abandon the idea it urged them not to set a date for a hunger strike unless it all looked hopeless – that is if it became clear that the protest outside the prison had failed to bring about the necessary change. The Republican Movement on the outside promised a better organised protest campaign.

The IRA offensive

At the beginning of 1979 the IRA had significantly stepped up its military offensive against commercial and military targets. In March Omagh and Dungannon town centres were blasted by car bombs. Kinawley, Co Fermanagh and Newtonhamilton, South Armagh British army/RUC barracks were destroyed by IRA bomb attacks killing one British soldier and injuring 4 British soldiers and 2 RUC men. On 22 March 19 towns across the Six Counties were hit within one hour, 9.30pm-10.30pm, in a coordinated IRA bomb blitz. Prime targets were banks – 'symbols of the economic oppression of the nationalist people'.[6]

On 22 March 1979 outside the British embassy at the Hague the IRA shot and killed the British ambassador to the Netherlands, Sir Richard Sykes. He had been in charge of the investigation of the assassination of Ewart-Biggs the British ambassador to Dublin, who had been killed by the IRA in July 1976 when a road-mine blew up his car. The General Election campaign in Britain had the issue of Ireland dramatically imposed on it when Airey Neave was assassinated on 30 March by INLA after a bomb which had been planted in his car went off in the precincts of the House of Commons. Airey Neave was the Conservative spokesman on Northern Ireland affairs and would almost certainly have become the Secretary of State for Northern Ireland after the Conservative election victory. He was an extreme right-wing reactionary and had called for the strengthening of the SAS and UDR and for the reintroduction of hanging and internment in the Six Counties. Faligot reports the claim of an ex-SIS (MI6) agent that Airey Neave, a week before his death, was discussing plans for the assassination of Tony Benn and the formation of an underground paramilitary force in the event of a Labour victory in the 1979 election.[7] INLA, the military wing of the IRSP, was to become more active over the next period. INLA/IRSP had about 40 members in prison by early 1980, who took part in the blanket protest.

In April the IRA shot and killed seven members of the 'security forces' in seven days. Senior officers obviously shaken by the dramatic increase in IRA military activities (Mason had been boasting for nearly two years that the IRA was 'reeling') began to consider the reintroduction of internment. Reports of British soldiers beginning to break down under the pressure of the war began to circulate. At the end of February Trooper Edward Maggs had gone berserk in Woodburn Barracks, West Belfast and shot dead a corporal and seriously injured an officer in his regiment the Blues and Royals, Household Cavalry. He was killed by other soldiers. A Corporal Schofield of the Royal Green Jackets deserted – his girlfriend stated after his recapture that 'he cracked under the pressure of the war'.[8] There was a report of another soldier going berserk and killing his wife at his base at Aldergrove, north of West Belfast. That same month Dickie Elder one of the three top prison officers at Crumlin Road gaol resigned and notified the IRA of his resignation.

In May 1979 the IRA achieved a dramatic propaganda victory against British imperialism. Extracts of a secret British army document, which had been captured in the mail by IRA intelligence a few months earlier, were published in *An Phoblacht/Republican News*. The document, prepared by Brigadier JM Glover of British Defence Intelligence Staff, totally contradicts the picture of the IRA projected by British government and army officials and faithfully reproduced in the servile British media. Whilst Mason and other British spokesmen were publicly proclaiming the imminent defeat of the IRA the document said:

'The Provisional IRA (PIRA) has the dedication and the sinews of war to raise violence intermittently to at least the level of early 1978, certainly for the foreseeable future. Even if "peace" is restored, the motivation for politically inspired violence will remain. Arms will be readily available and there will be many who are able and willing to use them. Any peace will be superficial and brittle. A new campaign may well erupt in the years ahead.'

Far from the IRA being the 'mindless criminals' and 'hoodlums' of British government spokesmen and slavish accounts of the war in the British media, the document states:

'(a) LEADERSHIP – PIRA is essentially a working class organisation based in the ghetto areas of the cities and in the poorer rural areas. Thus if members of the middle class and graduates become

more deeply involved they have to forfeit their lifestyle . . .
Nevertheless, there is a strata of intelligent, astute and experienced
terrorists who provide the backbone of the organisation . . .

(b) TECHNICAL EXPERTISE – PIRA has an adequate supply of
members who are skilled in the production of explosive devices . . .

(c) RANK AND FILE TERRORISTS – Our evidence of the calibre
of rank and file terrorists does not support the view that they are
mindless   hooligans   drawn   from   the   unemployed   and
unemployable . . .

(d) TREND IN CALIBRE – The mature terrorists, including for
instance the leading bomb makers, are sufficiently cunning to avoid
arrest. They are continually learning from mistakes and developing
their expertise . . . '

The document concluded that the 'Provisional campaign of violence is
likely to continue while the British remain in Northern Ireland'. It
could not see any prospect of a 'political development' which would
seriously undermine the Provisionals' position:

'PIRA will probably continue to recruit the men it needs. They will
still be able to attract enough people with leadership talent, good
education and manual skills to continue to enhance their all round
professionalism. The Movement will retain popular support sufficient to maintain secure bases in the traditional Republican areas.'[9]

British lies and propaganda might suffice for British politicians and the
British public but the British army had to conduct a war against the
Provisional IRA and it could not do this unless it had a reasonably
accurate assessment of the liberation movement it was fighting.

On 11 May 1979 Kieran Nugent, the first man to go 'on the blanket'
was freed. John Deery had been released two weeks earlier – the first
prisoner on the 'no wash – no slop out protest' to be released. They had
both successfully defied the British government's attempt to 'criminalise' Republican political prisoners.

In June Alan Wright, leader of the Northern Ireland Police Federation, argued that 'if we are not to lose what small gains we may have
made, then the army must play a more active role in the security
field'.[10] The IRA's renewed military offensive was clearly delivering
another major blow to that other element in British imperialism's
'Ulsterisation' strategy – the 'primacy of the police' in maintaining
'security' in the Six Counties.

IRA attacks continued over the next few months. At the end of

August the IRA carried out the most dramatic operations of the ten year war. In the first on Monday 27 August 1979 the IRA assassinated Lord Louis Mountbatten. A 50lb remote controlled bomb was placed on board his boat and was detonated by the IRA when the boat was in Mullaghmore Bay Co Sligo killing Mountbatten and three others. The second took place some five hours later at Narrow Water Castle close to Warrenpoint in South Down. IRA explosives engineers planted a huge bomb and a landmine. A charge of over 1,100lb of explosives in a hay-trailer was parked at the side of the main Warrenpoint to Newry road. A 500lb landmine was also buried nearby beneath the stone gate-post of a derelict lodge. Both were to be detonated by radio-controlled devices. As the third vehicle of an army convoy containing members of the 2nd Battalion Parachute Regiment passed the hay lorry the bomb was detonated killing six soldiers and injuring others. The remainder of the force then took cover near the lodge gate where the second bomb had been planted. They radioed for reinforcements. Twenty-five minutes later three Wessex helicopters brought in extra troops from the Queen's Own Highlanders in South Armagh. When they took up position the IRA unit detonated the second bomb killing ten more soldiers from the Parachute Regiment and two Highlanders including Lieutenant Colonel David Blair, the most senior ranking British officer to have been killed in the last ten years of the war.

These operations had a devastating effect on the morale of the British army. Immediately the Prime Minister, Margaret Thatcher visited the troops and in a show of concern attempted to repair British army confidence. The 'Ulsterisation' strategy had suffered a major blow. Disputes over security arose between British army chiefs and the RUC. In October, Sir Maurice Oldfield, a former head of MI6 (British intelligence service responsible for intelligence gathering etc outside Britain) had to be sent to the Six Counties to try and coordinate overall security — co-ordinating operations between the British army and the RUC.

The prisoner campaign

The IRA had certainly lived up to its Easter promise of 'uncompromising revolutionary guerrilla warfare'. The number of British army/UDR/RUC forces killed in 1979 was 62, the highest since 1973. Over 230 members of the 'security forces' had been injured. Yet in spite of this and the growing campaign of street protests and demonstrations the British government had not yet been forced to change its position on political status. The struggle would have to be intensified at all levels if a hunger strike by the political prisoners was to be avoided. It was at this stage towards the end of 1979 that a fundamental change of direction in the prisoner campaign took place. Political forces from outside the Republican Movement and the nationalist working class were increasingly drawn into the campaign. Some had already been involved since the Coalisland Conference, January 1978 but over the next two years they were to exert an ever growing influence over the direction of the campaign.

In June 1979 the Republican Movement and the prisoners called for a boycott of the EEC elections. They regarded the EEC as another force and institution restricting the Irish people from asserting their independence. But Bernadette McAliskey stood as an anti-repression and anti-H-Block candidate in the EEC elections causing serious divisions among the Relatives Action Committees and in the nationalist community. The Republican Movement wrote at that time:

'In the six counties the Republican Movement and the H-Block blanketmen are totally opposed to the opportunism of Bernadette McAliskey who is running on an anti-repression ticket . . .

The EEC parliament (and not the H-Block prisoners nor the Irish people) will certainly gain if people vote for the birth of a monster which in the long run is out to strangle us'.[11]

A year later Bernadette McAliskey was to be a leading figure in the National H-Block Campaign working on the National H-Block Committee with leading members of Sinn Fein.

At the beginning of 1979 there had been some pressure for a campaign in support of the prisoners based on 'humanitarian' grounds but at this stage the Republican Movement rejected them out of hand. At a march in Loughguile Co Antrim, the Belfast Republican Liam Hannaway made it clear that:

'The men in the H-Block and women in Armagh are not protesting for better prison conditions. Their protest is for recognition as political prisoners, as prisoners of war. Let us never forget that point'.[12]

Again in April a letter from a prisoner in H-4 Block, Long Kesh, commenting on 'humanitarian appeals to the Brits' for better conditions said:

'These calls are understandable coming from our friends and relations, but when they come from anti-Republican sources they take on a more devious meaning.

'For this reason we feel it necessary to make our position "blanket" struggle clear. Our fight is not concerned with better conditions . . .

We are Republican soldiers fighting a national liberation war against British rule.

We demand the right when captured to be recognised and treated as Political Prisoners of War'.[13]

The change in direction took some time to develop. The prisoner campaign and support for the armed struggle continued to grow during the second half of 1979. A massive 'Brits Out' demonstration took place in West Belfast on 12 August marking ten years of war between the Irish people and British imperialism. An estimated 10-15,000 people were on this march which had been billed beforehand as an 'act of resistance':

'It is a march in support of our armed comrades, it is a salute to our prisoners everywhere, an especial salute to the courageous and heroic blanket men'.[14]

The street wide banners on the march declared 'Britain must go', 'Victory to the Blanket Men' and 'Victory to the IRA'. And when armed IRA volunteers paraded in front of the crowd at the rally in Casement Park, there were ecstatic cheers and chants of 'I . . . I . . . IRA'. The nationalist people were saluting their revolutionary vanguard – the IRA. Even the British press were forced to record the significance of this march:

Daily Express: 'The rally was one of the strongest displays of support for the Republican campaign in recent years'.

Daily Mirror: ' . . . the biggest show of Republican support since the Army began their security duties in 1969.'

Daily Telegraph: ' . . . a demonstration which indicated the continuing significant support for the Provisional IRA's terrorist campaign in Northern Ireland.'

The Guardian: ' . . . the most dramatic display of strength by the Republican Movement here in recent years.'[15]

The Pope visited Ireland at the end of September. His call for 'peace' and reference to the 'men of violence' was shamelessly exploited by Irish and British politicians not known for their opposition to British imperialism's campaign of repression and terror in the Six Counties. The IRA answered them with a clear reaffirmation of the need for armed struggle to force Britain out of Ireland and so create 'a climate for real peace with justice'.

'...force is by far the only means of removing the evil of British presence in Ireland...Church leaders, politicians and establishments are bankrupt and have also failed to resolve the massive social and economic problems suffered by our people and created by British interference.'[16]

The IRA statement argued that one should not talk of 'men of violence' and ignore the 33,000 strong armed forces in the Six Counties, the repressive laws, the torture of prisoners and the situation in the H-Blocks. It was, however, the situation in the H-Blocks that was now causing most concern.

National H-Block Campaign

In September 1979 a conference organised by the Six Counties Coordinating Committee of the RACs was announced for 21 October in Belfast to set up a national 'Smash H-Block' committee. There were to be no preconditions on those attending the conference or on committee members other than support for the 'four main demands' of the blanket men. These were that political prisoners should have no prison work, no prison uniform, free association and the right to organise. The task of the conference was 'to explore the coordination of all those groups and individuals who are opposed to the situation in the H-Blocks for whatever reason'.[17] A week later Sinn Fein had its own conference on the prisoner issue. During this conference the leadership of Sinn Fein made it clear that it was supporting a fundamental change of political direction in the prisoner campaign. Gerry Adams stated that while previously Sinn Fein had generally limited its cooperation on the H-Block issue to those groups and individuals who not only support the blanket men, but also the armed national liberation struggle:

'The Smash H-Block conference and committee will be different. Participants are not required to support the IRA.'[18]

A major consideration behind this change of direction, besides the general urgency of intensifying the protest outside the prison, appeared to be the need to build the campaign in the Twenty Six Counties:

'A discussion from the floor then centred around how to make people, especially those in the twenty-six counties, more aware of the horrors of H-Block and of how to provide those who are aware, and care, with meaningful lines of political action.

The question was raised that as the H-Blocks are the direct

responsibility of the British, and not of the Free State government, perhaps it is difficult for people in the twenty-six counties to focus their anger on a meaningful target'.[19]

More than 600 people attended the 'Smash H-Block' conference on Sunday 21 October held in Belfast's Green Briar Club. Organisations which attended the conference included Sinn Fein, the IRSP, Peoples Democracy, TUCAR, Women Against Imperialism, a variety of left political groups and remarkably the Peace People. An Phoblacht/ Republican News reported that 'it was hoped to draw a much wider circle of people to the discussion, for example Frank Maguire MP, Father Faul, Mickey Mullen (ITGWU), senior GAA officials and humanitarian groups'. In their absence provision was made for the subsequently elected 'Smash H-Block Committee' to co-opt ten additional members in the interests of 'a broad-based united front'.[20]

In February 1978 after the Coalisland Conference Republican News had argued against Peoples Democracy and Bernadette McAliskey attempting to turn the clock back to the Civil Rights type of campaigning. It had said that while not all united fronts on the prisoner campaign had to be on the 'basis of everyone openly supporting the IRA's armed struggle' the 'humanitarian approach of Father Faul and the polite parliamentary-type protests of Frank Maguire ... are not enough to win our aims in the short term let alone in the long term'. Now these forces, openly criticised in 1978, were being asked to play a central role in the prisoner campaign. These developments did not take place without some protest from Republican activists. Jimmy Drumm wrote angrily to An Phoblacht/Republican News that he was astounded that a platform had been given to Ciaran McKeown, the 'Peace People's' spokesperson, at the conference. The 'Peace People's' exhortation for people to inform on 'anyone involved in acts of terrorism' had probably resulted in some of the 'blanketmen' finding themselves in the position they are in today. Was this 'not carrying liberalisation and democracy too far'?[21]

The main resolution proposed and passed by the Conference came from the Republican Movement. The resolution called for the election of a 'seventeen person H-Block Committee to spearhead a national campaign ... to force the British government to concede political prisoner status'. It said that the campaign should be oriented towards mobilising national support for the prisoners' demands 'particularly amongst the organised labour movement, community organisations and cultural organisations and also mobilising international support'.

It called for a Dublin Conference to elect a 'southern-based committee' to be 'charged with the responsibility of building a support campaign in the twenty-six counties.' Should political status not be won then another open conference had to be organised within six months. The message sent to the conference from the 'blanketmen' made it clear they were 'prepared to die for the right to political status'. The Committee members elected included members of Sinn Fein, IRSP, Peoples Democracy, representatives from the RACs (appointed) and others active on the prisoner issue. Kathleen Holden was co-opted on to the committee as the mother of a 'blanketman'.[22]

The Dublin Conference took place on 18 December. More than 500 people attended and elected a Southern-based sub-committee to co-ordinate H-Block activity in the South. Sponsors of the conference included 'a number of leading trade unionists, several solicitors and cultural figures, and notably Donegal politician Neil Blaney'. There were a number of 'famous personalities in attendance' including actresses and playwrights. Gerry Adams (then Vice-President of Sinn Fein) reinforced the new political direction of the prisoner campaign when he said:

> '... for those who are unable to support the armed struggle in the North there is nothing in the demands put forward by the committee which cannot be supported on humanitarian grounds'.[23]

The demands of the committee were now in the form of 'five demands':

☆ The prisoners right not to wear prison uniform.
☆ The right not to do prison work
☆ Freedom of association amongst political prisoners
☆ The right to organise recreational and educational facilities, to have weekly visits, letters and parcels
☆ The entitlement to full remission of sentences.

The action the Conference agreed to take included: approaching prominent individuals, seeking sponsors for major advertisements in the national press, launching a national petition, organising days of action, holding indoor public meetings in as many towns as possible, supporting the formation of independent local committees, supporting the march to Long Kesh from Belfast on New Year's Day, and organising a national demonstration in Dublin.

The first National H-Block march took place in West Belfast on 1 January 1980. The well-supported march was banned from going to Long Kesh and was blocked by thousands of troops and RUC men. No attempt was made to breach the blockade and the marchers' conduct was later praised by a spokesman for the National H-Block Committee as 'disciplined in the face of severe provocation by the RUC and British army'.[24]

At the Sinn Fein Ard Fheis over the weekend of 19/20 January 1980 the President of Sinn Fein, Ruairi O'Bradaigh said in his Presidential address:

'Sinn Fein is gratified at the establishment of the broad-based National "Smash H-Block" Committee on the simple platform of the five demands made by the prisoners themselves for the restoration of prisoner-of-war status. We urge our members to redouble their efforts with the assistance of non-members on this great issue of human rights'.[25]

But not everyone in Sinn Fein agreed. Doubts were 'vociferously expressed' by some delegates about the efficacy of or the need for the National H-Block Committee in 'one of the most heated debates of the weekend'. In particular delegates were disturbed that the Committee had broken with traditional practice and had filed with (notified) the RUC for the Belfast New Year's Day march.[26] Jimmy Drumm, a member of the Ard Comhairle (Central Committee) of Sinn Fein, was, according to *Magill*, totally opposed to the whole concept of 'broad-based organisation' now central to the prisoner campaign.[27]

In February 1980 the 33 women political prisoners in Armagh prison were forced to step up their 'no work' protest. On 7 February the authorities at the prison seriously escalated their harassment of the women prisoners. They announced, when the women were out of their cells and lined up for a meal, that they intended to search the women's cells. The women political prisoners were suddenly surrounded by some sixty male and female warders, some of the former drafted in from Long Kesh. Almost immediately about forty male warders moved in on the women and attacked them. Plates were thrown and the women were punched and kicked until 'order' was restored. The women were placed in two association cells and locked up. Their cells were searched and wrecked. Subsequently a number of the women prisoners were dragged before the governor. All the women on protest were then denied washing and toilet facilities and their cells were soon in a filthy state and soaked with urine. The women began to pour the contents of their pots filled with urine and excrement out of the spy holes in their cells and, after these were nailed shut, out of the cell windows. Soon they were put in cells with the windows boarded up. By 12 February a full scale 'dirt strike' was in operation with the women smearing their excrement on the cell walls and refusing all clothing except what they stood up in. The women political prisoners were now faced with the same barbaric inhuman conditions as their comrades in the H-Blocks.

As the prison struggle escalated, the National H-Block Committee continued to organise marches and protests outside, all the time attempting to draw more people into the struggle 'on the basis of common humanity and regard for human rights' (National H-Block committee member Fr Piaras O'Duill).[28] When on 2 March a 'several thousand' strong Belfast march was prevented by a heavy force of British army/RUC from leaving West Belfast for Long Kesh, militant youth repeatedly attacked the 'security forces'. Nine year old Hugh Hamill was seriously injured by a plastic bullet when the British army fired on the H-Block marchers. *An Phoblacht/Republican News* commented at the time:

'The frantic overreaction by certain stewards to the young rioters demonstrates the urgent need in the future for stewards to be fully informed of how to respond in all situations which arise and how – most vitally – to channel the militancy of the young people for the overall good of the march'.[29]

This issue was to be raised time and again as the militant anger of the youth conflicted with the 'disciplined' peaceful protests demanded by the National H-Block campaign.

On 26 March the Secretary of State for Northern Ireland Humphrey Atkins made a proposal to allow political prisoners to wear sports gear to exercise, weekly letters and an extra visit per month. This was immediately rejected by the 380 'blanket men' as 'ridiculous'.

'... We could have one visit per week, any amount of letters and daily exercise but only if we accept criminal status and come off the blanket ... We are protesting for full political status. We recognise we have a long way to go yet, but we shall not weaken'.[30]

With Atkins' 'concessions' came the announcement that from 1 April even prisoners sentenced for political offences committed before 1 March 1976 would now be denied political status. This conclusively demonstrated the determination of the British government to defeat the prisoners in their legitimate struggle to be regarded as political prisoners. The 'concessions' were simply a British propaganda exercise.

At the beginning of June John Turnly, joint chairman of the Irish Independence Party and H-Block activist, was assassinated by loyalist gunmen. He was the first of the H-Block activists to be murdered.

Loyalist gunmen had become much more active towards the end of 1979 after the IRA's dramatic military successes. Between August and December 1979 there were ten known victims of loyalist murder squads.

An Phoblacht/Republican News 14 June 1980 carried a statement from the IRA that it was 'resuming hostilities against all prison officials'. The announcement was made in an IRA statement claiming responsibility for the shooting of a prison warder in Belfast the Tuesday before. The IRA statement explained the sudden unannounced halt in attacks on prison officials in March:

'In early March we took a unilateral decision when Cardinal O'Fiaich and Bishop Daly visited the H-Blocks to cease all hostilities against the prison regime in an attempt to create a climate for a just settlement of the political prisoners' demands'.[31]

The talks that Cardinal O'Fiaich had had with Atkins since March had proved fruitless and at the beginning of June four defenceless prisoners had been viciously beaten up in the H-Blocks. The IRA decided to resume attacks on prison officials. The announcement however indicated the growing importance being attached to the activities of the Catholic hierarchy in the present prisoner campaign.

Bishop Daly immediately denounced the resumption of IRA attacks on prison warders as 'extremely unfortunate, regrettable and detestable'. He appealed to the British government for 'an easing of the situation' in the H-Blocks on the grounds this would be a 'considerable setback' to what he called 'IRA propaganda'. The IRA in a strong reply to this criticism pointed out:

'There is no propaganda for the Irish Republican Army in the H-Block situation: if there were, and if it superseded the value of the H-Blocks to the British, then the British government would have resolved the problem long ago and removed such propaganda'.[32]

The IRA statement went on to challenge Bishop Daly to make his position clear on prison brutality given that he had no reservations or qualifications about condemning the IRA for actions he disagreed with. The IRA had continued with its military offensive against commercial and military targets since the formation of the National H-Block Committee and throughout the period when attacks against prison officials had been suspended.

The second National H-Block Conference took place on 15 June 1980. Its task was to assess the progress of the campaign so far. There were various problems and organisational difficulties raised which for example 'had led to the H-Block marches in Armagh and Newry being only partial successes'. It was agreed to appoint a full-time national organiser to establish offices in Dublin and Belfast to overcome this and to set up the necessary fund-raising committee. The need to involve the trade union movement in the campaign became a central issue in the debate stressed particularly by left groups such as Peoples Democracy. One group called for immediate strike action – a totally unrealistic demand given the character of the Irish labour movement and the amount of campaigning work so far done in the trade unions. Gerry Adams correctly argued that while industrial action might be one aim to work towards, strike calls were premature. He then endorsed the political direction of the campaign and argued:

> 'There is no conflict between "political status" and a "humanitarian" approach: the prisoners are undeniably political, but – outside of the five basic demands of the prisoners – it is up to individuals what approach they take'.[33]

However this was not necessarily the case. A conflict would and did arise between those who saw the continuation of the armed struggle and militant action by youths on the streets as complementary to the campaign of peaceful protest led by the National H-Block Committee and those who quite clearly didn't. A new committee was elected at the Conference – it included Bernadette McAliskey.

On 26 June Miriam Daly, a major figure in the IRSP and a member of the National H-Block Committee, was murdered – bound hand and foot and shot five times in the head. *An Phoblacht/Republican News* argued that there was evidence – the 'professionalism' of the assassins – that pointed to British army involvement and most probably the SAS.[34]

Towards the end of May *An Phoblacht/Republican News* reported that the Ardoyne Republican Martin Meehan had gone on hunger strike in protest against being framed on a kidnapping charge and being gaoled for twelve years. The 12 July issue of *An Phoblacht/ Republican News* carried banner headlines 'Don't Let Meehan Die!' and reported a 'well-attended march and rally' to highlight the protest. Martin Meehan had just completed 52 days on hunger strike. The next week there were reports of intensive street fighting between militant youths and the British army/RUC on the Falls Road after a more than 2,000 strong march in support of Martin Meehan had taken place. The fights went on for three further days. Martin Meehan agreed to come off hunger strike after 66 days as 'his case had been highlighted' and 'his appeal hearing would be the focus of public attention' and thus 'some guarantee he would get justice'. An Phoblacht/Republican News stated at the time:

'...one thing the Brits had better take note of is that a real bond exists between the nationalist people on the streets and the Republican political prisoners and that the militant reaction they saw is just a very small taste of what they'll get should anything untoward happen to any of the blanketmen in H-Block or the women protestors in Armagh jail'.[35]

Seamus Mullen, a Derry Republican, also went on hunger strike towards the end of May in protest against being framed, this time on a blackmail charge, and sentenced to ten years. He ended his strike after 71 days – he was seriously ill – after the intervention of Bishop Daly and on being given a date for his appeal.

On 23 July 16 year old Michael McCarten was murdered by the RUC as he painted political slogans on a hoarding. The RUC claimed they thought the paint brush was a gun. The youth responded by openly daubing slogans over walls on the Falls Road showing they would not be intimidated. Militant street protests followed and the stoning of RUC vehicles by youths continued for five nights. Angry women plastered an RUC jeep with a dozen hand made posters declaring – 'RUC murdered Michael McCarten'.

The second Dublin Conference of the National H-Block Committee took place on 14 September. Progress had been made in the setting up of over 30 local groups and resolutions of support for the prisoners from 9 Trades Councils and 4 trade unions were reported. Speeches from the floor showed concern that:

'...the establishment of a new twenty-six counties committee was partitionist and that marches to Leinster House and appeals to clergymen were ignoring the realities of the overall anti-imperialist struggle'[36]

Jim Gibney (Sinn Fein and National H-Block Committee) argued against this putting the 'majority view' in support of a Twenty Six Counties committee that:

'the different situation North and South meant pressure could be exerted on trade unionists and politicians in the South which was impossible in the North'.[37]

However on 27 September *An Phoblacht/Republican News* carried banner headlines 'H-Block hopes dashed'. The talks between Cardinal O'Fiaich and Bishop Daly and Atkins, which had been renewed after June, finally collapsed for good. The blanket men were on the brink of total frustration. The National H-Block Committee's campaign had failed to move the British government. A hunger strike by the prisoners was now inevitable. A statement smuggled out of the H-Blocks on Friday 10 October announced a hunger strike to commence on 27 October 1980.

POLITICAL FORCES IN BRITAIN

The Labour Party's treacherous record on Ireland is second to none. The flag of the Labour Party is red only because it is stained with the blood of the Irish people and of oppressed peoples who have had to fight British imperialism to obtain their freedom in many parts of the world. However, the Labour Party's record on Ireland says it all:

1913/14 Betrayed the Dublin workers during the Dublin strikes and lock-out.

1916 Was party to the murder of James Connolly and applauded the suppression of the Easter Rising.

1921/22 Supported the partition of Ireland and the creation of the reactionary neo-colonial Twenty Six County 'Free State'.

1939 Supported the anti-Irish Prevention of Violence Act.

1949 Legitimised the loyalist police state in the Six Counties by introducing a new Government of Ireland Act.

1969 Sent British troops into the Six Counties of Ireland.

1974 Introduced the racist, anti-Irish Prevention of Terrorism Act.

1974-6 Laid the basis for a regime of terror through British imperialism's 'Ulsterisation' policy.

1976-9 Administered a regime of terror. Withdrew Special Category status from Irish political prisoners. Built and opened the H-Blocks. Institutionalised torture of Irish political prisoners first in police cells and then in the H-Blocks.

1978-9 Agreed to give extra seats to the Loyalists to keep the Labour government in power.

This totally reactionary Labour Party throughout its history has had the support of the official trade union movement in carrying ot its treacherous and barbaric policies. No significant section of the Labour

Party has or could take up a consistent fight against these policies without breaking with the Labour Party. For the Labour Party gives political expression to that privileged layer of the working class that has a material interest in the continuation of imperialism – for it is the source of its economic and political privileges. In the recent period not one so-called 'Left' Labour MP opposed the introduction of the Prevention of Terrorism Act. Mr Tony Benn sat in numerous Labour Cabinets and raised no objections to the Labour Party's record of brutality and terror in the Six Counties of Ireland. To argue that an effective alliance could be built with any section of the Labour Party in support of the Irish political prisoners' struggle for political status (or later the 'Five Demands') was at best to spread a cruel deception, at worst to openly betray the Irish cause.

Given the record of the Labour Party, the responsibility for building a movement in solidarity with Irish political prisoners would fall on those organisations which regard themselves as part of the revolutionary socialist left. The omens were not very good. After the massive Bloody Sunday demonstration of 1972 had been broken up by the police and three of the organisers had been arrested, the British left retreated from any confrontation with the British state. The retreat turned into headlong flight after the IRA's military campaign began in Britain.

The relative prosperity in the imperialist nations during the post-war boom – a prosperity based on the rebuilding of the major imperialist powers after the Second World War under the domination of US imperialism – allowed bourgeois 'democracy' a certain lease of life. It gave rise to new privileged sections of the working class – sections of which were able to obtain lucrative positions as trade union officials, journalists, lawyers, politicians, academics, economists, teachers, civil servants and the like. The privileges and status of these layers depend directly on the continuation of imperialism – the attempt to shore up the prosperity of the post-war boom through the super-exploitation of oppressed peoples.

The British socialist groups, on the whole, draw their membership from these new privileged layers of the working class. As the crisis of imperialism deepens these layers are faced with a choice. *Either* to side with the most oppressed sections of the working class in Britain – black and Irish workers, unemployed youth – as well as the liberation movements struggling against imperialism. *Or* to seek relative respectability respectability and security in alliance with other privileged layers in the Labour and trade union movement. There is no middle road. After the election of the Labour government in 1974 the main organisations of the British left made their choice. Increasingly they sided with those supporting imperialism and attacked those taking up the armed struggle against imperialism. For their opposition to the violence and brutality of imperialism only existed because they recognised that it created a revolutionary opposition to imperialism amongst the oppressed.

The class standpoint of the British left – middle class socialism – is the foundation of its consistent search for a 'progressive' side to British imperialism and underlies its attempt to build an alliance with the imperialist Labour Party. As we shall see, the promotion and protection of this alliance at all times took priority and often led to the British left ignoring or openly betraying the Irish peoples' struggle for freedom. The history of the Troops Out Movement (TOM) bears this out.

TOM was formed in October 1973 on the *formally* principled basis of accepting two demands – Troops Out Now! and Self-determination for the Irish People as a whole. However, given TOM replaced the Anti-Internment League, its demands, however formally principled, constituted a turning away from the very urgent issue of internment without trial in the Six Counties, which was not to end for another two years. After the election of the Labour government in 1974 TOM ceased campaigning for its formal demands.

The TOM acts on the basis that the Labour Party, or at least significant sections of it, can be won to an active campaign against British imperialist rule in Ireland. This position ignores the split in the working class movement and the fact that the Labour Party represents the interests of the labour aristocracy and other privileged sections of the working class. Members of the Labour Party who actively oppose British rule in Ireland would be forced into direct confrontation with the organised Labour and trade union movement. At all critical points in the Irish struggle a choice is inevitably faced: either loyalty to the Irish people's struggle or loyalty to the British Labour and trade union leadership. During the 1913 Dublin lock out, for example, Ben Tillett, 'militant' trade union leader, supported Larkin and the Dublin workers until it became necessary to confront the British Labour and TUC leadership. At that point Ben Tillett took the side of British imperialism, denounced Larkin and betrayed the Dublin workers.[38]

The TOM, in expressing the political standpoint of middle class socialism, attempts to avoid this choice by limiting all its actions and policies so that no real confrontation with the Labour and trade union leadership is forced out into the open. The more pressing the revolutionary challenge from Ireland is, the more dangerous it is for TOM to act in any decisive way or, indeed, at all. This was demonstrated during the period of institutionalised torture 1976–9 conducted by the Labour Party in power.

In July 1977, after a split in TOM, the United TOM was launched on exactly the same principles as the 'old' TOM. It declared that its 'major national focus . . . during 1977' was to be an International Tribunal on Britain's Crimes against the Irish People. This event, the brainchild of the International Marxist Group (IMG), was aimed at drawing in trade unionists, Labour Party members, MPs, prominent personalities etc. In pursuit of this end the title was changed to International Tribunal on Britain's Presence in Ireland. Concession after concession was made to avoid an open fight with the Labour government itself, even to the extent of holding a 'preliminary hearing' in November 1978 where a 'panel of judges' would 'establish whether or not there is a prima facie case for the Tribunal to investigate'.[39] These legalistic niceties came after Amnesty International itself had conclusively established the existence of torture in Castlereagh and other interrogation centres. Instead of using the *Amnesty Report* and other well-known material to mount an exposure of the British government and British rule in Ireland, the United TOM together with its IMG and Socialist Workers Party (SWP) backers mounted a Tribunal to 'investigate' whether or not there was a case to investigate! The reason for this refusal to seize the opportunity to expose British torture in Ireland is simple: the government in question was a Labour government.

On 7/8 July 1979 *two years* after its launch the Tribunal's final 'hearing' was a flop. Only 70 attended the first day and even fewer the second. The Tribunal called on Britain to 'reconstitute' its relations with Ireland – no call for immediate withdrawal of troops. Two years' work ended in a pointless farce – despised by anti-imperialists and, in fact, ignored by the Labour Party and trade union movement.[40]

In 1978 the failure of TOM to produce any results and the rampant anti-Republicanism of the British middle class left drove Sinn Fein (Britain) into calling its own Bloody Sunday march under its own leadership. Sinn Fein (Britain) called on United TOM and the British left to support its demonstration. Again, faced with a choice, United TOM, IMG and SWP decided to go ahead with their own march in order to avoid public identification with a march called by Sinn Fein. On 29 January 1978 there were two Bloody Sunday marches: one called by Sinn Fein, supported by the Prisoners Aid Committee (PAC),

Revolutionary Communist Group (RCG) and supporters of its anti-imperialist Bulletin *Hands Off Ireland!*, and others; the other an anti-Republican alliance of the British middle class left supported by United TOM, IMG, SWP and others. The anti-Republican demonstration had Tony Cliff (SWP), Tariq Ali (then IMG, now Labour Party), Bernadette McAliskey and Eamonn McCann billed as speakers. However, a positive development was to result from this split. The PAC, supported by Sinn Fein (Britain), RCG and supporters of Hands Off Ireland, launched a campaign in defence of Irish prisoners in Irish and British gaols. This campaign called for POW status for Irish political prisoners and an amnesty for all Irish POWs pending complete British withdrawal from Ireland.

The campaign organised two demonstrations of 5,000, 9 July, and 6-7,000 on 26 November 1978. The average size of Irish demonstrations at that time was 800-1,000. So these marches were considerably more successful. More importantly they proved that it was possible to build successful anti-imperialist demonstrations, drawing in wider forces, without making concessions to reactionary sections of the Labour and trade union movement in Britain. Of interest in this respect is the fact that trade union support for these marches, though tiny, was actually much greater than previous demonstrations. There were 15 trade union contingents, including 5 Trades Councils, on the 26 November march. Winning this trade union support required a political battle. For example, in the case of Edinburgh Trades Council the Scottish TUC intervened in an attempt to force the Trades Council to withdraw its support. Edinburgh Trades Council, in fact, supported both demonstrations. These demonstrations were built in spite of the indifference and, at times, open hostility of the British middle class left.

On 30 March 1979, as campaigning for the General Election had just begun, Airey Neave was assassinated (see above). The British middle class left responded in a fairly predictable way. The *Morning Star*, paper of the CPGB, expressed, in the language it reserves for the Republican Movement,

'...its utter and total condemnation of those who brutally and cold-bloodedly murdered Mr Airey Neave...

'The problems facing the people of Northern Ireland cannot be solved by such acts of barbarism. In fact they can only be made worse...'[41]

It went on to say that the 'right wing lobby' which had just received a 'severe blow to its credibility by the exposure of the crimes of torture and brutality in the RUC interrogations centres' will utilise this 'latest act of terrorist barbarity' to 'wriggle off the hook and justify their own barbarous practices'. The *Morning Star* fails to tell us that it was a Labour government, with Tony Benn in its Cabinet, directing the 'barbarous practices'. And that the *Morning Star* never actively campaigned, or gave support to those campaigning against such practices in the large demonstrations during 1978.

Socialist Challenge (IMG) also saw reactionary consequences following the assassination:

'But whether Neave was killed by a revolutionary nationalist or by a provocateur, the end result will be the same. A wave of repression . . . '[42]

Socialist Worker (SWP) agreed; 'It will be grist to the mill of the "law and order" brigade's campaign for greater police powers . . . One thing it will NOT do is to help the cause of the unification of Ireland'.[43] Terrified that the violence of the oppressed would lead to problems for their own 'so-revolutionary' organisations they condemned it under the guise of concern for the Irish cause – a cause they had done little to promote in the recent past. All the organisations of the British middle class left called for a vote for the Labour Party in the General Election. No doubt on the grounds that a Tory government would be worse for them – it could hardly be worse for the Irish.

In the period leading up to the election, the RCG conducted a Boycott campaign under the banner of Hands Off Ireland! Supporters of Hands Off Ireland! attended over 35 major Labour Party rallies throughout the country, raising the question of torture in Ireland and heckling and disrupting the meetings of Prime Minister James Callaghan and his Cabinet Ministers. In spite of every effort by all political parties to prevent Ireland becoming an election issue this intensive disruption of Labour Party meetings attracted widespread publicity in the media and brought the issue of Ireland into the election. The campaign of disruption was joined by Sinn Fein, PAC, RCT and sections of United TOM, although the latter was opposed to the boycott of the Labour Party. In boycotting the election the RCG gave expression to the stand already taken by thousands of Irish workers and sections of black workers. The *Irish Post* 5 May 1979 reported the results of a poll of the intentions of Irish workers in the general election. 31.5% indicated that they did not intend to vote. The vast majority of these traditional Labour supporters were taking this position because of Labour's record in the North of Ireland. Labour lost the election. The middle class left were horrified. The SWP told us that 'The ruling class is back in office'. *Socialist Challenge* immediately started to campaign; 'Kick out the Tories for a Labour Government'.[44] The Irish would not notice any difference. British imperialism's campaign of terror would continue. All that was different was that the British middle class left could use the issue of Ireland to attack a Conservative government and quickly bury the record of the Labour Party.

When the PAC withdrew from public campaigning soon after the General Election, the middle class left and TOM seized the opportunity to reassert their own claims to lead the Irish solidarity movement in Britain. They were fortunate because the new direction that the prisoner campaign in Ireland was to take could be exploited by them to confine any campaign in Britain to what was acceptable to their allies in the Labour Party. Support had to be won from 'broad forces'. The influence of communists and anti-imperialists in Britain was very small. The middle class left quickly moved in to reassert its claims.

When the Young Liberals called a march for August 1979 the middle class left saw its opportunity and jumped at it. While the 12 August march in Belfast was a jubilant celebration of the revolutionary national struggle (see above), in Britain, on the same day, a march of an entirely different character took place under the pacifist slogan 'End the War'. The London march called by Young Liberals was supported by SWP, IMG and TOM in the guise of the Committee for Withdrawal from Ireland. The political standpoint of this march was made clear by the East Midlands Young Liberal Federation who declared:

'. . . its support for the long term ideal of a united Ireland. However, EMYLF rejects and condemns outright the use of violence, as a means to achieving this end'.[45]

The contrast with the Belfast march could not be clearer.

The march itself was about 8,000 strong, led by a handful of Young Liberals and a handful of MPs. These included: Kevin McNamara who, in Parliament, compared IRA and INLA volunteers to 'rapists, burglars and murderers'[46] and, in a TV programme on Ireland, refused to appear alongside Sinn Fein President Ruairi O Bradaigh; Leo Abse who supported the Peace People; and Cyril Smith, Liberal MP, who voted for the death penalty. The organisers of the march forced a Sinn Fein H-Block cage to the back of the march. So this was a march led by anti-Republican reactionaries. It was also by the far the largest mobilisation of the middle class left seen since 1972. The very people who, in 1978, refused to give serious support to the prisoner campaign led by PAC and Sinn Fein, now turned out in their thousands for the Young Liberals.

The British middle class socialist left did next to nothing to aid the heroic 'blanketmen' with their four year long prison struggle in the torture chambers of the H-Blocks Long Kesh. In May 1979, significantly after an intensification of the armed struggle by the IRA in the Six Counties, and with the prison struggle in the H-Blocks and Armagh Prison reaching a critical stage they stage-managed what they regarded as a prisoner campaign. It was 'Charter 80: Human Rights for Irish Political Prisoners' organised by the SWP and supported by most of the British middle class left, including the CPGB, and a few left Labour MPs and trade union General Secretaries, such as Tony Benn and Alan Sapper. It used the 'Five Demands' of the National H-Block Campaign to plead for more humane treatment of Irish prisoners. There was no opposition to imperialism here, only the request that it be less brutal. The obvious association with the anti-Soviet/pro-imperialist Charter 77 was an insult to Irish revolutionaries who had taken up the armed struggle against British imperialism. But there was a method to all this. Under what other banner could the Labour Party, the CPGB, the SWP, the IMG and even the Young Liberals unite without confronting the organised Labour and trade union movement? The interests of the prisoners had to play second fiddle to this unprincipled alliance of the British middle class left.

The political forces in Ireland, North and South and also in Britain were now lined up. The first hunger strike was soon to begin. Could the balance of political forces be changed to force the British government to grant the prisoners political status. The strategy laid down in Ireland and adopted in Britain was now to face the decisive test.

NOTES

1   *An Phoblacht* 15 June 1977.
2   *An Phoblacht/Republican News* 8 July 1982.
3   *The Irish Times* 12 May 1977.
4   *Aspect* 13–26 May 1982.
5   *An Phoblacht/Republican News* 21 April 1979.
6   *An Phoblacht/Republican News* 31 March 1979.
7   Faligot R. *op cit* p. 112
8   *An Phoblacht/Republican News* 28 April 1979.

9   All extracts of Document 37 are taken from *An Phoblacht/Republican News* 12 May 1979. The full document is reprinted as an appendix in Faligot R, *op cit* pp. 221–242.

10   *An Phoblacht/Republican News* 9 June 1979.

11   *An Phoblacht/Republican News* 2 June 1979.

12   *An Phoblacht/Republican News* 17 March 1979.

13   *An Phoblacht/Republican News* 21 April 1979.

14   *An Phoblacht/Republican News* 11 August 1979.

15   Cited in *An Phoblacht/Republican News* 18 August 1979.

16   *An Phoblacht/Republican News* 6 October 1979.

17   *An Phoblacht/Republican News* 15 September 1979.

18   *An Phoblacht/Republican News* 29 September 1979.

19   *ibid.*

20   *An Phoblacht/Republican News* 27 October 1979.

21   *ibid.*

22   *ibid.*

23   *An Phoblacht/Republican News* 22 December 1979.

24   *An Phoblacht/Republican News* 5 January 1980.

25   *An Phoblacht/Republican News* 26 January 1980.

26   *ibid.*

27   *Magill* August 1981.

28   *An Phoblacht/Republican News* 8 March 1980.

29   *ibid.*

30   *An Phoblacht/Republican News* 5 April 1980.

31   *An Phoblacht/Republican News* 14 June 1980.

32   *An Phoblacht/Republican News* 21 June 1980.

33   *ibid.*

34   *An Phoblacht/Republican News* 5 July 1980.

35   *An Phoblacht/Republican News* 26 July 1980.

36   *An Phoblacht/Republican News* 20 September 1980.

37   *ibid.*

38   See chapter 3 p. 36.

39   Cited in Colfer K, 'Whose Tribunal?' in *Hands Off Ireland* No 5 September 1978.

40   *Hands Off Ireland* No 8 August 1979.

41   *Morning Star* 31 March 1979.

42   *Socialist Challenge* 5 April 1979.

43   *Socialist Worker* 7 April 1979.

44   *Socialist Worker* 12 May 1979 and *Socialist Challenge* 10 May 1979.

45   *Nottingham News* 7 September 1979.

46   Cited in Fox D, 'August 12 What it means' in *Hands Off Ireland* No 9 November 1979.

CHAPTER SIXTEEN

HUNGER STRIKE

In a remarkably explicit interview given to Ulster TV's 'Counterpoint' documentary programme on 24 September 1980, Michael Alison, then the British Minister for prisons in the Six Counties, explained why the British government gave Irish political prisoners 'Special Category status' in 1972:

> 'Special category status was won not just by a hunger strike, it was won by the enormous outburst of lawlessness, concentrated like a dam bursting into a particular moment in history which made it impossible to build in our prisons, to introduce a normal prison regime.'

The political prisoners, some of whom had been on hunger strike for nearly five weeks, had, in fact, been granted Special Category status in 1972 as one of four IRA conditions for truce negotiations with the British government. The British government had been forced to agree to truce negotiations and the four IRA conditions because of the intensity of the IRA's military and sabotage operations, and the growing militancy in nationalist areas as street fights with the British army and RUC, and large protests and demonstrations in support of the hunger strikers, took place. In the language of the imperialists, Special Category status was indeed won by an 'enormous outburst of lawlessness'. That is to say, the anti-imperialist struggle was beginning to undermine the stability of British rule in the Six Counties of Ireland. British imperialism would only give ground when confronted by revolutionary force.

On 10 October 1980 a statement smuggled out from the H-Blocks announced that a hunger strike would commence on 27 October 1980.

'We, the Republican Prisoners-of-War in the H-Blocks, Long Kesh, demand, as of right, political recognition and that we be accorded the status of political prisoners. We claim this right as captured combatants in the continuing struggle for national liberation and self-determination . . .

'Bearing in mind the serious implications of our final step, not only for us but for our people, we wish to make it clear that every channel has now been exhausted and, not wishing to break faith with those from whom we have inherited our principles, we now commit ourselves to a hunger-strike.'[2]

The British government was all too aware of the serious implications for its rule in Ireland if it recognised the political legitimacy of 'captured combatants' in the revolutionary national struggle for self-determination. That is why it had made a determined stand on the issue of political status. The prisoner campaign of disciplined peaceful protest led by the National H-Block Committee had so far failed to move the British government. As a result the political prisoners felt they had no alternative but to go on hunger strike. The question now raised was whether a prisoner campaign built on a specific appeal to those 'wider forces' who did not support the revolutionary national struggle for self-determination could force the British government to grant the prisoners the 'five Demands' – demands which the political prisoners and the British government viewed as tantamount to political status. The courage and example of the hunger strikers would undoubtedly lift the whole protest campaign. The strategy of the National H-Block Committee was now to face a decisive test.

THE FIRST HUNGER STRIKE

The same issue of *An Phoblacht/Republican News* which carried the announcement of the hunger strike also reported the brutal murder of two leading H-Block campaigners and members of the IRSP, Ronnie Bunting and Noel Lyttle. At 4am on 15 October two gunmen broke down the front door of the Buntings' home, ran up the stairs and cold-bloodedly fired on the Bunting couple who had come out on the landing. The gunmen then burst into the bedroom of their 18-month-old son, Ronan, and shot dead Noel Lyttle who was sleeping in the same room. It was said at the time that the shootings were either carried out by Loyalist assassins with the assistance of the British army/RUC who pinpointed the targets, or by the SAS, given the brutally efficient style of the murders and their location in the heart of nationalist West Belfast. Dramatic evidence of British army/RUC involvement in the assassinations of H-Block activists was, in fact, revealed in early 1982 at the trial of three UDA men convicted of the murder of John Turnly. At the end of the trial one of the three UDA men, Robert McConnell, stood up in court and read out a statement. In it he gave details of how two members of the SAS had supplied him with weapons and other equipment and had discussed with him the activities of H-Block activists such as John Turnly, Miriam Daly and Bernadette McAliskey.

On 19 October 1980, a few days after the murder of Ronnie Bunting and Noel Lyttle, 20 masked armed SAS men smashed their way into two homes in the nationalist West Belfast Twinbrook estate, and terrorised the occupants at gunpoint. The occupants were manhandled and tied up and two young men, who understandably attempted to get out of one house fearing assassination, were shot and then severely kicked and beaten. A widely-publicised Twinbrook Relatives Action Committee meeting to organise support for the forthcoming hunger strike was due to start in one of the houses belonging to H-Block activist Moyra Berkery an hour after the SAS hit it. These developments clearly indicated the determination of the British government to use all means available to crush the H-Block campaign.

On 26 October, the day before the hunger strike began, Belfast saw the largest demonstration to date in support of the H-Block and Armagh prisoners. Over 25,000 took to the streets led by a cavalcade of 32 black taxis and a lead banner across the street proclaiming 'Victory to the hunger-strikers'. *An Phoblacht/Republican News* said that the march 'served a clear warning to the British government of the consequence of the anger of the Irish people should any of the seven hunger-strikers die'.[3]

The seven H-Block men who began the hunger strike on 27 October 1980 were: Leo Green (Lurgan), Brendan Hughes (Belfast), Ray McCartney (Derry city), Tom McFeeley (Co Derry), Thomas McKearney (Co Tyrone), Sean McKenna (Newry) and John Nixon INLA (Armagh city). A few days earlier the British government had made an offer of 'civilian-type clothing' for all prisoners. The political prisoners issued a statement on 24 October rejecting this offer as 'meaningless' and as a 'cruel attempt to diffuse the growing support for the blanketmen'. Their statement pointed out that the women political prisoners in Armagh had the basic right of wearing their own clothes and this had not 'met their requirements'. It made it clear that the 'wearing of our own clothes' was 'only one of our five demands' and concluded by stating

'We are not criminals and we are ready and willing to meet an agonising death on hunger-strike to establish that we are political prisoners'.[4]

A week after the hunger strike began *An Phoblacht/Republican News* was reporting a 'tremendous and heartening tidal wave of support' throughout Ireland and abroad for the H-Block men and Armagh women political prisoners. This support, it said, had been evoked by the 'courageous commencement' of a hunger strike to the death by seven blanket men. The lead article, in commenting on this support, gave very clear expression to the political thinking behind the ongoing prisoner campaign:

'People are taking to the streets in public displays of solidarity in such impressive numbers that the British collaborators in the leadership of Fianna Fail and the SDLP are going to quake in their shoes and go crawling to their British masters pleading with them to grant the prisoners' five demands on a humanitarian basis in order to restore "normality".[5]

This confidence was however immediately tempered by the warning that there must be 'no false illusions'. That despite the tens of thousands on the streets and the movement on the political status issue 'even amongst British and Irish establishment circles' not nearly enough had been done to break 'the cruel instransigence of the British government'. However what was now clear was that an important aim in attempting to break that intransigence was to build massive street protests and demonstrations to pressurise the Fianna Fail and SDLP leaderships into supporting the prisoners. And this in turn was to dictate the political character of the protests and demonstrations organised by the National H-Block Campaign.

An Phoblacht/Republican News argued that:

'This necessity of building street protests of unprecedented size dictates . . . , in order not to alienate potential support during this building process, that all street protests be as dignified as possible, with the natural temptation to riot in the North, against British troops and RUC gunmen, being resisted.'[6]

Further, winning the Fianna Fail and SDLP leaderships behind the prisoners would open the way to even wider support.

'The effect of forcing Britain's chief nationalist collaborators, both North and South, into a stance behind the prisoners will have the double benefit of embarrassing the British and opening up, through "the seal of establishment respectability", unprecedented fresh channels for winning further massive support, especially in the South.'[7]

The political standpoint behind the National H-Block Campaign contained a number of crucial assumptions and begged a number of important questions. First, given that the massive, disciplined and peaceful protests of the 'wider forces' were built, could they force the leadership of the SDLP and Fianna Fail to act – against their will – in the interests of the political prisoners? Second, if they were forced to act in such a way, could their political pleading with the British government force it to change its determined stand on political status? Finally, in placing reliance on collaborationist forces, was there not an inherent danger that far from forcing them to fight for the prisoners' cause they would be placed in a position of such influence that they could eventually betray the prisoners?

These questions were not unreasonable ones to ask. Fianna Fail had a consistent history of betrayal of the revolutionary national struggle, and, as has been argued, its collaboration with British imperialism was designed to undermine and crush the struggle of the Republican Movement. The SDLP was only of value to British imperialism if it could be used to draw support in the nationalist minority away from the revolutionary national struggle to unite Ireland. The SDLP was used in this way during the power-sharing period. It had taken no part in the H-Block campaign. Less than two months before the hunger strike began, *An Phoblacht/Republican News* had reported on an RUC document, which had fallen into the hands of the IRA, giving 'sinister details' of private meetings the RUC held with middle class nationalists and unionists in the Six Counties. These private talks were aimed at improving the RUC image and acceptability, and discrediting the Republican Movement. They were primarily concerned with helping the RUC gain credibility within the nationalist areas of the Six Counties. Those involved in one or more of the 'seminars' held between October 1979 and June 1980 included representatives of the Catholic Church, the entire Northern Ireland Committee of the ICTU, members of the SDLP and other middle class nationalists – members of the legal profession, businessmen, and the medical profession. *An Phoblacht/Republican News* commented at the time:

'The leaders of the nationalist middle-class should note that their attempts to worm the RUC back into the ghettos, their advisory role to these butchers and torturers, who lie behind the painted smiles, will not only fail, because of nationalist hostility, but will rebound on them.'[8]

Collaborators would only get the ear of the British government and their views be given prominence if they were thought to have some real influence amongst the nationalist minority and were acting in the interests of British rule in Ireland. Only in such circumstances were they of use to British imperialism. Was it now possible that such people, having refused to back the prisoners so far, and rapidly losing nearly all credibility with the nationalist minority, could positively influence British policy in favour of the political prisoners? It would not be long before the answer to this question was given.

On 6 November the seven hunger strikers were isolated from their fellow blanket men and placed in individual cells in 'A' wing of H-Block 3. Reports of continual harassment of the hunger strikers and baiting by warders soon began to filter out. Harassment and beatings of political prisoners on protest were stepped up in the H-Blocks. They were especially aimed at men who had gone back on the blanket protest in support of the hunger strikers. This however did not break their resolve. By December there were over 500 men on the blanket protest.

In November the women political prisoners in Armagh prison decided to go on hunger strike 'in an intensification of their campaign for political status'.[9] This was in spite of appeals from the Republican Movement advising them against such action. This decision immediately undermined the attempts of the British government and others to make the issue of 'civilian clothing' the central point of dispute in order to confuse and divide the supporters of the prisoners. This courageous action of the women political prisoners made it clear to all those involved in the prisoner campaign that the political prisoners were fighting for political status. On Monday 1 December 1980 Mary Doyle, Mairead Farrell, and Mairead Nugent, all from Belfast, began a hunger strike to the death. In a statement they said:

> 'We women in Armagh wear our own clothes, but we refuse to do prison work, or to co-operate with the prison regime, which is under orders from the British government to criminalise us in an attempt to criminalise what we believe in and have struggled for – Irish freedom. The cause of Irish freedom is not a criminal cause, but a political cause, and in order to assert this we are going on hunger-strike . . .'[10]

The hunger strike evoked a massive public response which grew continually throughout the period. Militant protests – marches, torchlight processions, road blocks, occupation of shops, banks and government offices, and pickets on RUC and British army barracks – took place daily throughout the Six Counties. Industrial action also was taken on several occasions in support of the hunger strikers. The lead was given by 400 dock workers in Belfast, members of the ITGWU, who walked out on 11 November and marched to the Northern headquarters of the ICTU to protest at the inaction of the ICTU on the H-Block issue. The following afternoon workers from all over Derry walked out in solidarity with the hunger strikers and converged on the city centre where a crowd of nearly 10,000 listened to speeches in support of the hunger strikers.

On 27 November workers stopped work in Dungannon, Coalisland, Omagh, and Cookstown in Co Tyrone. The most widespread action took place on 10 December in response to a call for a National Day of Action by the National H-Block/Armagh Committee. Thousands of workers throughout the Six Counties defied the ICTU leaders and stopped work in support of the hunger strikers. In Belfast the walkout was followed by a rally in Dunville Park where trade union speakers attacked the ICTU leadership for refusing to support the Day of Action. Many nationalist councillors left the council chambers refusing to return until the hunger strike was honourably settled.

In the Twenty Six Counties there were numerous marches and meetings but the most significant events were the two mass marches in Dublin. On 22 November nearly 30,000 marched to the Parliament buildings at Leinster House bringing the centre of Dublin to a standstill. On 6 December an estimated 60,000 people converged on the British Embassy and were stopped short by riot-clad gardai. The marchers showed their hatred of the British government – burning Union Jacks and effigies of Margaret Thatcher and Humphrey Atkins – as well as Charles Haughey and the 'Free State' government – chanting *Who's a Brit? Gerry Fitt! Who else! Haughey!* and *Brits Out! North and South!* directed at the massive force of gardai around the embassy. As the marchers approached the line of gardai blocking their path about 200 yards from the Embassy, some of them reacted violently looking for stones and other missiles to throw. They were stopped from this by stewards determined to preserve the peaceful character of the march. *An Phoblacht/Republican News* commented at the time:

'As the head of the march arrived at this point a number of over-enthusiastic and unthinking marchers allowed their natural feelings full rein and reached for stones and whatever missiles came to hand.

But immediate order was restored from the platform and a line of stewards was quickly interposed between marchers and gardai.'[11]

The clash between the militant youth, who wanted to fight on the streets and the National H-Block/Armagh Committee, which wanted peaceful protests in order not to alienate 'broad support', was to be a recurring event especially in the Twenty Six Counties.

This massive protest however had so far failed to move 'Britain's chief nationalist collaborators, both North and South, into a stance behind the prisoners'. Not only had the SDLP and Fianna Fail not come out in support of the five demands but neither had the Catholic Church, the Gaelic Athletic Association or the ICTU. In commenting on this failure in an interview given to *An Phoblacht/Republican News* Gerry Adams, then Vice-President of Sinn Fein, argued:

> 'The nature of these organisations means that prominent members have indicated to H-Block activists and prisoners' relatives that they support the prisoners' five demands, but that they can't – for whatever reason – do this publicly. To get over this obstacle it is vital that pressure be exerted from grass-roots.'[12]

Adams believed that these organisations could still be won round as grass-roots pressure built up and that even John Hume (leader of the SDLP after Fitt's resignation in November 1979) and Charlie Haughey might be forced to do something about the five demands 'when they see the way the land lies'.

International support for the hunger strikers rapidly built up. In the USA, Belgium, Denmark, Norway, France, West Germany, Holland, Italy, Canada, Australia, Portugal and Greece marches, pickets and protests were organised. In the USA 4,000 marched on the UN to hand in protests and resolutions including resolutions from six State legislatures – New York, New Jersey, California, Massachusetts, Pennsylvania and Connecticut. In Iran a massive anti-imperialist demonstration of a million people cheered banners calling for Victory to the Irish Hunger Strikers.

A measure of the worldwide support was the fact that the Portuguese National Assembly on 17 December voted unanimously in support of a motion condemning British treatment of the prisoners and calling for political status. The Soviet Union gave support to the hunger strikers describing them as 'freedom fighters', reporting their struggle in *Pravda* and printing a letter from the prisoners to the Soviet people.

Major trade union organisations throughout the world including the World Federation of Free Trade Unions, the CGT in France, the OUT in Portugal, the Saskatchewan Federation of Labour in Canada and the Australian CTU gave support to the prisoners. The Longshoremen's Union in the USA voted to boycott all British goods if any prisoner died. And the California Labor Union sent a telegram demanding that the British TUC gave support to the prisoners.

In Holland, militant supporters of Irish prisoners burnt down a factory owned by the honorary British Consul. The British Consul office in Aarhus, Denmark, was burnt down. In Lyon, France, supporters of the hunger strikers petrol bombed the British Leyland Agent's offices, while Belgian supporters, protesting against the British Queen's visit, battled with the police.

On 4 December there appeared to be some movement in the British government's position. Humphrey Atkins, Secretary of State for Northern Ireland, made a statement in the House of Commons soon after a ninety minute meeting with SDLP leader John Hume. In it he said:

'We have always been, and still are, willing to discuss the humanitarian aspects of the prison administration in Northern Ireland with anyone who shares our concern.'[13]

The National H-Block/Armagh Committee requested a meeting with Atkins. Atkins refused. The SDLP offered to negotiate but urged the hunger strikers to abandon their strike. The SDLP got the backing of both Fianna Fail and Fine Gael. John Hume offered his services as mediator. Nine of the ten hunger strikers' families (one could not be contacted) immediately issued a statement pointing out that neither John Hume, nor even they, were in a position to negotiate on behalf of the hunger strikers nor the 500 protest prisoners who they represented.

On 8 December the 'Dublin Summit' took place. Thatcher, Carrington, Atkins and Howe met Haughey and his ministers in Dublin. A meaningless communiqué was put out, which typically was open to contradictory interpretations by the two sides. The communiqué noted the close co-operation at all levels between the two governments since the May 1980 meeting in London at which Haughey had accepted the loyalist veto on constitutional changes in the Six Counties of Ireland. Haughey had also promised the relatives of the hunger strikers to raise the issue with the British government. However all that came out of the meeting was a restatement of the Atkins 4 December position. A commotion and contradictory interpretations arose over the mention of the setting up of 'joint studies covering a range of issues including possible new institutional structures . . . '[14] This empty drivel was used by Haughey to claim that 'historic progress' had been made on the issue of the Six Counties. Thatcher, of course, vigorously denied it. The only 'co-operation' that both parties were really interested in was that of 'security co-operation' primarily directed at defeating the IRA.

However pressure was clearly building up on the British government to avoid the dangerous political consequences in Ireland, both North and South, which could follow the death of a hunger striker. On Wednesday 10 December, after 44 days of the hunger strike, a senior member of the Northern Ireland Office, Mr Blellock, met the seven hunger strikers in prison and informed them of the prison reforms that were then available. The prisoners immediately issued a statement stating that the concessions fell short of their demands and that the hunger strike would continue.

On Friday 12 December six loyalist prisoners in the H-Blocks went on hunger strike demanding political status and segregation from Republicans. The UDA was split on the strike and the prisoners were persuaded to give up after only six days.

After the Blellock meeting, the Republican prisoners in the H-Blocks decided to step up their protest. On Monday 15 December another 23 prisoners joined the hunger strike and on Tuesday 16 December a further 7 joined them. There were now 37 Republican prisoners on hunger strike in the H-Blocks and three in Armagh prison. At this stage the hunger strike reached a crisis point. Sean McKenna, after 51 days on hunger strike, had completely lost his sight and by Wednesday 17 December was unable to keep down the drinking water which was barely keeping him alive.

On Thursday afternoon, 18 December, Atkins postponed a statement he had been due to make in the House of Commons and ensured it was delivered to the original seven hunger strikers now in the prison hospital, together with a 34-page document explaining the prison rules. This document was a major elaboration on how far the British government was prepared to go to meet the 'five demands'. Atkins stated that if the hunger strike was called off by the prisoners 'the conditions available to them meet in a practical and humane way the kind of things they have been asking for'.[15] Sean McKenna was on the verge of death. The document appeared to meet the prisoners' demands by a more flexible interpretation of the prison rules. The hunger strike was called off.

Speaking at a 1,000 strong march and rally in Belfast on the Sunday after the hunger strike ended, Gerry Adams, while seeing the outcome of the hunger strike as a victory warned the people to 'be vigilant, be alert, be patient'. He called on Churchmen and politicians to now ensure 'perfidious Albion' behaves in a manner 'to actually resolve the "blanket/no-wash" protest'. The weeks ahead he said would be the most crucial since the protest began.[16]

The ending of the hunger strike initially brought about a conciliatory atmosphere within the H-Blocks. Bobby Sands, Officer-in-Charge (O/C) of all IRA prisoners in the H-Blocks, was given facilities to meet the O/Cs of the four other H-Blocks to discuss the terms of settlement. He had regular meetings with the prison Governor, Stanley Hilditch, and even met an official from the Northern Ireland Office. But this atmosphere ended within a matter of days. All the document's phrases about the situation not being static, work not being interpreted narrowly and the prison regime being progressive, humane and flexible were shown to be worthless as soon as the pressure on the British government was removed.

The blanket men hoped to move about 30 men off the blanket and no-wash protest before Christmas day but were stopped by Governor Hilditch. He told them that nobody could move anywhere until they put on prison-issue clothing and conformed. In Armagh prison, the women prisoners met with a similar response. The prison Governor refused even to discuss with them the self-education classes as outlined in the document until they conformed. On 9 January 1981, Atkins, in a public statement reversed the order in which the men in the H-Blocks would receive their own clothes. Initially, it was said that the men would first receive their own clothes and then be given civilian-style prison clothing. Now this was to be reversed. The prisoners made another attempt to de-escalate the protest step by step in a principled fashion after further discussions on Sunday 11 January between Bobby Sands and the prison authorities. They agreed to move the next day to clean cells and not soil them. They expected they would receive their own clothes by the end of the week. At the end of the week the prison Governor asked for a week's grace to give them time to ensure things were running smoothly. The prisoners agreed. On 20 January after two requests to have their own clothes they were told that they could not have them until they conformed. On 27 January 96 prisoners smashed up their cell furniture in an act of determined anger and opposition to the treachery of the prison authorities. The prison authorities reacted savagely. Men were brutally beaten and left in cold urine-soaked cells overnight without bedding and clothes of any kind. It was back to square one. A new hunger strike was inevitable.

THE SECOND HUNGER STRIKE

It was clear that the Atkins' document and statement were used by the British government as a 'holding operation'. And as soon as the immediate pressure was off with the ending of the hunger strike and the cessation of active campaigning the British government reverted to its original intransigent stand. They possibly believed that demoralisation would set in both inside and outside the prisons and that it would be some time before they would be confronted with another campaign on anything like the same scale as before.

The National H-Block/Armagh Committee announced on 5 January that it was remobilising local action groups throughout Ireland due to the deterioration of the situation in the H-Blocks and Armagh prison following the end of the hunger strike. A special conference was held in Dublin on 25 January to discuss remobilising the campaign in support of the prisoners. The large number of people attending the conference (more than 600) from all parts of Ireland indicated the readiness of activists to resume the campaign. It became clear in the course of the conference, however, that opinions were divided as to how the new campaign should be conducted.

Speakers from the National H-Block/Armagh Committee argued that the campaign should again be conducted on a 'broad front' basis, with more pressure being put on the SDLP and Fianna Fail to support the five demands of the prisoners. This view did not by any means receive universal support at the conference. Members of H-Block/Armagh Action Groups in Derry and Belfast in particular called for a different strategy this time. The Chairperson of the Derry H-Block/Armagh Action Group argued that in Derry during the hunger strike there had been a very militant campaign which had disrupted the city, but there had been little to show for it when the hunger strike ended. He emphasised that those who took part in the campaign in Derry did so not on a 'humanitarian' basis but because they were Republicans. He wanted the issue clearly defined this time – political status and Brits Out. His speech received loud applause and was endorsed by a number of other speakers from Belfast and Dublin.

Two issues attracted particular attention at the conference – the attitude to be adopted to Fianna Fail and the SDLP, and the question of industrial action. The call by the National Committee for greater pressure to be put on the SDLP and Fianna Fail to support the demands of the prisoners was strongly challenged by a number of speakers who argued that such a tactic served to foster illusions about these parties, both of them in fact completely being on the side of British imperialism. Several speakers, in backing up this argument, reported the intense harassment of H-Block/Armagh activists by the Twenty Six Counties gardai during the last campaign. Later it was reported that people leaving the conference itself were being stopped and questioned by the Special Branch.

On the question of industrial action, a number of speakers argued that a much more systematic and determined attempt should be made to mobilise the working class in support of the prisoners with a general strike as the ultimate goal, rather than merely organising token days of action as in the previous campaign. Speakers from the National Committee correctly described this view as unrealistic and a general resolution calling for workers 'when necessary to show their solidarity with the prisoners through industrial action' was passed. A number of speakers in the debate pointed to the pro-imperialist nature of the trade union leadership, which had been exposed by their actions during the hunger strike and by their call 'in chorus with Mrs Thatcher, on the hunger strikers to capitulate'. This fact alone showed the massive barrier against a general strike.

The conference approved the resolutions put forward by the National H-Block/Armagh Committee and backed by Sinn Fein. These included demands on the Fianna Fail government to end all diplomatic and military collaboration with the British government and to end the harassment of H-Block activists. The SDLP and the Irish Independence Party were called on to withdraw from council chambers in the Six Counties until the demands of the prisoners were met. John Hume, the SDLP leader, Cardinal O'Fiaich and the ICTU, all of whom had called on the prisoners to end the hunger strike, were now called on to demand publicly that Britain honour the settlement. Activities including a mass picket of Armagh prison on 8 March, International Women's Day, and a demonstration in solidarity with the prisoners on 1 March in the Six Counties were agreed. The conference, however, had shown that many activists in the local H-Block/Armagh Groups were not satisfied with the tactics of the previous campaign. They wanted the new one to be a strong and militant campaign based on the nationalist working class.[17] This view was very clearly expressed in a letter from the Markets/Ormeau H-Block/Armagh Action Group in Belfast published in the *Irish News* on 26 February after a new hunger strike had been announced. It said:

'While many groups are calling on the British to "honour their word'' we in the Markets/Ormeau area believe this is to a degree naive. We see this coming hunger strike as the most crucial development and believe that it is only through our strong, unified, militant agitation that the British will concede. We must accept the limitations of calling on establishment, political and Church leaders to call on the British to implement the five demands. Instead we should ensure that we are on the streets in force and determined to employ any methods necessary to end the British policy of criminalisation in Ireland and to win the five just demands for the men and women in the H-Block/Armagh.'[18]

On 5 February 1981, in an agreed statement jointly issued by the blanket men and the women on protest in Armagh prison, a new hunger strike was announced for 1 March. The British had been given 'every available opportunity' to resolve the issue but had failed to do so, placing 'obstacle after obstacle' in the way of the prisoners. The statement contained a bitter rebuke of those who had called on them to end the previous hunger strike in order to allow the resolution of the prison protest.

'Our last hunger-strikers were morally blackmailed by a number of people and politicians who called upon them to end the fast and allow the resolution of the protest. The hunger-strikes ended seven weeks ago and in the absence of any movement from the British we have not seen or heard from these people since.
    'It needs to be asked openly of the Irish Bishops, of Cardinal O Fiaich and of politicians like John Hume, what did your recommending ending of the last hunger-strike gain for us? . . . '[19]

The leadership of the Republican Movement again attempted to stop the hunger strike. According to *Magill*, Gerry Adams again wrote to Bobby Sands – during the first hunger strike Adams had told Sands that 'we are tactically, strategically, physically and morally opposed to a hunger-strike' – and stated categorically that he believed that Sands would die as the British would not concede in the present climate.[20] The prisoners, however, believed they had no choice. This time the hunger strike would be staggered, with men going on strike with intervals between them. Bobby Sands, as O/C, insisted he led it off. Once decided upon by the prisoners the Republican Movement gave the hunger strike their full backing.
    There had been almost an unofficial 'ceasefire' with very few operations by the IRA during the period of the first hunger strike. Once the

treachery of the British government became clear, after the strike had been called off, the IRA stepped up its military offensive. On 9 January 1981 the IRA in a statement claimed a number of recent operations in Britain – the bomb attacks on the Hammersmith Territorial Barracks in London on 2 December 1980, the gasworks explosions at Bromley-by-Bow on 31 December 1980, and the bomb attack on the Uxbridge barracks on 8 January 1981. The IRA also claimed responsibility for the shooting attack on Christopher Tugendhat, Britain's EEC Commissioner, on 3 December 1980 in Brussels. But it was in the Six Counties where the IRA significantly stepped up its military operations.

In the first two months of 1981 eight members of the 'security forces' were killed (including one killed by INLA) and several others were seriously injured. The RUC barracks at Clogher in Co Tyrone was devastated by a bomb attack on 25 February. There were numerous bomb attacks on commercial targets, the most spectacular being the sinking of a British ship in Lough Foyle on 6 February. On two occasions there were simultaneous co-ordinated bomb attacks on commercial targets in different towns. On 26 January bombs exploded in towns throughout the Six Counties, targets being hit in Belfast, Derry, Armagh, Portadown, Newry, Omagh and Lisnaskea. Nearly 100 commercial premises were either destroyed or damaged by these attacks, and at the same time a bomb attack closed the railway line between Belfast and Dublin. Less than a month later, on 21 February, a co-ordinated series of fire-bomb attacks destroyed or damaged fifteen commercial targets in Belfast, Derry and Armagh. In all the attacks on commercial targets warnings were given to avoid civilian casualties.

On 21 January the IRA assassinated two 'unionist aristocrats', Sir Norman Stronge and his RUC Reservist son, James, and destroyed their mansion at Tynan in Co Armagh. An IRA statement said that 'this deliberate attack on the symbols of hated unionism was a direct reprisal for a whole series of loyalist assassinations and murder attacks on nationalist people and nationalist activists which has gone on far too long'.[21] It pointed out that such reprisals represented a real departure from previous IRA policy. A number of H-Block activists had been recently murdered (see above) and a few days earlier on 16 January a loyalist (UDA) murder gang shot and seriously wounded Bernadette and Michael McAliskey after breaking into their house with a sledgehammer. The Loyalists were arrested 'on the scene' by a British army patrol which 'by chance' happened to be in the area.

The loyalist bigot Ian Paisley chose February to deliberately incite Protestant sectarian hatred in pursuit of his own personal political ambitions. He was able to exploit the ambiguous pronouncements of the Thatcher/Haughey December communiqué, in particular the section on 'joint studies' (see above), to mobilise and build up his own loyalist following under the banner of protecting the loyalist heritage. On 5 February at about midnight on an Antrim mountainside, near Ballymena, Paisley laid on a sinister show of strength in front of a selected half-dozen pressmen. In the semi-darkness five hundred Loyalists were drawn up in military formation. At the blast of a whistle they jumped to attention and each displayed what Paisley described as 'a legally held firearms certificate'. 'This is a token of the many thousands who are at the ready to defend our heritage', Paisley warned the pressmen.[22] There were, it appeared, no British army, UDR or RUC patrols in sight. RUC and UDR men were thought to be numbered among Paisley's 500 men.

On 9 February, at a press conference in Belfast's city hall, the venue for the launching of Carson's original 1912 covenant to resist Home Rule, Paisley launched his own covenant to be circulated for signatures. It was aimed at committing the signatories to 'using all means which may be found necessary' to defeat what he claimed was a British government conspiracy through the Thatcher/Haughey Dublin summit to bring about the re-unification of Ireland. He also announced eleven mass rallies throughout the North culminating in a major demonstration at the Carson monument at Stormont the following month. As there was no conspiracy, but only a British government determined to hold on to the Six Counties of Ireland, these rallies did not amount to a great deal.[23] However Paisley was giving clear notice that any attempt to undermine Protestant ascendancy would be met with naked sectarian force on the streets.

Bobby Sands began the hunger strike on 1 March 1981. A 'several thousand' strong march took place in atrocious weather in Belfast on that day. Also, on the 1 March Bishop Daly, addressing a conference of Catholic youth in Derry, attacked the hunger strike as not being 'morally justified' and urged the nationalist youth not to support hunger strike protests by H-Block action groups unless such groups dissociate themselves from 'groups which have a policy of guerrilla warfare'. Bishop Daly also attacked the continuation of the no-wash/no-slop-out protest. In fact the prisoners had decided to end the no-wash/no-slop-out protest and announced this a day later on 2 March. They did this to 'highlight the hunger-strike and the issues behind our demand for political status'. This decision, needless to say, brought no response from Bishop Daly.[24]

On 5 March the Independent anti-unionist Westminster MP for Fermanagh/South Tyrone, Frank Maguire, died suddenly. Immediately there was speculation as to who would succeed him. Sinn Fein declared that they were 'actively considering contesting the seat'.[25] There was talk of Bernadette McAliskey, Noel Maguire (Frank's brother) and an SDLP candidate being put forward. Eventually it was agreed that Bobby Sands would be the anti-unionist candidate. The electorate would be called upon to vote for Bobby Sands to save his life and show their support for the political prisoners' struggle against Britain's criminalisation policy. The by-election was called for Thursday 9 April.

On Sunday 15 March Francis Hughes (South Derry) joined the hunger strike. *An Phoblacht/Republican News* described him as 'one of the most fearless and active young republicans to emerge out of the armed struggle against British occupation forces in Ireland this decade'.[26] A week later, 22 March, Ray McCreesh from South Armagh and Patsy O'Hara (INLA) from Derry city went on hunger strike.

Election workers for Bobby Sands were continually harassed by the RUC and UDR in the run up for the Fermanagh/South Tyrone by-election. The SDLP told its supporters to boycott the by-election. A despicable and desperate intervention on polling-day came from British Labour Party opposition spokesman on Northern Ireland, Don Concannon – a man who had played a full part in implementing the British government's 'criminalisation' policy from 1976–79. He arrogantly told the voters of Fermanagh/South Tyrone that they had 'a unique opportunity to denounce the men of violence'. He said a vote for Bobby Sands was a vote for the perpetrators of 'senseless murders'.[27] His outburst was fully reported in the media on the day of the election. However it totally backfired.

In a very high poll of 86.8% Bobby Sands (Anti H-Block/Armagh Political Prisoner) received 30,492 votes against the 29,046 for the Official Unionist Harry West. The people had indeed denounced the real 'men of violence' – those like Concannon who were responsible for the whole apparatus of torture and repression by which Britain maintains its hold on the Six Counties of Ireland. Even the British media were forced to acknowledge the significance of the result. *The Guardian* said:

'Years of myth-making go out of the window with the election of Bobby Sands as MP for Fermanagh and South Tyrone. And the biggest myth is that the IRA in its violent phase represents only a tiny minority of the population.'[28]

The Guardian also pointed out that if Sands should die after such a vote of confidence, 'how can the electoral system be said to reflect the views of the people'. *The Guardian* chooses to forget that parliamentary democracy and constitutionality are only evoked by British governments in Ireland when they strengthen British imperialist rule. Just as the results of the 1918 election were ignored and brushed aside so would the victory of Bobby Sands be ignored. Indeed so great is the British ruling class' contempt for democracy that it soon changed the 'rules' of the game by passing a new law which would effectively prevent political prisoners from standing in elections.

By mid-April tension in the nationalist areas began to rise as Bobby Sands moved close to death having passed 45 days on hunger strike. Widespread and persistent street fighting between the nationalist youth and the British army/RUC took place over a period of ten days in Derry city as 'a genuine expression of popular anti-British sentiment'. The anger and determination of the youth intensified when British troops and RUC gunmen fired lethal plastic bullets randomly at nationalist youth on the streets. One youth, 15 year old Paul Whitters, shot at very close range, suffered a massive fracture of the skull and later died. Another youth lost an eye having been hit in the face. On 19 April two army landrovers driven at very high speed ploughed into a crowd of fleeing youths. Two Bogside youths, Gary English (19) and Jimmy Brown (18) were deliberately run over and killed. This double killing was cynically described by the RUC as a 'road accident'. The angry youths' reply to these murders was soon evident. They fought the 'security forces' with bricks, petrol bombs, acid bombs and the occasional hand grenade. *An Phoblacht/Republican News* reported at the time that the youths, 'with the approval of a community', turned the Bogside and Creggan into semi 'no-go' areas for the 'security forces', erecting barricades throughout the nationalist areas.[29]

On 20 April three Irish Euro MPs, independents Neil Blaney and Dr John O'Connell and Fianna Fail's Sile de Valera, were, at the request of Bobby Sands, permitted to visit him in the prison hospital. No doubt the British authorities hoped they would persuade him to come off hunger strike. In the event only one tried – John O'Connell – but to no avail. After the visit the MPs requested a meeting with Mrs Thatcher but were arrogantly rebuffed on the grounds that it was not her 'habit or custom to meet MPs from a foreign country about a citizen of the United Kingdom resident in the United Kingdom'.[30]

A few days later there was an attempt to 'resolve' the hunger strike through a Haughey-inspired intervention of the European Commission of Human Rights. This came about at a meeting in Haughey's home between himself and the Sands family – a day after he had refused to meet the family. At this meeting, using a combination of deceit and emotional exploitation, Haughey bulldozed Bobby Sands' sister Marcella into signing a form to get the Commission to intervene. He told her that if she didn't sign it, she could go home and prepare a funeral. He also said that the British government wanted to get 'off the hook' and would accept the recommendations of the European Commission – which would satisfy the prisoners – and thus end the hunger strike.

The political prisoners were extremely reluctant to co-operate with the European Commission. Four H-Block prisoners had petitioned the European Commission in 1978 on nine specific breaches of human rights. The prisoners did not seek a ruling on political status. Nevertheless in its report two years later in June 1980 while criticising the British government's 'inflexibility', the Commission ruled that there was no case for 'political status'. Bobby Sands, therefore, was opposed to the intervention of the Commission because he realised it could not possibly come up with anything in time to save his life – it appeared that 18 days would be required for the Commission to agree to an enquiry – and it could possibly be used at a later stage to undermine the position of the other hunger strikers, as the initial report of the European Commission had been. However not wanting to appear intransigent and allow Haughey's manoeuvre to be turned against the prisoners, he agreed to meet the Commissioners (who arrived in Belfast on 25 April) in the presence of Brendan McFarlane (O/C of prisoners on protest) and two external advisors, Gerry Adams and Danny Morrison. The British government would not permit this and so the European Commission did not intervene.

Towards the end of April the Pope dispatched to Ireland his personal secretary Fr John Magee, as a moral envoy to plead with the hunger strikers to end their protest. He got nowhere with the hunger strikers nor with the British government.

As Bobby Sands came closer to death leading H-Block organisers were arrested. In the week beginning Sunday 26 April nearly 60 were pulled in and put on 7-day detention orders. The arrests began on the day of a massive 20,000 strong march in support of the hunger strikers in Belfast. On 5 May 1981, after enduring 66 days on hunger strike Bobby Sands died. He was buried with full Republican military honours in Belfast on 7 May. Over ninety thousand people, many carrying black flags, joined the funeral procession or lined the five mile route as the procession made its way from Twinbrook to Milltown cemetery. The coffin, covered by a tricolour and a black beret and gloves, was flanked by an IRA guard of honour. When the procession reached Andersonstown, it stopped briefly while a volley of shots was fired over the coffin. At the graveside the mood of the thousands of mourners was not just one of grief at the loss of a brave comrade but also one of defiance and determination to continue the struggle for which Bobby Sands gave his life.

On 12 May Francis Hughes died after 59 days on hunger strike. Just over a week later on 21 May Raymond McCreesh and Patsy O'Hara died after 61 days on hunger strike. British imperialism had slowly and brutally murdered four heroic fighters for Irish freedom. Massive crowds of Irish working class people attended their funerals to pay their last respects to these courageous men. Other political prisoners determined to carry on the fight against criminalisation immediately joined the hunger strike and replaced those who had died. On 9 May Joe McDonnell (Belfast), 14 May Brendan McLaughlin (North Derry), 22 May Kieran Doherty (Belfast), and on 23 May Kevin Lynch INLA (North Derry) began their hunger strikes. When Brendan McLaughlin was forced to call off his hunger strike after 14 days due to a perforated stomach ulcer he was replaced on 29 May by Martin Hurson (South Tyrone).

In May the anger and outrage of the Irish people exploded throughout Ireland. In the Six Counties the British army and RUC came under constant attack in nationalist areas as working class youth took to the streets with stones and petrol bombs. These battles and street fights intensified as the British army and RUC went on the rampage and fired thousands of rounds of lethal plastic bullets killing and maiming predominantly young people as they stood on the streets. Julie Livingstone, 14 years old, was shot at from the rear of an armoured car with a plastic bullet on 12 May as she walked home from a local shop. She died two days later. A group of people, mainly women and children, were banging binlids in a protest following the death of Francis Hughes when two British army Saladin armoured cars came up the road. As the protesters ran for cover plastic bullets were fired and Julie was found lying on the ground, fatally injured. Carol Ann Kelly, 12 years old, was shot at by British soldiers on 19 May and knocked unconscious by a plastic bullet striking her head. She died three days later. There was no trouble in the area at the time. A widower with seven children, Henry Duffy, aged 45, was hit in the chest and temple by plastic bullets on 22 May as he was returning to his Creggan home from a city centre pub. He was in the vicinity of a street fight taking place in the Bogside soon after Patsy O'Hara's death. He died on the same day. Of the many people injured by plastic bullets in May, one lost an eye, others received serious head injuries, fractures and severe bruising. In May alone, 16,656 rounds of these lethal plastic bullets were fired – more than the total fired from 1973 to 1980 (13,004). British army and RUC gunmen had clearly been ordered on to the streets to terrorise the nationalist people into submission. They could not and did not succeed.

In May Dublin saw the emergence of a new force in the prisoner campaign – the dispossessed working class youth of Dublin. These youth from the worst areas of poverty in Dublin brought a new revolutionary spirit to the hunger strike campaign in the Twenty Six Counties. They followed the lead given by the nationalist working class in the Six Counties and took to the streets determined to take on the forces of reaction in the Twenty Six Counties. Their most popular slogan 'Gardai – RUC' expressed their understanding of the close relation between the Twenty Six Counties regime and British imperialism.

Following the murder of Bobby Sands on 5 May the Dublin youth took action. On 7 May a group of gardai in riot gear were driven out of the Sean McDermott Street/Gloucester Diamond area by masked youth hurling petrol bombs. This area is at the heart of the worst slums in Dublin. The youth hijacked and burned buses and cars in protest at the murder of Bobby Sands. They attacked shops which had refused to close on the day of mourning. On 12 May following the murder of Francis Hughes, a peaceful march to the British Embassy in the luxurious Ballsbridge area was met by a horde of helmeted, baton wielding gardai. The youth met this threat with a hail of stones. The gardai, in the tradition of imperialist police forces throughout the world, baton charged and viciously beat anyone they could get hold of. A nurse who tried to attend wounded victims of gardai brutality was beaten to the ground. The youth moved back into the city centre attacking symbols of British domination as they went. In particular two of the imperialist banks, Lombards and Ulster bank, were attacked.

On 13 May the youth came back armed with the weapons of the revolutionary youth in the Six Counties, petrol bombs and bricks. As another protest march moved into O'Connell Street it passed ranks of gardai, with shields and batons ready, ostentatiously guarding the British Home Stores. Petrol bombs were hurled into the British Home Stores. Litter bins, bricks and other missiles were thrown at the gardai and British owned shops. As the youth disappeared into the tenements and estates of Sean McDermott/Gardiner Street the gardai proceeded to beat up any demonstrators caught in O'Connell Street. Men, women and children were knocked to the ground batoned and kicked. The emergence of the youth in the hunger strike campaign sent a wave of fear through the Irish ruling class. It also had a dramatic effect on the National H-Block/Armagh Committee. It began to expose the weaknesses and contradictions inherent in the strategy of the prisoner campaign.

On 14 May the National H-Block/Armagh Committee announced that a vigil that night at the GPO, a march on the British Embassy the next evening, and another in the city centre the following Saturday afternoon were cancelled. The Committee expressed concern at the events of the previous night:

'Small and unrepresentative elements seem set on obstructing the national committee's stated policy of peaceful and dignified demonstrations by engaging in ill-advised and counter-productive confrontations.'[31]

The events had been cancelled to prevent the recurrence of such confrontations.

The *An Phoblacht/Republican News* report of the Dublin events began to reflect the confusion that the action of the militant youths had created among certain forces in the prisoner campaign. The article by Kevin Burke, which had earlier pointed out that 'condemnation of the ... rioters displayed small effort to understand the justifiable anger of newly-aroused youth', spoke of evidence of a tiny group of 'agents provocateurs' at work distributing leaflets calling for an end to peaceful protests and for people to come to demonstrations 'prepared to defend themselves'. Kevin Burke went on:

'This group apparently wishes to turn the anger of concerned youths away from British targets, against Free State "cops, courts and prisons" and presumably see the demonstrations fizzle out in total confusion.'[32]

The youth, however, quite obviously did not require 'leaflets' to turn their anger against the Free State 'cops, courts and prisons' protecting British imperialism's interests in the Twenty Six Counties. The real issue at stake was the direction of the prisoner campaign in the Twenty Six Counties.

On the whole, with certain qualifications, the actions of the youths taking to the streets and fighting the 'security forces' in the Six Counties was given support. After the murder of Bobby Sands *An Phoblacht /Republican News* reported:

'The intensity of the rioting, spearheaded by angry youths, and with the approval of the bulk of the nationalist community, has provided a welcome sign of the revived spirit of republican resistance amongst a saddened people.'[33]

And after the murder of Francis Hughes *An Phoblacht/Republican News* was reporting in an article 'Popular anger flares' that:

'...it was clear that within the nationalist areas there are growing numbers who are losing faith in the feasibility of peaceful protests in the face of British intransigence in the H-Blocks and armed force on the streets.'[34]

Why then was the new development of the dispossessed youth of Dublin following the lead and example of the nationalist youth in the Six Counties being condemned? The report, by Seamus Boyle, of an emergency open conference organised by the National H-Block/Armagh Committee on 9 May after Bobby Sands' death begins to answer this.

'Genuine impatience was expressed by the speakers ... fearful that the national committee's strategy of peaceful mass mobilisation and hard lobbying work, particularly of Fianna Fail and the SDLP, and among the trade unions in the South, would be incapable of saving the life of the next hunger-striker ...

However, such speakers, and the sizeable numbers who voted with them (who were defeated on a crucial vote threatening the existence of the committee) seemed unable to grasp that our strategy for success (of destabilising the six and twenty-six county states, and thus forcing the British government to grant the prisoner's demands) needs to encompass two sharply differing, but mutually re-inforcing, aspects: one peaceful, the other involving physical force.

On the one hand, there needs to be the ongoing vital work of the national committee strategy, particularly in the South, but also in the North, of drawing the broadest possible forces on to massive peaceful parades, of building towards a workers' indefinite general strike, and of committing the bulk of the rank-and-file of Fianna Fail and the SDLP to the five demands.

On the other hand, and generally restricted to the North, there urgently needs to be popular street riots, the erection of barricades against the British forces, and other violent acts of civil disobedience building towards the establishment of no-go areas in the nationalist ghettos; plus, of course, the armed action of IRA volunteers against military occupation forces ...

Many of those speaking, and especially those voting, for a different role of the committee, along implicitly "violent" lines, were mistaking the necessary role of the broad-based committee of organising protests, with the revolutionary role of the Republican Movement.'[35]

With the death of the hunger strikers it became increasingly clear that the British government would not respond to peaceful protests however popular, widespread and well supported. Further, Fianna Fail, the SDLP, the ICTU etc had not been forced by the 'broad-based' protest campaign to 'quake in their shoes and go crawling to their British masters pleading with them to grant the five demands' (see above). On the contrary the leadership of these organisations had played a central role in undermining the prisoners' struggle. To accept that a strategy for success would require 'destabilising the six and twenty-six county states' was realistically to call for a mass revolutionary campaign directed not only at British imperialism but also *against* its collaborationist agents North and South. Such a campaign was *not* compatible with the 'broad-based' campaign of the National H-Block/Armagh Committee and the dignified and peaceful protests it called for 'in order not to alienate potential support'. The 'broad forces' the National H-Block/Armagh Committee wished to attract were opposed to the revolutionary national struggle to free Ireland from British rule and were only prepared to support the prisoners on a 'human rights' basis. These 'broad forces' were totally against the growing revolutionary violence of the youth on the streets and the armed struggle of the IRA being used to force the British government to grant the prisoners' five demands. The two 'aspects' the 'one peaceful and the other involving revolutionary force' were not in reality 'mutually reinforcing' as events after the deaths of the hunger strikers so clearly demonstrated.

This had less immediate consequence in the Six Counties where a tradition of revolutionary street fighting had existed for over a decade and support for the armed struggle was widespread amongst the nationalist minority. But in the Twenty Six Counties that tradition had long since disappeared and if the prisoner campaign was to succeed it had to be rebuilt. When the courage, determination and example of the hunger strikers led to the dispossessed youth of Dublin taking to the streets attacking the symbols of British domination and taking on the 'Free State' forces of collaboration, the National H-Block/Armagh Committee called a halt. The violence of the youth would have alienated the 'broad forces' thought necessary to put pressure on Fianna Fail etc to support the prisoners. But the refusal of Fianna Fail to move and the resulting deaths of the hunger strikers was precisely what led to the youths taking to the streets in the first place. To go forward it was necessary to build on their revolutionary spirit and risk alienating the, on the whole, ineffectual 'broad forces'. This the National H-Block/ Armagh Committee refused to do. As a result of this the militant youth and the nationalist working class in the Six Counties were to become increasingly isolated. The inevitable consequence of such isolation was the defeat of the hunger strike.

During the first hunger strike the IRA had restricted its military campaign in order to create, what were considered at the time to be the most favourable circumstances for the settlement of the prison crisis. Once the treachery of the British government was clear for all to see the IRA renewed its military offensive. In May this offensive was significantly stepped up. After the murder of Francis Hughes *An Phoblacht/ Republican News* reported, under a headline 'A fitting response', an IRA RPG-7 rocket attack on a RUC jeep killing one RUC man and wounding 4 others. On 9 May an IRA bomb went off at the Sullom Voe oil terminal on the Shetland Islands only a quarter of a mile away from where the Queen and Prince Phillip were attending an inauguration ceremony. Throughout May there were almost daily attacks on the 'security forces' with one RUC man killed and other RUC men and British soldiers injured. Bomb attacks on commercial premises added to the massive damage to property from the petrol bombs thrown by the nationalist youths.

The result of the local election which took place in the Six Counties on 20 May indicated the increasing polarisation of political forces as a result of the hunger strike. Paisley nearly doubled the seats of his Democratic Unionist Party from 74 to 142. The Official Unionists won 152. Gerry Fitt got his just deserts for his despicable stand against the hunger strikers. He lost the council seat he had held for 23 years. While the SDLP won 105 seats, SDLP chairman Sean Farren and Alisdair McDonnell leader of the SDLP on Belfast city council were defeated. 3 (Official IRA) Republican Club councillors were also defeated. The Alliance Party lost 32 seats. Among those elected on an anti H-Block/ Armagh ticket were 2 IRSP members, 2 members of Peoples Democracy, a dozen independents and 21 members of the Irish Independence Party including Francis Hughes' brother, Oliver. Sinn Fein did not stand.

A general election in the Twenty Six Counties in June saw the defeat of Haughey's Fianna Fail administration and the eventual return of the Fine Gael/Labour Party Coalition with the help of the anti-republican independent Jim Kemmy. The most important development during the election was the intervention of nine H-Block/Armagh prisoner candidates. This took place despite the opposition of several members of the National H-Block/Armagh Committee who wanted 'prominent personalities' to contest the election on behalf of the prisoners. The election victories of H-Block man Paddy Agnew for Lough – he topped the poll on first preferences – and hunger striker Kieran Doherty in Cavan/Monaghan, and the 42,798 first preference votes amassed for all the prisoner candidates, dramatically indicated the support for the hunger strikers in the Twenty Six Counties. The votes for the prisoners came almost entirely from border areas, working class areas, and poor rural areas in the West of Ireland – areas which have been and still are hardest hit by the British imperialist domination of Ireland.

Four more prisoners joined the hunger strike in June: Thomas McElwee (South Derry) on 8 June, Paddy Quinn (South Armagh) on 15 June, Micky Devine INLA (Derry) on 22 June and Laurence McKeown (Co Antrim) on 29 June. In June another 'attempt' to resolve the hunger strike was made through the intervention of the Irish Commission for Justice and Peace (ICJP), a body established by the Irish hierarchy in 1967. Its five members included two Catholic clergymen, an academic, a solicitor and a member of the SDLP. The ICJP kept in regular contact with the Dublin government and other Free State parties and almost certainly with the SDLP. It attempted to use the hunger strikers' relatives as a vehicle for an imposed settlement and drew up proposals for the settlement of the hunger strike which it put to the British government and the prisoners. The prisoners rejected them as they were 'so far removed from our five demands'. But the ICJP continued meeting hunger strikers' families, the Northern Ireland Office, the National H-Block/Armagh Committee, politicians, and members of the Republican Movement. Eventually they met the hunger strikers.

On 4 July the prisoners put out a 'conciliatory' statement on the five demands. They explained they were not seeking treatment different from that which would be on offer to other prisoners and that the granting of the five demands would not 'mean that the administration would be forfeiting control of the prison'. It was as far as they could go without abandoning their demands.[36] At the same time the ICJP believed it had achieved an agreement with the British government on an acceptable basis (to the ICJP but not the prisoners) for resolving the prison crisis. Joe McDonnell was on the point of death. It was imperative to act quickly. The NIO, through Michael Alison, agreed to send a senior official into the prison on 7 July to explain the 'agreement' to the prisoners. This did not occur and on 8 July at 5.12am Joe McDonnell died after 61 days on hunger strike. That same day at 10am a senior NIO official was present when the prison Governor read a statement to the hunger strikers which reiterated previous public positions of the British government. The ICJP accused the British government of 'duplicity' but the damage had been done.

On 8 and 9 July two teenagers, Danny Barrett and John Dempsey, were shot dead by the British army and a woman, Nora McCabe, died after being hit by a plastic bullet. On 10 July the funeral of Joe McDonnell was attacked by the British army while it tried to arrest the IRA firing party. The British government was not out for compromise. Its only concern was to undermine the prisoners and their steadfast supporters. The prisoners remained unbowed and the nationalist youth gave their answer on the streets. The IRA continued its military actions. Pat McGeown joined the hunger strike on 10 July. On 13 July Martin Hurson died after 46 days on hunger strike. He was replaced by Matt Devlin on 15 July. In Dublin on 18 July the gardai brutally attacked a demonstration in support of the hunger strikers outside the British Embassy. The homes of H-Block activists in Dublin were raided. Many were arrested.

On 31 July Paddy Quinn's family asked for medical intervention to save his life when he became unconscious after 47 days on hunger strike. Kevin Lynch died on 1 August after 71 days on hunger strike. Kieran Doherty died on 2 August after 73 days on hunger strike. Tom McElwee died on 8 August after 62 days on hunger strike. Nine political prisoners had now been slowly and brutally murdered by the British government. In spite of all this *An Phoblacht/Republican News* continued to argue for the very strategy adopted by the National H-Block/Armagh Committee which had so clearly failed to shift the British government:

'The key to real progress, which is the saving of the hunger-strikers' lives, remains, whether palatable or not, the ability of the prisoners' supporters to move the Catholic hierarchy, the SDLP, and the Free State government.'[37]

The prisoners remained unbroken. Five more joined the hunger strike on a week by week basis in August; Liam McCloskey, Pat Sheehan, Jackie McMullan, Bernard Fox and Gerry Carville. Three more joined in September, John Pickering, Gerard Hodgins and Jim Devine.

On 20 August Micky Devine, the tenth and final hunger striker to give his life for political status, died after 60 days on hunger strike. The same day Owen Carron won a significant victory in the Fermanagh/ South Tyrone by-election standing on behalf of the political prisoners. Not only did Owen Carron gain even more votes and a larger majority than achieved by Bobby Sands but he did so in the face of interventions by the pro-British Alliance Party and the (Official IRA) Republican Clubs. This victory indicated the mass popular support for the demands of the hunger strikers.

During August pressure began to be put on the relatives of the hunger strikers to end the hunger strike, with Catholic priests and bishops calling on them to seek medical intervention as soon as the prisoners went into a coma. The Catholic hierarchy, far from putting pressure on the British government, was again undermining the hunger strike by pressurising the relatives. Fr Faul was the leading figure in this 'insidious campaign of moral exploitation'.[38] On 20 August medical intervention was sought to prevent Pat McGeown from dying after 42 days on hunger strike. The same occurred in the case of Matt Devlin on 4 September, and Laurence McKeown on 6 September. Bernard Fox dropped out of the hunger strike on 25 September after a serious premature deterioration which would have led to his death within days. On 26 September Liam McCloskey came off the hunger strike after 52 days on being told his relatives would intervene in the event of him lapsing into a coma. Eventually all but one of the families of the hunger strikers, after attending a meeting with Fr Faul, indicated they would seek medical intervention. Faced with this development the prisoners had no choice – they formally announced the ending of the hunger strike at 3pm on Saturday 3 October 1981.

In their statement ending the hunger strike the prisoners said that it had exposed 'the true face of the present Irish establishment, consisting of the Catholic church, the Dublin government and the SDLP'. They claimed a 'massive political victory' because the 'hunger strikers, by their selflessness, have politicised a very substantial section of the Irish nation'. They paid special tribute to the families of their dead comrades and thanked all those who had supported them. They would continue to struggle for the five demands.[39]

THE HUNGER STRIKE AND THE BRITISH LEFT

A decisive political factor in the defeat of the hunger strike was the fact that no political pressure was placed on the Thatcher government in Britain itself. While demonstrations, pickets, protests and even street fighting took place in Europe, Asia, America and Australia, the British Labour and trade union movement not only remained passive and silent but actually collaborated with the British government. The most despicable example of this was the Labour MP Don Concannon visiting Bobby Sands – close to death – in order to tell him that the Labour Party did not support him. How shameful then that the main emphasis of the British 'left' during the hunger strike was to seek an alliance with a section of the imperialist Labour Party. At the start of the first hunger strike the main political groups on the left in Britain mobilised on the basis of the demand 'Don't let Irish Prisoners die'. The vehicle for this campaign was 'Charter 80', an alliance of the Labour Party 'left', the CPGB, the SWP, the IMG and a small group of Young Liberals. The dominant force in it was the SWP, backed by IMG and a few people still active in the Troops Out Movement. Groups such as Militant and the WRP did nothing at all. The RCG and supporters of Hands Off Ireland, now organised through the paper *Fight Racism! Fight Imperialism!*, attempted to build a campaign around the demands 'Victory to the Hunger Strikers! Political Status Now!'.

The SWP-backed 'Charter 80' campaign from the beginning attempted to depoliticise, in order to defuse, the Irish prisoners' struggle. It declared that if the prisoners die:

> 'It will mean, as the Guardian said "that there is little hope of preventing the undying conflict from taking on an even more bitter form now or in another generation"'.[40]

This was not a call to support the prisoners' struggle but a plea to avoid further conflict. When the prisoners were near to death a statement instigated by Gerry Fitzpatrick (SWP) implicitly attacked the Republican struggle by calling for concessions for the prisoners on the grounds that any death would 'strengthen the hand of those who favour force rather than democratic political campaigning'.[41] This standpoint was taken as part of the continuing attempt to find a middle road between British imperialism on the one hand, and the Irish people on the other. And to avoid confrontation with the organised Labour and trade union movement which cannot and will not oppose British imperialism. It was argued for on the grounds that 'broader forces' had to be drawn into the campaign. But these 'broader forces' had over the years of the prison struggle refused to take any action at all. And so the British middle class left in order to maintain the unprincipled 'alliance' with the 'broader forces' refused to demand they actually do anything, and eventually was forced into a position itself of doing nothing at all.

At the Hunger Strike Coordinating Committee set up during the period of the hunger strike, consisting of British left and Republican organisations, the RCG proposed that the Labour MPs who signed the 'Charter 80' petition on the five demands be asked to attend a picket of Parliament on its opening day. This was *rejected* on the grounds that it was an attempt to 'expose' Tony Benn and the Labour Party. It was Gerry Fitzpatrick who argued strongly against this attempt to make Tony Benn and others back up their signatures with action – something which would have been of real *practical* assistance to the campaign. Not once did the SWP, IMG or TOM mobilise a sizeable proportion of their members and supporters on activities.

When the first hunger strike ended on 18 December 1980 the SWP attacked the prison struggle and described the hunger strike as an 'elitist tactic'. It went on to attack any renewal of the armed struggle of the IRA:

'There will be pressure on the IRA to adapt its tactics to the new situation. A return to isolated military acts will be hard to justify.'[42]

In so doing it was following in the footsteps of one of the 'broad forces' in the 'Charter 80' alliance – the CPGB. It had called on the IRA 'to declare a ceasefire here and now, for all time' two weeks after the hunger strike started.

The only really positive development during the hunger strikes occurred in Scotland. On 20 December, two days after the ending of the first hunger strike, 1000 people, predominantly workers, marched through Glasgow in support of the prisoners. The march initiated by the Scottish Hunger Strike Action Committee was built mainly by Sinn Fein and the RCG around the slogans. 'Victory to the Hunger Strikers! Political Status Now!'. This success was built on when on 14 February 1981 over 1500 marched two miles into Glasgow for a rally in the city centre. The march organised by the Glasgow H-Block/Armagh Action Committee fended off loyalist attacks to reach the city centre – the first pro-Republican march to go through the city centre for 10 years. The march again mainly built by an alliance of Republicans and commun-ists, was supported by TOM and the IMG. The SWP and CPGB refused to support it. So successful were these Glasgow marches that a third march called by the Glasgow Hunger Strike Action Committee for 4 April came under a 3-month ban enforced in the Strathclyde region under the guise of 'loyalist threats'. A huge march of over 3,000 had been expected. Needless to say all the 'broad forces', including the SWP, CPGB and IMG refused to campaign against the ban.

During the first hunger strike the SWP, IMG and TOM strategy of limiting the campaign to the prejudices of Labour MPs and other dignatories totally failed. So for the second hunger strike they consciously decided not to expose their chosen allies any further by doing next to nothing. In April a national demonstration came under a ban. It was decided to ignore it. Less than 500 turned up. A demonstration – all-London – in Staines, the constituency of Humphrey Atkins, mustered only 50. While, internationally, the murder of Bobby Sands led to massive protests and demonstrations in many capital cities, in London it was marked by a picket of Downing Street of only 300. A demonstration in London on 13 June mobilised only 2000. The 'national' demonstrations after six hunger strikers had died called for 18 July in Manchester and 29 July in Leeds, were both around 400-500 people. For the 29 July demonstration – timed to coincide with the Royal Wedding – only the RCG of all the left groups mobilised fully. The London H-Block/Armagh Committee meetings dwindled in attendance, pickets, marches etc became no more than token gestures. By the end the SWP and IMG were hardly pretending to campaign. With the exception of a handful of individuals and certain branches, TOM too had ceased to campaign. When the second hunger strike ended – after 10 political prisoners had been murdered – on 3 October, FRFI with some justification declared:

> 'The list of those who must take responsibility for the murder of the ten Irish revolutionaries who died in the hunger strike includes these traitors to the cause of the Irish prisoners: the Labour Party, TUC, CPGB, SWP, IMG and TOM.'[43]

These organisations put every obstacle in the way of communists, anti-imperialists and others who fought to build a serious campaign. The official British Labour and trade union movement had shown yet again that they will never be allies of the Irish people in the struggle for Irish freedom. And the middle class socialist standpoint had been shown to be indeed at best 'a cruel deception' and at worst an open betrayal of the Irish cause.

THE END OF THE HUNGER STRIKE AND ITS POLITICAL CONSEQUENCES

In their statement announcing the end of the hunger strike in October 1981 the political prisoners in the H-Blocks drew out a number of important political lessons. The first was that the prisoner campaign confirmed the necessity for revolutionary violence in the national liberation struggle.

'Despite the electoral successes, despite the hundreds of thousands at hunger-strikers' funerals, despite massive and unprecedented displays of community support and solidarity, the British government adhered rigidly to the precept that "might is right" and set about hammering home the point that nothing has really changed since the fall of Stormont or from the inception of this state. That is, that nationalist Ireland must always be subjected to the British and loyalist veto.'

From this they concluded that 'nationalist pacifism in the Northern Ireland context' would condemn the nationalist population to subserviency, perpetuate partition and undermine the struggle for a just and lasting peace in Ireland.

The second lesson was the exposure of the real face of the Irish establishment: the Catholic Church, the Dublin government and the SDLP. On the Catholic church:

'From the outset the Catholic hierarchy opposed the hunger-strike even though they offered no alternative course of action . . . their stance has been extremely immoral and misleading . . . they are intricately immersed in the field of politics and deceit . . . '

On the Dublin government:

'We believe that the Dublin bloc of Fianna Fail, Fine Gael, and Labour are accessories to the legalised murder of ten true and committed Irishmen . . . They sat idly by and thus encouraged the British to continue with the death policy . . . If John Bull doesn't actually rule the twenty-six counties physically, he still rules in spirit . . . '

And on the SDLP:

'There was only one positively injurious action available to the SDLP which would help save the lives in the H-Blocks and that was to isolate the British administration by withdrawing from the council chambers. This they consistently refused to do . . . This party should now be recognised for what it is, an amalgamation of middle-class Redmondites, devoid of principle, direction, and courage. This party is spineless and weak and is very capable of selling-out to unionist intimidators for imperialist perks . . . '

Although the hunger strike had been defeated and the political prisoners had not achieved the 'five demands', the statement, nevertheless, claimed a 'massive political victory'. This was because the courage and example of the hunger strikers had 'politicised a very substantial section of the Irish nation' and exposed the 'shallow, unprincipled nature of the Irish partitionist bloc'.[44] A claim that one year later was vindicated by the remarkable political gains made by Sinn Fein at the expense of the SDLP in the Assembly elections of October 1982. Sinn Fein fought the election on a 'Break the British connection! Smash Stormont!' platform pledging itself to boycott the proposed Assembly.

The denial of political status for Irish political prisoners was central to British imperialism's overall strategy of 'Ulsterisation' adopted soon after the failure of the 'power-sharing' Executive. A whole apparatus of emergency legislation, arrest, systematic torture in police cells, forced 'confessions', long remands, Diplock (non-jury) courts, imprisonment and torture in specially built concentration camps, the H-Blocks, had been set up to deny political legitimacy to the national liberation struggle to free Ireland from British rule and 'criminalise' Irish Republicans. So critical was this 'criminalisation' policy for Britain's continued domination over Ireland that the British ruling class was prepared to slowly murder 10 Irish political prisoners and risk undermining the stability of British rule not only in the Six Counties but over Ireland as a whole.

A victory for the political prisoners in the struggle for political status would strike at the heart of British domination over Ireland. To recognise the legitimacy of the prison struggle was to acknowledge the legitimacy of the revolutionary struggle of the IRA to drive British imperialism out of Ireland. Such recognition would also have important consequences in Britain. It would legitimise the use of revolutionary force against British imperialism. It would give strength and example to any developing forces of revolution in Britain. Finally it would not only expose the reactionary and brutal character of British imperialism but also of the British Labour Party and official trade union movement which gave, and still gives, British imperialism consistent support in the oppression of the Irish people. Such a development was not one the British ruling class could accept. It is in this context that the failure of the campaign to win the 'five demands' of the political prisoners was a defeat for the political prisoners and a setback for the national liberation struggle.

A year after the hunger strike ended the political prisoners in the H-Block and Armagh prison continued to face the petty and vindictive harassment of the British prison regime. The promised 'reforms' had, in the main, still not been fully granted. While all prisoners now wear their own clothes, the prison regime continued to insist that Republicans do any kind of work asked of them by the prison authorities. As a result several hundred Republicans in both the H-Blocks and Armagh prison maintained a 'no-work' protest after the hunger strike ended and were penalised as a result by loss of remission – ten days for every 28 on protest – and loss of other 'privileges' including the denial of educational facilities. The 'no-work' protest was ended in November 1982.

The failure to win the demands of the political prisoners was a setback for the national liberation struggle. It led to the demobilisation of the masses of Irish people who had been drawn into the struggle at every level and who had been politicised during the more than five years of the prisoner campaign. In the Six Counties British imperialism made a concerted effort to try to confuse and demoralise the nationalist population by the use of informers, increased British army raids, wholesale arrests and a barrage of anti-Republican propaganda. In the Twenty Six Counties the cross border collaboration between the Dublin government and British imperialism directed at Republicans intensified involving co-ordinated searches etc and the use of direct radio and computer links. The arrest, trial and sentencing in Twenty Six Counties courts of Gerry Tuite and the Republicans who escaped from Crumlin Road gaol in June 1980, showed the far-reaching measures the Twenty Six Counties government was now prepared to take to help British imperialism in its efforts to defeat the IRA.

In spite of all this it is undeniable that the overall result of the prisoner campaign was a growing politicisation of the Irish people. The experience of the hunger strike deepened the hatred of British imperialism and its collaborationist forces both North and South. In the Six Counties this was shown by the dramatic results in the October 1982 Assembly elections, already referred to, when Sinn Fein won 5 out of 12 seats it contested on an anti-imperialist platform. In the Twenty Six Counties the growing disaffection with British imperialism made it impossible for the Dublin government to support British imperialism's reactionary war in the Malvinas/Falkland Islands. And since the proposed Assembly did not offer any so-called 'Irish dimension', which the Fianna Fail government might have been able to get its supporters to swallow, the government was forced to oppose the Assembly. However the political developments, which occurred during the hunger strike in the Twenty Six Counties, have still a very long way to go if significant political support for revolutionary Republicanism is to be built. This was reflected in the February 1982 election results in the Twenty Six Counties. It is true that media predictions were proved wrong. The high votes achieved in the June 1981 elections did not completely disappear when the immediate emotional issue of the hunger strike ceased to be present. Although media attention focussed on the budget issue and Sinn Fein, fighting on an abstentionist, anti-imperialist platform, were denied broadcasting time, the election results still showed significant support for the Republican Movement especially in the border areas. Nevertheless no seats were won and the number of first preference votes obtained (17,000) was less than half those achieved during the hunger strike.

The defeat of the hunger strike also represented a defeat for the democratic and socialist movement in Britain. The most reactionary Tory government since the Second World War was considerably strengthened by the defeat of the prison struggle in Ireland. It gave that government increased confidence to continue with the attacks on working class living standards and with the gradual destruction of the 'welfare' state. It meant that the Thatcher government had no serious opposition in Britain to its reactionary war in the Malvinas/Falkland Islands. It encouraged the government to press on with legislation directed against fundamental trade union rights, action aimed at increasing police powers (emphasised by the appointment of Kenneth Newman, torturer-in-chief in the Six Counties of Ireland, as head of the Metropolitan Police) and racist legislation directed at the rights of immigrants and their families. All these developments took place with little or no opposition from the British Labour and trade union movement.

The history of the Irish people's struggle for freedom has always, at decisive moments, exposed the forces of collaboration with British imperialism as well as pointing to the new forces of revolution. The prison struggle and the hunger strike were no exception to this. In both Ireland and Britain the enemies of the Irish people were clearly exposed. So were the forces that could be relied on and those that could not.

In Ireland, in the words of the political prisoners, the 'shallow unprincipled nature of the Irish partitionist bloc' was exposed for all to see. Not only do the Dublin governments, Fianna Fail and Fine Gael/ Irish Labour Party and the SDLP come under this category but also the hierarchy of the Catholic Church and the ICTU. Everything they did was designed to undermine the hunger strike at critical points. In

Britain the British Labour Party and official trade union movement not unexpectedly gave full backing to the Thatcher government's murderous policies in Ireland. However new 'forces of collaboration' now clearly exposed themselves. The British middle class socialist left (CPGB, SWP, IMG, WRP, Militant, TOM etc) when faced, in practice, with a choice of siding with the Irish prisoners or with the imperialist Labour Party and its treacherous trade union backers chose the latter. The campaign in support of the hunger strikers was so completely sabotaged that it practically ceased to exist towards the end.

Finally in both Ireland and Britain the real allies of the Irish revolution began to emerge. In the Six Counties of Ireland behind the prisoners were the relatives, the Republican Movement and the nationalist working class – particularly the youth who came out on to the streets and fought the British army/RUC with stones and petrol bombs. In the Twenty Six Counties the Republican Movement gained the support of new sections of the Irish working class and, most important of all, new supporters of the political prisoners, the dispossessed youth of Dublin, came out on the streets after the murder of Bobby Sands. In Britain while a small number of communists and anti-imperialists were fully behind the political prisoners, the most significant development was not directly related to the hunger strike. This was the uprisings of the black and white youth in the major cities of Britain in 1981. These youth, taking their example from the revolutionary nationalist youth in the Six Counties, took to the streets to fight the repressive forces of the British imperialist state. These will be the new forces of revolution in Britain and therefore potential allies of the Irish revolution.

NOTES

1   *An Phoblacht/Republican News* 4 October 1980.
2   *An Phoblacht/Republican News* 18 October 1980.
3   *An Phoblacht/Republican News* 1 November 1980.
4   *ibid.*
5   *ibid.*
6   *An Phoblacht/Republican News* 8 November 1980.
7   *ibid.*
8   *An Phoblacht/Republican News* 6 September 1980.
9   *An Phoblacht/Republican News* 22 November 1980.
10 *An Phoblacht/Republican News* 6 December 1980.
11 *An Phoblacht/Republican News* 13 December 1980.
12 *ibid.*
13 *ibid.*

14 *ibid.*
15 Cited in *Belfast Bulletin* No 10 Spring 1982.
16 *An Phoblacht/Republican News* 27 December 1980.
17 *An Phoblacht/Republican News* 31 January 1981.
18 Cited in *Fight Racism! Fight Imperialism!* No 9 March/April 1981.
19 *An Phoblacht/Republican News* 7 February 1981.
20 *Magill* August 1981.
21 *An Phoblacht/Republican News* 31 January 1981.
22 *An Phoblacht/Republican News* 14 February 1981.
23 *ibid.*
24 *An Phoblacht/Republican News* 7 March 1981.
25 *An Phoblacht/Republican News* 14 March 1981.
26 *ibid.*
27 Cited in *Financial Times* 10 April 1981.
28 *The Guardian* 11 April 1981.
29 *An Phoblacht/Republican News* 25 April 1981.
30 Cited in *ibid.*
31 *An Phoblacht/Republican News* 16 May 1981.
32 *ibid.*
33 *An Phoblacht/Republican News* 9 May 1981.
34 *An Phoblacht/Republican News* 16 May 1981.
35 *ibid.*
36 *An Phoblacht/Republican News* 11 July 1981.
37 *An Phoblacht/Republican News* 15 August 1981.
38 *Iris* November 1981. This issue gives a detailed history of the prison campaign and the hunger strikes.
39 *An Phoblacht/Republican News* 10 October 1981.
40 Cited in *Fight Racism! Fight Imperialism!* No 7 November/December 1980.
41 Cited in *Fight Racism! Fight Imperialism!* No 8 January/February 1981.
42 *Socialist Worker* 3 January 1980.
43 *Fight Racism! Fight Imperialism!* No 13 15 October–15 November 1981.
44 *An Phoblacht/Republican News* 10 October 1981.

CHAPTER SEVENTEEN

BRITAIN AND THE
IRISH REVOLUTION

The events of the hunger strike and its outcome confirmed once again the main positions of the communist standpoint on the national liberation struggle to free Ireland from British rule. At this stage it is important to summarise the main elements of that standpoint and what it means for building an anti-imperialist movement in Britain today.

BRITISH IMPERIALISM CANNOT PLAY A PROGRESSIVE ROLE IN IRELAND

Imperialism will never voluntarily relinquish political control over an oppressed nation because such control enormously strengthens its ability to economically exploit that nation. Any movement by British imperialism to make concessions to the demands of the Irish people has, therefore, only been brought about by revolutionary force. On a number of occasions it took an insurrection or a direct threat to the stability of British rule over Ireland to force the British ruling class to move. Peaceful and constitutional methods of protest have always been ignored. Time and again British imperialism has resorted to outright terror to retain its domination over Ireland.

From the end of the 1870s until the turn of the century, it was the alliance of Michael Davitt's Land League and Parnell's Irish (Home Rule) Party which forced the British government to pass the concessionary Land Acts granting limited rights to the Irish peasantry and which forced the issue of Home Rule for Ireland into British politics. The peasantry organised in the Land League resisted evictions and seized land from the landlords in a land war which lasted over two decades. Parnell by becoming the President of the Land League used it to reinforce his parliamentary campaign and 'obstruction' tactics in the

House of Commons with the implied threat of a resort to force should his efforts to obtain Home Rule fail.

The aftermath of the Easter Rising led to revolutionary nationalism being given political expression in a new Sinn Fein movement led by Eamon de Valera. It stood firmly for an Irish Republic. In the December 1918 General Election Sinn Fein achieved a massive electoral victory winning 73 of the 105 seats in Ireland. The vast majority of the Irish people, nearly 70%, had voted for an independent Irish Republic. The British government simply ignored the democratic expression of the will of the Irish people. Sinn Fein set up an Irish National Assembly, Dail Eireann, in January 1919. There were then two 'governments' in Ireland: the one, Dail Eireann backed by the majority of Irish people; the other that of British imperialism operating from Dublin Castle and using repressive force and institutionalised violence to impose its decrees.

To prevent Dail Eireann establishing a democratic government of the Irish people, British imperialism unleashed a war of terror on Ireland. Dail Eireann was suppressed and all national movements were banned as thousands of British mercenary troops were poured into Ireland in an attempt to drive the Irish people into submission. It was not until the Irish people led by their revolutionary army, the IRA, had fought British imperialism to a standstill that the British government was forced to make concessions to Irish demands for self-determination.

Britain however retained its control over Ireland by signing a deal with a section of the national movement which was prepared to compromise the interests of the Irish people for limited self-government. To do this it partitioned Ireland and created and consolidated a reactionary loyalist police state in the Six Counties of Ireland. A totally reactionary, viciously repressive loyalist statelet became the medium through which British imperialism exerted its political and, therefore, economic domination over Ireland as a whole.

In partitioning Ireland and establishing a neo-colonial Twenty Six Counties 'Free State' in the South and a loyalist statelet in the North, British imperialism had the support of the Irish capitalist class. The Irish capitalist class, North and South of the border, had no real interest in fighting for a united Ireland. The partition of Ireland had divided the Irish working class and severely weakened the opposition to capitalist rule in Ireland which had developed during the war of independence. The Irish capitalist class was quite prepared to play a subservient role to the British ruling class as long as it could have a share of the profits arising from imperialist exploitation of Ireland as a whole.

The artificial statelet created by British imperialism in the Six Counties of Ireland was designed to maintain loyalist dominance in that part of Ireland. The loyalist (Protestant) working class in the Six Counties was among British imperialism's most resolute supporters in the partitioning of Ireland. The loyalist workers were, and still are, a privileged section of the working class and the maintenance of their privileges (higher wages, jobs, housing etc) depended on the union with Britain. For this reason they were, and still are, the most implacable enemies of a united Ireland. And for this reason they were, and still are, opposed to any improvement in the conditions of the nationalist (Catholic) working class in the Six Counties. For any improvement in these conditions, any reform of the reactionary loyalist statelet was, and is regarded as a direct threat to their own interests.

In the late 1960s the inherently reactionary character of the loyalist statelet was exposed for the world to see when sections of the nationalist minority took to the streets demanding basic democratic rights and were battered, beaten and shot at by the paramilitary forces of the loyalist state. Faced with this brutality and intransigence the nationalist people of Derry staged an insurrection in August 1969 and drove the loyalist forces out of their area. It was only at this stage that the British Labour government intervened. British troops were sent in to the Six Counties of Ireland to aid the 'civil power'. This action was designed to have one and only one effect – to support loyalist supremacy, the basis of British imperialism's rule in Ireland. The British troops were necessary precisely because the state was unreformable and the nationalist minority could not be bought off. However it took the rise of the Provisional IRA, an effective modern guerrilla army with growing support amongst the nationalist minority to force the British government to abolish Stormont and replace it with direct rule from Westminster nearly two-and-a-half years after the troops were sent in. The British government had no choice after the institutionalised terror of internment without trial (August 1971) and the Bloody Sunday massacres (January 1972) not only had failed to undermine support for the Provisional IRA but had driven hundreds of nationalist youth into its ranks. After Bloody Sunday, nationalist Ireland exploded and the British Embassy in Dublin was burned down. The Six Counties became rapidly ungovernable. The British government suspended Stormont in March 1972. No-one could have any doubts that it was the Provisional IRA which brought it down.

British imperialism had some room for manoeuvre after the suspension of Stormont. The Dublin government, the SDLP and the Catholic

Church welcomed direct rule from Westminster and the British government used the opportunity to try to undermine the unity of the nationalist minority and draw support away from the Provisional IRA. The
period 1973–5 saw the rise and fall of the power-sharing Executive.
The 'carrot' of power-sharing with the Unionists was offered to the
Catholic middle class in return for them giving legitimacy to a new
Stormont Assembly and accepting, for the time being, 'the status of
Northern Ireland as part of the United Kingdom'. The SDLP took the
bait.

Having no credibility in the nationalist working class the whole venture came to the inevitable sticky end after loyalist opposition to the
Executive, in the form of the Ulster Workers Council strike, brought
the Six Counties to a standstill in May 1974. The British Labour government refused to intervene to guarantee essential services. The UWC
strike had forcefully reminded it that the price of 'loyalty' to British
imperialism was the preservation of loyalist privileges and loyalist
supremacy in the Six Counties of Ireland. It was a price that the British
Labour government was quite prepared to pay. Loyalist ascendancy,
after all, was, and is, the key to British domination over Ireland as a
whole.

After the fall of the power-sharing Executive the British state resorted to outright repression in a new attempt to defeat the real threat to
its interests in Ireland – that from the nationalist masses led by their
revolutionary army, the Provisional IRA. It took almost two years to
prepare the way for this new 'regime of terror' in the Six Counties of
Ireland. The new policy was called 'Ulsterisation'. It involved the
'primacy of the police' in fighting the IRA and the 'criminalisation' of
the revolutionary national struggle to free Ireland from British rule.
The fundamental feature of this new period of terror was judicial
internment – the 'conveyor belt' process of arrest, systematic torture in
police cells, forced 'confessions', long remands, Diplock (non-jury)
courts and imprisonment in specially built concentration camps in the
H-Blocks. This process demanded the torture and brutalisation of
political prisoners in interrogation centres and in the specially built
prisons. It was to culminate in the slow and brutal murder of ten Irish
political prisoners who had gone on hunger strike to demand their
rights to be treated as political prisoners.

In spite of the evidence to the contrary there have been those who, at
times, have misread the situation and have seen in the statements of
politicians or the editorials of newspapers signs that Britain wants to
withdraw from Ireland, and see Ireland united again. One such occasion occurred after the fall of the power-sharing Executive when the

political initiatives of the British government were in disarray, and the British were preparing the ground for 'Ulsterisation'. In May 1974, the Liberal MP John Pardoe had called for the withdrawal of British troops by 31 December 1974. Britain's economic crisis was rapidly deepening and many felt that Britain could not afford the expenditure involved in subsidising the Six Counties of Ireland. Evidence of British withdrawal was said to be the substantial pulling out of businesses and closing down of factories. This belief was a factor in the truce negotiated by the Provisional IRA early in 1975. It was later admitted by the IRA that it had misread the signs and that Britain was committed to stabilising the Six Counties 'to assure loyalists' support for the long haul against the Irish Republican Army'. The truce had, in fact, given the British valuable breathing space to reorganise RUC/British army intelligence gathering and resulted in significant damage to the IRA.

In August 1978 the *Daily Mirror* ran an editorial under the headline 'Ulster: Bring home the troops'.[1] The British middle class left immediately hailed this as 'a move in the right direction'. It was nothing of the kind. The *Daily Mirror* was simply responding to the growing strength of the anti-imperialist movement in the Six Counties. Massive demonstrations of 10,000 and over in support of the political prisoners regularly took place in 1978. The IRA, far from being defeated, was about to launch a major offensive. The worldwide condemnation of the torture of Irish political prisoners in the interrogation centres of the Six Counties was additional pressure especially after the Amnesty Report. The *Daily Mirror* was not calling for a united Ireland. It was, as *Republican News* pointed out, 'merely calling for a change in the way Britain props up Loyalism; in effect it is calling for an "Ulsterisation" of the war'.[2] The *Daily Mirror* recognised that British imperialism had been unable to defeat the IRA and so it was calling for 'a government of Irishmen' to do the job. It wanted the British government to help create a 'stable government' to succeed it and to that end 'the troops should be the last to withdraw'. The *Daily Mirror* made this call – and for the same reasons – following Sinn Fein's victories in the October 1982 Assembly elections.

After the Labour Party had lost the March 1979 election a small section from the 'left' of the Party, very concerned about the fact that Irish workers were refusing to vote Labour, began to challenge the pro-Unionist orthodoxy of the imperialist Labour Party. They forced a short debate on Ireland at the Labour Party Conference in 1979. In the Spring of 1980 the Labour Committee on Ireland (LCI) was set up to build on this development. It was mainly composed of ex-members of the

Troops Out Movement and British left groups who had gravitated to the Labour Party. At the 1980 Labour Party Conference, Tony Benn, beginning his campaign for the leadership of the Labour 'left', told a fringe meeting of the LCI that 'the partition of Ireland was a crime' and 'there was no future for a policy based upon partition'. He apologised(!) for his previous silence on Ireland[3] – sitting silently in Labour Cabinets that introduced and implemented the regime of terror and torture in the Six Counties of Ireland. There were many now who were all too ready to believe that a significant section of the Labour Party could be won over to support for a united Ireland. With Benn fighting for the deputy leadership in 1981 and in the wake of the worldwide condemnation of Britain during the hunger strikes, the LCI trend became more outspoken. But action speaks louder than words.

During the second hunger strike the LCI did next to nothing to force the Labour Party to defend the hunger strikers, apart from calling a tiny march in Mansfield. Throughout the two hunger strikes only one Labour MP, Paddy Duffy, made any kind of protest in Parliament. Benn, although pressed to make a statement on a number of occasions, refused to support the hunger strikers. By the 1982 Labour Party Conference things were very much back to normal. A motion calling on the Labour government to 'withdraw from Ireland, without conditions being imposed by the Unionist minority' and to 'implement a comprehensive Bill of Rights' was placed on the agenda. The proposer of the motion from the LCI trend asked for it to be remitted on the grounds the Labour Party was already committed (sic!) to a united Ireland. This clumsy attempt to cover up for Labour's support for partition was exploded when the Conference overwhelmingly defeated the motion, thereby reaffirming the Labour Party's long tradition of support for the imperialist occupation of Ireland.

British imperialism has no interest in uniting Ireland precisely because a divided Ireland and the existence of the loyalist police state is the key to its domination over Ireland as a whole. After the fall of the power-sharing Executive in May 1974 British imperialism introduced and implemented a regime of terror to try and crush the revolutionary national movement led by the IRA. The British government steadfastly refused to grant Irish political prisoners political status because it cannot acknowledge the political legitimacy of a national liberation movement it has to destroy if it is to maintain its rule over Ireland. Ireland will only be free when British imperialism has been defeated.

NATIONALISM AND SOCIALISM
IRELAND THE KEY TO THE BRITISH REVOLUTION

Over 100 years ago Marx and Engels laid the foundation for a consistent communist standpoint on Ireland. It was they who first established that the question of Irish self-determination stands at the heart of the British revolution. At first, Marx and Engels thought Ireland would be liberated as a result of the victory of the working class movement in Britain. Deeper study, however, convinced them that the opposite was true. The British working class would never accomplish anything until it had got rid of Ireland. Ireland is the key to the British revolution.

They reached their new position on the basis of a concrete analysis of the relationship between Britain and Ireland. That relationship significantly changed over a twenty year period. The national liberation movement in Ireland assumed revolutionary forms with the rise of the Fenian movement – a 'lower orders' movement based on the land. The working class movement in Britain not only lost its revolutionary drive with the defeat of the Chartist movement in 1848 but also fell under the influence of the liberal bourgeoisie for a long period of time.

The British ruling class was divided into two main sections – the old landed aristocracy and the bourgeoisie. Ireland was not only a bastion of power and wealth for the old landed aristocracy but it was a point of unity of both sections of the British ruling class. For the bourgeoisie also benefited from British domination over Ireland. Ireland was not only a source of cheap food and raw materials for British capitalists, but also the impoverished Irish peasantry, driven off the land and forced to emigrate to England, was a source of cheap labour. This forced emigration of Irishmen divided the working class in Britain into two hostile camps. It allowed the ruling class to provide a relatively superior position for British workers as against the Irish and so support and nourish the hostility between these two sections of the working class. This antagonism between British and Irish workers, argued Marx and Engels, 'is the secret of the impotence of the English working class despite its organisation'. For the oppression of Ireland united the ruling class and divided the working class.

The British ruling class was most vulnerable in Ireland where the power of the landed aristocracy was being challenged by a revolutionary national movement based on the land. A defeat for the British ruling class in Ireland would open the way for the British revolution. Provided, of course, that the British working class made common cause with the Irish. The national emancipation of Ireland was the first condition for the victory of the British revolution. And unless the British working class made 'common cause with the Irish', the British working class would never accomplish anything. This is the sense in which Marx and Engels argued that Ireland is the key to the British revolution.

In defending their stand on the Irish question in the First International, Marx and Engels came up against the opportunist leaders of the British labour movement who at that time were moving closer to Gladstone and the leaders of the liberal bourgeoisie. They were forced to deal with political attacks on the Irish liberation movement which have recurred ever since. These included those of the 'English would-be liberators' who thought Fenianism was 'not altogether wrong' but wanted the Irish movement to use the 'legal means of meetings and demonstrations...' by which the English movement conducted its struggles. Supporters of Marx and Engels argued that the Irish had every right to use force since force was used to deny them their freedom. When Marx, in supporting the call for an amnesty for Irish political prisoners, accused Gladstone 'of deliberately insulting the Irish Nation' and attacked the conduct of his government, there were those who thought he went too far. Marx's reply is a political guideline for today: 'It is more important to make a concession to the Irish people than to Gladstone'. Finally Marx and Engels faced defenders of British rule over Ireland who argued that Ireland could not be independent because it would undermine the security of Britain. That the International was able to build a demonstration of nearly 100,000 people in support of the demand for an amnesty for Irish political prisoners was mainly due to the political fight Marx and Engels conducted in support of Irish self-determination in the First International.

By the turn of the century capitalism had entered its imperialist phase – a world-wide system of colonial oppression and financial domination of the overwhelming majority of the world by a small number of imperialist countries. Imperialism divides the world into oppressed and oppressor nations. It also divides the working class. A handful of imperialist countries obtain high monopoly profits out of the brutal exploitation of oppressed peoples world-wide. Out of these super-profits imperialism is able to create and sustain a small privileged and influential layer of the working class in the imperialist countries whose conditions of life isolate it from the suffering, poverty and temper of the mass of the working class. This privileged layer has a material interest in the continuation of imperialism for it is the source of its economic and political privileges. Such workers, a labour aristocracy, constitute the social base of opportunism in the working class movement. So critical was this development for the working class movement and so great the damage done to the interests of the working class as a result of the activities of these opportunist layers that Lenin, at the Second Congress of the Communist International (1920), said that:

'Opportunism is our principal enemy. Opportunism in the upper ranks of the working class is not proletarian socialism but bourgeois socialism. Practice has shown that the active people in the working class movement who adhere to this opportunist trend are better defenders of the bourgeoisie than the bourgeoisie itself. Without their leadership of the workers, the bourgeoisie could not remain in power.'[4]

In the middle of the nineteenth century Britain already revealed at least two major distinguishing features of imperialism, vast colonies and monopoly profits. Marx and Engels were soon to come into conflict with the opportunist layers of the working class movement in Britain especially in relation to Ireland. And these developments in Britain in fact proved to be the forerunner of developments worldwide. So that by building on the political experience of Marx and Engels on the Irish question, Lenin was able to formulate the tasks of communists in relation to national oppression in the epoch of imperialism. In particular, he was able to make clear the attitude the working class of the imperialist nations should adopt towards national movements.

The mass of the working class in the imperialist countries cannot liberate itself without uniting with the movement of oppressed peoples to destroy imperialism. Only such an alliance will make it possible to wage a united fight against the imperialist powers, the imperialist bourgeoisie and its bought-off agents in the working class. The unity of all forces fighting imperialism can only be achieved on the basis of the internationalist principle 'No nation can be free if it oppresses other nations'. And this is expressed through the demand for the right of nations to self-determination. Far from being counterposed to the socialist revolution, communists insist on this demand precisely in order to promote the socialist revolution. For unless imperialism is fatally weakened and opportunism defeated the socialist revolution cannot succeed.

This standpoint demands that the working class in the imperialist nation 'make common cause' with the oppressed peoples fighting imperialism. And, as Lenin argued, socialists could not, without ceasing to be socialists, reject such a struggle right down to an uprising or war. For the working class to side with its own ruling class, or not actively oppose it, in the imperialist domination of oppressed peoples necessarily means to strengthen the domination of opportunist forces over itself. Further, it undermines the unity of the working class in the oppressed and oppressor nations and hence the possibility of defeating imperialism and beginning the socialist revolution.

Since the rise of the Fenian movement in the 1860s up to today, the most critical revolutionary challenge to British imperialism has come from Ireland. The dominance of opportunist forces in the British working class movement however has not only held back the working class struggle in Britain but has also limited support for the Irish revolution. The failure of the working class movement in Britain to rid itself of its opportunist leadership and make 'common cause' with the Irish revolution has meant a severe set-back for the socialist revolution in both Ireland and Britain. Ireland is undoubtedly still the key to the British revolution.

It was the alliance of the leaders of the British working class with the Liberals which enabled the land question in Ireland to be resolved from above at the expense of the mass of the Irish peasantry, so avoiding the revolutionary consequences of the land war. There were however efforts by revolutionary socialists and others to carry out agitational work on the Irish question and a massive demonstration of 100–150,000 took place in April 1887 against the recently passed Irish Coercion Bill – even Gladstone, out of office, supported the demonstration. Eleanor Marx and Edward Aveling played a leading role in this agitational work so carrying on the tradition of Marx and Engels. However, the opportunist forces in the British labour movement proved to be too strong. Engels said at the time in an interview published in 1888:

> 'The masses are *for* the Irish. The organisations and the labour aristocracy in general, follow Gladstone and the liberal bourgeois and do not go further than these.'[5]

When the revolutionary workers of Dublin led by the ITGWU challenged Irish capitalism and its British imperialist backers during the Dublin strike and lock out of 1913/14 the leadership of the British Labour and trade union movement did everything it could to undermine real solidarity action from British workers. The ITGWU was a revolutionary union. It organised the most oppressed workers in Ireland. It was born out of bitter struggles against the capitalist class, and in 1913 it was led by two revolutionary socialists, James Larkin and

James Connolly. It spurned the tradition of 'moderation' and 'compromise' of the official British trade union movement. It was a fighting organisation with a political programme which included the demand for Irish self-determination. A victory for that union against the Dublin employers would have struck a mighty blow not only against the Irish capitalists but against British imperialism as well.

The British working class had been involved in a whole series of bitter strikes in 1911 and 1912 but it failed to rise to the revolutionary challenge of the Dublin workers. It proved unable to prevent its leaders, including those like Ben Tillett previously associated with militant trade unionism, from selling out the revolutionary workers of Dublin. As a result these same leaders were able to draw the British working class into support for the First Imperialist War and so lead it to political defeat.

Just before the First Imperialist War the Liberals announced an amendment to the Irish Home Rule Bill to exclude part of Ireland from the operation of Home Rule. Ireland was to be partitioned to preserve British rule. The national movement was split. The Irish Party, representing the interests of the Irish capitalist class, accepted partition. The revolutionary wing of the national movement supported by Irish labour was against partition. Once again the British labour movement was faced with a choice. And it chose to support partition and stand with the Irish bourgeoisie and British imperialism against the Irish working class. Having betrayed the revolutionary unionism of Larkin and Connolly during the Dublin lock out, the British labour movement went on to oppose the Easter Rising 1916 and applauded the judicial murder of its leaders, including the revolutionary socialist James Connolly. Arthur Henderson, the Labour MP, was in the War Cabinet which brutally crushed the Easter Rising and ordered Connolly's execution.

During the Imperialist War the Irish Party organised recruiting meetings up and down the country in defence of Britain and its Empire. But British imperialism was prevented from introducing conscription into Ireland. For Irish labour and the revolutionary wing of the national movement united in a successful mass campaign against the attempt of Lloyd George to introduce conscription into Ireland in 1918. Ireland saw the only general strike against the Imperialist War in any Western European country.

After the Irish people had overwhelmingly voted for an Irish Republic, had set up Dail Eireann and been forced to wage a revolutionary war to win its fundamental rights to self-determination, the British

Labour and trade union movement still refused to give it support. Trade union leaders in Britain did everything they could to prevent workers in Britain taking strike action in support of the Irish war, eg refusing to load munitions bound for Ireland. When the British government signed the Treaty with a section of the national movement prepared to sell out the interests of the Irish masses, and partitioned Ireland, it received the wholehearted support of the British labour movement. Only the small British Communist Party took a principled stand opposing the Treaty and supporting the revolutionary national wing of the IRA in the civil war.

At every stage in this period the British labour movement refused to 'make common cause' with the Irish. As a result the British working class found itself still dominated by the same opportunist leaders who betrayed its struggles before and after the Imperialist War and who were to betray its struggles right up to the defeat of the General Strike in 1926. Marx and Engels were right. By refusing to make 'common cause' with the Irish the British working class accomplished nothing.

From the ending of the Irish civil war (1923) until the late 1960s the social and political conditions did not exist to unite a mass movement behind a military and political campaign to destroy the loyalist statelet and unite Ireland. In the late 1960s, however, what began as a struggle of the nationalist minority in the occupied Six Counties of Ireland for basic democratic rights, was soon turned into a revolutionary war directed at British imperialism. In that period it was conclusively demonstrated in practice that the loyalist statelet was unreformable. Basic democratic rights for the nationalist population could only be achieved by ending partition and driving British imperialism out of Ireland. The 1970s saw the rise of the Provisional IRA as a revolutionary army with mass support amongst the nationalist minority in the Six Counties of Ireland. Again the direct revolutionary challenge to British imperialism was coming from Ireland.

Throughout the 14 years duration of this latest phase of the Irish national liberation struggle, the British Labour Party backed by the official trade union movement has played a direct role in oppressing and terrorising the nationalist minority in the Six Counties of Ireland. In 1969 the British Labour government sent troops into the Six Counties of Ireland to support loyalist supremacy, the basis of British imperialism's rule in Ireland. In 1974 a Labour government introduced the racist, anti-Irish Prevention of Terrorism Act designed to provide a legal cover for the systematic harassment of the Irish community in Britain in general, and for all, in particular, who were prepared to fight for a united Ireland. Finally, nothing has exposed the moral and political bankruptcy of the British Labour and trade union movement more sharply than its collaboration with the regime of terror and torture administered by the British Labour government in the Six Counties of Ireland from 1976–1979. It is of little surprise that the British labour movement not only remained passive and silent but actually collaborated with the British government in the slow and brutal murder of 10 Irish political prisoners on hunger strike during 1981. Far from making 'common cause' with the Irish people in their struggle for freedom, the British Labour Party and official trade union movement has become the zealous servant of their oppressor, British imperialism.

A working class movement from an oppressor nation which refuses to support an oppressed people fighting for the democratic right to self-determination will not be able to defend itself. It is, therefore, not surprising, that faced with the most reactionary Tory government since the war, faced with massive unemployment and growing attacks on living standards the British Labour and official trade union movement has done next to nothing to defend the working class. By refusing to make 'common cause' with the Irish the British working class has strengthened the hold of opportunist forces over itself. The struggle for socialism in Britain has been dramatically set back.

Imperialism will only be destroyed and opportunism defeated by the alliance of the British working class with the revolutionary national movement in Ireland. There can be little doubt today that, once again, the revolutionary challenge to British imperialism comes from Ireland. The ruling class understands this very well. As T E Utley of the *Daily Telegraph* said in 1976:

'... British security is hardly compatible with the existence of a Cuba a few miles from her Western shores.'[6]

And John Biggs-Davidson, Tory MP, backs him up:

'... if we lose in Belfast, we may have to fight in Brixton and Birmingham.'[7]

Ireland is the key to the British revolution.

BRITISH MIDDLE CLASS SOCIALISM AND THE IRISH REVOLUTION

The British Labour Party gives organised political expression to the interests of the upper ranks of the working class – the labour aristocracy. Its standpoint is bourgeois socialism. The Labour Party has always been a zealous defender of British imperialism's interests in Ireland and, when in power, has directed the oppression of the Irish people. No significant section of the Labour Party has or could take up a consistent fight against British imperialism's policies in Ireland without breaking with the Labour Party. This has however not stopped all the major organisations of the British middle class socialist left active on the Irish question from trying to find some section of the imperialist Labour Party prepared to take a 'progressive' standpoint on Ireland.

Politically the organisations of the British left have vacillated between the communist and bourgeois socialist standpoint on Ireland so reflecting their class position in society. As the crisis in Ireland has deepened, and especially in periods when the revolutionary challenge to British imperialism has intensified, more and more of these organisations, in the absence of a strong anti-imperialist current, have adopted a bourgeois socialist standpoint.

When confronted with an IRA bombing campaign in Britain in the late 1930s the Communist Party of Great Britain started to move away from its earlier principled, communist position on the Irish national liberation struggle. While supporting the 'just aims' of the IRA, the CPGB attacked its 'methods of struggle' particularly the armed struggle and the bombing campaigns in Britain. This position was transitional to its openly reactionary standpoint today. As soon as the latest phase of the war began, the CPGB entered the bourgeois socialist camp.

In the 1968 edition of its programme the *British Road to Socialism* the CPGB stated clearly and unequivocally:

'The enforced partition of Ireland should be ended and British troops withdrawn from Northern Ireland, leaving the Irish people free to realise their united republic'.

On the very day the British troops were sent into Derry on 14 August 1969 the Political Committee of the CPGB issued a statement which said:

'Any basic constitutional changes are questions of a *longer-term* nature which can only be settled by consulting with the people of Ireland. The immediate question is that of civil rights and democratic rights.' (*our emphasis*)

For the CPGB 1969 was the year when the fundamental democratic right to self-determination suddenly became a 'basic constitutional change' of a 'longer-term nature'. British imperialism was called upon to reform the loyalist state – to introduce a programme of democratic rights (a Bill of Rights), to end repression and discrimination and give financial and economic aid to provide jobs, housing and industrial development in Northern Ireland. Only after this programme had been carried out would it be possible to 'overcome sectarian divisions' and withdraw British troops from Ireland allowing the Irish people to rule the whole of their country – a process to be brought about, it seems, by consent.[8]

This is 'socialist colonial policy' with a vengeance – the plea for a 'colonial policy, which under a socialist regime [read 'left' Labour government], may have a civilising effect'. But who is to guarantee this 'civilising effect'. It appears that this is to be left in the hands of the British army guided by the British labour movement:

'And when the violence does come, the British Labour movement must be prepared to use every ounce of its strength to force the army command to use its military power in defence of democracy'.[9]

British imperialism which created and sustained a sectarian loyalist police state in the Six Counties of Ireland to preserve British rule in Ireland as a whole was now to destroy it. The guarantor for this was to be a British labour movement which had consistently betrayed the Irish people's struggle for freedom over the last hundred years. The CPGB has used this middle class idealist fantasy to justify its reactionary standpoint over the last 14 years.

There are none so blind as those who will not see. In 1977 the activities of loyalist paramilitary organisations had declined, as is always the case in a period of growing repression by the British army and RUC. There had also been action taken by the RUC and British army to end the Loyalist Strike in May 1977. The CPGB put this all down to the English moderation of the new Chief Constable Kenneth Newman.

'Politically isolated by their crushing defeat at the hands of the organised trade union movement, the Unionist paramilitary groups have come under the RUC hammer in an unprecedented way during the Summer.

The new chief constable of the RUC, Kenneth Newman with his background in the English police not the RUC, has played a key part in moderating the tacit toleration of known Unionist gunmen by the RUC special branch.'[10]

At the time Kenneth Newman was in the process of organising and

administering the systematic torture of political prisoners during interrogation in police cells. For the CPGB a progressive side to British
imperialism has to be found come what may. It is little wonder that the
CPGB has never missed an opportunity to attack the national
liberation struggle led by the Provisional IRA, arguing that its 'campaign of violence' gives a cover for British repression.

In February 1976 the loyalist dominated Northern Ireland Committee of the ICTU launched the 'Better Life for All Campaign'. One of its
'democratic' demands was the right 'to advocate political change by
peaceful means', a clear attack on the national liberation struggle led
by the Provisional IRA. The CPGB has used this campaign ever since
in an attempt to block all support in the British trade union movement
for the national liberation struggle in Ireland. The 'Better Life for All
Campaign', needless to say, had no support in Britain or Ireland.
Nevertheless it has been used to cement an alliance of the official British trade union movement with the loyalist working class, under the
guise of trade union unity. The support the CPGB has given to that
alliance has significantly strengthened the hold of opportunist forces in
the British labour movement.

The other major organisations of the British left are a variety of
Trotskyist groups which, in common with Trotsky on the Irish revolution, have an abstract and idealist understanding of the national question. As the pressure resulting from the very real war of national liberation in Ireland has built up most of these groups have been driven
towards the bourgeois socialist camp.

The Militant Tendency in the imperialist Labour Party joined the
bourgeois socialist camp as soon as the troops were sent in on 14
August 1969. It not only supported the troops being sent in but regards
those who call for withdrawal of British troops from Ireland 'as attor-
neys of the Provos'.[11] It still believes that British imperialism wants to
wash its hands of Ireland completely, on the grounds that the border
has 'outlived its usefulness' for the British capitalist class. Thinking
that you can overcome the partition of Ireland and the division of the
Irish working class by ignoring it, Militant calls for an all-Ireland
Labour Party and a trade union defence force to defend all working
class areas, Catholic and Protestant, from sectarian attacks . . . All this
idealist drivel is designed to cover up its very *real* support for British
imperialism in Ireland.

Most of the other Trotskyist groups claim to be opposed to British
imperialism's presence in Ireland. All of them however consistently
attack the armed struggle of the IRA – terrified that the revolutionary

violence of the oppressed might create problems for their own so 'revolutionary' political work. *Socialist Worker* has argued that IRA methods are opposed to those of the socialist movement:

'While the IRA have bombed factories in Northern Ireland as part of their struggle, as part of ours we campaign for workers to take over those factories – a completely different approach.'[12]

In this the SWP only repeats the arguments of the 'English would-be liberators' of Ireland who limited their support for the Irish movement on the grounds that the Irish did not use the same methods as English workers. Over 100 years ago such arguments were adequately dealt with by supporters of Marx and Engels.

In July 1982 the SWP and WRP went so far as to argue that the IRA bombing campaign in Britain against military personnel in Central London distracted British workers from fighting back against Thatcher's reactionary policies. 'The front pages were cleared of unemployment figures . . . ' whined *Newsline*.[13] And *Socialist Worker* had the nerve to say:

'On the very day when the depths of the government's callousness, hypocrisy and incompetence were laid bare, Thatcher was presented with the perfect distraction'.[14]

Socialist Worker conveniently forgets that the Tory government's callousness, like the Labour government's before it, has been clear for a long time – in Ireland. Had not Thatcher's government, so recently, cruelly and brutally murdered ten hunger strikers? What more evidence should British workers want? No-one can seriously believe that IRA bombs have distracted British workers from fighting back. The fact is that so far there has simply been no fightback. And the reason is that the British labour movement, with leaders and organisations long corrupted through their support for British imperialist oppression of the Irish people, has proved incapable of fighting back. Far from cringing before backward and reactionary attitudes in the British labour movement, real socialists and communists would be arguing for British workers to 'make common cause' with the Irish liberation movement in fighting their common enemy: British imperialism.

Like the CPGB, many of the Trotskyist organisations believe that British imperialism can play a progressive role in Ireland. So the SWP, for a period of time, allowed the pressure of events to force it into the bourgeois socialist camp when it supported British troops going into Ireland in August 1969. The SWP has also consistently argued, in spite of all evidence and arguments to the contrary, that British imperialism has an economic interest in uniting Ireland. Chris Harman, a leading SWP 'theoretician', even went so far as to see progressive develop- ments in the Thatcher/Haughey December 1980 talks, just before the end of the first hunger strike:

> 'Today the much greater depth of the economic crisis means that at least a section of the ruling class is thinking that it can no longer afford either the war or the aid. It is looking to cutting its costs any- where it can, and would be as glad to rid itself of "the dreary steeples of Fermanagh and Tyrone" as the hospitals of South London. Hence the indications that the Tory government is looking once again at possible ways of disengaging itself'.[15]

What would this political babe-in-arms say after the Malvinas/Falk- lands war and, of course, the collapse of the Thatcher/Haughey talks? The British middle class left fundamentally will never be prepared to accept that British imperialism will only leave Ireland when driven out by the revolutionary force of the Irish masses.

This is further demonstrated by the attitude of the British left to the loyalist working class. *Socialist Worker*, in yet another article by Chris Harman on 'The rights and wrongs of the IRA' argues that support for the Provisionals to 'beat the British state' cannot be won unless the Provisionals move:

> '...from talking merely of national unity and independence to fighting about the issues that affect all workers, North or South, Catholic or Protestant, Irish or British – issues of unemployment, working conditions, welfare services.'[16]

That is, as Harman put it in the article cited earlier, they have to speak to the 'best Protestant workers' in a language they can understand. This doctrine which James Connolly described as 'almost screamingly funny in its absurdity' simply ignores the existence of national oppres- sion and the reality of British imperialism's presence in Ireland. The loyalist working class is hand in glove with British imperialism because it guarantees loyalist workers their privileged position in relation to nationalist workers. For the same reason the loyalist working class is an implacable enemy of Republicanism and a united Ireland. Unless British imperialism is driven out of Ireland the unity of Irish workers cannot be achieved.

The belief that the Irish working class can be united before British imperialism is defeated is designed to avoid facing this reality. The

Communist Party wants to unite the Irish working class from above by British imperialism reforming the loyalist statelet. The Militant grouping wants the agents of British imperialism, the Labour Party and the official trade union movement to do it from above by creating an all-Ireland Labour Party and a non-sectarian trade union defence force. And the SWP wants to do it from below by Republicans appealing to loyalist workers on economic issues. And they all do this to cover up for their own refusal to 'make common cause' with the Irish national liberation struggle led by the IRA against the common enemy British imperialism.

The British left have rejected out of hand the Marxist standpoint on Ireland. Harman in the *Socialist Review* article cited above actually states clearly that if Marx's position means 'that the Irish struggle is the detonator that will explode British society, it is probably wrong'. For him Marx's position 'was connected to the struggle to overcome racialist division within the British working class, with aroused Irish workers playing a vanguard role in the struggle of the class as a whole'. But this ignores the most significant component of the Marxist position still relevant today: that a revolutionary challenge to the British ruling class was taking place in Ireland, its weakest point. If British workers made 'common cause' with the Irish, the national liberation struggle in Ireland would be the 'detonator' which set off the British revolution – a revolution in which Irish and British workers would be united. If they refused, they would strengthen ruling class domination over themselves.

The SWP quite clearly holds to the position Marx and Engels had before 'deeper study' had forced them to reverse their position on Ireland, before Britain had revealed two major distinguishing features of imperialism (see above). For the SWP, and the rest of the Trotskyist left in Britain, a deeply ingrained imperialist 'superiority' allows them to believe that it will be the victory of the British working class which will make Ireland and other oppressed nations free. Nothing expresses this more clearly than the patently chauvinist statement made by the leader of the SWP, Tony Cliff in 1975 on the South African revolution:

'After the revolution in Britain, the BBC (perhaps renamed the Workers' Revolutionary Broadcasting Station) could carry out a very simple appeal to workers around the world: Take into your own hands former British capital. Black workers of South Africa! With your sweat and blood you created the gold mines. They are yours! Workers throughout the world – take!'[17]

The South African and Irish working class have, in reality, nothing they can learn from British workers. On the contrary it is British workers who have much to learn from them. The focal point of the world revolution shifted long ago from the working class in the imperialist nations. The British middle class socialist left have obviously still to come to terms with this.

The main vehicle for the British left's 'solidarity' work on the Irish question, if it has been carried out at all, has been the Troops Out Movement (TOM). From the very beginning TOM's activities have been directed to building an alliance with the left of the imperialist Labour Party, thus holding to the position that British imperialism can be made to play a progressive role in Ireland. For this reason TOM has never carried out or supported any political campaign in solidarity with the national liberation struggle led by the IRA. Nor has TOM called for the defeat of British imperialism in Ireland. In this it merely reflects the class position of the British left groups.

To sustain its alliance with a section of the imperialist Labour Party, TOM soon dropped the anti-imperialist demand Troops Out Now as a campaigning slogan. It refused to give political support to the 1978 anti-imperialist prisoner campaign led by the PAC and supported by Sinn Fein and the RCG, preferring to conduct an innocuous and ineffective International Tribunal on Britain's Presence in Ireland instead. By the end of the second hunger strike TOM was barely active. Faced with the fact that the so-called 'left' of the Labour Party simply refused to take any effective action on the 'five demands', TOM in alliance with the SWP/IMG took all the pressure off them by not campaigning at all. The hunger strike showed that the whole strategy of TOM had completely failed – the imperialist Labour Party could not be moved.

In Autumn 1982 a document was circulating in TOM. This document drew out the inevitable logic of TOM's position. In arguing for a 'British withdrawal movement' it stated:

'The question of withdrawal [of British troops] *now* is not a principle but a diversion . . .
. . . a supposedly principled pro-IRA movement is unnecessarily too advanced in its stance and impractical to build . . .
. . . campaigns for example on IRA prisoners in English jails are about the last topic any British withdrawal movement should concern itself with, as their plight is the most difficult and fruitless aspect to take up of the whole Irish question . . . '

There you have it. Something that has always been implicit was now made explicit. Any anti-imperialists still remaining in TOM will be forced to make a choice. Are you for the victory of the Irish liberation movement against British imperialism or are you more concerned to build an alliance with the imperialist Labour Party? Which side are you on?

DEMOCRATIC RIGHTS IN BRITAIN AND THE IRISH REVOLUTION

Precisely because the Irish question is at the heart of the British revolution those campaigning in Britain in solidarity with the Irish national liberation struggle have necessarily had to confront the forces of repression of the British imperialist state. After Bloody Sunday 1972 the largest demonstration on Ireland for many years, 20,000 strong, was batoned off the streets by the British police and the organisers were arrested. The Prevention of Terrorism Act 1974 has been used as a weapon to deter people, especially the Irish community in Britain, from politically campaigning in support of the Irish revolution. Political organisations have been consistently harassed and often prevented from selling their newspapers and conducting street meetings on the question of Ireland.

The Revolutionary Communist Group (RCG) has engaged in Irish solidarity work ever since its foundation in 1974. First through the TOM (1974–1976), then through its anti-imperialist bulletin *Hands Off Ireland!* (1976–1980), and most recently through its newspaper *Fight Racism! Fight Imperialism!* (1979 to date) and the Irish Solidarity Movement (founded 1983). Throughout this period the RCG and supporters have faced continual police and right-wing harassment aimed at disrupting street work in working class areas and censoring anti-imperialist activity on Ireland. Significantly this harassment has been most intense from the launching of the boycott campaign against the Labour Party during the May 1979 General Election. By Autumn 1982 over 60 arrests involving 85 charges had taken place. These figures relate to a small group of people engaged in legal political activity, and reflect, in miniature, the fact that in fighing to build a solidarity movement on Ireland it is necessary to defend the basic democratic rights essential to the working class as a whole – rights which are under ever increasing attack. The fact that 33 aquittals, against 26 convictions, in cases completed by Autumn 1982, have been won through organised political campaigning, demonstrates it is possible to gain victories which strengthen the movement in Britain.

The major instrument of intimidation and censorship against Irish people and those engaged in Irish solidarity work is, of course, the PTA. By the end of 1982, 5,500 had been arrested under this racist, anti-Irish legislation. The PTA was used against the Glasgow 2, the most serious instance out of the 21 arrests which had taken place in Scotland up to that time. The two were arrested selling *Fight Racism! Fight Imperialism!* – an issue containing an interview with an IRA Volunteer – outside Celtic football ground in Glasgow on 9 August 1980. They were charged under the PTA and remanded in prison for one week. A massive campaign drawing in support from many MPs, councillors and political organisations forced the Scottish authorities to drop the PTA charges, although the Glasgow 2 were eventually convicted on a fraudulent charge of breach of the peace. In Scotland too there were three bans on marches during the hunger strike as well as arrests. This bare summary of police harassment against a very small number of communists and anti-imperialists over a limited period, whilst not at all comparable to the terror directed against the Irish people, nor unique to the RCG and its supporters, does confirm that those in Britain determined to build a real Irish solidarity movement will play a central role in the defence of democratic rights for all workers in Britain.

FORCES OF REVOLUTION

It has been demonstrated time and again over the last 14 years that the national liberation struggle to free Ireland from British rule cannot be won if confined to the Six Counties alone. The neo-colonial state in the Twenty Six Counties is a fundamental barrier to a united Ireland and will have to be destroyed if British imperialism is to be driven out of Ireland. Finally the important obstacle of British working class support for British imperialism must be overcome if the Irish revolution is to open the way for the struggle for socialism in Ireland and Britain.

The last 14 years of the Irish war of national liberation has also exposed the forces of collaboration with British imperialism and pointed to the forces of revolution. This is true in the Six Counties and Twenty Six Counties, and in Britain as well as Ireland. Which are the forces of revolution?

British imperialism faces its most immediate political threat from the nationalist working class in the Six Counties led by its armed vanguard the IRA. For 14 years the IRA has kept at bay the British army, the most highly trained counter-insurgency force in the world. British imperialism can only retain its political domination of the Six Counties of Ireland by terror. It can offer no future to the nationalist working class. Poverty, unemployment and some of the worst housing in Europe is the legacy of British rule in Ireland. Under Britain's control, unemployment stands at over 20% in the Six Counties, far higher than any area in Britain. And given the sectarian character of this police state many nationalist areas suffer unemployment rates of over 50%. In some nationalist areas nearly all the young people have no job and no chance of getting one. The nationalist youth are the implacable enemies of British imperialism. They demonstrated their revolutionary spirit during the hunger strikes when night after night they took to the streets and fought the British army with stones and petrol bombs. They are the forces of revolution. They will follow the revolutionary lead of the IRA.

The Twenty Six Counties neo-colonial state is facing a political and economic crisis of unprecedented proportions. Having mortgaged itself to imperialism it can only pay back its debts by savagely attacking the Irish working class. One third of all industrial jobs are in imperialist firms attracted by massive profits subsidised out of heavy taxes on the working class. American imperialism boasts a profit rate of 33.7% in Ireland, its highest rate of return in the world, and twice the European average. The neo-colonial state has a staggering foreign debt of IR£4bn (1982), more than one-third of the Irish GNP, and twice as high per head of population as Poland's. With the official unemployment rate (1982) at 12.5% – the real figure is certainly much higher – inflation still in the region of 17%, and, according to official statistics, one quarter of the Irish population living in poverty, it is little wonder that the Twenty Six Counties of Ireland staggers from one political crisis to another.

While unemployment is rising everywhere it is chronic amongst the youth. During the hunger strike sections of the youth in Dublin, enraged by the inactivity of the Twenty Six Counties government after the murder of Bobby Sands by British imperialism, took to the streets and fought the Gardai, in the manner of their comrades in the Six Counties, with stones and petrol bombs. With the hunger strike and the economic crisis increasingly exposing the bankruptcy of the neo-colonialist regime, its governments and its agents in the Irish working class such as the ICTU, the opportunity now exists for winning the masses of Irish workers led by the youth to the anti-imperialist struggle.

It is no coincidence that in 1981 as the revolutionary youth of Derry, Belfast and Dublin fought pitched battles on the streets against the

British imperialist forces and their loyalist and 'Free State' puppets, so the unemployed youth – black and white – rose up throughout Britain against the British imperialist state.

British imperialism, itself in deep crisis, has nothing but oppression and poverty to offer these youths. They have no illusions in the institutions of British imperialist democracy. They, like the Irish, have been forced to take the revolutionary and insurrectionary road. This reality was recognised by the ruling class media when the first uprising – in St Pauls, Bristol – took place in 1980:

'It was like a scene from Belfast without the bombs.'[18]

'These are things that we have regarded with horror when they happen in Ulster. We never dreamed that in the England of 1980 we could have "no-go" areas like those of Londonderry. It must never, never happen again.'[19]

The uprisings conclusively demonstrated that forces exist in Britain which are capable of the dedication and sacrifice that is necessary in the struggle against British imperialism here at home. These are forces which will risk the arrest, imprisonment and immense hardship which comes through participation in this fight. These are forces which will, by following the courageous lead set by Irish revolutionaries, give a lead to the mass of the British working class.

Only by following the example of these revolutionary forces and making 'common cause' with the revolutionary national struggle to free Ireland from British rule, can the British working class undermine and destroy the common enemy; British imperialism. Ireland is the key to the British revolution. Only by taking this stand will the British working class make a reality of the revolutionary slogan of the Communist International.

Workers of all countries and oppressed peoples unite!
Victory to the Irish People!

NOTES

1   *Daily Mirror* 14 August 1978.
2   *Republican News* 19 August 1978.
3   Bell G, *Troublesome Business op cit* p. 138.
4   Lenin, *On Britain op cit* p. 523. Also *LCW*, Vol 31 p. 231.
5   Engels F, *MEOI op cit* p. 460.

6   Utley T E, *op cit* p. 134.
7   Cited in Troops Out Movement, *No British Solution op cit* p. 22.
8   These quotes are cited in Marlowe T and Whittaker P, 'The CPGB and Ireland' in *Revolutionary Communist* No 7 November 1977.
9   *Morning Star* 24 October 1974, cited in Revolutionary Communist Group, *Ireland: British Labour and British Imperialism* London 1976 (pamphlet) p. 22.
10   *Morning Star* 23 September 1977.
11   *Bulletin* November/December 1979.
12   Chris Harman, *Socialist Worker* 14 August 1982.
13   *Newsline* 21 July 1982.
14   *Socialist Worker* 24 July 1982.
15   *Socialist Review* January/February 1981.
16   *Socialist Worker* 14 August 1982.
17   Cliff T, *The Crisis, Social Contract or Socialism* London 1975 pp. 191–2.
18   *Daily Mail* 3 April 1980.
19   *Sun* 5 April 1980. The major series of uprisings occurred in 1981.

POSTSCRIPT

Political developments both in Ireland and in Britain since the original articles were completed (November 1982) have confirmed all the main political points made.

IRELAND: THE KEY TO THE BRITISH REVOLUTION

As argued above, a decisive political factor in the defeat of the 1981 hunger strike was the fact that no political pressure was placed on the Thatcher government in Britain. This failure on the part of the working class movement in Britain considerably strengthened the most reactionary Tory government since the Second World War. The most dramatic proof of this was the landslide victory of this government in the 1983 General Election. The events of this period provide further evidence that a working class movement which fails to 'make common cause' with the Irish people in their struggle for freedom cannot defend itself against the British imperialist state. Indeed, the British ruling class, almost unopposed, has been able to use its experience in Ireland to prepare to meet any resistance here in Britain.

There has been no significant opposition to the appointment in July 1982 of General Frank Kitson as head of the UK Land Forces, or, three months later in October 1982 to the installation of Kenneth Newman as head of the Metropolitan Police. These two men represent the accumulated experience of the British ruling class in oppressing national liberation movements, particularly in Ireland where they both served during crucial periods – Kitson 1970–72, Newman 1973–79. These appointments make it clear how the British ruling class intends to deal with the inevitable resistance to its rule in Britain. It is important to examine this development in some detail.

Kitson is an 'expert' in counter-insurgency, that is, putting down revolutionary democratic struggles against imperialism. His book *Low Intensity Operations* is designed to gather together this experience and is easily adapted for use in a crisis-ridden Britain. Kitson argues that it is necessary ruthlessly to stamp out 'subversion' that is, revolutionary opposition, whilst simultaneously strengthening 'moderate' elements who support the state. Intelligence gathering operations are an essential feature of this process to target those capable of organising serious opposition.

His method of gathering intelligence relies heavily on a 'large number of low grade sources' – small pieces of information acquired by the police and army – fed into computers to build up a total picture of the community and its inhabitants.

At the same time 'psychological operations' are used in an attempt to isolate the opposition from the people. These include propaganda against the opposition cause, use of the press and media to put over the government side, government schemes to win 'moderate' opinion and support, 'dirty tricks' such as fake leaflets and eventually provocateurs and agents who masquerade as oppositionists to discredit the cause, and finally, if necessary, the assassination of leading oppositionists. The aim in Kitson's words is:

'. . . to discover and neutralise the genuine subversive element . . .'

and:

'. . . to associate as many prominent members of the population, especially those who may have been engaged in non-violent action, with the government.'[1]

'Intelligence gathering' and 'psychological operations', Kitson emphasised, had to take place before the emergence of subversion or an offensive phase of conflict had begun. This is the significance behind Newman's and Kitson's appointments in Britain. The ruling class is preparing for the major unrest and popular rebellion which is inevitable even here in Britain. They are acutely conscious of the depth and severity of the imperialist crisis and know it can only be solved by imposing intolerable levels of unemployment, poverty, homelessness and repression on the British working class. Already Newman's reorganisation of the Metropolitan Police as outlined in the 1982 Metropolitan Police Report (June 1983) shows him putting phase I of Kitson's overall strategy into operation. The strategy developed in Ireland is being put into practice in Britain with no opposition from the British working class.

Newman's proposed reorganisation of the Metropolitan Police to make it an effective intelligence gathering force is outlined in the 1982 Report. Newman's plan is to centralise and computerise information gathered from a variety of 'low grade sources'. Its emphasis is on information obtained in local police districts through police/community 'consultative committees', 'neighbourhood watch schemes', 'inter-agency co-operation' which involves liaison with social security, social services, schools etc, and increased police foot patrols in priority areas.

Newman calls this making the police 'responsive to local needs'. What he actually means is a centralised and directed police response to community-based intelligence and consultation with middle class 'moderates' for the purpose of isolating and attacking those liable to organise opposition or create problems for the police.

Intelligence and surveillance units will be set up in each of London's four police districts and will undoubtedly operate in black and poorer areas. All the information gathered is to be stored on massive computer systems to enable the police to target opposition and deal with it before it takes root in the working class. Newman carried out a strikingly similar reorganisation of the RUC in Ireland to make it an effective intelligence gathering force directed at Republicans.

Newman is also an expert at psychological operations, including manipulation of the media. In the 1982 Metropolitan Police Report Kenneth Newman attacked political activists, who had exposed the repressive role of the police, as 'dedicated denigrators', and 'a threat to public order'. At a press conference he went further and associated political activists with drug dealing and other criminal activity – he particularly mentioned the Colin Roach campaign. In this way Newman attempts to criminalise political opposition to the police. This is the first step to turning any effective political opposition to the British state into a criminal act. In Ireland Newman supervised the 'criminalisation' strategy, he denounced all exposure of RUC torture as IRA propaganda, and continually attacked the IRA as 'gangsters, mafia etc'.

'Psychological operations' at this stage also consist of building links with 'moderate' community figures and projecting a favourable image of the police through police-organised sports events, visits to schools and youth clubs. Newman's emphasis on community relations is clearly designed to control rebellious forces especially black youth. Newman unsuccessfully attempted to do this in Ireland through the RUC with 'blue lamp' discos etc.

Should all this fail and disorder break out the Metropolitan Police have been well prepared for offensive operations. The Instant Response Units, riot control police dressed for combat and armed with shields and truncheons, have already been used swiftly and violently to crush any street resistance. In 1982 there were '21,775 single day attendances' on riot shield training courses and '14,398 single day attendances' on courses for Instant Response Units. The number of police authorised to use guns is now 4,476. It is certain that stocks of CS gas and plastic bullets are available should they be needed. And should all this fail to contain opposition – behind Newman stands his brother-in-torture and repression General Kitson with his UK Land Forces.

The case of Newman/Kitson dramatically confirms the relationship between the Irish people's struggle for national liberation and the struggle to defend the working class here in Britain. The consequences of failing to make 'common cause' with the Irish people are plain to see. There are other obvious examples of this.

The Jellicoe Report on the Prevention of Terrorism Act 1983, which the government is implementing, aimed at strengthening and extending the PTA. Jellicoe recommended the extension of the PTA to 'suspected international terrorists of any group, cause or nationality'; that the word 'temporary' be dropped and the PTA be enacted for five years and then replaced by a new act; that loyalist paramilitary groups should not be proscribed. His report stressed the true role of the PTA as an instrument of political censorship and intelligence gathering. The extension of the PTA to so-called 'international terrorists' will allow the police in Britain free rein to harass and intimidate supporters of national liberation movements, especially those challenging the interests of British imperialism. The recommendation to drop the word 'temporary' and replace annual renewal by a period of five years is exactly the same process as took place with the Special Powers Act in the Six Counties. That Act was introduced as a temporary measure in 1922, renewed annually until 1928, when it was renewed for five years, then in 1933 it was made permanent. The PTA road has been travelled before. In December 1982 Sinn Fein elected representatives, Gerry Adams, Danny Morrison, and Martin McGuinness were banned under the PTA from entering Britain in a blatant act of political censorship.

Shoot-to-kill came to London on 14 January 1983 when the police ambushed, shot and very nearly killed Stephen Waldorf. He was shot several times without warning by an armed squad of policemen who claimed to be hunting David Martin. While David Martin got 25 years for grievous bodily harm the police officers involved in the Waldorf incident were acquitted. The *Sunday Times* revealed the use of hooding by the Birmingham serious crimes squad to extract confessions. According to the report four men said they suffered hooding.[2] Hooding is the technique used in Ireland in August 1971 during the internment operations and involves putting a plastic bag over the head of suspects and tightening it so that they cannot see or breathe. Britain was condemned in the European Court for this technique and gave a pledge that it would not be used again.

Finally, the Police and Criminal Evidence Bill, which is going through Parliament, proposes extended police powers including powers to: detain people for 96 hours; set up road blocks; fingerprint and photograph detainees; conduct forcible intimate body searches; stop and search people on 'reasonable suspicion'; and make it easier for statements extorted by police pressure to be accepted in court. This Bill, alongside a strengthened PTA, will give the British police the same kind of sweeping powers as the RUC in the Six Counties of Ireland. Little wonder that the British state has plans to build fourteen more prisons over the next period to house an extra 5,000 prisoners.

None of these developments have met any significant resistance from the organised Labour and trade union movement in Britain. Successes against this growing repression in Britain have in fact so far only come from the impact of the Irish people's struggle. The election of Gerry Adams as MP for West Belfast forced the British government to lift the PTA ban on him. It was fear of mass resistance in Ireland which prevented the ruling class from reintroducing judicial murder through hanging in July 1983.

BRITISH IMPERIALIST REPRESSION

Today the repression of the nationalist minority continues unabated in the Six Counties. Daily the fact that British imperialism cannot play a progressive role in Ireland is borne out by its actions. A major new weapon has been added to the armoury of repression being used in the British government's war against the Irish people – the informer. There were, in November 1983, over 350 people on remand and 55 had been convicted on the uncorroborated 'evidence' of informers. This figure compares with the internment operations of August 1971 – it is a major escalation of judicial terror against the nationalist people of the Six Counties.

The use of informers is not new. What is new is the scale of the operation. This massive use of informers reflects the successful campaign against torture in Castlereagh. The Diplock non-jury courts rely on confessions for convicting and imprisoning nationalists. However, the international exposure of the use of torture and the unbroken resistance of the nationalist people has forced the imperialists to turn to the 'informer' tactic whereby a single 'confession' can be used to imprison scores of nationalists. Raymond Gilmour's 'evidence', for example, led to 71 arrests; 38 nationalists were arrested on Christopher Black's 'evidence' – 22 were given prison sentences totalling over 4,000 years in all in a trial costing over £1m; 23 were arrested on Jackie Goodman's 'evidence', and 16 on that of informer Robert Lean. The efficiency of the tactic is clear: the maximum number of arrests on the minimum possible evidence. In non-jury Diplock courts there is no fear of the uncorroborated claims of touts being rejected. The real character of the Diplock court system stands exposed: judicial internment. That such methods as kidnap, brainwashing and bribery are necessary to maintain British imperialism's rule in Ireland is yet further evidence that this rule can only be maintained by terror and corruption. There have been a number of important victories against the informer system. By November 1983 six informers had retracted their evidence. The most dramatic case was that of Robert Lean who escaped from RUC 'protective' custody and retracted his evidence at a Sinn Fein press conference. Eleven people were subsequently released.

Alongside the use of the informer there has been a revival of shoot-to-kill operations. The first round of these operations took place from November 1982 to February 1983, that is to say, they started after the Sinn Fein success in the Assembly elections of October 1982. The latest round of shoot-to-kill operations involves murders by all the British forces of repression – the RUC, UDR and British army. And again the use of shoot-to-kill follows the Sinn Fein electoral success in the June 1983 General Election. Since November 1982 at least 15 nationalists have been murdered in such operations. These deliberate murders are the response of the British government to the legal, constitutional and peaceful Sinn Fein electoral campaign. Once again British imperialism has replied to peaceful protest with bloodshed and terror.

The repression in the prisons is continuing, particularly in Armagh women's prison. Since the reintroduction of strip-searching on 9 November 1982 the Armagh women have been subjected to continual brutality and harassment. The women are constantly being given punishments for trivial offences but the most serious repression consists of brutal and degrading strip-searches. The women POWs have resisted strip-searching which is a form of torture. For this they have been viciously attacked. In January 1983 three of the women,

Philomena Lyttle, Catherine Moore and Lorraine Nichol were beaten to the ground and forcibly stripped.

Finally, it is clear that British soldiers will continue to get away with murder in the Six Counties. The inquest into the murder of Stephen McConomy held in 1983, established beyond doubt that when he was shot dead with a plastic bullet there was no 'riot' or any other disturbance going on. Yet the soldier who killed him has not been charged. Stephen McConomy was eleven years old in April 1982 when he was murdered. On 8 September 1983, two soldiers were acquitted of the murder of Eamonn Bradley whom they had shot in Derry on 25 August 1982.

FREE STATE REACTION

The reactionary character of the Irish 'Free State' and the bourgeois parties within it has been demonstrated again and again. In the 'Free State' elections in November 1982, the Irish Labour Party treacherously abandoned its pre-election promises, formed a coalition government with the ex-blueshirts Fine Gael and thus created the first stable government for 18 months. This stability has allowed continuous repression against the Republican Movement and an all-out attack on the Irish working class.

One of the first acts in the first Cabinet meeting of the coalition government was the banning of the INLA. This attack on the Republican Movement was quickly followed up by an emergency budget which raised the price of petrol, tobacco and drink, hitting hardest at the working class and the poor. In February 1983 Republican POWs in Portlaoise gaol were assaulted during strip-searching. One of the prisoners, Angelo Fusco, was given two months solitary confinement for being assaulted. In the very same month the Irish Labour Party-supported coalition government started imprisoning Rank Flour mill workers who were on strike. The Rank workers had to fight not only their Fine Gael/Irish Labour Party gaolers but also the ITGWU which had withdrawn official recognition from the dispute. Supporters of the workers picketed the prison, the mill and Liberty Hall, headquarters of the ITGWU, underlining the alliance of reactionary 'Free State' forces ranged against them. And finally still in February the coalition government introduced its second budget in two months of further tax and price increases alongside cuts in public expenditure and public sector employment.

In April and May 1983 the 'Free State' Gardai carried out a series of raids, arrests and detentions of Sinn Fein members. On 1 May IRSP member Nicky Kelly, framed for the Sallins train robbery, was forced to go on hunger strike in an effort to gain his release. He ended his hunger strike on 7 June after 38 days and after a nationwide campaign for his release. He still remains in prison for a robbery he had nothing to do with.

The collaborationist forces north and south who betrayed the hunger strikers have set up their New Ireland Forum. Fianna Fail, Fine Gael, Irish Labour Party, and SDLP are involved in this 'fools forum' as a desperate attempt to shore up the 'partitionist' bloc against the military and political successes of the Republican Movement. The 'Free State' ruling class knows that it will inevitably face rising opposition to poverty, unemployment and homelessness. They know that the dispossessed and the poor of the 'Free State' will increasingly turn to the revolutionary national struggle to defeat British imperialism and its neo-colonial agents in the Twenty Six Counties. They, therefore, are forced to attack the Republican Movement before mass resistance breaks out all over the 'Free State'.

The neo-colonial status of the 'Free State' and its consequent poverty for the masses is undeniable. In July 1983 the official unemployment figure reached 192,000 which is more than the total number of people employed in manufacturing industry. For the youth the position is even worse. One in three under 25s are unemployed. More poverty is on the way as the Irish ruling class seeks to pay its staggering debt to the imperialist banks at the expense of the Irish masses. Its overall debt of IR£5bn (Autumn 1983) is equal to 40% of GNP and equivalent to one year's total export sales. This crushing burden of debt is higher per person than that of Mexico or Poland standing at IR£1,500.

REVOLUTIONARY FORCES IN IRELAND

The Republican Movement has continued the military and political resistance to British imperialist rule scoring important successes on both fronts. In January 1983 the IRA struck back against both the shoot-to-kill operations and the corrupt British-controlled judiciary. In Rostrevor the IRA executed two members of the RUC Divisional Mobile Support Unit believed responsible for RUC shoot-to-kill operations. In the same month the IRA executed Judge William Doyle. In the run up to the June General Election the IRA mounted a military offensive of commercial bombings and attacks on the security forces.

At least four members of the security forces were killed and 10 injured. The most spectacular attack took place on 17 May when the IRA destroyed the hated Andersonstown RUC barracks. On polling day itself INLA bombed the British army/RUC Stewartstown Road barracks. And on 13 July 1983 – the day of the hanging debate – the IRA executed four UDR soldiers. This was the worst blow suffered by the UDR since its formation in 1970.

On 25 September 1983 the complacent propaganda of the British imperialists was shattered. 38 Republican prisoners broke out of the H-Block concentration camp in the most daring escape in recent history. The news was greeted with jubilation in the nationalist areas and amongst anti-imperialists everywhere. The propaganda of the imperialists was in one mighty blow turned against them. The supposedly 'demoralised' and 'panic-stricken' IRA sent waves of demoralisation and panic through the British ruling class and its agents in the Six Counties, who turned on each other to find a scapegoat to get them off the hook. The now liberated prisoners (19 in all) include some of those framed and gaoled on the evidence of informers and also Gerard Kelly who was gaoled in Britain and was one of four POWs repatriated to Ireland following the long and courageous hunger strike in 1973.

On the political front the gains made in the Assembly elections of October 1982 were carried forward with the victory in March 1983 of Seamus Kerr in the Carrickmore local council by-election and most dramatically of all in the General Election of June 1983. Despite systematic harassment of Sinn Fein candidates and election workers and a propaganda onslaught from the British ruling class and neo-colonial agents north and south, Gerry Adams won West Belfast destroying arch-traitor Gerry Fitt and the collaborationist SDLP. Sinn Fein won 40% of the nationalist vote. Over 100,000 nationalists voted for the revolutionary national struggle to free Ireland from British rule.

Sinn Fein has destroyed the SDLP's lying claim to represent the nationalist people. The *Irish Times* pointed to the contrast between Sinn Fein and the SDLP saying it was:

' . . . youth versus middle age, working class versus middle class and enthusiasm versus weariness'.[3]

The unprecedented electoral successes of Sinn Fein have inevitably generated pressure from bourgeois nationalist and opportunist forces aimed at undermining the revolutionary nationalist strategy of the Republican Movement. This pressure takes many forms: the alleged 'conflict' between military and political activity; the need for 'purely political' campaigning in the Twenty Six Counties; and the need to abandon abstentionism in relation to imperialist imposed parliaments – the Assembly in the North, Leinster House in the South and the Westminster Parliament. This pressure has revealed differences of view on the way forward within the Republican Movement.

At the November 1983 Sinn Fein Ard Fheis a motion affirming the ban on discussion of abstentionism in the Sinn Fein constitution was defeated by 180 votes to 140. This abstentionist position, which was a central issue in the split between the revolutionary nationalists who formed the Provisionals and the revisionist Official Republicans in 1969/70, is now no longer seen as beyond question. At the same Ard Fheis it was agreed to allow any successful Sinn Fein candidates in the EEC elections to take their seats 'under the guidance of the Ard Comhairle' (leading committee of Sinn Fein).[4]

The way forward in the Twenty Six Counties has also become a crucial and immediate issue for the Republican Movement. The social base of opportunism in the Twenty Six Counties is very powerful as was shown in the exposure of the collaborationist 'Free State' forces – the 'partitionist bloc' – during the hunger strike campaign. The continued strength and influence of these forces creates a powerful pressure for 'purely political' campaigning by the Republican Movement. The tension created by this was seen during the hunger strike campaign in the attitude adopted towards the militant street fighting of the Dublin youth by the National H-Block/Armagh Committee.[5]

At the same time the rapidly accelerating economic and social crisis in the Twenty Six Counties, throwing more and more Irish workers into poverty and unemployment, is once again creating the mass social base for the revolutionary national struggle. These forces are inevitably brought into conflict with the increasingly repressive 'Free State' regime. The slogan of the Dublin youth during the hunger strike campaign – 'Gardai–RUC' – showed that the connection between the neo-colonial 'Free State' and its British imperialist masters is already being drawn. Reality daily demonstrates that the neo-colonial regime cannot be reformed. It has to be destroyed if Ireland is to be free. It is in this context that the issues of abstentionism, the question of the armed struggle in the Twenty Six Counties and the way forward for the Republican Movement are being raised.

Following the assassination of the Ulster Unionist Assembly member Edgar Graham by the IRA in November 1983 James Prior, Tory Secretary of State for Northern Ireland, declared that he was seriously considering breaking off all contact with Sinn Fein. He demanded that

Sinn Fein choose between the ballot box and the gun. In doing this he is attempting to separate the electoral campaign of Sinn Fein from the revolutionary national struggle and draw a section of the Republican Movement into constitutional politics. He is attempting to counterpose a legal 'constitutional' Sinn Fein to the illegal 'unconstitutional' IRA. The British imperialist ruling class, masterly in such manoeuvring, is attempting to use the very success of Sinn Fein's electoral work to divide the Republican Movement.[6] In the face of revolutionary nationalist resistance these manoeuvres, as in the past, will undoubtedly fail.

In an important interview in *Magill* magazine (July 1983) the IRA summarised the revolutionary nationalist strategy to free Ireland from British imperialist rule.

One point was made clear: the IRA will not abandon or restrict the armed struggle in favour of electoral campaigning. Recognising the propaganda value of Sinn Fein's electoral successes, the IRA said:

'For years the political establishment claimed that the IRA had very little support. The election results have answered that conclusively . . . '

And went on:

' . . . They will not lead to any real change in the strategy or tactics of the IRA . . . The military struggle will not slow down to relate to Sinn Fein's political activity. If anything . . . the war is likely to be stepped up.'

The IRA also made clear what their strategy is:

'Our strategy has been, by military and political action, to frustrate the British aim of making the six counties governable through local power-sharing-type institutions. So far we have succeeded in this and the Brits can only govern in a direct colonial way, using 30,000 armed men.'

The last 14 years confirms this success: from the abolition of Stormont to the impotence of the Assembly British imperialism has been unable to secure any bogus local arrangement to disguise its colonial rule. And British parliamentary elections have been transformed from a means of legitimising British rule into a means of legitimising the revolutionary national struggle. This has been achieved by a combination of the armed struggle and successful use of abstentionist candidates. British imperialism has been prevented from disguising the fact that it can only rule by force – and that it can only be driven out by force.

However, as the IRA pointed out in line with the position laid down by veteran Republican Jimmy Drumm at Bodenstown 1977, the struggle cannot be confined to the Six Counties. The 'colonial rulers' of the Irish type – the 'Free State' ruling class – must also be destroyed if Ireland is to be free. As the IRA said:

'We recognise that even if the entire nationalist population in the six counties voted for Sinn Fein, that wouldn't be enough. There must be an increase in political activity in the 26 counties so that they also demand that the Brits get out. Even that wouldn't be enough, because the only thing colonial rulers will listen to is force . . .'[7]

As argued above, the eruption of Dublin youth in the hunger strike campaign and the massive poverty imposed on the Irish working class by the 'Free State' regime shows that the material exists for an escalation of the revolutionary national struggle in the Twenty Six Counties. Such an escalation, exposing the 'legitimacy' of the 'Free State' as it has already exposed the 'legitimacy' of British rule in the North, would meet 'Free State' repression every bit as fierce as British repression in the Six Counties. The 'Free State's' use of non-jury courts, censorship, torture, rigged laws and imprisonment against Republicans puts this fact beyond doubt.

REVOLUTIONARY FORCES IN BRITAIN

The period since November 1982 has produced even more evidence of the bankruptcy of the organised Labour and trade union movement in Britain. The Prevention of Terrorism Act came up for renewal in March 1983. Despite official Labour Party policy of opposition to the PTA only 129 MPs voted against the act and not all of these were Labour MPs. The parliamentary Labour Party refused to put a three line whip on the vote, thus allowing the likes of Concannon, Rees, Mason, Callaghan and others to abstain. The real character of Labour's opposition was exposed by Kevin MacNamara who said:

'Ordinary decent coppers using ordinary decent police methods apprehended those responsible for the Birmingham outrages.'[8]

The ordinary decent police methods referred to were in fact vicious beatings, threats against the families of those arrested and the framing of the Birmingham 6. It is no surprise that these same people did nothing to oppose the PTA ban on the Sinn Fein delegation of December 1982 or protest against the Home Office refusal to allow Gerry Adams to visit Irish POWs in English gaols.

When Ken Livingstone in August 1983 compared Britain's treatment of Ireland with Hitler's treatment of the Jews he was subjected to the usual barrage of ignorant abuse in the British press and, predictably, from his Labour Party 'colleagues'. All the contenders for the leadership of the Labour Party rushed to disown him. Peter Shore said that Livingstone's remarks 'justified all the murders and maimings of the IRA'; Neil Kinnock called him 'eccentric', and said Livingstone's remarks were a 'misreading of both Irish history and the history of Nazism'; Roy Hattersley called Livingstone 'absurd and offensive'; Eric Heffer said Livingstone's remarks were 'unfortunate'.[9] The speed with which these 'rivals' rushed to disown Livingstone's statement was eloquent testimony to their united commitment to continued British oppression in Ireland.

No significant section of the organised Labour and trade union movement has done anything to oppose the use of 'informers' or the 'shoot-to-kill' operations. In the face of this the significance of the trend in the Labour Party represented by Ken Livingstone must not be exaggerated. How weak this trend is in reality, and how little influence it has, was shown in two examples. When the Sinn Fein delegation visited the House of Commons after the June 1983 election only six Labour MPs had sufficient courage to meet them. The September 1983 'fact-finding' delegation to the Six Counties led by Clive Soley publicly and shamefully grovelled and apologised for meeting the Sinn Fein representatives.[10] Little wonder that such a labour movement cannot and will not defend the working class in Britain. The 8 months long strike of low-paid workers in the NHS was defeated in December 1982 by the treachery of a trade union leadership which has always opposed the Irish people's struggle for freedom. The Tory government as a result has now announced plans for thousands of redundancies which will devastate hospitals and health care throughout the country. And yet it is now that the TUC leadership under the guise of facing the 'political reality' has decided to discuss with this viciously anti-working class Tory government. Nothing but reaction can be expected from such a labour movement on the Irish question.

The struggles which have taken place against growing repression in Britain have come from outside the organised Labour and trade union movement. A determined and courageous struggle is now taking place inside the prisons against the brutal and inhuman prison system here in Britain. In Albany prison in May 1983 prisoners rose up against intolerable conditions and arbitrary punishments. The protest was brought to public attention by the courageous act of 10 prisoners who broke out on to the roof. Four of them were Irish POWs, one was a Palestinian freedom fighter and the others were ordinary long-term prisoners. This showed the growing anti-imperialist unity and solidarity of a section of prisoners. Throughout the roof-top protest prisoners displayed banners calling for prison reform, repatriation for Irish POWs and condemning Zionism. After the protest prisoners were given long sentences, loss of remission and solitary confinement by internal kangaroo courts. But through legal and political organisation they fought back and forced the Home Office into an unprecedented retreat, abandoning all mutiny charges and overturning all punishments meted out. The prisoners also won important new rights in internal disciplinary proceedings.

The protest quickly spread to Wormwood Scrubs D-Wing where long-term prisoners on 16 June staged their own protests in solidarity with the Albany prisoners. In order to undermine Home Office and press attacks on Irish POWs, this protest was carried out solely by ordinary long-term prisoners. They were viciously beaten and also given long sentences of solitary confinement. They too fought back through legal and political organisation. Finally on 24 June a prisoner, Tommy Tangney, carried out a courageous solo protest in support of his Wormwood Scrubs comrades. The prisoners are also now contesting Leon Brittan's vicious new policy on parole for long term prisoners. These protests show how a determined, united, and politically organised resistance can achieve some victories even under the most difficult conditions. The movement outside the prisons has a great deal to learn from these prisoners.

These protests have confirmed the revolutionary role of Irish POWs. Through their consistent defence not only of their own rights as political prisoners but also of the rights of all prisoners, they have placed themselves in the forefront of the struggle against the repressive British prison system. They therefore occupy a unique position, uniting the struggle of the Irish people for national liberation with the struggle for basic democratic rights in Britain.

Since 1981 there has been no repeat of the widespread uprisings that took place in the Spring and Summer of that year. However, throughout the country local, smaller-scale campaigns against the racist police, racist laws and fascist attacks have taken place. In Dewsbury Asian youth have mobilised against police and fascist attacks in their area. The campaign to defend the Newham 8, Asian youth arrested by the police after they defended themselves against fascist attacks, is continuing and a 2,000-strong march took place in September 1983. The Newham 8 trial began in November 1983 at the Old Bailey with militant daily pickets. In the court police racism has been exposed and the Newham 8 have asserted the right of black people to defend themselves against racist attacks. The best-known campaign of 1983 has been the campaign for an independent public enquiry into the death of Colin Roach in Stoke Newington police station. The fight to expose the truth about Colin Roach's death drew in widespread support from the Hackney black community especially the youth. Predictably the police sought to crush the campaign with over 100 arrests and repeated attacks on demonstrations. The Stoke Newington and Hackney Defence Campaign was formed to defend the youth against this police harassment. It is an anti-racist, anti-imperialist campaign. Throughout its short history it has not only given legal and political defence to the youth but has exposed the connection between racism in Britain and British imperialism. The SNHDC has consistently pointed out the role of Kenneth Newman in Ireland and the significance of his appointment as Head of the Metropolitan Police. It has given active support and solidarity to anti-imperialist movements and other campaigns – on South Africa, Ireland and anti-racist struggles in this country.

BUILD THE IRISH SOLIDARITY MOVEMENT

Following the end of the hunger strike in 1981 communists and anti-imperialists including the RCG, established Irish Solidarity Committees in different parts of the country. Whilst most of the left stopped campaigning on the Irish question, these forces redoubled their efforts. The first step in the national co-ordination of a new movement was taken on 20 November 1982 when a conference of 250 delegates formed Building an Irish Solidarity Movement. A further conference in October 1983 formally launched the Irish Solidarity Movement (ISM). The RCG played a central role in creating the ISM which has won support from a number of POWs, other left organisations, Republican individuals, TOM and Labour Party supporters, and unaffiliated individuals. The founding policy of the ISM is to direct its work towards the most oppressed sections of the British working class as the basis for a new solidarity movement.

Since November 1982 the ISCs and organisations affiliated to the ISM have worked to build a democratic, non-sectarian, anti-imperialist Irish solidarity movement. By working on the streets in working class areas ISM supporters have directed their work towards the most oppressed sections of the working class. Through this work it has been proved that there is indeed widespread sympathy with and interest in the Irish people's struggle for freedom. Nearly 50,000 people have signed the ISM petition calling for the immediate withdrawal of British troops and the work of the ISCs is financed by donations given by people on the streets. Where, as in Edinburgh, local working class youth have been drawn in to active work, it has led to important political gains such as when the Edinburgh ISC open-air rally fought off and roundly defeated loyalist attempts to disrupt it. Elsewhere black and Irish workers, unemployed youths, have been involved in the work but not yet on anything like the scale needed.

The ISCs have everywhere worked in unity with other forces and individuals wherever possible. Nationally the ISM has supported all national solidarity events on Ireland despite the fact that restrictions were placed by the organisers on the ISM's participation. And in response to the Albany POWs' letter in April 1983 calling for a united solidarity movement,[11] the ISM initiated a unity campaign culminating in a demonstration and conference in October 1983. Locally too, such unity efforts have been pursued. An important success was made in Manchester in August 1983 with a 150-strong march that gained support from local Women and Ireland, the LCI and the IRSP. It has to be said, however, that the ISM has not yet overcome the sectarian refusal, particularly of the national Troops Out Movement and the Irish Freedom Movement, to unite in such campaigns.

The ISCs have firmly defended the democratic right of free speech and public assembly vital to any work in this country on Ireland. When Lambeth Tories attempted to ban South London ISC from the use of Lambeth Town Hall in March 1983, SLISC successfully mobilised to defeat this move with support from South London Troops Out Movement and Labour Party councillors amongst others. A similar successful campaign took place in Manchester.

When the Albany roof-top protest began the ISM immediately responded calling two pickets of the Home Office. Those pickets were also supported by South London TOM, and the IFM. When Ken Livingstone was attacked for telling the truth about British barbarism in Ireland and was disowned by his own so-called 'colleagues', SLISC produced a special leaflet defending Livingstone's right to speak out on Ireland. These examples demonstrate the point made above: that those in Britain determined to build a real Irish Solidarity Movement will play a central role in the defence of democratic rights of all workers in Britain.

The experience of this work, the political developments which have taken place, have shown that a new Irish Solidarity Movement can be built and must be built in Britain. The overall political stand of this book has been confirmed in all its major points: Ireland is the key to the British revolution – if the British working class fail to make common cause with the Irish struggle it will be incapable of defending itself; British imperialism cannot play a progressive role in Ireland; and finally, forces exist in Britain which can be won to an anti-imperialist solidarity movement on Ireland.

The new Irish Solidarity Movement can be built basing itself on the anti-imperialist slogans *Victory to the Irish People! Troops Out Now! The Right to Repatriation for all Irish Prisoners of War!*, directing its work towards the most oppressed sections of the working class and fighting for unity of all forces and individuals supporting the Irish people's struggle for freedom. Such a movement will not only be a contribution to the Irish revolution but will also be a major step forward for the British working class.

NOTES

1 Kitson F, *Low Intensity Operations; Subversion, Insurgency and Peacekeeping* London 1971 p. 87.
2 *Sunday Times* 28 August 1983.
3 Cited in *An Phoblacht/Republican News* 24 March 1983.
4 *An Phoblacht/Republican News* 17 November 1983.
5 See chapter 16.
6 In the aftermath of the Harrods bombing, in December 1983, the British ruling class threatened to ban Sinn Fein in yet another attempt to divide the Republican Movement and counterpose Sinn Fein's electoral campaigning to the IRA's military offfensive.
7 The deployment of thousands of 'Free State' soldiers and Gardai against the IRA unit involved in the Tidey kidnapping, in December 1983, and the shooting of a 'Free State' soldier and Garda by IRA volunteers acting in self-defence, underlines these points.
8 *Hansard* 7 March 1983 Column 606.
9 *Fight Racism! Fight Imperialism!* No 32 September 1983.
10 In January 1984 the 'left' Labour Sheffield Council banned the annual Bloody Sunday Commemoration March in response to media-created anti-Irish hysteria.
11 See *Fight Racism! Fight Imperialism!* No 29 May 1983

BIBLIOGRAPHY

BOOKS, PAMPHLETS AND ARTICLES

Amnesty International, *Report of an Amnesty International Mission to Northern Ireland* London 1978.

Association of the families of innocent victims of loyalist, UDR, RUC and British army violence, *Silent Too Long* Dublin nd.

Bell G, *The Protestants of Ulster* London 1976.

Bell G, *Troublesome Business* London 1982.

Bell J Bowyer, *The Secret Army: The IRA 1916–1979* Dublin 1979.

Bernstein E, *Evolutionary Socialism* (1899) New York 1961.

Berry S, *To the bitter climax of death if necessary* London 1980.

Bew P, Gibbon P and Patterson H, *The State in Northern Ireland 1921–72* Manchester 1979.

Birchall I, *'The smallest mass party in the world' Building the Socialist Workers Party 1951–1979* London 1981.

Boulton D, *The UVF 1966–73* Dublin 1973.

Boyce D G, *Englishmen and Irish Troubles* London 1972.

Boyd A, *The rise of Irish Trade Unions 1729–1970* Tralee 1972.

Boyle K, Hadden T and Hillyard P, *Ten Years on in Northern Ireland* London 1980.

Brady S, *Arms and the Men* Wicklow 1971.

Braunthal J, *History of the International* Volume 1 *1864–1914* London 1966, Volume 2 *1914–43* London 1967.

Broom J, *John Maclean* Scotland 1973.

Buckland P, *Irish Unionism* Volume Two *Ulster Unionism* Dublin 1973.

Callaghan J, *A House Divided* London 1973.

Campaign for Free Speech on Ireland, *The British Media and Ireland* London nd.

Challinor R, *The Origins of British Bolshevism* London 1977.

Clarkson J D, *Labour and Nationalism in Ireland* New York 1925.

Cliff T, *The Crisis, Social Contract or Socialism* London 1976.

Cole G D H, *Chartist Portraits* (1941) London 1965.

Cole G D H, *A History of Socialist Thought* Volume 3 Part 1 (1956) London 1974.

Cole G D H and Postgate R, *The Common People 1746–1946* London 1949.
Colfer K, 'Whose Tribunal' in *Hands Off Ireland!* No 5 September 1978.
Collins H and Abramsky C, *Karl Marx and the British Labour Movement* London 1965.
Communist International, *The Second Congress of the Communist International* Volume 1 London 1977.
Communist International, *Theses, Resolutions and Manifestos of the first four Congresses of the Third International* London 1980.
Communist Party of Ireland, *Outline History* Dublin nd.
Connolly J, *The Connolly–Walker Controversy* Cork 1974.
Connolly J, *Erin's Hope The End and Means and The New Evangel* Dublin and Belfast 1972.
Connolly J, *Ireland Upon the Dissecting Table* Cork 1975.
Connolly J, *Labour and Easter Week* Dublin 1966.
Connolly J, *Labour in Irish History* Dublin 1973.
Connolly J, *The Reconquest of Ireland* Dublin and Belfast 1972.
Connolly J, *Selected Writings* London 1973.
Connolly J, *Socialism and Nationalism* Dublin 1948.
Connolly J, *The Worker's Republic* Dublin 1951.
Coogan T P, *The IRA* London 1980.
Coogan T P, *On the Blanket* Dublin 1980.
Cummins I, *Marx, Engels and National Movements* London 1980.
Curriculum Development Unit, *Divided City, Portrait of Dublin 1913* Dublin 1978.
Davis H B, *Nationalism and Socialism* New York and London 1973.
De Paor L, *Divided Ulster* London 1973.
Deutsch R and Magowan V, *Northern Ireland a Chronology of Events 1968–1974* Volume 1 *1968–1971* Belfast 1973 Volume 2 *1972–1973* Belfast 1974 Volume 3 *1974* Belfast 1975.
Devlin B, *The Price of My Soul* London 1969.
Devlin P, *The Fall of the NI Executive* Belfast 1975.
Devlin P, *Yes We have no Bananas: Outdoor Relief in Belfast 1920–1939* Belfast 1981.
Dillon M and Lehane D, *Political Murder in Northern Ireland* London 1973.
Ellis P B, *A History of the Irish Working Class* London 1972.
Faligot R, *Britain's Military Strategy in Ireland the Kitson Experiment* London 1983.
Farrell M, *Arming the Protestants* London 1983 (this book appeared after *Ireland: the key to the British revolution* was finished).
Farrell M, *Northern Ireland: The Orange State* London 1976.
Farrell M, *Struggle in the North* London nd.
Faul D and Murray R, *The Castlereagh File* Dungannon 1978.
Faul D and Murray R, *The Shame of Merlyn Rees* Dungannon 1975.
Feeney H, *In the care of... Her Majesty's Prisons* Belfast 1976.
First International, *Documents* Volumes I to V *1864–1872* London nd.
First International, *The Hague Congress September 2–7 1872 Minutes and Documents* Moscow 1976 *Reports and Letters* Moscow 1978.
Fisk R, *The Point of no Return* London 1975.

Fitzgerald J, 'The Loyalist Strike whose Defeat?' in *Hands Off Ireland!* No 2 June 1977.

Fox D, 'August 12 What it Means', in *Hands Off Ireland!* No 9 November 1979.

Fox R, *Marx, Engels and Lenin on the Irish Revolution* London 1932.

Fox R M, *Jim Larkin: The rise of the Underman* London 1957.

Geraghty T, *Who Dares Wins The Story of the SAS 1950–1980* London 1981.

Gilmore G, *The Irish Republican Congress* Cork nd (second edition).

Greaves C D, *The Irish Question and the British People* London 1963.

Greaves C D, *Liam Mellows and the Irish Revolution* London 1971.

Greaves C D, *The Life and Times of James Connolly* London 1972.

Haines J, *The Politics of Power* London 1977.

Harman C, 'Ireland after the Hunger Strike' in *Socialist Review* January/February 1981.

Harman C, 'The rights and wrong of the IRA' in *Socialist Worker* 14 August 1982.

Harman C, *The Struggle in Ireland* London nd.

Harvey R, *Diplock and the Assault on Civil Liberties* London 1981.

Hobsbawm E J, *Labouring Men* (1964) London 1979.

Holton B, *British Syndicalism 1900–1914* London 1976.

Information on Ireland, *They Shoot Children* London 1982.

International Socialist Congress, *Proposals and Drafts of Resolutions 18–24 August 1907* Published by International Socialist Bureau.

Interview with Cathal Goulding in *New Left Review* No 64 November/December 1970.

IRA (Provisional), *Freedom Struggle* Dublin 1973.

Irish Freedom Movement, *An anti-imperialist guide to the Irish War* London 1983.

Jackson T A, *Ireland Her Own* (1947) London 1971.

John D W, 'Ulsterisation and Loyalist Terror' in *Hands Off Ireland!* No 7 April 1979.

Kapp Y, *Eleanor Marx* Volume One *Family Life 1855–1883* London 1972, Volume Two *The Crowded Years 1884–1898* London 1976.

Kautsky K, *Ireland* (1922) London 1974.

Kee R, *The Green Flag* Volume One *The Most Distressful Country* London 1979 *Volume Two The Bold Fenian Men* London 1979 *Volume Three Ourselves Alone* London 1980.

Kelly H, *How Stormont Fell* Dublin 1972.

Kelley K, *The Longest War Northern Ireland and the IRA* London 1982.

Kendall W, *The Revolutionary Movement in Britain 1900–1921* London 1971.

Kenzo M, 'Marx and "Underdevelopment" His Thesis on the "Historical Roles of British Free Trade" Revisited' in *Annals of the Institute of Social Science* Tokyo 1978.

Kitson F, *Low Intensity Operations; subversion, insurgency and peacekeeping* London 1971.

Klugmann J, *History of the Communist Party of Great Britain* Volume 1 *Formation and early years 1919–1924* Volume 2 *The General Strike 1925–6* London 1980.

The Labour Party, *Commission of Inquiry into the Present Conditions in Ireland January 1920* reprinted in *Ireland Socialist Review* No 3 Autumn 1978.
The Labour Party, *Report of the Labour Commission to Ireland 28 December 1920.*
Larkin E, *James Larkin Irish Labour Leader 1876–1947* London 1965.
Lenin V I, *Collected Works* Moscow (1960–1970).
Lenin V I, *On Britain* Moscow nd.
Lenin V I, *Lenin on Ireland* Dublin 1970.
Levenson S, *James Connolly* London 1977.
Leviné-Meyer R, *Leviné the Life of a Revolutionary* Glasgow 1973.
Longford Lord, *Peace by Ordeal* London 1972.
Longford Lord and O'Neill T P, *Eamon De Valera* London 1970.
Lyons F S L, *Ireland since the Famine* London 1974.
Lysaght D R O'Connor, *The Republic of Ireland* Cork 1970.
Macardle D, *The Irish Republic* London 1968.
McCann E, *The British Press and Northern Ireland* London nd.
McCann E, *War and an Irish Town* London 1980.
Macfarlane L J, *The British Communist Party Its origin and development until 1929* London 1966.
McGuffin J, *The Guineapigs* London 1974.
Maclean J, *In the Rapids of Revolution* London 1978.
McLennan G, *Britain and the Irish Crisis* London 1973.
Mac Stiofain S, *Memoirs of a Revolutionary* Edinburgh 1975.
Mansergh N S, *The Irish Question, 1840–1921* London 1965.
Marlowe T, 'The Easter Rising' in *Hands Off Ireland!* No 10 April 1980.
Marlowe T, 'Review of "Troublesome Business"' in *Fight Racism! Fight Imperialism!* No 26 February 1983.
Marlowe T and Palmer S, 'Ireland: Imperialism in Crisis 1968–1978' in *Revolutionary Communist* No 8 July 1978.
Marlowe T and Whittaker P, 'The CPGB and Ireland' in *Revolutionary Communist* No 7 November 1977.
Marx K and Engels F, *Articles on Britain* Moscow 1975.
Marx K and Engels F, *Collected Works* London (1975–).
Marx K and Engels F, *Ireland and the Irish Question* Moscow 1978.
Marx K and Engels F, *Selected Correspondence* Moscow nd.
Miliband R, *Parliamentary Socialism* London 1975.
Milton N, *John Maclean* London 1973.
Mitchell A, *Labour in Irish Politics 1890–1930* Dublin 1974.
Moran B, '1913, Jim Larkin and the British Labour Movement' in *Saothar 4* Dublin nd.
Murphy J T, *Preparing for power* (1934) London 1972.
Neeson E, *The Civil War in Ireland* Dublin 1969.
O'Brien N C and Ni Sheidhir E, *James Connolly Wrote for Today…* Dublin 1978.
O'Dowd L, Rolston B and Tomlinson M, *Northern Ireland Between Civil Rights and Civil War* London 1980.
O'Neill T, *The Autobiography of Terence O'Neill* London 1972.
O'Neill T, *Ulster at the Crossroads* London 1969.
Pankhurst S, *The Suffragette Movement* London 1977.

Paul W, *The Irish Crisis (1921)* Cork 1976.
Prisoners Aid Committee, *Irish Political Prisoners in English Jails* London 1980.
Prisoners Aid Committee, *Irish Voices from English Jails* London 1979.
Purdie B, *Ireland Unfree* London 1972.
Reed D, *Building an Irish Solidarity Movement* London 1982.
Reed D, 'Marx and Engels: The Labour Aristocracy, Opportunism and the British Labour Movement' in *Fight Racism! Fight Imperialism!* No 27 March 1983.
Revolutionary Communist Group, 'Britain and the Irish Revolution' in *Revolutionary Communist* No 2 May 1975.
Revolutionary Communist Group, *Ireland: British Labour and British Imperialism* London 1976.
Robertson G, *Reluctant Judas* London 1976.
Ryan W P, *The Irish Labour Movement* Dublin 1919.
Sands B, *One Day in My Life* Dublin and Cork 1983.
Sinn Fein, *Eire Nua* Dublin 1971.
Sinn Fein, *The Informers* Dublin 1983.
Sinn Fein, *Special Category A* Dublin 1980.
Sinn Fein – The Workers' Party, *The Irish Industrial Revolution* Dublin 1977.
Socialist Workers Party, *Why we say Troops out of Ireland* London 1980.
Spring R, 'Connolly and Irish Freedom' Part Two in *Hands Off Ireland!* No 5 September 1978.
Strauss E, *Irish Nationalism and British Democracy* London 1951.
The Sunday Times Insight Team, *Ulster* London 1972.
Taylor A J P, *English History 1914–1945* London 1975.
Taylor P, *Beating the Terrorists?* London 1980.
Troops Out Movement, *No British Solution* London nd.
Trotsky L, *Writings on Britain* Volume Three London 1974.
Utley T E, *Lessons of Ulster* London 1975.
Wilson H, *The Labour Government 1964–1970* London 1974.
Woddis J, 'Ireland – Common Cause of British and Irish People' in *Marxism Today* July 1973.

GOVERNMENT AND OFFICIAL REPORTS

Bennett Report, *Report of The Committee of Inquiry into Police Interrogation Procedures In Northern Ireland* London 1979.
Cameron Report, *Disturbances in Northern Ireland: Report of the Commission Appointed by the Government of Northern Ireland* London 1969.
Compton Report, *Report of the Enquiry into Allegations Against the Security Forces of Physical Brutality in Northern Ireland Arising Out of Events on 9 August 1971* London 1971.
Diplock Report, *Report of the Commission to Consider Legal Procedures to deal with Terrorist Activities in Northern Ireland* London 1972.
Gardiner Report, *Report of a Committee to consider, in the context of civil liberties and human rights, measures to deal with terrorism in Northern Ireland* London 1975.
Green Paper, *The Future of Northern Ireland* London 1972.

Hansard, *House of Commons Official Report Parliamentary Debates.*
Hunt Report, *Report of the Advisory Committee on Police in Northern Ireland* London 1969.
Newman K, *Report of the Commissioner of Police of the Metropolis for the Year 1982* London 1983.
Northern Ireland Cosntitutional Convention, *Report* London 1975.
Scarman Report, *Violence and Civil Disturbances in Northern Ireland in 1969: Report of a Tribunal of Enquiry* London 1970.
Secretary of State for Northern Ireland, *The Northern Ireland Constitution* London 1974.
White Paper, *Northern Ireland Constitutional Proposals* London 1973.
Widgery Report, *Report of the Tribunal appointed to Enquire into the Events on Sunday, 30th January 1972 which led to Loss of Life in connection with the Procession in Londonderry on that day* London 1972.

BRITISH NEWSPAPERS AND PERIODICALS

Bulletin (Militant Tendency, internal).
The Call (British Socialist Party, 1916–1920, weekly).
The Communist (British Communist Party, 1920–1923, weekly).
Daily Express.
Daily Herald.
Daily Mail.
Daily Mirror.
Daily Telegraph.
Daily Worker (Communist Party of Great Britain, 1930–1966).
Fight Racism! Fight Imperialism! (Revolutionary Communist Group, monthly).
Financial Times (daily).
The Guardian (*Manchester Guardian* up to 1959, daily).
Hands Off Ireland! (Revolutionary Communist Group 1976–1980, quarterly).
Ireland Socialist Review (occasional).
Irish Post (weekly).
The Irish Prisoner (Prisoners Aid Committee, occasional).
Justice (Social Democratic Federation, 1884–1928, weekly).
The Labour Leader (Independent Labour Party, 1894–1922, weekly).
Marxism Today (Communist Party of Great Britain, monthly).
Militant (Militant Tendency, weekly).
Morning Star (Communist Party of Great Britain, daily).
Newsline (Workers Revolutionary Party, daily).
PAC News (Prisoners Aid Committee, occasional).
Red Mole (International Marxist Group – replaced by *Red Weekly*).
Revolutionary Communist (Revolutionary Communist Group 1975–1979, occasional).
The Socialist (Socialist Labour Party, 1902–1924, monthly).
Socialist Challenge (International Marxist Group – later *Socialist Action*, weekly).
Socialist Review (Socialist Workers Party, monthly).
Socialist Worker (Socialist Workers Party, weekly).

Sun (daily).
The Sunday Times.
Troops Out (Troops Out Movement, monthly).
The Woman's Dreadnought (Workers Suffrage Federation, 1914–1917, monthly).
The Workers Dreadnought (Workers Socialist Federation, 1917–1924, weekly).
Workers Press (Socialist Labour League, 1969–1976)

IRISH NEWSPAPERS AND PERIODICALS

An Phoblacht (Sinn Fein, 1970–1979, weekly).
An Phoblacht/Republican News (Sinn Fein, weekly).
Aspect (monthly).
Belfast Bulletin (Workers Research Unit, occasional).
Combat (Ulster Volunteer Force, occasional).
Hibernia (1970–1980, weekly).
Iris (Sinn Fein, quarterly).
Irish Independent (daily).
Irish News (daily).
The Irish Times (daily).
Magill (monthly).
Protestant Telegraph (Democratic Unionist Party, monthly).
Republican News (Sinn Fein, 1970–1979, weekly).
Sunday Independent.

INDEX

Also from **Larkin Publications:**

The revolutionary road to communism in Britain

Manifesto of the Revolutionary Communist Group

British imperialism, the oldest imperialist power, is in the throes of a deep economic and political crisis. Its economic and political interests are threatened by the international banking crisis, the growing inter-imperialist rivalries and the challenge to British imperialism from anti-imperialist movements throughout the world – in particular from the Republican Movement in Ireland, and SWAPO and the ANC in Southern Africa.

In Britain, in these early stages of the crisis, British imperialism faces the challenge from the most oppressed sections of the working class, black and immigrant workers, particularly the youth.

In 1981 the British state faced the most serious political confrontation since the beginning of the crisis. The youth rose up throughout British cities in the spring and summer of 1981 and fought the racist British police on the streets with stones and petrol bombs. The lead of the most oppressed will eventually be followed by other workers as unemployment and cuts in public expenditure threaten to drive millions of families into dire poverty.

British imperialism will face a revolutionary challenge from within as new forces of revolution emerge in Britain itself.

£1.50 + 30p postage and packing
From Larkin Publications BCM Box 5909 London WCIN 3XX

ISBN 0 905400 03 8